# The Political Economy
# of Oil in Alaska

# THE POLITICAL ECONOMY OF OIL IN ALASKA

## Multinationals vs. the State

JERRY MCBEATH
MATTHEW BERMAN
JONATHAN ROSENBERG
MARY F. EHRLANDER

LYNNE
RIENNER
PUBLISHERS

BOULDER
LONDON

Published in the United States of America in 2008 by
Lynne Rienner Publishers, Inc.
1800 30th Street, Boulder, Colorado 80301
www.rienner.com

and in the United Kingdom by
Lynne Rienner Publishers, Inc.
3 Henrietta Street, Covent Garden, London WC2E 8LU

**Library of Congress Cataloging-in-Publication Data**
The political economy of oil in Alaska : multinationals vs. the state /
Jerry McBeath . . . [et al.].
    p. cm.
 Includes bibliographical references and index.
 ISBN 978-1-58826-557-9 (hardcover : alk. paper)
 1. Petroleum industry and trade—Alaska. 2. Petroleum industry and
trade—Political aspects—Alaska. 3. International business
enterprises—Alaska. I. McBeath, Jerry.
 HD9567.A4P65 2008
 338.2'728209798—dc22
                                                    2007036119

**British Cataloguing in Publication Data**
A Cataloguing in Publication record for this book
is available from the British Library.


Printed and bound in the United States of America

The paper used in this publication meets the requirements
∞ of the American National Standard for Permanence of
Paper for Printed Library Materials Z39.48-1992.

 5  4  3  2  1

# Contents

# Tables and Figures

■ **Tables**

## ▪ Figures

# Acknowledgments

We began this study in 1999 and thank President Mark Hamilton and the University of Alaska (UA) Natural Resources Fund for assistance at that time. President Hamilton was also instrumental in allocating support from the University of Alaska Foundation, specifically from the BP/ConocoPhillips Fund, to support work on the project in 2007. We thank, too, these senior UA administrators for their assistance: UA vice president Jim Johnsen; former director of the Institute of Social and Economic Research, University of Alaska Anchorage (UAA), and now interim chancellor, Fran Ulmer; University of Alaska Fairbanks (UAF) chancellor Steve Jones; and former UAF provost Paul Reichardt.

We are grateful to these colleagues and friends, who provided critiques and insightful commentary on individual chapters: Claus-M. Naske, professor emeritus of history (UAF); Jim Gladden, professor of political science (UAF); Jenifer Huang McBeath, professor of plant pathology and biotechnology (UAF); Scott Goldsmith, professor of economics (UAA); Mary Nordale, former state revenue commissioner and Permanent Fund trustee; and Tom Williams, former revenue commissioner and now with BP-Alaska. We would also like to thank Stephen Smyth, formerly of the Yukon territorial government, for steering us toward "mature dependency" as a way to comprehend Alaska's political economy. Thomas Morehouse, professor emeritus of political science (UAA), assisted us by reviewing the entire manuscript and making suggestions for improvement of integration and consistency. His deft editorial work greatly enhanced the logic and readability of the text.

Alaska agency staff were generous with their time in answering our questions. We especially thank the following: in the Department of Natural Resources, Kevin Banks, William Nebesky, Anthony Scott, and Brian Havelock; in the Department of Revenue, Roger Marks and Patrick McKnight; in Legislative Finance, Rob Carpenter and David Teal; and in the Alaska Permanent Fund Corporation, Laura Achee.

In conducting research for the book, we made ample use of the Alaska and Polar Regions collection of the Rasmuson Library at UAF. We thank the librarians for their assistance and expertise. Dixon Jones at UAF Graphics redrew maps, converted figures, and helped format tables, for which we are grateful. Also, we thank the administrative assistants and student workers in political science, women's studies, history, and northern studies at UAF, and especially Julia Parzick, Courtney Pagh, and Celine Gonon.

At Lynne Rienner Publishers, we thank three anonymous reviewers for their constructive criticism of the manuscript. We especially appreciate the assistance of Claire Vlcek and Leanne Anderson, who patiently answered our questions and assisted us in rooting out inaccuracies. We also thank Sonia Smith for the exceptional care she took in copyediting the manuscript and Shena Redmond for skillfully guiding the manuscript through the production process. For remaining errors and omissions, we cheerfully absolve all the foregoing from responsibility.

# 1

## Introduction:
## Oil, Political Economy,
## and Alaska

On January 23, 2003, the newly inaugurated Republican governor of Alaska, Frank Murkowski, opened his first State of the State Address with the following words: "[O]n election day Alaskans spoke with a loud voice. They voted for leadership, accountability. They wanted a future for our state to be built on a foundation of hard work and on resource wealth. They asked for a government that could learn to live within its means and that will invest in jobs and prosperity."[1]

The address made two other things perfectly clear about the new governor's plans for the state and the state's role in the national and international political economies. First, as promised in the 2002 gubernatorial campaign against Democratic lieutenant governor Fran Ulmer, Murkowski would address the state's fiscal problems with a combination of budget cuts and increased revenues from natural resource extraction—especially oil and natural gas—avoiding, if possible, new taxes and tax increases. Second, as an incentive to investors, the governor would seek to streamline the state's regulatory and licensing practices for resource extraction. In short, oil would continue to dominate the Alaska economy, as it has since the 1950s, and the oil industry would continue to be a major force in state politics.

It would be easy to write off the new governor's approach as dictated by partisan politics—the natural ideological affinity between corporate interests and the Republican Party—but that would be misleading. Although the 2002 elections were hotly contested, the fundamentals of Alaska's resource-based economy were never at issue. While opening the coastal plain of the Arctic National Wildlife Refuge (ANWR) to oil exploration has divided Democrats and Republicans in the US Congress and in national elections since the early 1990s, in 2002, only the tiny Alaska Green Party actively opposed the opening of ANWR in its electoral platform.[2] Democrats and Republicans differed mainly in their assessments of the severity of the state's fiscal crisis, the amount of new revenues and employment that could come from oil in the near

1

future, the need for more tax revenues, and the best ways to protect the sacrosanct Permanent Fund Dividend.

Clearly, the relationship between the state and the oil industry has been, and remains, at the center of Alaska's political economy, and the state is dependent on oil in ways that we will make apparent in subsequent chapters. But does the state's reliance on its substantial reserves of oil and natural gas also mean that it is penetrated and/or controlled by corporate energy interests? Does the industry—represented by giant multinational corporations (MNCs) like BP, ConocoPhillips, and ExxonMobil, and local exploration and service companies—dominate state politics, or has the state used its vast holdings to manage a more symmetrical relationship with the industry? Also, how has that relationship been shaped and changed by developments in the state and the industry?

To answer these and related questions, we conceive of the relationship between government and the oil industry in Alaska as a bargaining relationship between two competing actors. Each actor controls a set of different but complementary resources in pursuit of a common economic goal—the maximization of its revenues from oil and gas extraction. Each responds to similar constraints from the natural, economic, and political environments on the ways in which it can utilize its resources for its own gain. But the *political* goals and orientations of each actor need to be reconciled through bargaining, because it is the *political* goals and orientations that, at times, differ, leading to different responses to changing local, national, and international contexts for the exploration, extraction, and marketing of oil and gas.

Government's principal resources are political, including control over regulatory, fiscal, and social policy and the ability to affect and reflect public opinion. State government also owns and/or controls access to substantial amounts of land, subsoil rights, and permits and provides or licenses much of the infrastructure required by the industry. The industry's principal resources are its capital, technology, and expertise, and the refining and marketing capacity needed to extract value from the state's oil and gas reserves. The industry also possesses considerable capacity to affect public opinion and influence the political process, directly through lobbying, campaign contributions, and public relations efforts, and indirectly by providing employment for citizens and residents and revenue for the state.

Government and industry, therefore, share a fundamental interest in maximizing earnings from the state's oil and gas reserves, but each actor competes over how the costs and benefits of extraction and the political goods needed to support a viable oil industry are distributed between them. And while each actor places a high value on cooperation, changes in the bargaining context and the composition and orientation of each actor will change the nature of the bargain and the ability of each actor to shape the bargain in its interests. Government and industry may be differently affected by changes in the party composition and leadership of state government; in the regulatory environment (local, state, and federal); in the fiscal situation of state and local governments; in public opinion; and in the relationship between the state and federal governments. Such changes can affect a government's perception of its relationship with the industry and the industry's perception of its relationship with government. Likewise, both actors may react differently to changes in global markets and the industry brought on by fluctuations in supply and demand, mergers, acquisitions, bankruptcies, and changes in management and strategic plans. Furthermore, both sets of actors contend with an internal contradiction of resource dependency. On the one hand, government and industry wish to bind one another in a profitable relationship. On the other hand, each is constantly looking for a way out. Multinational oil firms, concerned with the depletion of the state's oil patch, global price fluctuations, increasing expenses, and political liabilities, will constantly measure the benefits of maintaining or increasing production levels in Alaska against the costs of moving operations elsewhere. For similar reasons, the state will (or should) take measures to diversify its revenue sources and limit its dependence on a single commodity. Finally, while the state is primarily concerned with stabilizing and maximizing its revenue streams, the industry is primarily concerned with profitability.

We trace the several aspects of the evolving political relationship between government and industry to understand the changing nature of the bargain struck between them. We try to discover the underlying conditions that can make this relationship symmetrical or asymmetrical, and we provide a detailed analysis of the ways in which each actor has attempted to shape this relationship to optimize its own benefits while providing incentives for the other to remain in the relationship.

The terms *dependence* and *dependency* have a special place in the literatures of political science, economics, and international political economy. Typically, when applied to societies with resource-based economies, they connote chronic underdevelopment and structurally asymmetrical relationships in which powerful MNCs dominate weak and vulnerable, if not subservient, governments. These connotations of resource dependence need to be modified if we are to understand the political economy of oil in Alaska (and elsewhere). As clearly indicated by the Organization of Petroleum Exporting Countries (OPEC) oil shocks of the 1970s, oil can be a source of political power as well as a source of political vulnerability. Furthermore, oil companies themselves depend on, and therefore must live within, particular policy frameworks.[3]

> The energy industry needs government. In many cases the energy industry operates with a government license, giving it a privileged access to resources or markets, but also giving the government the right to intervene and to levy special taxes to share the profit. The energy industry and energy markets cannot function without a regulatory framework, dependent on governments and politicians.[4]

Therefore, before proceeding with a more detailed analysis, it is important to establish the extent to which Alaska displays the structural characteristics of an oil-dependent state and to situate the study of the political economy of Alaska oil in a broader context by examining some relevant theories and concepts.

## ▧ Alaska's Dependence on Oil

In strictly economic terms, Alaska is an oil-dependent state, exhibiting the lack of diversification typical of all resource-dependent states. In 1991, approximately 86 percent of unrestricted general fund revenues came from oil and gas industry activities, and although that amount declined to 79 percent in 2000, with the price surges of subsequent years the share had increased to 88 percent by 2005. In addition, oil revenues invested through the state's Permanent Fund provided residents with direct annual dividend payments worth as much as $1.15 billion in disposable income in 2000 ($660 million in 2006) and provided the state with a savings account worth approximately $40 billion as of July 2007.

This situation can either stimulate or limit more diversified forms of development, depending on how state and federal governments use policy to shape incentives and opportunities. Theoretically, oil can be a source of economic and political strength if linked to a strategy of long-term capital formation aimed at diversification, or it can be a source of political vulnerability, even as it provides economic benefits. As George Philip has pointed out, "the essential problem with unbalanced oil economies is that there is more to development than merely money."[5] With a small population (approximately 670,000 in 2006) and an economy that rides the peaks and troughs of fluctuating international markets, Alaska could be expected to display all the advantages and disadvantages of similarly endowed nation-states, such as Saudi Arabia, Kuwait, or the United Arab Emirates. And with its economic fortunes linked tightly to demand for oil in the rest of the United States and the developed world, Alaska might be expected to suffer from the pressures and uncertainties typical of oil-rich states in other parts of the Americas, such as Mexico or Venezuela.[6] Furthermore, like present-day Nigeria and Angola, Mexico before 1938, Venezuela before 1958, and Saudi Arabia before 1980, giant MNCs play a central role in the production and sale of Alaska's oil reserves. In 2000, these corporations, including the recently merged British Petroleum (BP) and ARCO, ExxonMobil, and Phillips (which bought ARCO's Alaska operations as a federally mandated prerequisite for the BP-ARCO merger and has since merged with Conoco to form ConocoPhillips), accounted for 95 percent of the total petroleum corporate income tax paid to the state.[7]

Obviously, the political context for the relationship between the state and the industry in Alaska bears only a passing resemblance to any of the cases mentioned above. In addition, there is a great deal about Alaska that is unique within the United States. Still, we contend that it is not so unique that a study of Alaska would not benefit from a discussion of relevant concepts of international political economy and at least implicit comparison with other cases.

## ■ Oil and the International Political Economy: Through an Alaska Lens

Oil is the quintessence of modern international political economy, linking issues of trade, finance, development, and national security. Oil is traded on a huge and burgeoning global market, and its exploration, production, use, and trade touch virtually every aspect of every national and local economy. Oil markets are challenged and changed by rapidly evolving technologies that presently increase global demand for oil but may someday make it obsolete,[8] and although oil is of great intrinsic value, its production and consumption can also exact tremendous costs. It is a finite, nonrenewable resource for which there presently appears to be an infinite and inexhaustible demand. Using it and producing it makes life better or worse depending on where one is situated in the complex chains of benefit and cost.

Thus, governments everywhere and at every level (international, national, state/provincial, and local) become, at times, arenas of conflict among producers, consumers, and affected third parties. Nation-states engage powerful private interests, their own citizens, and each other over oil and oil-related issues. Access to oil, production of oil, pricing, and the methods of production, transportation, and consumption have catalyzed important political changes, from war to the development of new institutions for international cooperation.[9]

But the political economy of oil is also shaped by a variety of local, individual, group, and corporate interests linked directly to its availability as a source of revenues, profits, and employment, and to its impact on the environment and indigenous cultures. Nowhere is this more apparent than in Alaska, where the political economy of oil can overwhelm most other concerns and where the predominant role of oil can be traced directly to issues of national security, macroeconomics, and changing global markets. The particular array of local interests and the ways in which the local, national, and global intersect in Alaska may be unique, but the conditioning effects of global oil markets on state politics are not.

### The Case For and Against Alaska "Exceptionalism"

Alaska is unique among US states for its large size, extreme climate, and small but diverse population. Being a US state makes it unusual among relatively underdeveloped, resource-dependent regions, most of which are less-developed countries (LDCs) with authoritarian or newly democratizing governments (e.g., Mexico, Saudi Arabia, and Nigeria). Alaska also differs from oil-rich provinces and regions in *parliamentary* democracies (such as Alberta or Scotland) where different institutional structures, party orientations, and patterns of authority dictate different political tactics for shaping policy decisions. The question is, do these differences make the politics of oil in Alaska exceptional, sui generis, or unsuited to theoretical constructs developed for other resource-dependent states?

Our answer to the first part of the question is somewhat equivocal. When considering Alaska's relationship to global energy markets, we find significant similarities between Alaska and the oil-exporting states of Latin America, the Middle East, and Africa. But the profound local and domestic political differences warn against applying such sweeping social science concepts as dependency and underdevelopment without substantial revision.

Ken Coates has noted that the characteristics that make remote northern regions distinctive have caused scholars to shy away from comparisons with geographically distant regions or the use of theories of development derived from the study of LDCs. He argues that northern regions, although colder, more remote, and more sparsely populated than typical LDCs, are similar in important ways. They are shaped by recent histories of external political and economic control. They have been penetrated by MNCs, and they suffer net outflows of the profits derived from resource development. In addition, the internal politics of northern regions tend to be characterized by "intense internal struggles that have limited the regions' ability to present and protect their interests against outside forces."[10] So there is a basis for comparison and a reason to take seriously lessons derived from theories of development.

The constraints of global markets and MNCs are felt strongly in Alaska, but liberal democratic and federal structures, and competitive market forces provide a broader range of possibilities and more complex and open arenas for bargaining between Alaska policymakers and the oil industry. Authoritarian states may exercise more raw power vis-à-vis their own citizens, but democracies, because of their ability and need to reflect the policy preferences of powerful domestic interests, show greater resilience in their dealing with foreign and multinational actors.[11]

While democracy and a liberal economy may complicate negotiations and give policymakers more options, they also open the arenas of political competition to oil MNCs, which possess substantial resources for influencing voters and politicians. Therefore, at the most general level, we find in Alaska many of the same global patterns as in any other resource-dependent state or country. Powerful economic interests in the form of oil MNCs can drive the behavior of dominant private and public sector actors at the state and local levels. Private sector interests, acting separately, as entrepreneurs and workers, or in aggregations that include business partnerships, labor unions, and corporations (domestic and multinational), compete or collaborate with the political efforts of those MNCs. As private interests compete to discover, control, and extract oil and gas while retaining as much of the profit as possible, they inevitably become involved in efforts to affect land use and leasing policies, fiscal and regulatory policy, and social policy that affects labor, public health, safety, and the environment. Pluralism and federalism open up more points of access and more areas of vulnerability for both the state and the industry. Outcomes depend on how well the actors play a complex political game. In addition, as recent scandals have revealed, democratic transparency and rule of law do not prevent corrupt practices by business interests and legislators.

Not only do private interests compete within political and economic arenas shaped by governments, they compete with governments to reshape those arenas through, for example, pressures to make new lands available for exploration or to deregulate or privatize various aspects of production and distribution. Under federalism, governments compete among themselves based on interests of their own, in ways that may or may not complement those of particular private interests.

Generally, government interests are more complex than private interests. On the one hand, governments have income-related interests (i.e., the collection of revenues) that are similar to and to some extent competitive with private sector interests. But governments also have interests pertaining to "reasons of state," public service and social welfare that go beyond simply turning natural resources into revenue. The economic interests of government are captured by two fundamental concepts of political economy: public goods and externalities. The former refers to the responsibility of government to provide certain goods and services not adequately or equitably available through private market relationships. The latter refers to government responsibility to mitigate the costs (especially environmental) and distribute the benefits (especially economic) to citizens not directly involved in the oil industry. In addition, various levels of government within nation-states may compete with each other for control over policy and rents, even while national governments compete with each other for sovereign control of resources in international arenas. Because we seek to understand the nature of bargaining between the state and the industry, it makes sense now to explore some general theoretical propositions about politics in resource-dependent regions, first with reference to the international political economy and next with reference to other western US states.

## Dependency Theory Alaska-Style

Dependency, as a characteristic of nation-states in the international political economy, typically raises issues of compromised sovereignty for the commodity-exporting state. Host governments lose control over the direction and level of their state's economic development. MNCs with home offices in developed countries repatriate the lion's share of their profits, while local capital participates either by becoming an appendage of the MNCs' activities or by fleeing to more profitable and secure havens in the banks and stock exchanges of developed countries. Local economic activities are either adjuncts of the activities of resource-extracting MNCs or are limited to the declining share of local markets for cheap goods requiring low technological input. Leading political and economic elites (not to mention national political processes) coordinate their interests with those of the MNCs and their home-country governments, leading to trade, investment, fiscal, regulatory, and monetary policies favoring the export of raw materials and the import of manufactured and capital goods. In addition, although they dominate the dependent state's economy, MNCs provide relatively little direct employment for local workers.[12]

Resource-dependent states have attempted to regain a modicum of control over their economic destinies in a variety of ways. Using the constitutional and statutory instruments made available by formal sovereignty, they have nationalized private holdings (foreign and domestic), limited MNC activities, redistributed earnings using economic policy instruments, and negotiated agreements concerning capital flows, ownership, production, marketing, investment, labor, and profits. But control is limited by the relative powerlessness of these states in the international political economy.

Alaska too faces challenges to its ability to control the use and the fruits of its most valuable natural resources, and these challenges also stem from the asymmetries of power between the state and the MNCs, and between the state and the US government. For example, as Robert Gramling has noted, in the struggle between US states and the federal government over oil-related national security and macroeconomic interests, national interests usually take precedence. In particular, in time of crisis, the federal government has promoted expansion of domestic supply over environmental interests and over local interests in economic diversification.[13] In Alaska's case, this does not present a conflict between currently dominant state and federal interests, but it does illustrate how alliances among industry, the federal government, and particular local interests have shaped the local political arena.

Oil dependency, then, is an indisputable condition of the Alaska economy, but is it the defining condition of Alaskan politics? Building on Fernando Henrique Cardoso and Enzo Faletto's dependency analysis (1979) and Peter Evans's notion of dependent development (1979), Heather-Jo Hammer and John W. Gartrell (1998) argue that a country can be both developed and dependent. Canada, for example, enjoys high average standards of living, healthy aggregate rates of growth, and relatively low levels of income inequality; still, it is highly penetrated by multinational capital. To comprehend the Canadian case, they coined a new term—"mature dependence."[14]

Mature dependence displays the following characteristics that distinguish it from the dependent development that Evans found in Brazil. Some of these characteristics may be relevant to Alaska. First, the basic structure of a mature dependent economy is already in place at the time the tripartite relationship of foreign capital, local bourgeoisie, and the state is formed. Foreign capital does not impose itself but is invited in by established political and economic elites.[15] Therefore, the politics of the tripartite relationship under mature dependence is a consensual one, characterized by bargaining and "normal" politics.

Although a complete history of these processes in Alaska is beyond the scope of this book, we do consider these developments briefly in Chapters 2 and 3. Furthermore, existing studies of the development of the oil industry in Alaska seem to support the mature dependency thesis. Arrangements between the Alaska and federal governments, both before and after statehood, established a set of procedures for leasing potential oil lands to private interests. Those procedures were eventually structured to allow major oil MNCs a leading role in the discovery and development of new reserves, displacing the independents and wildcatters who had been essential to the earliest commercial discoveries.[16]

Second, the "masses" are not economically excluded or politically repressed in any conventional, authoritarian sense. In other words, mature dependency does not preclude liberal democracy.

This clearly applies to the formal aspects of government and politics in Alaska. It also raises important questions about the outcomes of both electoral and legislative political competition in Alaska. To what extent and in what ways do "normal politics" pit the interests of oil MNCs and their allies against those of more local, grassroots interests? We give careful consideration to those processes and outcomes in Chapters 3, 4, and 5. The more subtle and structural issues of discrimination based on race, ethnicity, gender, and region are beyond the scope of this book, as they are affected by, but more pervasive than, the political competition over oil policy.

Third, while mature dependence causes regions within rich, industrialized countries to be relatively underdeveloped, the domestic effects of underdevelopment can be mitigated by the state's own development policies. In other words, "the mature dependent has abundant social, economic, and political resources that can be mobilized to regulate the negative effects of dependency."[17]

We find this very descriptive of the Alaska situation and devote a substantial portion of the book to showing how, how well, and in whose interests the state's "abundant social, economic and political resources" are used to overcome the inherent limits of a resource-dependent economy (Chapters 4 through 8). These resources include, of course, the powers and authority assigned to state government by the Alaska Constitution; the relevant bodies of fiscal, regulatory, and administrative law; the Statehood Compact; and the federal US Constitution.

Furthermore, as we discuss in Chapters 5 and 9, the extent to which oil MNCs may have free rein in the Alaska political economy cannot be explained by asymmetries of power alone. Alaska political culture—alternatively described as "frontier," populist, and libertarian—embraces individualism, self-help, free enterprise, and private property rights and eschews regulation. It is consistent with these ideological affinities that the state seeks to profit from its *ownership* of land and resources and leaves the exploitation and marketing to a relatively unrestrained and putatively more efficient private sector.

Unfortunately, Hammer and Gartrell's assessment of the effects of mature dependence is not optimistic.[18] Although different in its timing from the classic dependency scenario, the structural effects are expected to be similar—i.e., loss of local control over investment, marketing, and employment. Therefore, the long-term effects on the mature dependent state's economic growth are negative, due to the state's lack of control over its relationship to global markets and the limited nature of its fiscal resources for mitigating the local effects of dependence. In sum, the mature dependent state's autonomy is still limited by resource dependency, the vagaries of international markets, and the prerogatives of foreign-based MNCs, despite its relative economic success.

Michael Pretes offers a different application of dependency theory to the Canadian case.[19] By returning to the work of earlier dependency writers, he shifts focus from a preoccupation with global patterns to inequalities among regions that divide or crosscut dependent nation-states.[20] Applying Andre Gunder Frank's analysis of the Brazilian Amazon to the Canadian Arctic, Pretes argues that the latter was underdeveloped as a function of the development strategies emanating from the wealthier, more powerful south, creating an intra-Canadian core and periphery. Citing boom-and-bust cycles related to fur, whaling, gold, and oil, he finds that the Canadian core treated the Arctic as a virtual economic and political satellite. Decisions about investment followed trends set in the south. Laws regulating everything from resource extraction and land use to native cultural practices were imposed on the Arctic by the south. Thus, the dependency relationship between resource-rich but politically weak regions and capital-rich and politically powerful regions of the same country was classically dependent. The applicability of these conclusions to Alaska is open to dispute but cannot be dismissed out of hand. Certainly, there have been times when the clout of Alaska's congressional delegation and its ability to attract federal funding argued against applying Pretes's thesis to Alaska. But many aspects of oil industry development in Alaska respond as much, or more, to national and global interests than to local ones.

So, there are reasons to apply these modifications of the dependency approach to Alaska, if we do it cautiously. The main advantage of dependency frameworks is that they allow us to both see and see beyond the obvious similarities between Alaska and other resource-dependent regions. They also show us that the significant differences between Alaska and the resource-dependent LDCs are primarily political.

Stephen Hymer, for example, argues that in a global economy dominated by multinational corporations, a state's ability to make its own development policy (including setting the terms of foreign direct investment) is inversely related to the state's distance from corporate decisionmaking centers. Furthermore, both Hymer and Evans argue that states that mainly contribute unrefined raw materials to multinational industrial activities will have the least leverage and extract the least value from their relationships with MNCs.[21] Is Alaska exceptional in that regard? That question is explored in depth in Chapter 4 and is touched on in Chapters 6 and 7 as well.

An alternative perspective comes from Cardoso's work on associated-dependent development in which he shows that when substantial control over economic and political resources is already in local hands, local bourgeoisies can extract substantial concessions from MNCs.[22] This point is further developed with Richard L. Sklar's introduction of the concept of postimperialism.[23] Sklar points out that in developing areas MNCs become an integral part of new dominant classes. In the process of class formation, the interests and orientations of the representatives of MNCs become an integral part of local economic, political, social, and cultural elites. In effect, local elites domesticate the multinationals, while the multinationals globalize the locals. The result is that we find a growing incongruence between national and dominant class interests in advanced industrial capitalist states and a growing congruence in countries in the early and intermediate stages of industrialization.[24] With that in mind, we might hypothesize that Alaska state politics display characteristics typical of late-developing, resource-dependent states. State oil policies are congruent with the interests of the state's leading social and economic forces, which include and are strongly influenced by local and multinational oil and gas interests. The state is strong enough to set many of the conditions under which oil MNCs operate; the result is a strong community of interests between state political elites, Native corporate elites, non-Native business elites, labor unions, and local representatives of oil MNCs. Oil MNCs, for their part, act consistently within the "doctrine of domicile."[25] They act as good corporate citizens, abiding by state regulatory and fiscal regimes while aggressively pursuing their economic interests through normal political means.

### Alaska, the Circumpolar North, and the American West

Alaska's oil-dependent political economy, then, is different but still comparable to oil-dependent developing countries and the northern Canadian periphery. Theories that consider the powers of states to bargain successfully with MNCs may be adapted to illuminate Alaska's situation. Does this characterization of Alaska as a different-but-not-exceptional oil region mean that it is just another resource-dependent state of the western United States—a frigid Oklahoma, Wyoming, or Idaho?

Clive S. Thomas has posited "ten enduring characteristics" of western US states, including "weak political parties and strong interest groups," "the dominance of the issue of economic development," and "an all-pervasive depend-ence on government."[26] All are evident in Alaska to varying degrees. World commodity prices and the decisions of a distant federal government may not exclusively "determine the economic well-being" of Alaska, but they do set parameters for state action. Some western states, such as California and Washington, have large internal markets and highly diversified economies that manage to insulate them from these powerful external influences, but Alaska's economy is much more vulnerable.[27] Even the Permanent Fund (discussed in Chapters 5 and 7), which invests some of the state's earnings in financial and real estate markets, still depends on oil rents for fresh infusions of capital.

Dependence on external sources of development capital and global com-modity markets contributes to boom-and-bust cycles, whether we are talking about the western United States, Latin America, Africa, or the Middle East.[28] As a "proprietary state," Alaska's bargaining leverage rests with its ownership of substantial amounts of land and subsurface rights. Therefore, the state's abil-ity to strike a good bargain rests, in part, with its ability and will to use politi-cal processes to counteract the cyclical effects of global commodities markets. In this regard, there are important differences between Alaska and other west-ern states. First, in most other western states, competing economic interests—such as ranching, farming, and mining—make for occasionally competing per-spectives on land-use policy, taxation, and other policies that affect and are affected by energy prices. That allows state policymakers to play interests against each other or at least hedge their bets on the best sources of revenues. In addition, most of these states have sales and income taxes that provide some revenue diversification and take some of the onus off the industries themselves for funding state services. In Montana, for example, where mining, oil and gas exploration, and timber accounted for the bulk of a 1.3 percent growth of employment in 2004, natural resource taxes provided only 2 percent and cor-porate income taxes only 5 percent of total general fund revenues for fiscal year 2005. Individual income taxes, on the other hand, contributed 48.4 percent.[29] In New Mexico, "severance, rents, and royalties" (a measure more directly com-parable to Alaska's oil and gas revenue stream) made up only 17 percent of gen-eral fund revenues in 2005, compared to 26 percent from income taxes (see Chapters 2, 4, and 5 for data on Alaska).[30] Therefore, Alaska's other powerful economic interests, such as fisheries and mining, may be influential in setting policy that pertains to them but do little to offset the influence of "Big Oil" in the political bargaining over fiscal policy.

## ■ Alaska: The Exception that Proves the Rule?

Alaska is not a classically dependent state due to several important political, social, and economic characteristics that set it apart from commodity-exporting LDCs. For example, despite severe problems of rural poverty and a boom-and-bust economy, Alaska is part of a developed country with high average per capita income and social indicators—such as literacy, life expectancy, infant mortality, nutrition, and infrastructure—that compare favorably with the rest of the developed world. Also, in contrast to putatively federal democracies like Mexico and Venezuela, Alaska really does enjoy a semisovereign relationship to its federal government, founded on deeply held and generally respected democratic principles and procedures. Within this federal structure, both state and national governments have regulatory authority and extract substantial rents from the activities of local and multinational enterprises involved in the oil and gas industries. Although at the national level, Alaska interests are subject to competitive pressures from states that consume oil and other states that produce it, the importance of Alaska oil to the energy and security needs of the entire nation give the state leverage.

Therefore, the instruments that Alaska has for bargaining with oil companies differ from those that have proven successful in oil-dependent LDCs. Rather than state enterprises, joint ventures, or the threat of nationalization, Alaska extracts rents through leasing, taxes, and royalties. Whether it has been as successful as it might be in that regard is a question we address in various ways throughout the book. Oil companies, for their part, seek to influence policy through conventional methods of interest-group activity such as lobbying, electioneering, and forming alliances with other local and national interests. If successful, such methods can lead to deep penetration of the political processes of this oil-dependent state—even though it is part of a democratic federal republic. We will show that in Alaska oil interests have been so successful that in the state political arena the interests of multinational corporations, local governments, state agencies, legislators and executives, local economic actors, and the federal government have become intricately interwoven. Nevertheless, we will also attempt to untangle some of these relationships in order to understand the ways in which the Alaska government has attempted to bargain with the industry on which it is so dependent.

So, while in classic studies of oil-dependent LDCs[31] the focus is typically on the formal and informal political alliances that are struck between political leaders (principally in the executive branch and/or the military) and MNCs, in this book we focus more on "normal" democratic politics. Whereas, in oil-exporting LDCs, elections are often less than transparent, state enterprises demand joint ventures, and legislative processes are often inconsequential, in Alaska, it matters that the industry attempts to influence elections, legislation, and public opinion. By examining the motivations for, methods of, and outcomes of those attempts, we see how and why the political economy of Alaska bears the unmistakable marks of oil MNCs, but we realize that those marks are also the results of the pursuit of revenue, employment, and other benefits by local and state governments committed to providing public goods and social services for their citizens while economically and politically locked into a structural condition of a resource-dependent economy.

## ▓ The Plan of This Book

Our first task is to establish that, in fact, the relationship between the state of Alaska and the oil and gas industry is a dynamic one resulting from attempts by each side to pursue its economic interests in the political arena. In Chapter 2, therefore, we provide a brief history of the exploration and commercialization of oil and gas in Alaska. We trace the development of the state's proprietary role, examining the ways in which the state has established and exercised proprietorship over oil- and gas-bearing lands and how the state's efforts to optimize rents from those lands while encouraging investment have shaped its relationship with the federal government and corporate and other organized actors. We take particular note of several key developments that have furthered or altered those relationships—including the Statehood Act of 1958, the Alaska Native Claims Settlement Act of 1971, the construction of the Trans-Alaska Pipeline System (TAPS) in 1975–1977, the Alaska National Interest Lands Conservation Act of 1980, the *Exxon Valdez* oil-spill disaster of 1989, and the battle over ANWR—and we introduce recent debates about the construction of a second major pipeline project to bring North Slope natural gas to market.

Chapter 3 examines industry influence on the "normal politics" of elections. For the most part developments in state legislation and regulations governing campaign finance and interest groups have shadowed national trends, including a tightening of formal controls to match the federal post-Watergate reforms of the 1970s and McCain-Feingold in 2002. But we also show that issues of influence, access, and accountability persist, mainly due to the overwhelming presence of industry money in elections, industry lobbyists working the halls of state government, close personal ties among legislators and industry officials, and occasional acts of corruption.

We focus on elections and the substantial role that industry money has played in supporting candidates for statewide office. We trace the connections between candidates and parties and industry support, and examine the relationship between industry support and electoral success in selected legislative and gubernatorial elections. Data presented in this chapter substantiate our modified dependency argument by detailing the considerable and costly efforts the industry makes to influence elections and gain access to lawmakers through mainly legal methods (although we do note important exceptions, especially a recent bribery scandal involving state legislators and an oil-field service corporation).

We find that oil money in the form of campaign contributions appears to have been influential in some tight races and that the industry tends to favor the state's Republican candidates and officeholders, but we also find that mainstream candidates from both major parties have received substantial support from the industry, that both parties support oil and gas development as instrumental to the state's economic interests and developmental needs, and that the industry will make substantial contributions even in noncompetitive and uncontested elections. These findings strike us as evidence of a mature dependent relationship. In the most general sense, for both major parties, the state's interests are tied tightly to oil and gas (if not always to the oil and gas MNCs), and the industry can count on substantial access to decisionmakers regardless of the party in office. However, the industry neither takes its privileged status for granted nor fails to recognize the autonomous power of the state to affect its profitability.

In Chapters 4 and 5 we address fiscal policy. Chapter 4 covers the methods employed by the state to extract revenues from its oil and gas. We provide a framework for understanding the multiple and changing strategies used by the state to optimize its share of oil and gas earnings through exercise of its sovereign authority. We apply the concepts "administrative distance" and "risk sharing" to show how the industry's positions and the state's policy responses have changed with changes in the available oil supply.

Early in the history of the state when the population was small and poor and the size and value of Alaska's known oil reserves was highly uncertain, proceeds from competitive lease sales provided the bulk of state revenues from oil, creating a regime with high administrative distance between industry and state that assigned most of the risk to the lessee. As proven reserves increased, especially with the discovery of major North Slope deposits, royalties and severance taxes became more important sources of revenue. The result was reduced administrative distance and a more equal sharing of risk. But the reduced administrative distance increased the influence of the industry on policymaking and accentuated the political effects of dependency. As the oil industry matured—from a geologic and economic standpoint—and the state matured—from a political and administrative standpoint—the administrative relationship changed as well. Each side has become more confident that its needs can be met through the political bargaining that produces revenue-raising policies.

The effects on dependency have been mixed. State agencies have developed a much stronger institutional capacity for analysis and bargaining with the oil industry, but the diminution of administrative distance over the past two decades has also resulted in a significant loss of transparency in the state's dealings with the industry. This problem was most recently illustrated by the closed-door negotiations between the Murkowski administration and the big three energy multinationals over the Petroleum Profits Tax and the proposed North Slope gas pipeline. However, the unpopularity of the governor's agreement with BP, ConocoPhillips, and ExxonMobil was a factor in his decisive defeat in the Republican gubernatorial primary in 2006; the incoming administration of Republican governor Sarah Palin promised a tougher bargaining position and a more transparent process in its dealings with the industry. Late in 2007 she developed a proposal for a new tax regime and called a special session of the state legislature to consider it. The session resulted in the second major revision to the state's oil tax regime in less than two years.

Chapter 5 examines the general parameters of state spending and changes in the value to the state of oil and gas as a revenue source. This chapter also introduces the state's two main savings accounts—the Constitutional Budget Reserve and the Permanent Fund—in the context of fiscal policy. We describe how fiscal policy reflects the complex and indirect linkages between state politics and global energy markets and how the state attempts to deal with the fiscal impact of variations in available in-state reserves. The chapter tracks the relationship between global oil price volatility and changing state fiscal policy responses from the mid-1980s to the present. We discuss tactics used by executives and legislators to live with price declines and take advantage of price surges, and we pay particular attention to the politics of the Alaska fiscal policy process, including the relationship between legislatures and governors, legislative and gubernatorial partisanship, the influence of interest groups, and the effects of political pressure on agency budgets. Along with Chapters 4 and 7, this chapter chronicles attempts by the state to stabilize revenue sources and control expenditures in order to manage the uncertainties of an oil-based economy while meeting constituent demands and budgetary commitments.

Chapter 6 provides a direct examination of development strategies—a major concern of dependency analysis and therefore a useful way to put the Alaska experience in a broadly comparative perspective. Here, as in Chapter 2, we identify the aspects of petroleum-based development that make Alaska both exceptional and a source of lessons for other resource-dependent regions.

The discovery of economically significant oil and gas deposits helped qualify Alaska for statehood but also set up the fundamental tension underlying economic policymaking for the state. Alaska's governors and legislators, from the beginning, have been pressed to satisfy their constituents' desire to make oil and gas earnings a source of capital for other types of development *and* a source of revenues to fund public services. The state faces a constant dilemma. It may be able to stimulate economic development by giving away its natural resources to the sponsors of projects that promise such long-term economic benefits as diversification of the tax base, more and higher skilled employment opportunities, and increased earnings from in-state refining of natural resources. Yet the state can ill afford to divert substantial portions of its oil rents to long-term investments at the cost of diminishing its principal revenue source for the immediate funding of public services. Overall, the state has been able to use its sovereign authority—including ownership of oil lands, royalties on production, and the power to tax property and incomes—to accomplish some of both. As our discussion of the royalty-in-kind program demonstrates, however, state-supported investments have achieved little real economic diversification, and the state remains dependent on its ability to bargain with oil and gas multinationals for its future development. Some of the state's failings in this regard are endemic to its challenging geography: remoteness from markets and processing and distribution centers; small population; and high overhead costs due to a harsh climate and limited but expensive infrastructure. Nevertheless, a substantial part of the problem, as we show in the next chapters, is political.

In Chapter 6, we also delve further into the plans and negotiations for the construction of a North Slope natural gas pipeline, heralded as "the next big thing" for bringing wealth to the state and saving Alaska from calamity due to the inevitable depletion of its oil reserves. The current struggle centers on efforts to win a firm commitment from energy MNCs to construct a pipeline to bring North Slope natural gas to national and global markets. By placing our examination of these negotiations in the context of economic development, we comprehend the controversies surrounding the gas pipeline as the most recent case of the state's attempting to engage MNCs as its agents for extracting rents from its natural resources at favorable rates.

In Chapter 7, we continue with issues related to investing state oil rents for economic diversification and fiscal stability. Effective government programs for wealth management can help even out the booms and busts that come from dependence on global commodities markets, provide a more equal distribution of the state's oil earnings, and create alternative sources of revenues and income to lessen vulnerability to the production decisions of MNCs. In this chapter, we offer a detailed account of the Permanent Fund (PF) and the Permanent Fund Dividend (PFD) program. We describe how the fund was established as an instrument of fiscal discipline to provide an additional and well-protected rainy day fund that would accumulate principal during boom times and continue to generate earnings during busts. We discuss the politics of the fund, especially its statutory insulation from political manipulation through the establishment of an independent management board and the "prudent investor" rule.

Chapter 7 provides data showing the solid success of PF investments and the economic and political effects of the PFD on the state. Since 1982, the PFD has provided equal, individual payments annually to all Alaska residents. The PFD provides a source of disposable income of great significance to lower- and middle-income households and local businesses. In addition, as intended, the PFD has served to lock in public support for the PF and constrain legislators and executives from tinkering with the program.

This chapter also contains a discussion of several "baby funds" established by city and borough governments to invest windfall earnings and provide local tax relief. We conclude the chapter by noting that the PF, as the centerpiece of Alaska's wealth management strategy, has been successful insofar as its earnings have now surpassed earnings from oil and gas rents. However, because of the politically sacrosanct nature of the PFD, it will take a major economic crisis to create the political conditions for tapping into the fund's earnings for other purposes or changing the formula for dividend distribution.

Environmental policy, when effective, illustrates key differences between oil dependency in developed democracies and authoritarian LDCs: the power that the state derives from the rule of law and high administrative capacity; the checks on political leaders that come from constitutionally mandated processes, rights, and requirements for accountability; and a strong civil society. In Chapter 8, we describe the environmental regulatory regime that governs oil and gas in Alaska. Focusing mainly on the North Slope, we describe the interactions of three tiers of government—local, state, and federal—with broad and varied constituencies. We review the public laws, executive orders, and regulations that govern the relevant federal agencies; the statutes, administrative orders, interagency agreements, and regulations administered by state agencies; and the authority delegated to the North Slope Borough (home to the giant Prudhoe Bay and Kuparuk fields) by state and local ordinances. This regulatory regime involves a complex mix of laws and regulations protecting wildlife; fisheries; waterways; marine resources; coastal zones; air, land, and water quality; and the use of related natural resources and infrastructure.

Permitting of industry activities is the key to controlling environmental impacts, and permitting has become a complicated process requiring careful coordination among all three levels of government, and attracting careful scrutiny from all interested parties. Governments have attempted to coordinate efforts at all three levels and to settle disputes among agencies. Three types of interest groups take an intense interest in the assessment and regulation of the environmental impacts of oil and gas production—industry groups, environmentalists (local, statewide, national, and international), and Alaska Native groups—as these decisions affect corporate profitability, environmental sustainability, traditional subsistence activities (hunting, gathering, and fishing), and local economic opportunities.

Normal democratic politics at the state and national levels open up multiple points of access to all of these groups. Although, as discussed in Chapter 3, industry groups have an advantage in campaign contributions and lobbying, all of these groups have proven effective to varying degrees at contacting officials, rating candidates for office, participating in public hearings, tracking and commenting on the various permitting processes, mounting public information campaigns, and using the courts. Their influence is enhanced by several institutionalized opportunities for public input and oversight, and the regulators' need for accurate and usable information, which is often in short supply.

The results for the environment and the industry have been mixed.

Arguments have been intense between industry supporters and critics in and out of government on the environmental dangers posed by oil and gas development and the sufficiency of regulatory measures at all three levels of government, but absent a disaster, judging the sufficiency of environmental regulations is often a question of explaining "the dog that didn't bark." Focusing mainly on the North Slope and TAPS, we find several reasons for concern related to scarcity of information for measuring and predicting environmental impacts; gaps and redundancies in regulatory authority; shortages of trained, local personnel (especially Alaska Natives); and lax security. Incidents of catastrophic environmental disturbances since the 1989 *Exxon Valdez* disaster (which had a pervasive effect not only on environmental policy but fiscal policy as well) have been few, leading to complacency by regulators and industry claims of diligence. However, in August 2006, a major leak was discovered in a Prudhoe Bay TAPS feeder line. The leak, it turns out, was directly attributable to mismanagement by the operator, BP Exploration Alaska, Inc. The effects of the leak and subsequent disruption of deliveries sent ripples throughout global energy markets. News of the leak revealed to a broader public the costs of insufficiencies in information and regulatory oversight and generated strong reactions from state and federal legislators.[32]

We conclude, in Chapter 9, by coming back to our organizing concepts of mature dependency and political bargaining and offering some suggestions about the relevance of the Alaska experience for understanding the political economy of other oil-dependent regions. We remain cautious in our application of dependency analysis to the state, finding particularly problematic the claims that orthodox dependency theory makes about the colonial nature of politics in dependent states. Instead, we argue that Alaska shares with other "single crop" economies around the world many of the characteristics of dependency in its domestic political economy and its relationship to the international political economy. These characteristics include extremes of wealth and poverty, particularly in underdeveloped rural areas, and easy penetration of the state's economy, political processes, and political culture by multinational corporations. We also argue, however, that in many ways Alaska is exceptional. Economically, the potential for diversification exists both in the form of other exploitable natural resources and in the human capital found only in a highly developed nation-state. Furthermore, the success and depoliticized management of the Permanent Fund, along with a replenished Constitutional Budget Reserve, could provide a soft landing when the oil runs out, provided that the political will can be found to make significant policy changes when the time comes.

Ultimately, we find that the most important deviations from the dependency thesis are political. The main role of energy multinationals in pursuit of their interests in Alaska is that of policy advocate. Recent scandals notwithstanding (which were exposed by a free press and prosecuted in federal court), the industry's political power is realized largely through conventional, legal means within constitutionally established and protected arenas of competition. MNCs, as registered legal entities in the state, enjoy the same rights and are held to the same constraints as competing interests.

The balance of interests in the bargains struck change with the changing circumstances that affect the influence of each party. For example, as noted in Chapter 4, new tax policies that reduce the administrative space between state and industry can increase industry influence, and in Chapter 9, we note the revolving door phenomenon that further enhances the ability of the industry to penetrate state legislative and executive branches. Nevertheless, we also note how the reactions of policymakers and the electorate to disasters and scandals can serve to rein in industry and allow the state to claim a larger take from oil earnings. These developments show that both sides bring considerable resources to the bargaining process.

We conclude our final chapter with an inventory and summative evaluation of the types of resources that industry and state bring to the table. As the state develops and matures, it builds capacity for bargaining on a more equal footing with the oil and gas industry. However, we urge caution. A careful analysis of developments over the state's first half-century shows that shifts in the distribution of power move both ways and frequently occur for reasons that are beyond the state's control.

## ◼ Notes

1. "The State of the State: An Address to the Twenty-Third Alaska State Legislature by the Honorable Frank H. Murkowski, Governor of Alaska, January 23, 2003," available from www.state.ak.us/local/sos12403.html.

2. Democrat Tony Knowles, Alaska's governor from 1994 to 2002, supported opening ANWR, using state funds to lobby the US Congress.

3. In addition, the state risks becoming mired in the "resource curse"—devoting the preponderance of its human and financial resources to oil and gas production and tailoring its policies to accommodate the needs of a single industry—thereby making itself incapable of timely responses to changing markets and opportunities for economic diversification. We discuss the "curse" briefly in Chapters 7 and 9.

4. Oystein Noreng, *Crude Power: Politics and the Oil Market* (New York: I. B. Tauris, 2002), pp. 41–42.

5. George D. E. Philip, *The Political Economy of International Oil* (Edinburgh: Edinburgh University Press, 2004), p. 204.

6. Philip also points out that "very large amounts of oil money may in fact work against the acquisition by LDCs [less-developed countries] of some of the other things upon which developmentally successful societies have relied. These have included a strong work ethic, an effective regulatory framework through which economic policy can be made, and a culture that rewards technological expertise." (Ibid., 204.)

7. "Green Light for BP-Arco Merger," *BBC News Online*, available from http://news.bbc.co.uk/1/hi/business/712962.stm (downloaded July 21, 2007); State of Alaska, *Spring 2007 Revenue Sources Book*, p. 6, available from www.tax.state.ak.us/sourcesbook/2007/Spr2007/index.asp (downloaded July 21, 2007).

8. Noreng observes that oil's share of international energy markets probably peaked in the late twentieth century. Since then, demand for natural gas has been advancing. But transitions to new energy sources are extremely capital intensive on both the supply and demand sides, therefore a complete transition, that would relegate oil to an obsolescing position similar to that currently held by coal, is still decades away (pp. 29–30).

9. Daniel Yergin, *The Prize: The Epic Quest for Oil, Money and Power* (New York: Simon and Schuster, 1992), pp. 12–16.

10. Kenneth Coates, "The Discovery of the North: Towards a Conceptual Framework for the Study of Northern/Remote Regions," *The Northern Review* 12/13 (1994): 25–26.

11. Peter Katzenstein, ed., *Between Power and Plenty* (Madison: University of Wisconsin Press, 1978).

12. Walter Rodney, *How Europe Underdeveloped Africa* (Washington, DC: Howard University Press, 1981). In 1998, oil and gas extraction directly employed less than 3.3 percent of the Alaskan resident workforce.

13. Robert Gramling, *Oil on the Edge: Offshore Development, Conflict, Gridlock* (Albany: State University of New York Press, 1996), p. 12. Gramling refers to federal attempts to control the leasing of offshore oil reserves during World War II and the Nixon administration's emphasis on increasing supply that led to federal support for the Trans-Alaska Pipeline after the first OPEC oil shock of the 1970s. The George W. Bush administration's national energy policy also reflects this continued tendency of the federal government to emphasize increased supply over curtailing demand. See Dick Cheney et al., *National Energy Policy: Report of the National Energy Policy Development Group* (Washington, DC: US Government Printing Office, 2001).

14. Fernando Henrique Cardoso and Enzo Faletto, *Dependency and Development in Latin America* (Berkeley: University of California Press, 1979); Peter Evans, *Dependent Development: The Alliance of Multinational, State and Local Capital in Brazil* (Princeton: Princeton University Press, 1979); Heather-Jo Hammer and John W. Gartrell, "American Penetration and Canadian Development: A Study of Mature Dependency." In Mitchell A. Seligson and John T. Passé-Smith, ed., *Development and Underdevelopment: The Political Economy of Global Inequality* (Boulder and London: Lynne Rienner Publishers, 1998), pp. 337–352.

15. Hammer and Gartrell, "American Penetration and Canadian Development," 340–341.

16. See Jack Roderick, *Crude Dreams: A Personal History of Oil and Politics in Alaska* (Fairbanks: Epicenter Press, 1997); John Strohmeyer, *Extreme Conditions: Big Oil and the Transformation of Alaska* (New York: Simon and Schuster, 1993).

17. Hammer and Gartrell, "American Penetration and Canadian Development," 341.

18. Ibid., 342.

19. Michael Pretes, "Underdevelopment in Two Norths: The Brazilian Amazon and the Canadian Arctic," *Arctic* 41, no. 2 (1988).

20. Andre Gunder Frank, *Capitalism and Underdevelopment in Latin America: Historical Studies of Chile and Brazil* (New York: Monthly Review Press, 1969); Stephen Hymer, "The Multinational Corporation and the Law of Uneven Development." In Jagdish N. Bhagwati, ed., *Economics and World Order: From the 1970s to the 1990s* (New York: The Free Press, 1972), pp. 113–140.

21. Hymer, "The Multinational Corporation," pp. 122–130; Evans, *Dependent Development*, pp. 163–213.

22. Fernando Henrique Cardoso, "Associated-Dependent Development: Theoretical and Practical Implications." In Alfred Stepan, ed., *Authoritarian Brazil: Origins, Policies and Future* (New Haven, CT: Yale University Press, 1973), pp. 142–178.

23. Richard L. Sklar, "Postimperialism: A Class Analysis of Multinational Corporate Expansion," *Comparative Politics* 9 (1976).

24. David G. Becker and Richard L. Sklar, "Introduction." In David G. Becker and Richard L. Sklar, eds., *Postimperialism and World Politics* (Westport, CT: Praeger, 1999), p. 4.

25. Richard L. Sklar, "Postimperialism: Concepts and Implications." In Becker and Sklar, *Postimperialism and World Politics*, p. 17.

26. Clive S. Thomas, "The West and Its Brand of Politics." In Clive S. Thomas, ed., *Politics and Public Policy in the Contemporary American West* (Albuquerque: University of New Mexico Press, 1991), p. 8.

27. Thomas, "The West and Its Brand of Politics," pp. 13–24.

28. John G. Francis and Clive S. Thomas, "Influences on Western Political Culture." In Thomas, *Politics and Public Policy*, pp. 23–27.

29. Jeffrey D. Greene and John R. Brueggeman, "Montana." In Carl Mott, ed., *Proceedings: Roundtable on State Budgeting in the 13 Western States, January 2006* (Salt Lake City: Utah Center for Public Policy and Administration, 2006), pp. MT-1 and MT-9.

30. Danice R. Picraux and Gilbert K. St. Clair, "New Mexico Budget—FY 2006." In Mott, *Proceedings: Roundtable on State Budgeting*, p. NM-8.

31. For example, George W. Grayson, *The Politics of Mexican Oil* (Pittsburgh: University of Pittsburgh Press, 1980).

32. Steven Quinn, "Prudhoe Bay One Year Later: BP Says Progress Has Been Made," *Fairbanks Daily News-Miner,* July 28, 2007, pp. A1, A10.

# 2

# A Brief History of Oil in Alaska

Oil and gas are Alaska's dominant natural resources in the early twenty-first century, but their economic prominence is relatively recent. Alaska's fish and game resources attracted its first residents—the indigenous population, arriving some 13,000–40,000 years ago. The fur trade (for sea otter) brought Russians to Alaska in the 1740s, and they left when the species neared depletion (as well as for other reasons pertaining to Russian weakness in post–Crimean War Europe). First gold and then fisheries created economic booms that were magnets for a large, transient population, some of whom remained when low world prices or depletion of the resource ushered in economic declines. Alaska's geopolitical position was a strategic resource attracting over 100,000 non-Natives in the 1940s and 1950s. The population base, developed through siting several large military installations in Alaska during World War II (1941–1945) and the early Cold War (1947–1953), became one of the compelling arguments for statehood in the 1950s.[1]

By a numbers count, petroleum is the fifth resource to be exploited in Alaska. Limited demand for oil and gas before the invention of the internal-combustion engine and development of the automobile industry in the early twentieth century explains much of the lack of early interest in this resource. Alaska's remoteness and distance from global markets was a second factor slowing growth. The multinational oil corporations that nearly monopolized global petroleum production could find cheaper and more accessible supplies in the contiguous forty-eight states, the Middle East, and Latin America. A related factor retarding growth was the lack of resolution of Alaska Native land claims and land status issues, which required congressional action, and the establishment of basic infrastructure to facilitate development. Alaska's territorial government was hobbled by excessive restrictions on its autonomy, yet it anticipated development by instituting some rules and regulations. Only in the 1960s did the Alaska state government begin to demonstrate the capability necessary to stimulate a robust petroleum industry.

In this chapter, we outline the history of the oil industry in Alaska in a narrative of six sections. First, we review the record of oil and gas deposits in early Alaska—discovered by Alaska Natives, by Russians during the colonial era, and by Americans in the colonial and territorial era. Then, we chronicle the development and exploitation of Alaska's first oil and gas province on the Kenai Peninsula in the late 1950s. The third section turns to the actions of the young state government as it selected lands on the North Slope as part of its statehood land grant, which inspired Native land claims mobilization. The fourth section discusses oil discovery and development at Prudhoe Bay, including construction of the Trans-Alaska Pipeline System. It also considers prospects for oil development in the Arctic National Wildlife Refuge and for construction of an Alaska natural gas line. The next section examines related North Slope discoveries, smaller in size than Prudhoe Bay, but the cumulative production from which has slowed the decline of the petroleum industry in Alaska. The final substantive section analyzes changes in the oil industry itself, in particular its increased degree of concentration.

## ■ Discovery of Oil and Gas in Early Alaska

It is not possible to say exactly when Alaska's indigenous population discovered oil, but archaeological evidence shows that early Eskimos used oil shale for fuel. It is clear that by the time they made contact with non-Natives in the eighteenth and nineteenth centuries, Natives living near surface oil deposits were using the resource. For example, the Inupiat Eskimos of Alaska's North Slope routinely burned oil for both heat and light. However, they used the oil locally, and it did not enter into trade between villages or across regions. Russian colonists did not engage in systematic mapping of Alaska's oil resources, yet before their departure in 1867 they had found both gold and oil. One site discovered to have oil seeps in the early 1850s was on the Iniskin Peninsula, located on the western side of the lower Cook Inlet.[2]

However, it was not until two decades after the cession of Alaska to the United States in 1867 that the national and international interest in oil exploration arose, and this was the primary determinant of the pace of development in Alaska. Four areas of the territory attracted the largest initial interest: the Alaska Peninsula, the Gulf of Alaska, the North Slope, and the Copper River Basin.

An area of intense activity, spanning from 1902 through the 1950s, was Cold Bay on the eastern shores of the Alaska Peninsula, near the Native village of Kanatak. Initially, groups of individual speculators drilled five oil wells from 1902 to 1904, but none of the wells produced oil in commercial quantities.[3] In the 1920s, independent wildcatters drilled another five wells in adjacent areas without producing significant output. At this point, Standard Oil

Company of California (now Chevron) entered the Cold Bay region, joining General Petroleum (now ExxonMobil) in 1921 in an exploration agreement. Company drilling of deeper wells from 1923 to 1938 did not produce commercial oil either. In the 1950s, Shell Oil acquired leases in Bear Creek near Cold Bay; then it partnered with Humble Oil (now ExxonMobil) in a drilling program in 1957 that dug the costliest well drilled in Alaska before Prudhoe Bay (14,000 feet costing $7 million), but found no oil.[4]

Exploration along the northern coast of the Gulf of Alaska initially seemed more promising. Three wells drilled from 1901 to 1903 produced from twenty-five to fifty barrels of oil a day, but the oil had a high paraffin content. The largest development venture in this region brought together Kerr-McGee Oil Industries[5] and Phillips Petroleum, which explored for oil at Icy Bay in the early 1950s. After spending $1.2 million and drilling to 12,000 feet without discovering good oil sands, Phillips shut down its Icy Bay operation, but many Alaska independents continued to explore in the region.[6]

The third area of interest was the North Slope, where the US Geological Survey (USGS) recorded geological and topological descriptions in 1919. Prompted by President Warren Harding, who believed that US Navy ships required a reliable source of fuel oil to replace coal, Congress set aside 25 million acres on the North Slope in Naval Petroleum Reserve No. 4 (called "Pet-4" until the 1960s, when Congress renamed it the National Petroleum Reserve–Alaska [NPR-A]). From 1944 to 1953, the navy drilled thirty-six test wells in this region, discovering three small oil and seven gas fields. Two accumulations were sizable—Umiat, with an estimated 50 million recoverable barrels of oil, and Gubik, with an estimated 600 billion cubic feet of recoverable gas.[7]

The final area of exploration before the discovery of the Swanson oil field on the Kenai Peninsula was the Copper River Basin. Independent investors drilled two wells northeast of Cook Inlet without discovering either oil or gas.[8] Later in the 1950s, explorers drilled three wells near Houston (some 40 miles north of Anchorage), because of reports of methane gas in the area. These, too, were dry wells.

Exploration for oil and gas during the late colonial and territorial period followed the lead of international events and technological change in the oil industry. Peaks of exploration activity occurred in the early 1900s, the 1920s before the Great Depression, and after World War II. Advances in technology enabled explorers to drill deeper wells and work at more remote sites.

The most interesting characteristic of this preliminary phase of Alaska's oil development history was the diversity of speculators, investors, and explorers who sought oil and gas. Speculation on Alaska's oil prospects attracted hundreds of individual Alaskans, limited partnerships, a large number of independent investors from the contiguous forty-eight states[9], and a bevy of national and multinational oil corporations, including the parents of today's global oil giants. Most responsible for the flood of investors, speculators, and wildcatters was the federal Mineral Leasing Act of 1920. Previous mining legislation had required prospectors to stake land for mineral claims and then work it annually. The new leasing act allowed any US citizen over twenty-one years old to file an oil and gas lease application in a federal land office. Paying a $10 filing fee and a rental fee of $0.25 an acre gave the lessee an exclusive ten-year right to the subsurface resources of the land filed for.[10] The new legislation encouraged entrepreneurs to file for large tracts of land in areas of probable oil and gas deposits and then sell the rights to oil operators. As we shall see, however, the first large oil discovery at Swanson River in 1957 transformed the Alaska oil industry.

### ■ Alaska's First Oil and Gas Discovery on the Kenai Peninsula

The Kenai Peninsula was not an area of early interest in Alaska's petroleum development. Individual investors and speculators had bought leases to Cook Inlet tracts in the early 1950s, but the first wells were not drilled until 1955, and they did not indicate substantial subsurface deposits. Nevertheless, Richfield Oil Corporation, a then relatively small West Coast oil company, filed lease applications in the middle of the north Kenai Peninsula. Its executive, Frank Morgan, believed that Alaska had huge oil potential, and company geologist, Frank Tolman, had noted a large topographic high on USGS maps and records in the north Kenai area.[11]

The oil company did not act alone, however. A group of Anchorage boosters had formed a leaseholders' club to promote oil development in Alaska. The core of the group included John McManamin and Glenn Miller (owners of the Army-Navy Surplus store) and hotelier Wilbur Wester (co-owner of the Westward, then the territory's largest hotel and center of Anchorage social life). Joining the group were Robert Atwood, publisher of the *Anchorage Daily Times,* and his brother-in-law Elmer Rasmuson, the territory's richest banker. Later associates included Willard Nagley, landowner; Fred Axford, a jeweler and owner of an ice cream and office supply store; George Jones, an accountant; Phil and Ray Raykovich, bar owners; contractor C. R. "Kelly" Foss; and vice president of the National Bank of Alaska Rod Johnston.[12] Locke Jacobs, who had developed expertise in oil leasing, soon joined them.

Several of the applications Richfield had made "top-filed" some of the group's leases, which prompted them to offer a no-cost assignment of the leases to Richfield if the corporation agreed to drill a well within two years anyplace in Alaska. Although the group stood to benefit substantially from an oil boom, Atwood dismissed profit as their chief objective: "Everyone knew that they would profit from their existing businesses even without striking oil. We just wanted a well. We weren't out to make a quick dollar like so many people who play with oil leases, get in, buy 'em, and make a quick buck. The price of our leases, we told the oil companies, was a drill hole."[13]

A complicating factor in the development of Swanson River oil was that the Richfield tracts lay completely within the Kenai National Moose Range. In early January 1955, Richfield filed for a Swanson River exploration unit with the USGS, which required that geophysical and drilling developments receive prior approval from the US Fish and Wildlife Service (FWS). Simultaneously, Congress was examining leasing in all US wildlife reserves, spurring Alaska's territorial governor Ernest Gruening and congressional delegate E. L. Bob Bartlett to urge that the moose range be opened to oil exploration. Congressional silence on the issue allowed both FWS and USGS to authorize drilling inside the unit.[14] In Alaska's first environmental protest action, the National Wildlife Federation opposed operational leases within the range for four reasons: "the potential damage to the moose population, the dubious legality of the leases, the availability of alternative areas for mineral exploitation outside wildlife refuges, and the danger of establishing a precedent inconsistent with the original purpose of the range."[15]

This protest notwithstanding, Richfield's drilling proceeded, and on July 19, 1957, a test of the Swanson River No. 1 well showed that it could produce 200 to 500 barrels daily of good quality oil. Later estimates indicated that the field, the only commercial production unit on the Kenai Peninsula, contained more than 250 million barrels of oil—a "giant" by industry standards in the United States, but only the fifth largest reservoir ever discovered in Alaska.

Discovery of commercial oil deposits on the Kenai had immediate ramifications on Alaska's statehood campaign. The chief issues in the statehood battle concerned the amount of the land grant and the impact that a state that had voted Democratic in recent elections would have on the delicate power balance of the US Senate, yet Alaska's ability to sustain itself economically was a nagging concern of both proponents and opponents of statehood. Discovery of an Alaska oil patch assuaged these concerns.

The Swanson River discovery unleashed a new land rush in Alaska, with more than a hundred oil companies and hundreds of individual investors and speculators frenetically filing applications for leases. The discovery drew attention to the immature state of the territory's oil and gas legislation. Two years prior to the Richfield find, the territorial legislature—at the urging of Governor Gruening and Territorial Senator Irene Ryan, a geological engineer—passed the Alaska Oil Conservation Act, which regulated well spacing and offset draining of oil from future state land adjacent to federal land. Also in 1955 legislators established a maximum economic recovery policy, and they passed two oil and gas taxes: a 1 percent gross oil and gas production tax and an $0.08-per-barrel conservation tax, which paid for administrative costs of the new Alaska Oil and Gas Conservation Commission.[16]

Then, in 1957, the territorial legislature passed the Alaska Land Act, modeled on the US Mineral Leasing Act. This legislation provided for competitive lease bidding only on three classes of lands—the 1 million acres of Mental Health Lands that Congress had granted Alaska in 1956, University of Alaska lands, and tidal and submerged lands (lying within 3 miles seaward of mean high tide).[17] In the Statehood Act, Congress gave Alaska the right to all minerals underlying its large land grant (unique for such a sizable land grant) and specifically required the state to retain this mineral interest when conveying property in the surface estate.[18]

The last session of the territorial legislature left unanswered the more perplexing issues of the new oil state—competitive versus noncompetitive leasing, the amount of royalty oil allocated to the state, and the formula for deriving oil and gas taxes. The new state legislature resolved these issues at its first session in 1959, with the active involvement of oil industry interests.

To craft regulations and lease forms for Alaska, the new commissioner of natural resources, Phil Holdsworth, inspected provisions from ten western and southwestern states and worked closely with the Western Oil and Gas Association (WOGA) in Los Angeles. The state Land Board held hearings on competitive versus noncompetitive leasing, and at one of the first meetings, Ryan, who had become a state senator, suggested that Alaska adopt the Canadian system, which allowed the government to harvest more of the profits of successful oil fields. Virulent oil industry opposition to this proposal removed it from the discussion table.[19]

Most individual investors and speculators wanted noncompetitive leasing, which required minimum capital to invest and allowed independents to sell their lease rights to oil companies for rich potential profits. In the uncertainty surrounding the new state's relationship with the oil industry, arguments of the independents made an impression on the public. The manager of Union Oil, representing a dozen West Coast oil companies, argued that noncompetitive leasing would lower exploration costs while bolstering Alaskans' acceptance of the oil industry. Richfield also supported the position of the independents. However, Exxon led other large firms in support of competitive leasing, contending that it would create an orderly and efficient business environment as oil companies would be able to negotiate with the state government instead of with many small independents.[20] Holdsworth attempted to satisfy both sets of interests in a compromise that restricted competitive leasing to state tide and submerged lands, while allowing noncompetitive leasing on state uplands.

The shape of the state's first oil and gas regulations and lease forms bore the strong imprint of the oil industry perspective, because Commissioner Holdsworth retained as his consultant Jim Wanvig, an attorney in Chevron's law firm recommended by Chevron's land manager and the WOGA. On Wanvig's recommendation, Holdsworth made two decisions that affected the price Alaska would receive for its oil:

First, he said the state, not producers, should in effect pay for the cost of transporting oil from offshore Cook Inlet wells to land before it was tankered to West Coast refineries. The companies could deduct platform-to-shore charges before making their royalty payments to the state. Second, the point at which the value of the state's royalty oil should be determined was outside Alaska. It was to be "netted back" from the price paid at the refinery. This netting back—subtracting the cost of transporting the oil from the well head to the refinery—to determine the oil's value was realistic, Holdsworth believed, because most Cook Inlet oil would be refined on the West Coast.[21]

These regulations won the support of the industry, for the obvious reason that they were written in the industry's interest. Wanvig's firm drew 30 percent of its business from Chevron, and WOGA paid for his expenses in Alaska. Twenty years later, Alaska Supreme Court Justice Alan Compton, ruling on Cook Inlet field costs in a 1978 royalty lawsuit, said the state's hiring of Wanvig was like having "a fox in the chicken coop."[22]

The state's new bureaucracy lacked expertise comparable to industry in oil and gas regulation. And certainly, the mood then in the new and impoverished state was strongly supportive of development. For example, when the first session of the First Alaska Legislature amended the Alaska Land Act, legislators added a provision to encourage oil exploration. Instead of the customary 12.5 percent royalty for discovery of commercial quantities of petroleum on state lease lands, companies would pay a royalty of only 5 percent for the first ten years. This was not the only occasion when state administrators and legislators made decisions favoring oil industry interests in the belief that it would promote long-term state interests.

The new state's compromises with the oil industry had an immediately positive impact on state finances. By 1963, oil and gas accounted for about three-fourths of all mineral production in Alaska.[23] New oil and gas production in Cook Inlet, adjacent to the Kenai, bolstered net petroleum receipts to the state. By 1967, Alaska's income derived from oil and gas (as well as other mineral deposits) surpassed federal military expenditures for the first time in Alaska's history; oil became the chief source of state income, and fisheries moved to a distant third place.[24] Yet it was the discovery of oil on the Alaska North Slope that secured Alaska's place as an international oil giant. To appreciate this event, we discuss briefly the context for Prudhoe Bay oil development in state land selections and the developing Alaska Native claims movement.

## ■ State Land Selections on the North Slope

Native land claims played a prominent role in the development of Alaska's oil economy. The source of the land claims issue lay in the fact that Native rights in the land, based on aboriginal use and occupancy, were recognized but never clearly defined and resolved after the US purchase of Alaska in 1867.[25] Unlike the Indians of the contiguous forty-eight states, Alaska Natives had not been defeated in war, treaties were not made, and reservations generally were not established. The Alaska Organic Act[26] of 1884 provided the legal foundation for the land issue. According to the act, Alaska Natives were not to be "disturbed in the possession of any lands actually in their use or occupation or now claimed by them but the terms under which such persons may acquire title to such lands is reserved for future legislation by Congress."

When Alaska became a state seventy-five years later, Congress had not yet acted on the issue. However, in the 1958 Statehood Act, Congress reaffirmed Alaska Natives' rights even as it authorized the state to select 104.3 million acres of land from a public domain of some 375 million acres. The act thus provided that "the state and its people . . . forever disclaim all right and title . . . to any lands or other property . . . the right and title to which may be held by Indians, Eskimos, or Aleuts."[27] Congress again reserved to itself the power to define and resolve the problem of Alaska Native claims, but it did not exercise this power. Instead, Congress authorized state land selections while attempting to maintain the status quo with respect to Alaska Native land rights. This set the stage for direct clashes between the state government and the Native people.

The state's land selections were to be made by January 1984 through a lengthy and complex process involving notifications, adjudication of conflicting claims, tentative approvals, surveys, and, finally, issuance of patents.[28] Before this process began, the interior secretary had received Alaska Native claims to 122 million acres of Alaska land. Indians and Eskimos made these claims and maintained that aboriginal title to the lands remained affirmed under the federal acts discussed above. Before the filing deadline of the Indian Claims Commission in 1951, ten Native groups filed claims.[29] These claims were still pending ten years later. In the rest of the state, Indians, Eskimos, and Aleuts still occupied or used lands where their homes were located and on which they hunted and fished.

The processes for the nomination and patenting of state land did not lead to Native participation or even notification in a form most understandable to them, despite the claim of the state that it did not intend to seek title to lands that the "Natives are clearly using or occupying."[30] However, in 1961, state nominations of lands did bring protests from the residents of the villages of Minto, Tanacross, Northway, and Dillingham. They filed claims with the federal Bureau of Land Management (BLM), which were dismissed because they were not claims to lands actually occupied by Alaska Natives. In February 1962, the federal Bureau of Indian Affairs (BIA) joined these villages in objecting to state selection of lands in their areas and in supporting the claims to the BLM. Yet the Alaska director of the BLM dismissed the protests, claiming he lacked authority to determine the "validity of aboriginal title."[31] This case was appealed to the interior secretary, but state land selections continued.

The pace of state land selections reflected some ambivalence in policy. Because of the state's need for revenues, it quickly selected those lands of obvious commercial value, but for a series of reasons, the state progressed slowly in nominating the balance of lands available for selection. First, the amount of money that the state received from the federal aid highway fund was based, in part, on the ratio of federal to state land; thus, the more land the state selected, the less money it received from the federal government for highway construction. Second, state officials were ignorant about where the most valuable resources lay. The state then had insufficient funds and expertise to conduct the inventories necessary for this purpose. Third, federal laws passed in 1964 provided that the federal government should classify public domain lands according to their best use and dispose of these lands in certain designated classes; 90 percent of the proceeds from sales of these lands would be transferred to the state, reducing the need of the state to select lands.[32] Finally, the state was required to pay for management and fire protection of the lands it selected.[33]

Nonetheless, this pattern of state land selections ignited Alaska Native protests. By 1966, 150 million acres were under Alaska Native protest in addition to the 122 million acres claimed at the end of 1951. Claims to 4.8 million acres affected state-selected lands (about one-quarter of the lands the state had selected since 1959).[34]

Native claims also affected state oil and gas leasing activity. When Native Alaskans of the south-central coast filed a protest, the state withdrew some tracts from sale. Then, in 1966, Alaska Natives objected to the plans of the state to sell oil and gas leases on the North Slope, on land the state had already selected and tentatively approved for patent. Following this, Secretary of the Interior Stewart Udall declared a moratorium on transfers of all federal lands to state jurisdiction until the Native claims were settled.[35] Consequently, BLM offices in Anchorage and Fairbanks were instructed to suspend all final actions, including granting of tentative approvals on state selections, mineral leases, and issuing of final patents—the start of the Alaska land freeze. Federal leasing activity in the Arctic Slope area also was largely curtailed because of this decision.

However, the state moved to develop its tentatively approved lands; it leased twenty tracts on the Arctic Slope area, including those in Prudhoe Bay that later produced the North Slope oil discovery. By then, Walter J. (Wally) Hickel, who had defeated William A. (Bill) Egan in the 1966 election and ordered the lease sale among his first acts as governor, remarked, "Alaska is on its way to becoming one of the major oil-producing states of the Union and artificial barriers to development must be broken down for the benefit of all."[36] Yet, the state Division of Lands noted that its actions were circumscribed by Alaska Native protests; it complained that state revenues from oil and gas had dropped from $4 million in 1966 to $3.5 million in 1967.

The federal policy of declining to take final action on lands under recorded Native land claims brought an end to most state selections by 1967.[37] Not even tentative approval was granted on state selections, and without tentative approval, the state could not assume management of the selected land. In 1968, the US Congress refused to extend beyond 1969 the deadline for state selections of mineral lands provided under the federal Mineral Leasing Act of 1920. (The statehood act gave Alaska the right to select mineral lands for five years; Congress granted an extension until January 1969.) This action caused an accelerated filing of state applications covering about 7.5 million acres on the North Slope and in the Bristol Bay and Copper River Basin areas.[38] The state's land selection program came to a complete halt in late 1968 when Secretary Udall expanded the land freeze by withdrawing for two years all unreserved federal lands in the state to protect Native rights.

In short, state efforts to select lands under Native claims initiated high reaching changes in communities throughout the state. When selections began after statehood, only villages directly affected protested. By 1969, however, Alaska Natives had mobilized; they recorded forty-two often overlapping claims, which covered 388.8 million acres (the state has only 375 million acres of land). The federal land freeze prevented any transaction—whether state selection or homesteading—on federal lands.

The Alaska Native claims movement did not invalidate the state's existing selections of North Slope lands, the sale of leases on tentatively approved lands, or the development and production of oil and gas from those lands. But Alaska Native claims protests effectively curtailed transportation of newly discovered oil, while they questioned the legitimacy of existing leases.

## ■ Prudhoe Bay and the Trans-Alaska Pipeline

### Oil Discovery at Prudhoe Bay

The state had sold leases to the Prudhoe Bay area in 1964. British Petroleum (BP), which had entered the Alaska oil market only in 1959, purchased more than half of the leases. Expelled from Iran a few years earlier, the oil multinational had reevaluated its global investment and development strategy and turned its focus toward Alaska.[39] BP's geologists, like those of other oil multinationals, recognized the unusual Sadlerochit formation near Prudhoe Bay that signaled a large oil and gas reservoir. In the 1965 state lease sales of remaining Prudhoe Bay–area parcels, BP spread its bids across the entire huge structure. Richfield (then partnered with Exxon) bid higher on the crest where seismic data showed more oil would be tapped. BP bid on the flanks as well and thereby captured more than half the oil in Prudhoe Bay.[40]

It was Richfield that again led the march in North Slope oil and gas development, but in a new form. Although the oil firm had been highly successful in exploiting Swanson River oil and had explored most of Alaska's sedimentary basins, antitrust action of the federal Justice Department jeopardized its status.[41] Two other oil companies—Sinclair and Cities Service—together owned more than 50 percent of Richfield's common shares and were ordered to divest themselves of the shares within seven years. Richfield sought a new partner, and Atlantic Refining Company, once owned by John D. Rockefeller, acquired it. The merged corporation, Atlantic Richfield Company (ARCO), became the seventh largest oil company in the United States.

ARCO began drilling on its North Slope leases in late 1967, somewhat later than BP and other companies, which had found no oil and planned to depart. It dug nine dry holes, but by the end of the year, the tenth well displayed massive natural gas deposits, which it announced in mid-January 1968;[42] two months later, ARCO announced oil discovery at the flow rate of 20 to 30 thousand barrels per day. Estimates of the size of Prudhoe Bay reserves at that time were 22 billion barrels of oil (9.6 billion of which were recoverable, a figure that has since increased to more than 13 billion barrels) and nearly 38 trillion cubic feet of natural gas.[43] The oil was a good quality medium gravity crude with less than 1 percent sulfur content. The discovery was the largest in the Western Hemisphere and the twelfth largest in the world.[44]

Several events flowed directly from the huge Prudhoe Bay discovery. North Slope oil and gas leases became extremely valuable. Oil companies pressured the state to sell off remaining leases, particularly those offshore that were thought to tap into the Sadlerochit formation. Natural Resources Commissioner Tom Kelly conducted a bonus lease sale in September 1969, which netted the state more than $900 million and inaugurated (briefly) a state spending spree. Governor Hickel sought to expedite development of the North Slope leases and directed the state Department of Transportation to carve a road through the tundra to Prudhoe Bay. Constructed in the winter of 1968–1969, the road carried 7,464 tons of heavy equipment to the North Slope oil fields. Affectionately dubbed the Hickel Highway by successor Keith Miller in 1969,[45] the highway quickly turned into ruts as roadbed permafrost melted. This ecological disaster focused the interest of national environmental organizations on Alaska at the starting point of US environmental consciousness.[46]

The three owner companies of most Prudhoe Bay oil and gas—ARCO, Exxon, and BP (which merged with Sohio in 1970)—were preoccupied with their search for a route to transport oil from the North Slope to market. Briefly, Exxon proposed a tanker route through the Northwest Passage. In 1969, it sent its largest oil tanker, the SS *Manhattan*, from a Pennsylvania port to Barrow, but it required assistance from US and Canadian icebreakers to escape pack ice. This indicated the possibility of an all-sea route for transport of oil to East Coast markets, but the waters of the Beaufort Sea were too shallow to allow construction of a tanker terminal.[47] Moreover, Canada asserted sovereignty over the Northwest Passage, which limited support for this alternative.

The companies also considered a route from Prudhoe Bay to Fairbanks and then to follow the Alaska Highway through Canada to the US Midwest. This route too was attractive to Exxon, which had more East Coast and Midwest markets than its partners, and it won support of political leaders in the Midwest. By the close of 1969, however, the companies had selected an all-Alaska route, beginning at Pump Station 1 in the center of the Prudhoe Bay field and traveling 800 miles south to the ice-free port of Valdez. Because the pipeline route would cross federal, state, and some private lands, it required both federal and state permits (the companies sought a right-of-way of 100 feet for the 48-inch diameter hot-oil pipeline) under new federal environmental legislation and ultimately an authorization from Congress. Because its route crossed lands claimed by Alaska Natives, it required resolution of Native land claims by Congress as well. These two issues dominated the congressional agenda from 1969 to 1973.

## Settlement of Native Claims

A number of bills were introduced in Congress from 1967 until final resolution of the Native land issue with passage of the Alaska Native Claims Settlement Act (ANCSA) in December 1971. The bills differed in sponsorship and substance but raised identical issues: (1) the size of the land settlement, with proposals from as few as 100,000 to as many as 60 million acres; (2) the amount of compensation for land already taken and the period over which this would be paid; (3) the extent to which Alaska Natives would share in income from state and federal mineral leases; and (4) the organizational structures and allocation of authority for administration of lands and funds. The active players were the Alaska Federation of Natives (AFN), formed in October 1967 to represent all Alaska Natives in their quest for a just claims settlement; the US Department of the Interior; the state's congressional delegation and governor; committee chairs in the Congress; and the oil industry.[48]

Initially, legislation proposed by the Department of the Interior and the AFN authorized courts to determine the amount of money paid to Alaska Natives for lost lands. The state's position had been adamantly opposed to a large land grant until Governor Hickel was forced by the land freeze to cooperate with AFN in forming a land claims task force. The task force recommended awarding 40 million acres of land; 10 percent of the federal income from Alaska's Outer Continental Shelf (OCS) oil lease royalties; and administration through statewide, regional, and village business corporations (the first mention of what became the vehicle for claims administration).

Before Congress seriously considered alternate bills, Henry Jackson, chair of the Senate Committee on Interior and Insular Affairs, called for comprehensive research as a basis for legislation, denominating the Federal Field Committee for Development Planning in Alaska to undertake the research. The field committee's publication *Alaska Natives and the Land* was influential because it documented Native aboriginal use and occupancy of large tracts of land; too, the report influenced Senator Jackson to author legislation raising the possible compensation to $1 billion.

The field committee also recommended revenue sharing from public lands and mineral leases, a proposal that entered a new AFN bill, written after the state's $900 million bonus lease sale. Two other bills, one sponsored by Senator Jackson, and the second by Representative Wayne Aspinall, chair of the House Committee on Interior and Insular Affairs, created a situation of uncertainty, which was clarified when AFN sought and obtained President Richard M. Nixon's support for a generous settlement. Lobbied by oil companies anxious to avoid further delay in construction of the pipeline, and persuaded by the sole Republican in the state's congressional delegation, Senator Ted Stevens, that a village-based settlement would not conflict with state land selections, in April 1971 the administration proposed 40 million acres, $500 million in direct compensation, and $500 million from mineral revenues.

White House support brought compromises in both House and Senate versions, with results in the conference committee favoring the AFN position, which emphasized the role of Native-controlled regional corporations for the administration of settlement land and money. Hearings on the various land claims measures had produced only moderate and predictable opposition: from the miners who objected to limits on mineral exploration they feared a large land grant would impose; from the Alaska Sportsmen's Council, which feared loss of the best hunting areas in the state to Alaska Natives; and from the conservative *Anchorage Times*.

Other major actors in the legislative campaign were always potential supporters of claims legislation. When Wally Hickel left for Washington, DC, in 1969 to become secretary of the interior, there was backsliding in Juneau, briefly, as the transitional Miller administration reasserted the contention that the land claims issue was a federal matter and that funds to settle it should not come from the state. However, the land freeze and perceived need to expedite oil and gas development made congressional legislation an urgent issue for Alaska's governors. By 1971, Governor Egan promised to accept even a 60-million-acre settlement and a 2 percent share of state mineral revenues for Natives.

The oil industry initially objected to the concept of a generous land settlement, and throughout the campaign, it refused to negotiate with regional or statewide Native associations.[49] However, the filing of claims to lands on which oil companies held leases, and particularly the filing of petitions for injunctions (primarily by the Arctic Slope Native Association) against their ongoing exploration programs, made their investments unstable. Even more unsettling was the prospect that no pipeline permit would be issued by the Department of the Interior until land claims were settled. The industry finally endorsed the congressional settlement of 44 million acres of land, $962.5 million, and ANCSA management by twelve regional for-profit corporations.

## Pipeline Authorization

Authorization of the Trans-Alaska Pipeline System was even more controversial. Part of the delay can be attributed to the oil industry itself. Although BP, ARCO, and Exxon owned most of the Prudhoe Bay oil and gas, four other companies had small shares. It took nearly a year for the seven companies to agree on the form of the consortium that would construct and manage the pipeline for the owner companies and to entrust its executive with sufficient authority to negotiate with federal and state legislators, bureaucratic officers, and Alaska Natives. In 1970, the companies announced the establishment of the Alyeska Pipeline Service Company, and hired engineer Edward Patton as its president.

A second factor in the delay concerned the implementation of new environmental legislation. In January 1970, President Nixon signed into law the National Environmental Policy Act (NEPA). Under its terms, any major federal action that might have a significant impact on the environment had to undergo an environmental impact statement (EIS) review.[50] The Department of the Interior's leasing of TAPS constituted such a major action and required an exhaustive review of the alternatives to construction along the proposed route and the design of the pipeline itself. The design needed to answer questions about the impact of the hot-oil pipeline on fish and wildlife (particularly the migrating caribou along part of the route); its impact on unstable soils, especially regions of continuous and discontinuous permafrost; and the impact of earthquakes on the oil pipeline. Initially, the companies proposed a pipeline that would be buried over most of the route (see Figure 2.1). The state's new Department of Environmental Conservation required that Alyeska build an elevated pipeline in all sections having unstable soils. Oil company engineers had not constructed a pipeline to address potential disturbances in an Arctic environment, and the redesign work delayed issuance of the final EIS until May 1972.

Environmental organizations that opposed TAPS construction made five basic criticisms: (1) the Interior Department was subservient to the oil industry; (2) federal construction and operations stipulations were vague and unenforceable; (3) insufficient attention had been paid to meeting energy needs

Figure 2.1 Trans-Alaska Pipeline System

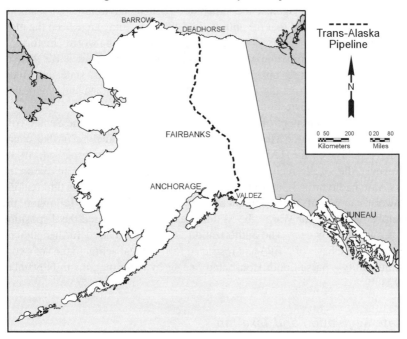

*Source:* Alaska Department of Transportation.

from other sources; (4) superior transportation alternatives, particularly a common oil and gas transportation corridor through Canada, had not been investigated properly; and (5) the Interior's economic and national security data, specifically to the effect that oil supplies from the Middle East were unreliable, were specious and distorted.[51] Nevertheless, Judge George Hart of the Washington, DC, District Court ruled that the final EIS complied with all NEPA requirements and lifted the injunction he had imposed. However, the US District Court of Appeals in Washington, DC, determined that the project could not be approved until Congress amended the Mineral Leasing Act to accommodate a broader right-of-way. (Alyeska had requested a 100-foot right-of-way, while the act provided for only 64 feet.) Thus, the TAPS issue left the courts and entered Congress.

A large array of environmental organizations opposed TAPS construction, with a fallback position that a Canadian route be used. They included the Sierra Club, the Wilderness Society, the National Wildlife Federation, the Wildlife Management Institute, Friends of the Earth, Defenders of Wildlife, Trout Unlimited, Zero Population Growth, Environmental Action, the Citizen Committee on Natural Resources, and the Alaska Action Committee. An umbrella organization—the Alaska Public Interest Coalition (APIC)—coordinated the campaign against the pipeline.[52] British environmental historian Peter Coates remarked that the antipipeline coalition "may have been the most powerful and broad-based conservationist force in world history."[53] Advocating for the pipeline were Alyeska and the oil companies; the state of Alaska and the state's congressional delegation; national, state, and local chambers of commerce; the Teamsters and other labor unions; and, importantly, the Nixon administration.

The critical moment of review was July 17, 1973, when the Senate considered Alaska Senator Mike Gravel's amendment to foreclose further court-ordered delays on the TAPS project. The first vote narrowly passed, 49-48. However, the vote to reconsider tied at 49-49 (because a senator absent on the first vote had returned), and Vice President Spiro Agnew used his tie-breaking power in favor of the amendment. The Arab oil embargo following the October Yom Kippur War in the Middle East quickly changed the disposition of Congress, however. The authorization act—which barred further judicial review on the basis of NEPA and restricted further legal action to the act's constitutionality—passed both House and Senate by large margins in November 1973.

## State Regulation and Taxation

A final issue related to the discovery of the Prudhoe Bay oil reservoir concerned state regulation and taxation. In 1971, Governor Egan proposed that the state build and own the pipeline. He argued that oil company ownership of the line would adversely affect the state's revenue from Prudhoe Bay oil. The pipeline owners would establish high charges for use of the pipeline to transport oil and then deduct these tariffs as transportation expenses before paying taxes and royalties to the state. He also believed that the oil companies would inflate the costs of construction and pipeline operation.[54] The legislature established a special committee to examine this issue and took testimony from oil company representatives. They vehemently opposed state ownership of the pipeline and questioned whether the state could finance construction, build the line expeditiously, and get throughput to market (the chief interest of those buying bonds). Oil industry opposition to the Egan proposal effectively killed it, and the state senate voted it down by a large majority.

A competing proposal for control of the pipeline came from Chancy Croft, an Anchorage Democratic state senator and political rival of Egan. In 1972, Croft proposed that the state impose right-of-way leasing fees on users of the oil pipeline. By the price the state charged, it would be able to regulate pipeline tariffs. (By adjusting the leasing fee, the state could counter high construction costs, pipeline earnings and tariffs.) This idea too met stiff oil industry opposition, but the state legislature supported it.[55] During the same session, the legislature also passed Egan's cents-per-barrel tax on oil companies. The tax guaranteed a minimum payment to the state for each barrel of oil produced and would serve as a replacement for the state's severance tax in the event oil prices dropped significantly.[56]

Both laws irritated Alaska's oil companies and ten (Amerada Hess, Amoco, BP, Humble Oil, Humble Pipeline, Gulf, Phillips, Skelly, Sohio, and Union) sued the state in superior court. They alleged that the laws violated the doctrine of federal preemption of interstate commerce regulation. Furthermore, the companies argued that litigation over the legislation would further delay construction of the pipeline. While Congress debated the TAPS authorization bill, pressure in Alaska intensified to construct the pipeline. Finally, during the 1973 legislative session, the governor authorized negotiations with the oil companies, which led to a compromise of Egan's cents-per-barrel tax and the repeal of Croft's right-of-way leasing law.[57] Egan then called the legislature into a special session in October 1973 to consider the package. However, he had not consulted legislative leadership during the discussion with the oil companies, which led to the perception, particularly by Democrats, that he had sold out the state's interests in order to expedite pipeline construction.

The elements in Egan's proposal included the following:

- a $0.25-per-barrel minimum tax,
- a 20-mill property tax on pipeline facilities,
- amendments that would cripple Croft's right-of-way leasing law,
- elimination of the tariff-setting authority of the just-established Alaska Pipeline Commission,
- a one-eighth-cent-per-barrel conservation tax,
- changes to the 8 percent severance tax,
- a common-purchaser/common-carrier pipeline bill, and
- a measure enabling pipeline owner companies to purchase the Valdez terminal site.[58]

Legislators operated under two constraints. First, the Arab oil boycott brought about instant increases in oil prices and increased pressure on legislators to facilitate pipeline construction. Second, the oil industry's lobbyists warned legislators that if the package did not pass intact, the pipeline would be further delayed and the industry would need to renegotiate its deal with the state. Legislators made few changes to the proposals. They allowed local governments along the pipeline corridor to share in the 20-mill tax on oil and gas production and pipeline assets. They also required the pipeline to operate as a common carrier, so that all oil producers would have equal access to it. And they lowered the ceiling for assessment of the severance tax, without raising the rate. Both houses supported the Egan proposals.

In retrospect, Egan's attorney general John Havelock, who negotiated the state's position with the oil companies, said he would have acted differently:

> I was concerned about flat well head prices. The industry opposed it bitterly, and churned a lot on that. If we had been more far-sighted, we would have just increased the ad valorem rate. Look at what goes on in other states. Head banging. Then, our rate was roughly comparable to the best rate of any state, but of course not foreign governments. We could have set a higher rate. This would have cut the industry's profit. No state ever built a pipeline on its own.[59]

In short, he thought that the state did not employ its power of taxation effectively.

Perhaps the state could have won better terms. As in the crafting of oil and gas regulations and lease forms in 1959, however, the state lacked expertise and did not have the resources to withstand a long legal battle with the oil industry.

### ■ Related North Slope Discoveries and Prospects

The period from discovery of Prudhoe Bay oil and gas resources in 1968 to the congressional authorization of TAPS in November 1973 marked a critical era in Alaska state history. External forces (the federal government, multinational oil corporations) and external events (the Arab oil embargo) narrowed the state's options. Pipeline construction starting in 1974 brought jobs and money to the state, and from the first barrel of oil coming out of the pipeline in 1977 to the start of the decline in Prudhoe Bay production in 1989, the state settled into a dependent relationship with the oil industry, a dependence prefigured by the 1973 special session of the legislature.

After the Prudhoe Bay discovery, however, there were no comparable oil finds. We review here the smaller fields discovered (see Figure 2.2) and brought into production by oil companies, the technological changes in the industry making development of smaller fields profitable, the state's self-imposed limits on oil company taxation established in 1981, and the two prospective developments most important to state economic development—oil exploration and development in ANWR and Prudhoe Bay natural gas.

### *Discovery of New Petroleum Resources*

Sinclair Oil Company made the next large discovery on the North Slope. After drilling seven dry holes between 1962 and 1966, Sinclair and BP (its partner of the time) closed down exploratory operations. ARCO's Prudhoe Bay discovery motivated Sinclair to reactivate its drilling program; in 1969, it discov-

**Figure 2.2  North Slope Oil and Gas Activity, 2006–2007**

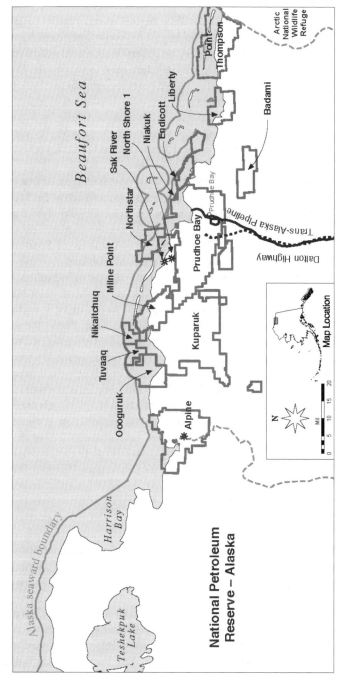

*Source:* State of Alaska Department of Natural Resources.

ered the Kuparuk River field, 40 miles west of Prudhoe Bay. This was Sinclair's largest and final discovery in its 65-year history.[60]

The Kuparuk field with about 3 billion barrels of recoverable reserves is Alaska's second largest and the second largest in North America. Without the discovery at Prudhoe Bay, the Kuparuk discovery well would not have been drilled. Without TAPS and the other infrastructure built to support the Prudhoe Bay field, the Kuparuk field would not have been economical to develop. The field came into production in 1981.

ARCO also made smaller discoveries at Lisburne and Point McIntyre, but it remained frustrated in its attempt to develop oil accumulations in West Sak. This field has an estimated 10 billion to 15 billion barrels of oil, yet it is cold, shallow oil—quite viscous and difficult to remove.[61]

During the late 1970s and early 1980s, BP conducted an active exploration program in the Beaufort Sea, leading to discoveries such as Endicott and Niakuk.[62] Endicott is the third largest major oil field after Prudhoe Bay and Kuparuk (a joint venture of BP, Exxon, and ARCO); the field has about 600 million barrels of recoverable oil. Development beginning in 1985 featured the construction of a 5-mile-long causeway and two gravel islands.

Alpine became the state's fourth largest oil reservoir (430 million recoverable barrels) and is the farthest western oil field on the Alaska North Slope. It is called the "gateway" to NPR-A, where drilling began in 1999, and it produced oil in 2000. BP developed three new fields in the 1990s, the first of which was the small (and now closed) Badami reservoir near ANWR. Northstar (with 160 million recoverable barrels of oil) is in the US OCS and is the first producing OCS field in the US Arctic. For this reason, it is particularly objectionable to the national and state environmental constituencies. Liberty, another BP development with about 120 million barrels, was shut down in 2001 because the company deemed its exploitation economically unfeasible. The Badami and Liberty closures notwithstanding, North Slope operators have established a pattern of aggressive oil field development that has partially offset the significant depletion of the aging Prudhoe Bay and Kuparuk oil reservoirs.

## Technological Change in the Oil Industry

It was technological developments in the oil industry that made it possible to profitably develop deposits once considered marginal. Costs of North Slope oil production have dropped to one-fourth of those in the late 1960s. Four technological changes bear mention. First in importance, petroleum engineers have enhanced recovery of oil from reserves by four methods: gas cap expansion/gravity drainage, water flood, miscible flood, and gas cycling.[63]

Second, directional (extended reach) drilling changed the way the oil industry taps distant petroleum accumulations. From a single pad, operators have access to a larger area, to a distance of four miles. Third, exploration and production footprints have been reduced by more than 80 percent through closer spacing of wellheads and construction of smaller pads. Fourth, drilling efficiency has increased because of the acquisition of advanced seismic data and interpretation. All four changes in technology lowered exploration and production costs, increased efficiency of recovery, and promised to minimize environmental disturbances.

## Limitations on Taxation of Oil Companies

The flush of oil production after the startup of TAPS in 1977 provided more royalty and tax revenues to Alaska than even the most optimistic booster had predicted. The motivation to change the oil and gas taxation regime was an outgrowth of the "Sunshine Boys" reforms of 1974–1980, when Democratic legislators inspired by the post-Watergate era in American politics controlled the House of Representatives.[64] Leading the charge against oil company dominance was Chancy Croft. In 1976, he persuaded the legislature to establish a $30 million fund for immediate cleanup of oil spills (declared later to be an unconstitutional infringement on interstate oil transportation).

Then, in 1978, Croft led the effort to change the way oil companies were taxed. To that time, the state taxed companies based on global profits and losses, which enabled them to transfer large Alaska profits and avoid heavier local taxes. The new legislation taxed oil based on profits of Alaska operations.[65] This "separate accounting" tax met an instant court challenge from oil companies.

By 1981, the Supreme Court had not resolved the issue, and Governor Jay Hammond, seeing that two states using separate accounting had lost their cases to oil companies, decided to support repeal of the method in the event Alaska lost its case and had to repay the disputed funds. Also, in 1981, the Sunshine Boys era came to an end in a legislative coup that installed Republican control. The legislative repeal, crafted by Revenue Commissioner Tom Williams (who later managed British Petroleum's Alaska tax office), easily passed the oil-friendly legislature.[66] Croft's assessment of the reversal pictured it as a juncture in the state's relationship with the oil industry:

> The demise of separate accounting marked the day that Alaska capitulated to the oil industry. That's when the state became a seller rather than a regulator of oil. Separate accounting not only gave us added revenue, but it also gave us important information. The state's power to tax is limited, but information can give you a good idea of what the limits are. It gave the state some basis to form an intelligent policy towards the oil industry, and Alaska lost that.[67]

The court upheld the validity of separate accounting in 1985, but the legislature did not restore it.

The post-coup legislature also declined to fix a loophole in legislation (called the Economic Limit Factor, or ELF) giving tax breaks to marginal oil fields. In 1981, the companies applied the ELF to both Prudhoe Bay and Kuparuk, lowering their taxes by nearly $150 million annually. Only in the negative mood toward the oil industry following the *Exxon Valdez* oil spill of 1989 (see Chapters 6 and 8) was it possible to remove the ELF and pass tough oil-spill and other environmental regulations. By this time, however, Prudhoe Bay production had begun its decline, and this environment made significant tax increases difficult to enact (except those directly related to oil-spill response and cleanup) for fear of losing oil company investments in the state.

An increased number of small fields may significantly increase oil production, but they cannot replace Prudhoe Bay; at its peak in 1988, it sent 2.1 million barrels of oil daily through the pipeline, which then constituted nearly 25 percent of domestically produced American oil. For this reason, oil companies and state policymakers have sought another Prudhoe Bay, focusing their attention on ANWR.

## The Arctic National Wildlife Refuge

The refuge occupies the eastern end of the 500-mile-long North Slope, a treeless plain between the jagged Brooks Range and the nation's only Arctic shore. The Alaska National Interest Lands Conservation Act (ANILCA), passed by the Congress in 1980, requires congressional action to open any section of the refuge for oil and gas development. In 1987, the Division of Oil and Gas of the Alaska Department of Natural Resources estimated that ANWR reserves stood at 29 billion barrels—over two times the size of the Prudhoe Bay field.[68] The federal Department of the Interior's final report on oil leasing in ANWR made a lower estimate of 9.2 billion barrels of recoverable oil. The Interior agreed that the area held the highest oil and gas potential of any unexplored US onshore frontier region, and it recommended to Congress that the coastal plain be opened for "orderly" oil development.[69]

However, ANWR has been the defining issue for US national environmental organizations. Notwithstanding very strong Alaskan support—consistently measuring 70–75 percent in public opinion polling—and unified advocacy of the legislature, governor, and the congressional delegation, ANWR has been a casualty of divided government (until the election of George W. Bush in 2000) and US Senate filibuster rules. The Reagan and Bush I administrations supported oil development in ANWR, but Democrats controlled both houses of Congress and opposed opening of the 1002 section thought to contain the largest reservoir. When Republicans captured both houses of Congress in the 1994 election, a Democratic president, Bill Clinton, occupied the White House, and opposed development. The election of George W. Bush initially gave the greatest momentum to the effort of developers.

Industry experts consistently contend that new technologies for efficiently finding and drilling for oil have sharply reduced pollution and other environmental problems and that wildlife generally is not harmed by oil and gas development. Scientists from conservation groups, however, believe that expansions of the oil fields would irrevocably mar one of the country's wildest and most fragile landscapes. Leaders of Native communities point to scars on their culture from development, notwithstanding the jobs and other benefits it provides.[70]

The first few months of the Bush II administration and the 107th Congress presented the most auspicious circumstances for a new push to drill for oil and gas in ANWR, but the national environmental community mobilized to keep the refuge closed. "This is the No. 1 issue facing national environmental groups," said Adam Kolton of the Alaska Wilderness League in Washington.[71]

Supporting the state's position was a prodrilling consortium, Arctic Power, which received nearly $2 million from the Alaska legislature to lobby Congress on ANWR that year and was not asked to provide details on how the money would be spent.[72] President Bush made drilling in ANWR the focus of his campaign to boost domestic energy production, arguing that drilling and wildlife preservation could go hand in hand. In opposition was most of the Democratic membership of Congress, which indicated that it was prepared to filibuster on any legislation touching the refuge issue. Nor was Republican support for ANWR drilling unanimous. Seven Republican senators, both conservatives and moderates, announced opposition to opening ANWR, believing it would be environmentally harmful to a pristine area.

President Bush's support weakened in the face of concerted opposition, as administration officials gave conflicting accounts of whether ANWR development should be pursued. The administration's energy plan did propose opening a portion of ANWR when the energy bill passed the House in 2002. However, the threat of a filibuster on the ANWR provision in the bill when it reached the Senate led to its removal.

To avert a filibuster in the Senate, the recent strategy of development proponents has been to incorporate potential federal earnings from ANWR oil and gas development in the executive budget proposal and to include the opening of ANWR in budget reconciliation legislation (which cannot be filibustered) in the House and Senate. Even this strategy did not work in 2005, which was the most dramatic year in the ANWR debate. ANWR passed the House but was three votes short of passing in the Senate, leading Senator Ted Stevens to call it "the saddest day of my life" (and threatening retaliation against ANWR opponents).[73] So it continued until the shift of both chambers to Democratic control after the 2006 elections. This, along with the mobilized opposition of national environmental groups, means that ANWR is not likely to be developed in the near-term.

## The Gas Line

Alaska natural gas production became realistic at the turn of the twenty-first century. Declining Prudhoe Bay production gave the owner companies a greater interest in sales of gas, which to the present has been reinjected into oil wells to boost production. The North Slope contains about 38 trillion cubic feet of proven natural gas—almost twice current annual US consumption, or 20 percent of known US reserves. In 2000–2001, natural gas prices in the US domestic market doubled, which increased the interest of owner companies in marketing the gas. BP and ConocoPhillips each owns 30 percent and Exxon holds a 40 percent interest in North Slope natural gas.

Natural gas production does not promise to solve state funding problems as taxes and other charges likely would produce only between $200 million and $400 million in annual revenues. Gas line construction, however, would significantly increase jobs and fuel growth in the commercial sector. The state's effort to develop the gas line began in 1998, when the legislature passed the Stranded Gas Development Act (SGDA). In late August 2000, Governor Tony Knowles announced his administration's commitment to see a gas line built within two years and to insure that natural gas development provided the resource for Alaska communities. "It's unacceptable for us to fuel America, or the world, while Alaskans freeze in the dark,"[74] said the governor brightly. Although the Knowles administration conducted negotiations with the producers, it did not develop a proposal. That fell to the Murkowski administration (2002–2006).

Under terms of the SGDA, the administration conducted negotiations with the producers in secret for nearly two years, and this made the process controversial. The Murkowski administration finally reached closure with the three owning companies in early 2006. However, the producers insisted they would develop the gas line only if the state provided certainty in its oil taxation regime. The governor introduced the changes to the state's oil taxation legislation (discussed in Chapter 4) in February, but kept the contract with producers secret. In fact, the legislature had to seek court intervention to force release of the contract,[75] and even after the court ordered release of the contract, the administration did not fully reveal it until the start of the first special session of the legislature.

Briefly, the administration proposed a 20 percent state-ownership share in the pipeline. The producers would pay the state's share of profits in gas and not cash. The contract spelled out a lengthy process to move toward construction in these stages: (1) feasibility studies, (2) engineering studies, (3) declaration of an "open season sale" for shippers to build capacity, (4) application for permits, (5) ordering the 6 million tons of steel necessary for the pipeline, (6) start of construction by 2012, and (7) completion, with gas flowing by 2015.[76] The contract did not commit the producers to build the gas line, and indeed consultants mentioned a 20–30 percent probability that the line would not be built. It held them harmless from litigation concerning construction of the line.

Although most commentators (like most residents in the state) wanted to see a natural gas pipeline constructed, opinions differed on these points: routing, state ownership and its implications, antitrust problems, guarantees, tax rates, viability of a gas line, and speed of the process. In the end, the legislature declined to approve the contract, and it died with the Murkowski administration. (Murkowski lost the August 2006 Republican primary to Palin.)

In the 2006 general election campaign, all candidates contended that the SGDA (revised in 2003) did not apply to Prudhoe Bay gas, which was now competitive on world markets; they also opposed concessions they believed Murkowski had made to producers. However, before the expiration of the Murkowski administration, Natural Resources Commissioner Mike Menge terminated the Point Thompson leases owned by ExxonMobil for failure to produce gas,[77] an action that newly elected governor Palin did not reverse.

After her inauguration, Governor Palin began a series of meetings with gas producers, including independents, and pipeline construction firms. She announced that her administration would not follow the SGDA, arguing that this was an insufficient authority for gas line development because North Slope natural gas was not "stranded." Instead, she proposed legislative adoption of an Alaska Gasline Inducement Act (AGIA).

AGIA resembled a request-for-proposals. The state would invite applications from interested pipeline builders and select the "best" proposal. The plan had specified goals, inducements, and a timeline. The six goals were

- employing Alaskans,
- creating a competitive marketplace for project proposals,
- ensuring long-term development,
- ensuring expansion of North Slope facilities,
- setting reasonable tariffs on gas moving through the pipeline, and
- guaranteeing a natural gas supply for Alaska.[78]

One inducement to potential producers was to match the initial state or federal permitting costs by up to $500 million. A second inducement would offer certain tax exemptions to producers for natural gas committed to the line. The timeline would be much shorter than that proposed by Murkowski. The application deadline was in late 2007 and by mid-2008, preparation for construction would begin.[79]

During legislative hearings, owners of the gas leases—BP, ExxonMobil, and ConocoPhillips—opposed key provisions of the bill. They questioned the economic viability of the state's proposal; they claimed that the requirements (or the state's "must haves") were too inflexible; and they insisted that the state provide "fiscal stability." The oil companies sought a thirty-five-year freeze on taxes (compared to AGIA's ten years), which had been part of the Murkowski-negotiated plan.[80] Also, the producers objected to the exclusive nature of the AGIA license.

Senator Hollis French (Democrat, Anchorage) explained the need for exclusivity in an interchange with an oil company executive:

> You can understand why it's (exclusivity) in the bill. . . . From the per-spective of many Alaskans, you (BP), ConocoPhillips and Exxon have sort of had exclusivity for 30 years, and we don't see a pipeline. We tried a process last year that produced a contract that was not acceptable to most Alaskans and to the folks here in the building. We understand that the market may someday bring you and ConocoPhillips and Exxon to the point where you're ready to build the pipeline. . . . But if you guys aren't ready to go next year, we're going to get on a different pony, and try to ride that one.[81]

At a period of intense state criticism of Big Oil, legislators from the start were sympathetic to the transparency of the governor's proposal and a gas pipeline construction process responsive to state direction and future expansion needs. In the end, both houses of the legislature passed AGIA with large majorities, making only cosmetic changes to the governor's proposal. On July 2, 2007, the governor and her pipeline team released a request for applications. Of the three producers of Alaska natural gas, BP indicated it would not complete an application and both ConocoPhillips and ExxonMobil were equivocal. Both the Alaska Gasline Port Authority and MidAmerican Energy Holdings Company indicated they likely would apply.[82]

Although AGIA clearly has the support of the Palin administration and legislature, the chief uncertainty is whether the lease owners will agree to transport the gas they own in a pipeline they neither own nor control, should a viable application be approved by the state. If they decline to do so, the sovereign powers of Alaska as an owner state will be sorely tested.[83]

## Oil Industry Changes and Relationships

An obvious change to the oil industry in its Alaska history has been the declining role of independents. Although multinational oil companies became involved in Alaska near the start of the twentieth century, independents played an active part also, encouraged by liberal provisions of federal and state leasing laws. The state's laws began to favor competitive leasing after changes in the First Alaska Legislature. However, the cost of exploration in the North Slope had an even larger impact on speculators and independent wildcatters without large investment capital.

The second significant change has been the increased concentration in the industry. Mergers and acquisitions were standard practice for oil companies in Alaska, as we noted with changes to ARCO, BP, Exxon, and other firms. Declining oil prices and depression in the global oil market of the late 1990s stimulated most of the recent merger and acquisition activity. In 1998, Exxon Corporation merged with Mobil, creating the world's largest oil company in an $81.1 billion deal. Although Mobil had been a small player in Alaska's oil fields, Exxon owned 40 percent of the gas in Prudhoe Bay. It had a 22 percent stake in oil in Prudhoe Bay and 20 percent of the Trans-Alaska Pipeline. The Federal Trade Commission (FTC), which along with the Justice Department, regulates antitrust violations and uncompetitive practices of oil companies, did not object to this merger.

The second instance of concentration was BP-Amoco's acquisition of ARCO. The two oil companies had dominated oil exploration and production in Alaska. ARCO, which located the Prudhoe Bay discovery well in 1968, was the longest-operating oil company in the territory and state; BP-Amoco is the third largest privately owned oil multinational and a prominent producer in Alaska since 1959.

ARCO looked for buyers when the low oil and gas prices of 1998 and 1999 made its refining and sales operations unprofitable. The $26 billion acquisition would have left BP-Amoco with a controlling interest in every producing field on Alaska's North Slope and 72 percent ownership of the Trans-Alaska Pipeline. The initial response of the Knowles administration was positive, and the state supported BP-Amoco's application to the FTC. The Knowles administration saw economies of scale in the merger of the two North Slope giants, which would reduce expenditures in the search for new North Slope oil fields, leading to accelerated production and more jobs for Alaskans. (BP-Amoco claimed it could save $1 billion through a consolidation of operations.)

Opposition to the plan developed quickly, however. Backers of a gas line from Prudhoe Bay to Valdez saw consolidation in the oil industry as antithetical to their plans, because BP owned relatively more of Prudhoe Bay oil than gas. Environmentalists thought a decline in North Slope competition would increase environmental risks of oil development. Also, oil industry critics feared that the development of a BP monopoly position on the North Slope would weaken the state's position and reduce its take of oil profits, as BP would be able to establish the oil tariff through the pipeline autonomously.

In response to these criticisms, the state hardened its negotiating position with BP somewhat, but the revisions did not mollify the FTC. In fact, it was this agency that focused most attention on the anticompetitive aspects of the acquisition and did so for reasons distant from the concerns of Alaskans.

The FTC had not challenged oil company mergers since it blocked the Mobil Corporation's $6.5 billion bid to buy Marathon Oil in the early 1980s.

Seemingly it welcomed consolidation in the industry when it declined to oppose Exxon's purchase of Mobil, BP's purchase of Amoco, and Texaco's entrance into a joint marketing venture with Shell. However, in the case of the BP-Amoco acquisition of ARCO, first the regulatory agency staff and then the commissioners objected, seeking a preliminary injunction against the agreement. Commissioners asserted that the merger would be strongly anticompetitive and could lead to significant rises in the price of crude oil for refiners in California and other West Coast states, where prices at the gas pump far exceeded the national average.[84]

Much of the joint BP-ARCO production of oil does end up in the gas tanks of Californians. The FTC's bureau of competition director Richard Parker said, "This deal will cement market power and harm competition by creating a significant risk that crude oil prices would be higher on the West coast than they would without the deal. . . . What this case is about at a fundamental level is a dominant firm that is already exercising market power buying the one firm, ARCO, that is the one threat to that market power."[85]

BP officials scoffed at the notion that "the price of oil can be controlled by any company, country or agency in today's market. . . . Alaska crude oil represents about 28 percent of the oil refined on the West Coast. What the government is suggesting is that we can push around an oil market whose producers include Saudis, Venezuelans, Mexicans and California. Can we do that? Of course not."[86] They prepared to file suit in federal court against the injunction, but they also found a buyer for the ARCO holdings in Alaska (Phillips Petroleum) that posed the greatest competitive concern.

Phillips had been a small player among the oil multinationals, with acreage in twenty-two countries, production in nine nations of about 222,000 barrels daily, and worldwide reserves of 2.21 billion barrels of oil. It had been active in Alaska since the 1950s and held interests in a Kenai liquefied natural gas plant; leases in Cook Inlet; and minority interests in Point Thompson, NPR-A, and thirteen blocks in the Beaufort Sea.

For $7 billion, BP-Amoco sold Phillips ARCO's Alaska interests, including the large Kuparuk field, the promising Alpine development, a substantial interest in Prudhoe Bay's oil and gas, a 23 percent interest in the Trans-Alaska Pipeline, ownership of a six-tanker fleet, and other Alaska-trade assets. To curry favor with the gasoline price-conscious public, BP-Amoco also announced it would halt the export of Alaska oil to Asia if the acquisition were approved. The disposition of ARCO's North Slope interests met the approval of the FTC, which withdrew its objections to the BP-Amoco purchase of ARCO.

Then Exxon, the world's largest publicly traded oil company, tangled the process. On the tenth anniversary of the *Exxon Valdez* oil spill, it filed suit to block the sale of ARCO's Alaska oil fields to Phillips. Exxon is the state's third-largest oil producer and holds a major stake in Prudhoe Bay and other fields in which ARCO Alaska was a partner. Exxon based its suit on a claimed right of first refusal to purchase certain ARCO assets included in the sale to Phillips. Such rights, it alleged, were given in 1964 and designed to protect a unique ownership split among North Slope producers.

Two other factors seemed more powerful in motivating Exxon to stop the BP-Amoco acquisition of ARCO. First, Exxon had an interest in forcing financial concessions from BP-Amoco. Jim Whitaker (Republican, Fairbanks), chair of the state House Special Committee on Oil and Gas, noted, "Exxon's significant concern is competing with BP-Amoco on the West Coast. . . . Alaska is a pawn in that game. It is a display of self-serving arrogance on the part of Exxon that must not be tolerated."[87] Second, Exxon sought to protect its gas holdings in Prudhoe Bay and resented the loss of the other North Slope operator, ARCO, with parallel interests.[88]

One part of Exxon's objection was resolved when negotiations with BP-Amoco and Phillips led to a single operator (BP) for the huge Prudhoe Bay oil field and an equalization of oil and gas ownership among the companies. This development promised greater production efficiency and investment at Prudhoe Bay, and also layoffs of duplicative employees. A second part of Exxon's concern was alleviated when Phillips Petroleum (which became ConocoPhillips in 2003) took over the Kuparuk field from BP-Amoco and ARCO, and when both companies guaranteed that they would consult Exxon on operational decisions affecting its interests. With these assurances, Exxon dropped its suit, and the acquisition took effect in 2000.

The takeover of ARCO brought a close to a dynamic era in the Alaska oil industry. One of ARCO's corporate ancestors, Richfield Oil, discovered Alaska's first large oil field near Swanson River on the Kenai Peninsula in 1957. This discovery invigorated Alaska's oil exploration prospects and it provided a steady stream of revenue to the cash-strapped territorial government, bolstering Alaska's chances for statehood. Richfield merged with a struggling East Coast refiner, Atlantic Refining, in 1966. The new company, renamed ARCO, discovered the super-giant Prudhoe Bay field in 1968, which without a doubt was the most important event in Alaska's economic history. Alaska became the center of ARCO's world, and it became a strong competitor with multinational oil companies for lease sales and the development of new oil fields. After the acquisition, many Alaskans questioned whether ConocoPhillips would follow ARCO's traditions, and whether the oil industry would remain competitive enough to safeguard the interests of the state.

## ▇ Conclusions

This accounting of the history of the oil industry in Alaska seems to support hypotheses about natural resource extraction economies and particularly those like Alaska at the periphery of the nation-state or world system. The constrained dominance of the oil industry in Alaska resembles the power of natural resource firms—coal, oil, copper—in other western states lacking diversified economies. As well, the dominance of oil companies resembles the power of multinational corporations in developing nations, which are dependent on the firms for capital, local jobs, infrastructure development, and access to world markets.

There is much to support these hypotheses in the history of the Alaska oil industry. The chapter points to easy access of oil industry lobbyists to legislators, governors, bureaucratic officers, and generally highly supportive public attitudes for the industry's role in state economic development. Overall, the industry gained favorable tax terms, making profits on Alaska operations likely higher than in other jurisdictions (but the risks were higher, too). Also, the oil industry was able to minimize its regulatory burden (as will be noted in Chapter 8, concerning government-industry partnerships).

However, we also pointed to constraints on the influence of the oil industry, because of both state and federal coalitions. After the Swanson River discovery, the oil industry did not seem to know how to change the taxation regime to suit its interests, and at that time gave the appearance of uncertainty in negotiations with the state. In the early 1970s, the governor did propose and put on the state agenda ownership by the state of the Trans-Alaska Pipeline. And in the late 1970s, the legislature did adopt the separate accounting system, which briefly increased taxes on the oil companies. Finally, after *Exxon Valdez,* the legislature and governor punished oil companies by reducing their tax breaks, making them pay for oil-spill cleanup and prevention, and taxed companies to establish a cleanup fund (see Chapter 8). These events at the state level suggest three qualifications to the hypothesis of oil industry dominance. First, the dominance was not immediate or instant but developed relatively slowly in the relationship of government and industry. Second, the dominance depended on Republican Party control of the legislature, which occurred in 1981 and remained for most of the next two decades (see Chapter 3).

Third, the dominance disappeared during and after crises and mobilization of opposition opinion. First came the *Exxon Valdez* oil spill in Prince William Sound.[89] This eco-disaster made it impossible for oil companies to conduct negotiations satisfying their interests privately in the presence of public uproar. Then, seventeen years later came a series of crises and untoward events, which poisoned public attitudes toward oil companies: BP's huge (267,000 gallon) onshore oil spill, historically high gasoline prices, and discrediting of pro-oil political leaders and particularly the governor because of lapses in ethics and political judgment. This prompted the legislature to reject a natural-gas-line contract favoring the oil and gas industry and adopt a new, more productive production tax on oil companies.

The dependence of the state upon the federal government, particularly in its early years of development, had advantages respecting state-industry relationships. The federal government is a magnet for multiple interests and pressures, and those of the oil industry must compete with others. The Alaska Native land claims movement showed the extent to which interests of a minority having a special relationship with the federal government could curb company plans. The development of national environmental consciousness and a vibrant environmental NGO community showed the possibility of the development of a countervailing interest affecting oil.

Finally, the chapter indicates that for most of their history in the state, multinational oil companies have competed with one another, a competition that until recently has softened the dominance of the oil industry collectively.[90] Overall, the history of the oil industry in Alaska shows incidences of oil industry dominance, but also instances when Big Oil could not attain its objectives, because of opposition from governments (federal as well as state) and an aroused citizenry.

### ▪ Notes

1. The US military itself advised against statehood, as did President Dwight D. Eisenhower, as the federal government would lose flexibility in the use of Alaska's lands. See Claus-M. Naske and Herman E. Slotnick, *Alaska: A History of the 49th State,* 2nd ed. (Norman: University of Oklahoma Press, 1987), p. 154.

2. Jack Roderick, *Crude Dreams: A Personal History of Oil and Politics in Alaska* (Fairbanks: Epicenter Press, 1997), p. 21.

3. Ibid., 24.

4. Ibid., 31.

5. The owner, Robert Kerr, was a powerful US senator from Oklahoma. See ibid., 42.

6. Ibid., 42–43.

7. Alaska Division of Oil and Gas, *Alaska Oil and Gas Report* (Anchorage: Department of Natural Resources, 2004), p. 7. A small gas field was also discovered, which produces today for Barrow consumers. See also Naske and Slotnick, *Alaska: A History,* 243–246.

8. Roderick, *Crude Dreams,* 49.

9. Including film stars Bing Crosby and Laurel and Hardy. See John Strohmeyer, *Extreme Conditions: Big Oil and the Transformation of Alaska* (New York: Simon and Schuster, 1993), p. 23.

10. See Roderick, *Crude Dreams,* 21.

11. Ibid., 73.

12. Ibid., 62.

13. Quoted in ibid., 74.

14. Ibid., 77–78.

15. Quoted in Peter A. Coates, *The Trans-Alaska Pipeline Controversy: Technology, Conservation, and the Frontier* (Fairbanks: University of Alaska Press, 1993), pp. 92–93.

16. Roderick, *Crude Dreams,* 99–100.

17. Ibid., 100.

18. Claus-M. Naske, "ANS Royalty Litigation: FGSO Sales as Royalty-Bearing," expert testimony before the Alaska Legislature, January 24, 1994; see also Alaska Division of Oil and Gas, *Alaska Oil and Gas Report,* p. 7.

19. Roderick, *Crude Dreams,* 106.

20. Ibid., 104–106.

21. Ibid., 114.

22. Ibid., 115.

23. Institute of Business, Economic, and Government Research (IBEGR), "The Petroleum Industry in Alaska," *Monthly Review of Alaska Business and Economic Conditions* 1 (University of Alaska, Fairbanks) (August 1964): 1.

24. IBEGR, "Alaska's Economy in 1967," *Monthly Review of Alaska Business and Economic Conditions* 5 (1976): 2.

25. This section follows Gerald A. McBeath and Thomas A. Morehouse, *The Dynamics of Alaska Native Self-Government* (Lanham, MD: University Press of America, 1980), pp. 19–22; for a history of US relations with Alaska's Native peoples, see Donald Mitchell, *Sold American: The Story of Alaska Natives and Their Land* (Hanover, NH: University Press of New England, 1997).

26. The Organic Act was the first in a series of laws passed by the US Congress constituting civil government in Alaska.

27. This disclaimer clause was also incorporated into the state constitution (Article 12, Section 12), further strengthening the legal base for aboriginal rights.

28. Alaska Division of Lands, *1966 Annual Report* (Anchorage: Department of Natural Resources, 1966).

29. Federal Task Force on Alaska Native Affairs, *Report to the Secretary of the Interior,* December 28, 1962, pp. 56–66.

30. Ibid., 62.

31. Ibid., 63.

32. This was the stated reason for Governor Egan's reluctance to nominate North Slope lands for selection, based on recommendations of his lands office and the commissioner of natural resources. See Roderick, *Crude Dreams,* 160. Governor Egan also feared that if he made these lands of high potential oil reserves available for competitive leasing, critics would allege that he was selling out the interest of the state to the oil companies.

33. Alaska Legislative Affairs Agency, *Public Lands of Alaska* (1966), pp. 7–8.

34. Alaska Division of Lands, *1966 Annual Report.*

35. Mary Clay Berry, *The Alaska Pipeline: The Politics of Oil and Native Land Claims* (Bloomington: University of Indiana Press, 1975), p. 49; see also Donald Mitchell, *Take My Land Take My Life* (Fairbanks: University of Alaska Press, 2001), pp. 83–94.

36. Berry, *Alaska Pipeline,* 49.

37. Alaska Division of Lands, *1967 Annual Report,* 9.

38. Alaska Division of Lands, *1968 Annual Report,* 17–18.

39. British Petroleum, *BP in Alaska: 40 Years of Risks and Rewards* (Anchorage: 2001), pp. 12–13.

40. Roderick, *Crude Dreams,* 186–187.

41. Strohmeyer opines that Robert Kennedy, then attorney general, acted against Richfield because it had made secret contributions to the Nixon campaign in the 1960 presidential elections; *Extreme Conditions,* 54.

42. Ibid., 56.

43. Roderick, *Crude Dreams,* 222.

44. The 13 billion barrels of recoverable oil made Prudhoe Bay a "super giant" oil field. A "giant" oil field contains at least 100 million barrels of recoverable oil. Only about 1 percent of oil fields are giants. However, the Prudhoe Bay field is 100 times

larger than a giant. See Alaska Review of Social and Economic Conditions, *Sustainable Spending Levels from Alaska State Revenues*, February 1983 (Anchorage: University of Alaska, Institute of Social and Economic Research), p. 3.

45. President Richard Nixon appointed Hickel to be secretary of the interior after his 1968 election. Miller had been Hickel's lieutenant governor.

46. See Ken Ross, *Environmental Conflict in Alaska* (Boulder: University Press of Colorado, 2000), pp. 148–149.

47. Roderick, *Crude Dreams,* 262–264.

48. For a brief summary, see McBeath and Morehouse, *The Dynamics of Alaska*, 57–60; the definitive study is Mitchell, *Take My Land Take My Life*.

49. Berry, *Alaska Pipeline,* 68–72.

50. Initially, the Interior Department produced an eight-page EIS finding no environmental dangers arising from the first phase of the TAPS project, construction of the North Slope Haul Road. In response, the Wilderness Society, Friends of the Earth, and the Environmental Defense Fund sued the Interior Department in the federal district court of Washington, DC. Judge Hart ruled that an impact statement covering the entire TAPS proposal had to be prepared. See Peter Coates, *Trans-Alaska Pipeline Controversy,* 189–190.

51. Ibid., 229.

52. Ibid., 217–218.

53. Ibid., 248.

54. Roderick, *Crude Dreams,* 335–336.

55. Ibid., 347–350.

56. Ibid., 355.

57. Ibid., 363–364.

58. Ibid., 369.

59. Interview with John Havelock, Anchorage, April 27, 2002.

60. Kay Cashman, "ARCO's 40 Years in Alaska," *Alaska Journal of Commerce*, September 18, 1995. Shortly after the discovery, Sinclair merged with ARCO to escape a hostile takeover bid by Gulf & Western.

61. Cashman, "ARCO's 40 Years," Mike Bowlin (President, ARCO), *Alaska Journal of Commerce*, September 18, 1995.

62. Other ventures were costlier and less successful, for example the Mukluk well, a dry hole costing Standard about $1 billion—more than any other exploratory well in history. About 65 miles northwest of Prudhoe Bay, the well was drilled from the largest gravel island built in US waters.

63. D. J. Szabo and K. O. Meyers, "Prudhoe Bay: Development History and Future Potential." Paper presented to the Society of Petroleum Engineers Western Regional Meeting, Anchorage, May 1993. A multiphased water expansion project began at Prudhoe Bay in 1982. It expanded water handling capacity throughout the Prudhoe Bay field and provided facilities to further strip oil from produced water. This project also created a distribution system to well pads for injection to increase secondary recovery. Simultaneously, the companies developed a low-pressure separation system, which increased productivity as well. In 1984, the companies invested $2 billion in a comprehensive water distribution system, sea-water treatment plant, and pumping systems to inject sea water into the reservoir to maintain oil pressure. In 1986, companies began injecting a miscible injectant throughout the reservoir to aid recovery. In the early to mid-1990s, a $1 billion project called Gas Handling Expansion created the largest gas handling system in the world at Prudhoe Bay.

64. See Stephen Johnson, "The Alaska Legislature." In Gerald A. McBeath and Thomas A. Morehouse, eds., *Alaska State Government and Politics* (Fairbanks: University of Alaska Press, 1987), p. 246.

65. Strohmeyer, *Extreme Conditions,* 205.

66. Ibid., 206.

67. Quoted in ibid., 207.

68. Peter Coates, *Trans-Alaska Pipeline Controversy,* 311.

69. Ibid., 311.

70. *New York Times*, January 10, 2001; see also Jerry McBeath, "Changing Capabilities of Northern Communities: Environmental Protection," *Northern Review* (2002).

71. *Fairbanks Daily News-Miner*, February 19, 2001.

72. Ibid., March 15, 2001.

73. Ibid., December 22, 2005.

74. *Anchorage Daily News*, August 28, 2000.

75. Ibid., April 22, 2006.

76. *Fairbanks Daily News-Miner*, May 23, 2006.

77. Ibid., November 28, 2006.

78. Ibid., March 6, 2007.

79. Ibid., March 6, 2007; also see *Alaska Budget Report*, March 29, 2007.

80. Ibid., March 24, 2007, April 7, 2007, May 1, 2007, and May 3, 2007.

81. *Alaska Budget Report*, April 19, 2007, p. 1.

82. *Fairbanks Daily News-Miner,* July 4, 2007. The Bradners' *Alaska Economic Report* argues that AGIA was written for an independent pipeline company, with the favored contender being MidAmerican Energy Holdings Co. Observers note that AGIA's state incentives of $500 million and an exclusive license mirror a proposal that MidAmerican made to former governor Murkowski in 2005. Reportedly, Murkowski initially favored construction of the gas line by an independent pipeline company, but then changed his mind and supported a producer-owned pipeline. Lending some credence to these reports, MidAmerican was the only pipeline firm that supported Governor Palin's proposal in its entirety.

83. For other criticisms of AGIA, see *Alaska Economic Report*, May 11 and June 11, 2007.

84. *Anchorage Daily News*, March 3, 2000.

85. *Fairbanks Daily News-Miner*, March 3, 2000.

86. Ibid.

87. *Anchorage Daily News*, March 25, 2000.

88. In most oil fields, owners resolve differences so that companies share equal interests in both oil and gas. When the companies formed an operating agreement at Prudhoe Bay, however, oil was easy to value but gas was not (because of uncertainty as to when North Slope gas would reach the market). Thus, the companies separated their oil and gas holdings into separate units. BP owned 51 percent of the oil but only 14 percent of the gas. ARCO and Exxon each held 23 percent of the oil and 43 percent of the gas. Consequent to these different interests, BP resisted plans to convert the natural gas to a liquid and send it through the Trans-Alaska Pipeline; instead it favored reinjecting the gas to produce more oil. Exxon and ARCO sought to maximize the value of the gas. Company spokesman Tom Cirigliano stated that with the loss of its partner, "We don't have information on how the field is going to be operated (*Anchorage Daily News*, March 31, 2000). The company suspected that BP would strike a side deal with Phillips, favoring the oil owners' interests.

89. In 2006, Alaskans perceived oil companies to be fat with profits and unconcerned about the public interest. This enabled the legislature to pass progressive oil taxation legislation.

90. The companies had a unified position on Governor Murkowski's gas-line proposal, and they were united in opposition to Governor Palin's AGIA plan.

# 3

## Campaigns, Elections, and the Influence of Oil

The oil and gas industry is a major player in Alaska campaigns and elections. In several recent elections, it has been the single largest industry contributor to candidates, although its contributions have declined in the past two election cycles (2004–2006). The industry heavily favors the Republican Party, and its political action committees (PACs) and individuals associated with the industry give generously to the party and Republican candidates. In a few close contests in recent history, industry contributions may have influenced outcomes. In other cases, it is clearer that large contributions from the industry to winners—Republican and Democratic—in uncompetitive races have enhanced industry access to legislators in positions to shape legislation affecting oil and gas policies.

There is no question that the oil and gas industry uses its financial resources to influence elections and to establish positive relationships with policymakers. The industry spends millions of dollars in the state on legislative lobbying, regularly promotes a public image of environmental responsibility and employment opportunity, and makes generous contributions to worthy causes throughout the state. All of this helps build and reinforce the favorable attitudes that a majority of Alaskans hold toward oil development.

Although approximately 60 percent of the state's registered voters identify as other than Republican or Democrat (most register as undeclared or nonpartisan),[1] Alaska is a "red" state, with nearly twice as many registered Republicans as Democrats.[2] Republicans have dominated the state legislature since the mid-1990s, and Alaska's three-member congressional delegation has been all Republican since 1981 (see Table 3.1). The electorate is generally pro-development, and both business interests and the oil and gas industry strongly favor the Republican Party with their donations. This is not to say that competing interests are not represented in government. Labor is strong in Alaska, heavily favoring the Democratic Party, and there is a large public sector whose employees strongly favor Democrats with political contributions and votes. Overall, however, the campaign contributions of business, the pro-development

**Table 3.1   Partisanship of Alaska State Offices and US Congressional Delegation, 1959–2007**

| Legislative Session | State Senate D | State Senate R | State Senate O | State House D | State House R | State House O | Governor | | US Delegation Senate | US Delegation House |
|---|---|---|---|---|---|---|---|---|---|---|
| 1959–1960 | 18 | 2 | | 34 | 5 | 1 | Egan | D | D D | D |
| 1961–1962 | 13 | 7 | | 19 | 20 | 1 | Egan | D | D D | D |
| 1963–1964 | 15 | 5 | | 20 | 20 | | Egan | D | D D | D |
| 1965–1966 | 17 | 3 | | 30 | 10 | | Egan | D | D D | D |
| 1967–1968 | 6 | 14 | | 14 | 26 | | Hickel | R | D D | R |
| 1969–1970 | 9 | 11 | | 22 | 18 | | Miller | R | R D | R |
| 1971–1972 | 10 | 10 | | 31 | 9 | | Egan | D | R D | D |
| 1973–1974 | 9 | 11 | | 20 | 19 | 1 | Egan | D | R D | D |
| 1975–1976 | 13 | 7 | | 30 | 9 | 1 | Hammond | R | R D | R |
| 1977–1978 | 12 | 8 | | 25 | 15 | | Hammond | R | R D | R |
| 1979–1980 | 9 | 11 | | 25 | 14 | 1 | Hammond | R | R D | R |
| 1981–1982 | 10 | 10 | | 22 | 16 | 2 | Hammond | R | R R | R |
| 1983–1984 | 9 | 11 | | 20 | 20 | | Sheffield | D | R R | R |
| 1985–1986 | 9 | 11 | | 21 | 18 | 1 | Sheffield | D | R R | R |
| 1987–1988 | 8 | 12 | | 24 | 16 | | Cowper | D | R R | R |
| 1989–1990 | 8 | 12 | | 24 | 16 | | Cowper | D | R R | R |
| 1991–1992 | 10 | 10 | | 23 | 17 | | Hickel | AIP | R R | R |
| 1993–1994 | 9 | 10 | 1 | 20 | 18 | 2 | Hickel | AIP | R R | R |
| 1995–1996 | 7 | 12 | 1 | 17 | 22 | 1 | Knowles | D | R R | R |
| 1997–1998 | 6 | 14 | | 15 | 25 | | Knowles | D | R R | R |
| 1999–2000 | 6 | 14 | | 15 | 25 | | Knowles | D | R R | R |
| 2001–2002 | 6 | 14 | | 14 | 26 | | Knowles | D | R R | R |
| 2003–2004 | 8 | 12 | | 13 | 27 | | Murkowski | R | R R | R |
| 2005–2006 | 8 | 12 | | 14 | 26 | | Murkowski | R | R R | R |
| 2007–2008 | 9 | 11 | | 17 | 23 | | Palin | R | R R | R |

*Source:* Table compiled by authors based on information provided at the Alaska State Legislature website at w3.legis.state.ak.us/infodocs/roster/ROSTERALL.pdf and w3.legis.state. ak.us/infodocs/infodocs/htm, accessed on June 30, 2006.

*Note:* D = Democratic; R = Republican; O = Other; AIP = Alaska Independence Party.

attitudes of most residents, and the state's "redness" complement oil and gas interests and give the advantage to Republican and pro–oil industry candidates.

Despite these complementary interests, and reflecting national electoral reform trends, Alaskans are increasingly concerned about the industry's influence in state politics. This is evidenced in part by the successful August 2006 ballot initiative titled "Take Back Our State." The initiative requires legislators to disclose all income sources over $1,000, provides stricter requirements for lobbyists to register, reduces campaign contributions from individuals, and limits donations to political parties.

Shortly after the initiative, the *Anchorage Daily News* shocked Alaskans statewide with the headline that FBI agents had raided the offices of six legislators in an investigation of campaign donations from a major oil field services corporation. Four executives of VECO Corporation, a multinational company with headquarters in Anchorage and hundreds of millions in annual revenues, admitted bribing state legislators with money and promises of future employment in return for their support of legislation favored by the oil and gas industry. Following the announcement of the raids, accusations of improprieties by legislators escalated, and the campaign season was one of the most acrimonious in recent memory. As of November 2007, three legislators had been indicted on corruption charges related to VECO bribes, and two had been tried and convicted, with the third awaiting trial. It is not clear as of this writing how many legislators will be indicted or whether others in the industry, in the legislature, and among Alaska's congressional delegation have engaged in similar practices. The scandal has led to calls for more reform in campaign financing and ethics reform in the legislature. Owing to the charges of corruption surrounding the passage of the petroleum production tax (PPT) in 2006, Governor Palin called a special session of the state legislature to revisit the legislation in October 2007. The legislature passed a new, higher tax rate with increased incentives for exploration.

The following analysis of campaign financing and election results in Alaska begins with an overview of campaign finance reform in the United States and national trends, noting the escalating costs of elections and the strong correlation between campaign spending and winning. Study of Alaska's circumstances shows a similar pattern of campaign finance reform, escalating costs, and spending correlating with winning. As is the case elsewhere, Alaska incumbents have name recognition, experience, perquisites of office, and the ability to attract more campaign money than challengers—factors contributing to their high reelection rates regardless of the sources of their campaign funds.

## ■ Campaign Finance Reform

### National Campaign Reform

Following the Federal Elections Campaign Act (FECA) of 1971, the Nixon-Watergate scandal spurred additional reforms in the mid-1970s and later. The main objectives were to inform voters about contributors to campaigns (disclosure) and to limit the influence of individuals and special interests on candidates. There were broad concerns about the rising costs of campaigns and the degree to which election outcomes and public policy may be compromised by moneyed interests. In *Buckley v. Valeo* (1976),[3] the Supreme Court upheld congressional limitations on individual contributions to campaigns and requirements for disclosure but struck down limitations on campaign expenditures, independent expenditures, and expenditures by candidates for their own campaigns. The court referred to the danger of quid pro quo arrangements between donors and politicians and the potential for harm to the democratic process because of the *appearance* of corruption.

Despite further campaign finance reform since the 1970s, perceptions of impropriety abound. Archibald Cox, the independent prosecutor during the Watergate hearings, said in 2000 he believed there was "much less trust in government" and there were "far worse" campaign abuses at the turn of the twenty-first century than during the Watergate years. Cox believed that the "threat to the democratic process [was] even graver," both because more money was involved and because the pressure for and expectations of quid pro quos were much greater, particularly among members of Congress.[4]

In 2002, Congress passed the Bipartisan Campaign Reform Act (commonly known as the McCain-Feingold Act), which sought to reduce the influence of soft money (that is, contributions that do not go directly to candidates and do not expressly endorse candidates) and the number of issue ads in federal campaigns. It also doubled the sum of money an individual may give a federal candidate from $2,000 to $4,000 per election cycle. Proponents of the measure claimed that it would increase competitiveness in congressional elections and decrease the time congressional candidates spent campaigning. These predictions did not come to pass, however. The 2004 elections saw an increase in small donor contributions, but this increase was more than offset by the increase in large contributions.[5] In the 2004 congressional elections, candidates who received more money than their rivals won in 97 percent of the races, up from 94 percent in 2002. In the 2004 general elections, winners raised three times as much as losers. The winners' money advantage was even greater in contributions of over $1,000, and the advantage of incumbents over challengers increased.[6] Nor was there any evidence that time spent campaigning declined.[7]

The US Public Interest Research Group (PIRG) has warned against a minuscule proportion of the electorate (.05 percent of the electorate made contributions of $2,000 or more in 2004) having increasing influence over elections and has predicted that, among other effects, there would be a reduction in the number of candidates for political office and a reduction in voter confidence in America's electoral system. "The need for big money favors candidates with personal wealth and access to networks of wealthy donors."[8] In sum, money influences outcomes in the following ways:

- Higher revenues correlate strongly with winning.[9]
- Campaign donations increase the advantage that incumbents derive from name recognition and media coverage.[10]
- The costs of campaigning are rising in real dollars, in terms of average and aggregate contributions and expenditures.[11]

## Campaign Reform in the States

As Congress has wrestled with national campaign finance reform, "a somewhat quiet revolution" of campaign finance reform has been underway in the states since the 1970s.[12] States have enacted a variety of reforms, ranging from public disclosure, to disclosure plus limitations on contributions, to public financing of campaigns. Political scientist Paul Schultz ascribes the increase in costs of campaigning at the state level to (1) devolution of federal policy to the states since the 1980s; (2) "nationalizing" of state elections as they become increasingly media-driven and run by professionals; (3) dealignment of the electorate and in some regions shifting partisan alignment, which has led to increasing competitiveness of elections; and (4) increasing use of state parties as conduits for contributions no longer legal at the national level, for example contributions from corporations and labor unions.[13] He notes that where restrictions have been placed on hard-money contributions, soft money has more than compensated.[14]

Research on the effects of campaign spending and reforms reveals complex relationships between spending and voter attitudes and between reform aims and effects. One study found that the effects of campaign finance reform varied greatly, depending on their specific formulas, and that more restrictive limits correlated with increased incumbent spending and with *greater disparities* in candidate spending.[15] Another study found that public disclosure of campaign contributions and expenditures increased feelings of efficacy among voters, as did placing limits on organizational donations. However, public funding of campaigns and limitations on individual donations had a negative effect on respondents' feelings of efficacy.[16] Still another study found that the effects of campaign advertising were strongest among those least knowledgeable and most in need of further information. The study concluded that rather than corrupting the democratic process, campaign contributions that fund advertisements "(fulfill) a vital democratic function,"[17] but the authors also warned that great disparities in funding among competitors could harm the democratic process.[18]

In sum, since the 1970s, many campaign finance reforms occurred at the national and state levels. They have included efforts to provide for public disclosure, reduce the costs of campaigning, broaden citizen participation while limiting the influence of large donors, increase the competitiveness of elections, and protect governmental legitimacy. Yet, there is little evidence showing that the objectives of such reforms have been achieved, as campaign costs continue to rise and perceptions of impropriety abound.

## Campaign Finance Reform in Alaska

Alaska has followed the national trend in adopting a series of campaign finance reforms since the 1970s. This section addresses these reforms and examines campaign contributions by the oil and gas industry, which has been the largest industrial contributor since the 1990s. In several cases, oil contributions appear to have affected outcomes, when contributions were substantial and winning margins were small. Even where victory margins were large and it is impossible to connect contributions to election outcomes, large donations may have had an influence on the policymaking process, as campaign contributions garner access to politicians and could make them more receptive to the donors' positions on matters of critical interest to the donors. Former VECO chief executive officer (CEO) Bill Allen has confessed to having on numerous occasions given campaign donations and other compensation to politicians in return for their supporting a tax formula favorable to the oil industry.[19]

Alaska's policymakers are not out of step with the majority of Alaska residents in promoting oil development in the state. However, as is illustrated by the VECO corruption case, the industry's large contributions to political campaigns could induce the recipients to produce legislation more favorable toward oil industry positions and less protective of state interests than they otherwise would. The same holds true, of course, for other sectors and special interests with significant influence.

Alaska's post-Watergate reforms were led by the "sunshine boys," a group of young, idealistic Democrats in the state House who sought to limit the influence of the oil industry in the state legislature and to plan for expected enormous revenues from oil production at Prudhoe Bay.[20] Alaska's legislature passed the Alaska Campaign Disclosure Law (Alaska Statute [AS] 15.13) in 1974, creating the Alaska Election Campaign Commission (renamed the Alaska Public Offices Commission), whose mission is "to encourage the public's confidence in their elected and appointed officials by administering Alaska's disclosure statutes and publishing financial information regarding the activities of election campaigns, public officials, lobbyists and lobbyist employers."[21]

The same year, Alaskan voters supported an initiative that resulted in AS 39.50, Alaska's Public Official Financial Disclosure Law (initially Conflict of Interest Law). Other reforms included the 1976 Alaska's Lobbying Law (AS 24.45), the 1990 Legislative Financial Disclosure Law (AS 24.60), and the 1997 Alaska Campaign Disclosure Law, the last of which provided for stricter limitations and disclosure, including prohibiting corporate and out-of-state group donations to local and state candidates.[22] The 1997 law also reduced the limit on individual campaign donations from $1,000 to $500. The 1997 law's stated purpose was to "substantially revise Alaska's election campaign finance laws in order to restore the public's trust in the electoral process and to foster good government."[23] This reform resulted from a citizen initiative begun in 1995, to which the legislature responded, moderating some of its components.[24] Finally, apparently in response to the McCain-Feingold Act, the state legislature raised contribution limits in 2004.[25] The state doubled individual contribution limits to candidates and political parties from $500 to $1,000 and $5,000 to $10,000, respectively. However, as mentioned above, in a ballot initiative titled "Take Our State Back," voters on August 22, 2006, reduced allowable contributions again. The new law took effect January 1, 2007; the resulting campaign contribution limits are shown in Table 3.2.

## ■ Campaign Costs and Their Implications in Alaska

In 1987, Larry Makinson, a longtime Anchorage journalist who subsequently served as executive director of the Center for Responsive Politics in Washington, DC, and later as a senior fellow at the Center for Public Integrity, published a thorough study of the financing of Alaska's 1986 legislative and statewide elections entitled *Open Secrets: The Price of Politics in Alaska*. Makinson found that overall spending had increased dramatically since the 1970s. The cost of successful House campaigns had risen by 350 percent. The cost of successful Senate campaigns had risen by 900 percent. The cost of gubernatorial campaigns was far higher than those of the 1970s, though down from the 1982 election when Bill Sheffield spent $2 million of his own money on his campaign.[26]

Incumbents enjoyed a strong advantage in fund-raising; 70 percent of the donations of the top fifty donors went to incumbents. And money correlated with winning. In thirty-three of the thirty-six contested legislative races, the candidates who spent the most money won.[27] This trend of money following incumbents and winners has continued through the 2006 elections.

Labor unions and the oil and gas industry were the biggest spenders, respectively, in the 1986 elections, both raising their contributions significantly from previous years. Labor favored Democrats heavily, while oil favored Republicans heavily.[28] Republicans received 80 percent of oil's campaign con-

**Table 3.2  Allowable Campaign Contributions Under Alaska's Campaign Disclosure Law**

| | | To | | |
|---|---|---|---|---|
| From | Candidate | | Group | Party |
| Individual | | $500 | $500 | $5,000 |
| Group | | $1,000 | $1,000 | $1,000 |
| Party | Governor | $100,000 | | |
| | Lieutenant Governor | $100,000 | | |
| | Senate Candidate | $15,000 | | |
| | House Candidate | $10,000 | | |

*Source:* Table compiled by authors from information found at www.state.ak.us/local/akpages/ADMIN/apoc/faq297.htm.
*Note:* Alaska Statute section 15.13.074(f) (1998) bans campaign contributions by corporations, business associations, and unions to candidates or groups.

tributions, which totaled $430,000.[29] This trend also continued through 2006, though the percentages varied, with oil and gas donating overwhelmingly to the Republican Party and to Republican candidates. However, the top fifty donors, whose contributions ranged from $103,368 to $15,329, donated more heavily to Democrats than to Republicans. Democrats received $1,020,943 from the top fifty donors (54 percent). Republicans received $853,574 from the same top fifty donors.[30]

In 1996, Republicans raised more total campaign contributions than Democrats.[31] Oil and gas industry donations followed a pattern similar to that of a decade earlier, although the industry now surpassed organized labor, leading all other campaign contributors by giving $870,873, which was 39 percent of all reported industry contributions. The industry gave more to winners than losers in all but four races, and it favored Republicans in 70 percent of races.[32] Among the top twenty-five recipients of oil money running for the state House, oil industry receipts amounted to a substantial proportion of the total receipts for several successful candidates, including Republicans Gail Phillips (13.5 percent), Joseph Green (17.3 percent), Pete Kott (18.5 percent), Con Bunde (22.8 percent), Pete Kelly (17.5 percent), Mark Hodgins (20.8 percent), and Alan Austerman (23.2 percent); and Democrats Richard Foster (19.5 percent) and Ivan Ivan (15.7 percent). Of the top twenty-five recipients of oil money who ran for state House seats, all but one won.[33] However, only in Phillips's race, where she won with just 51.6 percent of the vote, and Ivan's race, where he won with 54.7 percent of the vote,[34] does it appear that oil money was a factor in the outcome of the election, as the other races were not competitive or were unopposed.[35]

Although the industry's contributions could have affected outcomes in just two races, the largest contributions from oil and gas went to candidates who filled powerful positions in the legislature, including speaker of the House (Phillips), co-chair of House Finance, vice-chair of House Labor and Commerce, chair of the Special Committee on Oil and Gas, chair of Senate Labor and Commerce, co-chair of Senate Finance, and chair of Senate Resources Committee.[36] Thus, more money appears to have been channeled toward achieving access to legislators with disproportionate power over public policy affecting the oil industry than to controlling the outcome of specific races.

Oil money was somewhat less of a factor in state Senate than in state House races in 1996. Seven of the top eight recipients of oil money received between 5.8 and 9.9 percent of their campaign funds from oil industry employees. Republican Mike Miller received 21.1 percent from the industry;[37] however, his race was not competitive—North Pole is historically a conservative district, and Miller, the incumbent, won with 78 percent of the vote.[38] Thus, campaign contributions from the oil industry helped provide access to many of the most powerful members of the state legislature, which, following the

1996 elections was 70 percent Republican in the House and 62.5 percent Republican in the Senate and therefore already generally favorable toward the industry.

Though the industry favored Republicans, its contributions in 1996 were somewhat more evenly spread between Republicans and Democrats than they had been in 1986, providing it with better access to both parties. In a 1992 interview, George Findling, ARCO's Alaska manager of government and public affairs, explained ARCO's strategy with regard to campaign donations. He said that ARCO sought, through its political activities, to promote a stable tax and pro-business environment in Alaska. As a taxpayer, he said, ARCO participated legitimately in the political process by supporting candidates who shared its views, including those who opposed increases in industry taxes, those who supported limiting state government, and those who would consider "reasonable approaches" to regulating the industry. Findling said that ARCO tended to favor Republicans because they tended to take a more pro-development approach, but that it also supported Democrats who were supportive of the industry, and it contributed to incumbents, regardless of their views, because it was important to have working relationships with members of the legislature.[39] Political scientist Jonathan Rosenberg refers to such an approach as an "economistic" notion of citizenship. He notes that industry activities include public relations media campaigns, lobbying, educational programs, and encouragement of activism by employees.[40]

During the 1998 campaign, the oil and gas industry was again the largest single industry contributor to legislative campaigns, though industry contributions declined, owing to campaign reform. In 1998, oil and gas gave twice the amount that labor unions gave to legislative candidates. Of the top ten legislative recipients of oil industry donations, these contributions may have been a factor in four victories in the state House: Phillips, Ramona Barnes, Jerry Sanders, and Carl Morgan, all Republicans. Table 3.3 shows the percentages of their campaign receipts that came from oil interests and their victory margins.

All of these candidates strongly supported oil and gas exploration and development, and all opposed increasing taxes on oil company profits.[41] Although whether oil contributions tipped the scales is not known, with such large percentages of these candidates' campaign chests coming from oil, and with their small victory margins, outcomes may have differed without substantial support from oil companies. However, we can be reasonably sure that the industry contributions increased or reinforced industry access to the winners.

As for the 1998 gubernatorial contest, contrary to the general tendency to support Republican candidates, the industry favored the successful Democratic Knowles/Ulmer ticket. Knowles had a good relationship with the industry, while the Republican nominee, John Lindauer, had been discredited by serious charges of financial impropriety.

**Table 3.3    Campaign Donation Percentages and Votes Received in 1998 Races (where oil industry contributions may have been a deciding factor)**

| Candidate | Percentage of Total Campaign Receipts from Oil Interests | Percentage of Vote Received |
|---|---|---|
| Gail Phillips | 17 | 54.7 |
| Ramona Barnes | 24 | 50.5 |
| Jerry Sanders | 21 | 51.1 |
| Carl Morgan | 32 | 49.9 |

*Source:* Table compiled by authors with contribution information accessed at www.followthemoney.org and elections results accessed at www.elections.state.ak.us/elect98/general/results.pdf.

The 2000 campaign reports reveal similar patterns to those found in earlier election cycles. Again oil and gas donated more than any other single industry, with 8 percent of total contributions to legislative candidates, up from 7 percent in 1998.[42] Oil and gas again favored Republican candidates overwhelmingly, although less so than in 1998, donating $297,341 to Republican legislative candidates and $85,008 to Democratic candidates. The industry gave winners 4.8 times as much as losers.[43]

The year 2002 was an expensive campaign year, with total contributions at $10,998,279, of which $4,437,099 went to gubernatorial candidates. The difference in receipts between the gubernatorial candidates was relatively small. Murkowski, the Republican candidate and winner, raised only $100,000 more in contributions than Ulmer, his Democratic opponent, with Murkowski taking in $1,850,071 to Ulmer's $1,742,546. Murkowski was the clear favorite of oil and gas, receiving $84,191, compared to Ulmer's $23,921. Other notable differences between the two included Murkowski's receiving $199,358 from Republican Party sources, compared to Ulmer's $121,395 from Democratic Party sources, and Ulmer's receiving significantly more from retired persons, lawyers and lobbyists, civil servants and public officials, and education and general trade unions.[44] The Alaska Republican Party received $57,305 from oil and gas interests in 2002, which was 10 percent of the party's total receipts from donors. Yet, the contributions of oil and gas, direct and indirect through the Republican Party, which amounted to 5.6 percent of Murkowski's campaign fund, cannot be considered critical in his win. There was a 15 percentage point spread between his and Ulmer's vote totals, with Murkowski receiving 55.8 percent of the general election votes and Ulmer receiving 40.7 percent of the vote.

In the 2002 legislative campaigns, Democratic legislative candidates raised $2,008,861, while Republican legislative candidates raised a total of $3,455,098. Contributors identified with the oil and gas industry donated $574,575, of which 87 percent went to Republicans and only 13 percent went to Democrats. This was a 9 percentage point jump from 2000 in the proportion of industry support that went to Republican candidates.

There was an unusually high number of uncontested races in the 2002 general elections: 15 of 40 House positions and 3 of the 10 Senate seats. The oil and gas industry contributed $57,219 to these House races, including $11,277 to Lisa Murkowski, who would later be appointed to the US Senate by her father, Frank Murkowski, who resigned his Senate seat when he became governor of Alaska in 2002. In the Senate, the industry gave $7,849 to Scott Ogan and $26,932 to Ben Stevens, both of whom were unopposed. Stevens, the son of US Senator Ted Stevens, and Senate president following the election, is one of the legislators now under investigation by the federal government (discussed further in this chapter).

In several races, Republicans lost, despite receiving sizeable contributions from the oil industry. In the contest for Senate District Q, the industry donated $14,050 to Republican Jerry Ward, which was 12 percent of his total; Republican Moderate Thomas Wagoner, who received just $500 from oil and gas, won the seat.[45] In two close races, House District 21 and Senate District L, donations of $7,550 and $7,195, respectively, did not tip the balance for Republicans.[46] In House District 22, oil and gas gave Republican Michael Ryan $5,550 of his total $41,765, but he lost to Sharon Cissna, who raised only $30,704 in a grassroots campaign. Other notable industry donations were those to successful Democrats: Al Kookesh in House District 5 received $2,249, with nothing to Republican Gary Graham. Ethan Berkowitz received $8,149 of his total $101,454, with just $350 to his underfunded Republican challenger; Berkowitz was the clear favorite. The oil industry's $9,499 donation to Gretchen Guess may have contributed to her victory over Republican Tim Worthen, who received nothing from oil and gas; Guess received less than one percentage point more than Worthen in the final vote tally.

Oil and gas also gave large sums to Republicans Lyda Green ($9,300), Vic Korhing ($12,849), Lesil McGuire ($16,974), John Cowdery ($18,880), Con Bunde ($19,872), and Charles Chenault ($13,700), all of whom ran in noncompetitive races. Thus, the most notable pattern for oil and gas donations in 2002 was not heavy support for Republican candidates in competitive races (there were few), but heavy support for many unchallenged Republicans and Republicans in noncompetitive races, along with heavy support for a few favored incumbent Democrats.

The 2004 election cycle was less costly overall than that of 2002, mainly because there was no gubernatorial contest in 2004. Alaska legislative campaigns drew more contributions than in previous years. The average sum raised by House candidates rose from $33,191 in 2002 to $38,129 in 2004, a nearly 15 percent increase. The average sum raised by Senate candidates rose from $54,905 in 2002 to $66,699, a 21 percent increase. In 2004, Democratic candidates for the state legislature raised $2,243,012, whereas Republican candidates raised $3,513,328, for a nearly 57 percent advantage, about the same as the Republican advantage in fund-raising in 2002.

Oil and gas was once again the largest single industry contributor in the 2004 election cycle. Only candidate self-finance and party committees accounted for more contributions than did oil and gas. The industry gave $342,305 to candidates in 2004 and once again overwhelmingly favored Republicans. In 2004, 88 percent of the industry's contributions went to Republican candidates, up one percentage point from 2002, and only 7 percent went to Democrats in 2004, down from 13 percent in 2002. The difference went to third-party candidates in 2004.

As Table 3.4 shows, many Republican House candidates received large

**Table 3.4    Oil Contributions to House Candidates and Winning Margins in 2004**

| Candidate and District | Amount of Oil Industry Donations ($) | Percentage of Campaign Chest from Oil | Winning or Losing Margin in Percentage Points |
|---|---|---|---|
| J. Elkins (R), 1 | 4,350 | 9.3 | 8.46 |
| W. Thomas (R), 5 | 7,825 | 15.4 | 1.11 |
| W. Sattler (R), 6 | 4,087 | 17 | −1.12 |
| J. Miller (R), 8 | 1,625 | 2 | −3.55 |
| J. Holm (R), 9 | 7,085 | 11 | .77 |
| J. Harris (R), 12 | 5,990 | 7 | Uncontested |
| C. Gatto (R), 13 | 7,700 | 15 | 34.96 |
| V. Kohring (R), 14 | 17,759 | 18 | 24.15 |
| M. Neuman (R), 15 | 3,400 | 12 | 13.89 |
| B. Stoltz (R), 16 | 4,850 | 9.6 | 43.26 |
| P. Kott (R), 17 | 15,050 | 18 | 27.83 |
| N. Dahlstrom (R), 18 | 11,052 | 9.6 | Uncontested |
| T. Anderson (R), 19 | 12,905 | 9.9 | 11.86 |
| W. Moffatt (R), 20 | 3,600 | 4.9 | −4.78 |
| J. Gonnason (R), 21 | 3,587 | 8 | −1.43 |
| M. Ryan (R), 22 | 4,350 | 13.6 | −14.81 |
| R. Goodman (R), 23 | 3,684 | 14.6 | −39.9 |
| A. McLeod (R), 24 | 6,584 | 15.5 | −4.41 |
| N. Rokeberg (R), 27 | 11,950 | 10.6 | 17.54 |
| L. McGuire (R), 28 | 13,575 | 12.6 | 38.23 |
| R. Samuels (R), 29 | 5,725 | 13.8 | 21.81 |
| K. Meyer (R), 30 | 13,750 | 15 | 42.13 |
| M. Hawker (R), 32 | 14,225 | 15.9 | 17.93 |
| C. Chenault (R), 34 | 15,450 | 24.5 | 44.54 |
| P. Seaton (R), 35 | 4,650 | 8.4 | 17.17 |
| G. Ledoux (R), 36 | 3,100 | 3.5 | Uncontested |
| C. Moses (D), 37 | 3,000 | 14 | 26.81 |
| R. Foster (R), 39 | 5,650 | 14.7 | 28.55 |
| R. Joule (D), 40 | 2,800 | 12 | Uncontested |

*Source:* Table compiled by authors from campaign funds data at www.followthemoney.org and from election returns data at www.ltgov.state.ak.us/elections/vhist02g.htm.

campaign donations from the industry. In two contests, those for House Districts 5 (Haines) and 9 (Fairbanks), the oil industry contributions to Bill Thomas and Jim Holm, respectively, represented large enough proportions of their total campaign receipts that industry contributions may have been influential. Nine candidates received 15 percent or more of their campaign funds from oil and gas interests. One candidate, Charles Chenault, the winner from House District 34 (Kenai Peninsula), received 24.5 percent of his funds from oil and gas. He was the incumbent and in a noncompetitive race, as the large vote gap between him and his challenger shows. Several other candidates received large donations from oil and gas when they hardly needed it, which suggests that the donors were more interested in ensuring access and favorable views on their positions, rather than ensuring that their candidates won. Note that John Harris and Nancy Dahlstrom received large donations despite the fact that they had no challengers, and Gabrielle Ledoux and Reggie Joule (a Democrat from Kotzebue) received smaller donations despite their running unopposed.

On the other hand, the table shows that oil and gas donations did not always serve their intended purposes. In seven contests, the candidate favored by oil and gas lost, despite what were in some cases quite sizeable donations.

Table 3.5 shows oil donations and election outcomes in Senate races in 2004. As can be seen, substantial sums of money were donated, even in the case of Lyda Green, who had a large margin of comfort going into the race, presumably to ensure access. In two contests, those in which Democrats Hollis French and Don Olson were favored to win, oil and gas made contributions to

**Table 3.5    Oil Contributions to Senate Candidates and Winning Margins in 2004**

| Candidate and District | Amount of Oil Industry Donations ($) | Percentage of Campaign Chest from Oil | Winning or Losing Margin in Percentage Points |
|---|---|---|---|
| B. Stedman (R), A | 8,450 | 9 | 16.00 |
| C. Morgan (R), C | 7,100 | 16 | −7.76 |
| L. Green (R), E | 7,900 | 6.5 | 36.31 |
| K. Flynn (R), K | 7,837 | 14.4 | −6.14 |
| P. Pawlowski (R), M | 4,600 | 14.8 | −25.29 |
| H. French (D), M | 1,000 | 1 | 25.29 |
| J. Cowdery (R), O | 18,000 | 11.18 | 13.08 |
| T. Wagoner (R), Q | 7,950 | 5.58 | 54.74 |
| G. Stevens (R), R | 9,150 | 13 | 17.48 |
| T. Sweeney (Non), T | 17,955 | 18.96 | −30.19 |
| D. Olson (D), T | 5,575 | 6.2 | 30.19 |

*Source:* Table compiled by authors from campaign funds data at http://www.followthemoney. org and from election returns data at http://www.ltgov.state.ak.us/elections/vhist02g.htm.

the projected winners, as well as their favorite candidates, which would help ensure their access to these Democrats once they were in office.

Following the 2004 elections, Republicans held twelve of twenty Senate seats and twenty-six of forty House seats, one less House seat than in the previous session. To what degree oil and gas affects the complexion of the state legislature and executive office is difficult to determine. Alaska's electorate is generally Republican-leaning, pro-business, and in favor of oil development. Alaskans are unusual in terms of the high percentage of registered voters who identify as nonpartisan or undeclared. In 2004, fully 60 percent of registered voters identified as something other than Republican or Democrat, with the largest percentage identifying as undeclared (36 percent) and another 15 percent registering as nonpartisan. Others registered as Alaskan Independence, Green Party, Republican Moderate, and Other party members. Still, the major parties and their candidates garner the overwhelming majority of campaign donations and votes. Tables 3.6 and 3.7 show the numbers of registered voters per party and the money raised by the two parties, respectively, during the 2004 election cycle.

**Table 3.6    Alaskan Voters by Party in 2004**

|  | Total Voters | Democrats | | Republicans | | Other | |
|---|---|---|---|---|---|---|---|
|  |  | Number | Percentage | Number | Percentage | Number | Percentage |
| Registered | 474,740 | 71,961 | 15 | 118,328 | 25 | 284,451 | 60 |
| Who voted | 313,592 | 47,610 | 15 | 83,906 | 26.7 | 182,076 | 58 |

*Source:* Table compiled by authors from information provided by the Alaska Division of Elections at www.ltgov.state.ak.us/elections/vhist02g.htm.

**Table 3.7    Breakdown of Campaign Donations by Party in 2004 Election Cycle**

| Office | Campaign Donations | Democrats | | Republicans | | Other | |
|---|---|---|---|---|---|---|---|
|  |  | Amount Donated | Percentage | Amount Donated | Percentage | Amount Donated | Percentage |
| Senate | $1,867,581 | $742,613 | 39.8 | $1,030,275 | 55 | $94,693 | 5 |
| House | $4,079,752 | $1,500,399 | 36.8 | $2,483,053 | 60.8 | $96,300 | 2.36 |
| Totals | $5,947,333 | $2,243,012 | 37.7 | $3,513,328 | 59 | $190,992 | 3.2 |

*Source:* Table compiled by authors from information on Alaska's 2004 election cycle provided by the Institute on Money in State Politics at www.followthemoney.org.
*Note:* There was no gubernatorial election in 2004.

As can be seen from these tables, while most registered voters identify as neither Republican nor Democrat, a much higher percentage of Alaskans identify as Republicans than as Democrats (25 percent versus 15 percent). Republican candidates received significantly more contributions than Democrats, $3,513,328 versus $2,243,012, in 2004. Thus the proportions of campaign donations to the two parties correlate fairly well with their proportions of registered voters.[47]

By the elections season of 2006, the political climate in the state had changed considerably, owing to several unpopular decisions made by Republican governor Murkowski[48] and to contentious discussions in the legislature and between the legislature and governor regarding the petroleum production tax (see Chapter 4). Concern about the oil industry's influence in state politics was rising.

An August 2006 raid on the offices of six state legislators by FBI agents with warrants to search for connections between political contributions by VECO employees and legislative action on the proposed natural gas pipeline and the petroleum production tax dramatically heightened misgivings within the electorate about the oil industry's political power. The warrant named top executives of the oil services company, Bill Allen, Peter Leathard, Roger Chan, and Rick Smith, who had donated over $570,000 to candidates for state offices over the previous ten years. Donations had increased since talks with Governor Murkowski on the proposed natural gas pipeline began in 2004. Agents raided the offices of Senate President Ben Stevens, Senator John Cowdery, Representative Pete Kott, Representative Vic Kohring, Representative Bruce Weyhrauch, all Republicans, and Senator Donald Olson, a Democrat. Stevens, in addition to receiving campaign donations from VECO, had received $252,000 in consulting fees since 2001 from the company; he was not required to report details of the services rendered, presuming these were legitimate consulting fees for non-legislation-related work, which he claimed they were.[49]

In September 2006, Michael Carey, former editorial page editor of the *Anchorage Daily News,* wrote a scathing editorial in the *News*, blasting the Republican Party for its indulgence of VECO interests and predicting disastrous consequences in the upcoming elections. He declared,

> Everybody in the Capitol building knew VECO's money bought the company exceptional access to lawmakers. Everybody in the building knew many lawmakers, mostly Republicans, were inordinately dependent on VECO dollars for their campaigns. Everybody in the building knew VECO wanted to make the state lobbying laws less restrictive so corporate officials could report less of their activities. And succeeded when compliant lawmakers passed a measure known as "the Bill Allen bill."[50]

Carey was referring to the 2002 revision of the lobbying law, which sought to reduce restrictions on "citizen" (nonprofessional) lobbyists. Carey's reference in the editorial to a group of legislators who reportedly called them-selves the "Corrupt Bastards Club" increased campaign rhetoric to a fevered pitch, with the public speculating about which legislators were members of this notorious club.

Democrats capitalized on the allegations and speculation, and they cam-paigned against a climate of corruption in Juneau. It worked. The highly con-tentious Fairbanks race between Republican incumbent Ralph Seekins and Democrat challenger Joe Thomas exemplified this pattern. Thomas ousted Seekins by nearly 20 percentage points. Thomas accused Seekins of being a member of the "Corrupt Bastards Club," while Seekins denied the allegation. Although Seekins had attracted other criticism of his performance while in office, the allegations of his having close ties to VECO appeared to be the most damaging. Following the elections, Republicans controlled one less seat in the Senate (Seekin's seat), which resulted in a shake-up in leadership and the formation of a bipartisan working group. In the House, Republicans lost three seats, which reduced their numbers to 23, with 17 Democrats. Republican Bruce Weyhrauch's seat (Juneau) went to Democrat Andrea Doll (Weyhrauch had not run for reelection). Republican Jim Holm (Fairbanks) lost to Democrat Scott Kawasaki. And Republican Norman Rokeberg's seat (Anchorage) went to Democrat Bob Buch (Rokeberg had run for the state Senate and had lost in the primary).

Reports on campaign donations for the 2006 election cycle show that the cost of elections continued to rise. Total contributions (with 94 percent of data complete) were $14,980,300, up from $10,906,871 in 2002, the last year there was a gubernatorial competition. The average gubernatorial candidate raised $219,635 in 2006, up from $158,468 in 2002. The average state House candi-date raised $40,964, up from $38,129 in 2004, while the average Senate can-didate raised $65,033 in 2006, down from $66,699 in 2004. These figures include both the primary and general elections and both major and minor can-didates. High-stakes ballot measures, particularly Ballot Measure 2 discussed later in this chapter, drew $3,036,267 in contributions, raising the total cost of the elections significantly.

Oil and gas again was a major contributor, though industry contributions fell from $342,305,000 in 2004 to $273,125,000,[51] and the industry dropped in contributor rankings from third to ninth place, behind candidate self-finance, party committees, retired persons (contributors who were retired and not actively associated with a trade or profession), general trade unions, lawyers and lobbyists, health professionals, public sector unions, and real estate, respectively. In 2006, oil and gas industry contributions went even more exclusively to Republicans (91 percent, up from 88 percent in 2004). We have no evidence that these contributions were influential in affecting out-comes.

Winning margins generally were large in the 2006 elections, and the industry's contributions tended not to make up a large percentage of the candidates' total receipts regardless of whether the industry's candidates won or lost. In the gubernatorial competition, the industry supported Republican incumbent governor Murkowski with $16,080 in donations, but he lost to challenger Sarah Palin in the primary. In the general election, oil and gas contributed $14,195 to Democrat (and former governor) Tony Knowles, whom the industry had supported in 1998, as well, and only $4,125 to Palin, but Palin won with a 7.36 percentage point margin. Palin's more reserved posture toward the oil industry appeared to be one of the factors that explained her comfortable winning margin.

Republican candidates received additional support indirectly from oil and gas through campaign contributions from the Republican Party and party committees. Oil and gas (through its employees) was the largest industry contributor to the Republican Party, contributing $53,800 to the party, 16 percent of its total contributions. Of the five $10,000 contributors to the Republican Party, three were VECO executives.[52]

The industry exerted its greatest influence in the 2006 election cycle in its successful effort to defeat Ballot Measure 2, the "Alaska Gasline Now Act." The initiative would have levied a new tax on certain oil and gas leases over known deposits of natural gas until the leasers produced the gas. Sponsors argued that the tax would push producers to extract the gas sooner, which would result in large sums going to state coffers in production taxes. Oil producers strongly opposed the initiative and, in an expensive media campaign, convinced Alaskans that it would be detrimental to the business climate in the state. Voters defeated the measure by 65 percent to 35 percent.[53] Most state policymakers had opposed the measure as well. ExxonMobil contributed $455,000, BP Alaska contributed $457,000, and ConocoPhillips contributed $252,000 to the effort to defeat the initiative. Their contributions composed 68.5 percent of the total $1,698,960 campaign against Ballot Measure 2.

Patterns of campaign donations in Alaska mirror national trends as costs have escalated tremendously in recent decades. Incumbents attract the majority of campaign donations, which enhances the advantages they already enjoy from name recognition and media coverage; more money correlates with incumbency, which correlates with winning. The oil and gas industry supports Republicans over Democrats by overwhelming margins, but it also supports incumbents, especially strong incumbents who are not hostile to the oil industry.

Providing campaign contributions is but one tactic the oil and gas industry uses to influence public policies in Alaska. The industry spends millions of dollars a year in lobbying to influence legislation and administrative policies. In 2006, oil and gas corporations spent $3,088,929 in Alaska on fees to lobbyists, and an additional $812,470 to cover their expenses. Oil and gas industry lobbyists stand out for being among the highest paid lobbyists in the state. Seven industry lobbyists earned over $100,000 (two of them earned over

$200,000) from a single employer in 2006, while only five other lobbyists in the state earned more than $100,000 from one employer. Oil and gas corporations spent another $8,107,509 in support of attempts to influence legislative or administrative action, for a total of $12,008,908 in all three fields of lobbying expenditures that they are required by law to report to the Alaska Public Offices Commission (APOC). The "big three" producers far outspent others in the oil and gas industry on lobbying efforts. BP Alaska spent $5,981,875, ConocoPhillips spent $3,351,268, and ExxonMobil spent $1,126,300 on lobbyists and lobbying activities in 2006. The only other industry that spent over $1 million on lobbying activities reportable to APOC was the healthcare industry, which spent a total of $1,186,087.[54] Thus, the industry spends far more in its efforts to influence public policy in the state than what it spends in its attempts to influence elections. Exact figures are difficult to obtain, but clearly additional millions are spent each year by oil and gas corporations in their media and charitable-giving campaigns aimed at promoting a positive image of the industry to the public.

In early May 2007, Representative Vic Kohring and former representatives Pete Kott and Bruce Weyhrauch were indicted on charges of bribery and extortion related to negotiations on the petroleum production tax and the gasline proposal. A few days later, Bill Allen, CEO, and Rick Smith, vice-president of VECO, pled guilty to bribing state legislators with money, promises of future employment, and other favors for their support of legislation favored by the oil services company. The three indicted legislators pled not guilty. However, on June 19, Kohring, pressured by Governor Palin and House leaders, announced that he would resign his House seat. On September 25, Kott was found guilty of bribery, extortion, and conspiracy.[55] On November 1, Kohring was convicted of attempted extortion, bribery, and conspiracy to commit bribery for his taking money from VECO in return for action on legislation favorable to VECO and the oil industry.[56]

Although former Senate president Ben Stevens had not been indicted as of November 2007, the factual basis for Bill Allen's guilty plea relates payments made to a "Senator B" for purposes of corruptly influencing legislation. The figures for these payments to "Senator B" coincide with the consulting fees Stevens reported from VECO mentioned above. The plea document states that "the value of the payments from VECO to State Senator B far exceeded the value of the non-legislative consulting work done by State Senator B." The document further relates that Allen and "State Senator B" discussed the latter's becoming an executive at VECO after his senate term ended. The total value of the illegal benefits Allen and Smith provided to elected officials and their family members or campaigns exceeded $400,000, according to the Factual Basis for Plea that Allen signed.[57] At the time of this writing, the federal investigation continued and it had expanded to include connections between VECO executives and Stevens's father, Alaska's powerful US senator Ted Stevens.

The investigation appeared to focus on VECO's involvement in a substantial 2000 addition to Stevens's Girdwood, Alaska, home, and it also appeared to extend to Allen's large campaign donations over the past ten years to Alaska's congressman Don Young.[58]

As to the question of the corrupting influence of oil lobby money on state politicians, former Republican state senator Steve Frank (Fairbanks)[59] believes that corruption is the exception, rather than the rule. "[Legislators] nearly always vote their constituencies," and Alaska residents are generally pro-development and pro-oil, though it varies markedly from district to district, he says. "People who run for office are rarely ideologues. They're usually people-pleasing public servants who want to serve their constituents. They want to be in step with their constituents." Frank contends that legislative decisionmaking has little to do with campaign contributions, noting that most legislators don't care simply about what their own supporters (campaign contributors) want. They care on a human level about what their nonsupporters (within their districts) think of them. "You'll sometimes see them reaching across . . . trying to please constituents on the other side of the aisle who will never vote for them." Frank says he never saw anyone during his tenure in the legislature who didn't, as a matter of course, vote his or her constituency, and he does not believe that oil lobby money has an improper influence on the state legislature. He notes that the oil industry represents huge interests in Alaska and employs many people with high incomes who are well-informed and who vote. Thus, the oil industry is organized and effective in that sense. He emphasizes, "Money doesn't get you elected. Votes get you elected." Frank estimates that money could have a more corrupting influence on politics in Washington, DC, because members of Congress can become rather distanced from their constituents.[60]

Former state representative John Davies (Democrat, Fairbanks)[61] believes that more public discussion on how money affects politics is in order. He observes that money's influence on policymaking is nebulous. There is "a whole spectrum from completely benign to totally bought." Contributors' motives reflect the same spectrum, he says. Some contribute "because it's Democracy 101"; they support a candidate and expect nothing specific in return. They merely want to be a part of the political process.[62] At the other end of the spectrum are special interests that have a high stake in specific legislation, and they visit legislators' offices several times during the legislative session. VECO lobbyists would do this, he says, noting that in his last campaign, "VECO folks were very active against me." Davies says that "everyone knows" that such intense politicking takes place.

On the other hand, Davies believes that most large campaign donations are not generally made as quid pro quos. Most donors simply support candidates who think as they do. "Where the process goes awry is where the money gets pretty big and where it's big enough that legislators are acutely aware of the amount of the contribution while they are making legislative decisions, in particular when they're concerned that if they vote the wrong way, they may not get a contribution again." Sometimes it's a fine line, Davies says, between just getting support and getting support with expectations for specific actions. He points out that it's not the size of the donation, but the proportion of the candidate's total funding that a single donation represents that raises concern. He concludes that disclosure of campaign financing is essential and that limits on donations are another appropriate line of defense against undue influence.[63] Both Davies and Frank feel that undue influence related to campaign donations is the exception in Alaska politics.

Clearly the potential for corruption exists when campaigning is expensive and special interests have much at stake in the policies that government enacts. At the start of the 2007 legislative session, Governor Palin introduced revisions to the state's executive and legislative branch ethics acts. By the end of the session, both houses had enacted reform rules, and they did so unanimously. The changes prohibited legislators from representing clients before the legislature or executive branch boards, assessed criminal penalties on lawmakers who traded votes for campaign contributions, and revised other provisions, such as the amount of gifts that could be received.

Yet, campaign finance regulation is complex, not only because of the difficulty in defining what is appropriate and what is inappropriate in terms of expectations of donors, but because political contributions fall within US citizens' freedom of expression, and because funding is necessary to wage effective campaigns that inform voters. Regardless of how the federal investigation of possible political corruption in Alaska unfolds, the specter of corruption has been raised, and public debate likely will continue about potential safeguards against wrongdoing. Alaskans' tendency to be skeptical of government will contribute to demands for high ethical standards and responsibility. However, the small size of the population, the tendency of citizens to know their representatives, and the accessibility of politicians, coupled with Alaskans' sense that Alaska is "different and somewhat better"[64] than other states may contribute to complacency.

## ■ Conclusion

The oil and gas industry's influence on state politics reflects its dominance of the state's economy. Historically the dominant financial actors in the state have wielded significant political power. As Alaska historian Terrence Cole writes, "For most of its history either the federal government or the canned salmon industry paid Alaska's bills, and as might be expected, those who paid the piper were those who called the tune."[65] From the 1880s to the 1940s, it was the salmon and gold industries that dominated the state's economy and influenced politics. In the 1950s, the pulp industry was large and influential. From the 1960s forward, oil and gas have composed the leading industry.[66]

Since the 1970s when oil first began flowing through the Alyeska pipeline, oil and gas taxes have provided between 65 and 90 percent of state revenues. However, the influence that the industry wields in state politics derives not merely from the effects of lobbying and campaign contributions to state office holders, as well as its media campaigns and generous charitable contributions, but also from the fact that Alaskans are well aware of how dependent the state's economy is on oil and gas extraction. Of course, this is the aim of the industry's media and goodwill campaigns.

The University of Alaska Institute of Social and Economic Research estimates that one in three Alaska jobs depends on the oil industry, including employment within the industry itself, employment supported by state spending of oil revenues, and employment supported by the spending of Alaskans' Permanent Fund dividends.[67] Furthermore, Alaskans' lives are greatly enhanced by the myriad services provided by the state, thanks to oil revenues. In short, Alaskans know who butters their bread, and Alaskans overwhelmingly favor oil and gas development. For instance, in 1995 and 2000 surveys, 75 percent of Alaskans favored drilling for oil in ANWR.[68] Thus, the composition of Alaska's legislature and the generally pro-oil and pro-development attitudes of legislators, especially Republicans, reflect not simply the purchasing power of the oil industry's PAC money, lobbying dollars, media campaign, and charitable donations, but the attitudes of the electorate, which is eager to maintain a robust economy that provides employment for Alaska residents and sustains the high levels of services provided by the state.

Alaska's dependence on the oil industry is reinforced by broad public awareness as well as political leaders' awareness of the state's vulnerability and their eagerness to encourage more exploration and development, especially as reserves in Prudhoe Bay continue to decline. The oil tax debates of the 2006 legislative session exemplify the problem: Ideally the state would tax the oil industry at the maximum rate possible without creating disincentives that would reduce production and state revenue to a greater degree than the tax rate would increase revenue. This is what Alaskans—politicians and other residents—want. The trick is finding that formula.

Dependency is nothing new for Alaska, but today the state is in a much better position than it was historically to protect its interests. Alaska's economic dependence on oil and gas has grown dramatically, if one measures that dependence in terms of the size of the state budget, the level of services to which Alaska residents have become accustomed, and the fact that approximately 80 percent of state revenues derive from oil and gas taxes. Yet, Alaska's political process has become much more permeable to interests other than oil in recent years. Organized labor is strong in Alaska, and unions overwhelmingly favor Democrats. Numerous environmental groups inside and outside the state actively and successfully challenge the oil industry's interests and positions, as can be seen in the thus far successful efforts to protect ANWR from oil exploration. Numerous other interests, such as health professionals, restaurant and bar owners, telecommunications, and the travel industry, make major campaign contributions that purchase access to lawmakers and arguably increase their reception to those sectors' concerns, which are not always congruent with those of the oil and gas industry.

In recent Alaska elections there have been several close contests in which it appears that sizeable donations from oil and gas may have made a difference between winning and losing, but we cannot say that such donations made the difference. In other contests, industry employees have given large sums to virtually certain winners, suggesting that these donations were intended to buy or maintain access, which of course is not illegal. Public awareness of the potential for impropriety related to large donations from the oil and gas industry (or other interests) is on the rise, as evidenced by the successful August 2006 ballot initiative to reduce allowable campaign contributions by individuals and groups to candidates, groups, and parties, and the requirement that legislators disclose their sources of income. These changes in the law, as well as further disclosures in the current federal investigation of political corruption, may lead to changes in oil industry tactics and practices in campaigns and elections, but clearly the industry will remain active and influential in state politics in any case.

## ■ Notes

1. Alaska's open primaries contribute to the high percentages of nonaligned voters. Nonpartisan and undeclared voters may participate in Alaska's primaries, requesting one of the Republican, Democratic, or other parties' ballots.
2. Alaska voters have favored the Republican nominee for US president since statehood (1959), except for in 1964, when they chose Lyndon Johnson.
3. *Buckley v. Valeo* 424 U.S. 1.
4. Charles Lewis and the Center for Public Integrity, *The Buying of the President 2000* (New York: Avon Books, 2000), p. 5.
5. Contributions of under $200 to congressional candidates rose by $37 million from 2002 to 2004, apparently as a by-product of interest in the presidential election, but individual contributions to congressional candidates of $1,000 or more rose by $129 million from 2002 to 2004. See Gary Kalman and Adam Lioz, *Raising the Limits: A Bad Bet for Campaign Finance Reform* (Washington, DC: US PIRG Education Fund, 2006), p. 10. While the nominal gaps between winners and losers in funds raised and spent widened between 2002 and 2004, the ratio of funds raised and spent of winners to losers decreased significantly (ibid., 23).
6. US PIRG suggests that this increase in fund-raising advantage for incumbents explains the decrease in candidates for federal elections from 2,416 in 2000 to 2,219 in 2004. However, there has been a significant decline in number of federal candidates in each presidential election year since 1992, the steepest decline occurring between 1992 and 1996 when the number of candidates dropped from 2,950 to 2,605 (ibid., 8–9).

7. Ibid., 12.

8. Ibid., 6–7.

9. In the 2002 congressional elections, winners raised four times as much as losers; in the 2004 congressional elections, the revenue ratio of winners to losers was 3.1 (ibid., 23).

10. US PIRG reports that in the 2002 congressional elections incumbents raised 4.5 times what challengers raised, and in 2004 incumbents raised 4.1 times as much as challengers (ibid., 24).

11. Paul Schultz, "Laboratories of Democracy: Campaign Finance Reform in the States," *Public Integrity* 6, no. 2 (Spring 2004): 120.

12. Ibid., 115.

13. Ibid., 121.

14. Ibid., 127.

15. Donald A. Gross, Robert K. Goidel, and Todd G. Shield, "State Campaign Finance Regulations and Electoral Competition," *American Politics Research* 30 (March 2002): 143–165.

16. David M. Primo and Jeffrey Milyo, "Campaign Finance Laws and Political Efficacy: Evidence from the States," *Election Law Journal* 5, no. 1 (2006): 34–36. On the other hand, the study of campaign finance reform by Schultz suggests that public funding produces more competitive races (Schultz, "Laboratories of Democracy").

17. Paul Freedman, Michael Franz, and Kenneth Goldstein, "Campaign Advertising and Democratic Citizenship," *American Journal of Political Science* 48, no. 4 (October 2004): 723.

18. Ibid., 735.

19. *United States of America vs. Bill J. Allen* (2007), Case 3:07-cr-00057-JWS. Factual Basis for Plea (Document 5-2), accessed June 18, 2007, at http://adn.com/static/includes/alaskapolitics/indictments/Allen_plea_agreement_facts.pdf.

20. Gerald A. McBeath and Thomas A. Morehouse, "Reforming Alaska's Political and Governmental System." In Clive S. Thomas, ed., *Alaska Public Policy Issues: Background and Perspectives* (Juneau: Denali Press, 1999), pp. 240–241.

21. Alaska Public Offices Commission website, www.state.ak.us/apoc/index.htm, accessed May 25, 2006.

22. "History," Alaska Public Offices Commission website, www.state.ak.us/apoc/apocomm.htm.

23. 1996 Alaska Sess. Laws 48 ss 1(b). The Court of Appeals for the Ninth Circuit in *Jacobus v. State of Alaska* (2003) upheld Alaska's limitations on "soft money" contributions to parties, reversing the federal district court for the State of Alaska. However, the appeals court upheld the lower court's ruling that struck down as unconstitutional Alaska's $5,000 limit on contributions of professional services to political parties. The appeals court held that Alaska "failed to demonstrate that there is an actual danger or appearance of corruption if contributions of volunteer professional services go unrestricted." (*Jacobus v. State of Alaska*, CV-97-00272-JKS [No. 01-35666], pp. 11045–11046.)

24. McBeath and Morehouse, "Reforming Alaska's Political and Governmental System," 243.

25. Kalman and Lioz, *Raising Limits,* 14.

26. Larry Makinson, *Open Secrets: The Price of Politics in Alaska* (Anchorage: Rosebud Publishing, 1987), p. 8.

27. Ibid., 7.

28. Ibid., 6.

29. Ibid., 10.

30. Ibid., 16–17.

31. Jonathan Rosenberg, "Persistent Patterns: Oil and Gas Industry Contributions to Alaska Legislative Races, 1986 and 1996." Paper delivered at the Western Regional Science Association Conference in Hawaii in February 1997, pp. 6–7.

32. Ibid., 8–9.

33. Ibid., 11.

34. State of Alaska Division of Elections website, www.gov.state.ak.us/ltgov/elections/results/summary.txt.

35. Ibid.

36. Rosenberg, "Persistent Patterns," 12.

37. Ibid., 11.

38. State of Alaska Division of Elections website.

39. "Contributions Part of AAI's Political Activities," *Alaska Spark* 9, no. 3 (Fall 1992): 8–9, cited in Rosenberg, "Persistent Patterns," 7–8.

40. Rosenberg, "Persistent Patterns," 1.

41. Jerry McBeath, "Campaign Finance Reform and Alaska's 1998 Elections: A Preliminary Report." Paper presented at the Western Regional Science Association Conference in February 2000 on Kauai, Hawaii, pp. 10–12.

42. Burr Neely, "Oil and Gas Industry Campaign Contributions and Election Outcomes: An Analysis of the 1998 and 2000 Legislative Elections in Alaska." Paper delivered at the Western Regional Science Association Conference in Monterey, California, February 2002, p. 19.

43. Ibid., 21–22.

44. All figures on campaign financing from the 2002, 2004, and 2006 elections are provided by the National Institute on Money in State Politics at www.followthemoney.org.

45. Ward's total campaign receipts were $115,610, of which $14,050 came from oil and gas. Wagoner's total receipts were $50,284, of which $500 came from oil and gas.

46. In House District 21, Republican Art Nelson received $7,550 from oil and gas, and a total of $49,581 in receipts. In Senate District L, Republican Harold Heinze received $7,195 from oil and gas and a total of $65,511, whereas winner Democrat Johnny Ellis received a total of $52,180 in campaign donations. All campaign funding figures are from the National Institute on Money in State Politics website.

47. Republicans have not always dominated the state. The first legislature following statehood was overwhelmingly Democratic—90 percent in the Senate and 85 percent in the House. Democrats dominated heavily for about a decade, but the 1966 elections swept in Republican Governor Walter Hickel and an overwhelmingly Republican legislature. From the mid-1960s to the mid-1980s, the Senate tended to be fairly evenly divided, though it was consistently organized in Republican-led coalitions. The House, though dominated by the Democrats, more often than not was organized into Republican-led coalitions, as well (McBeath and Morehouse, "Reforming Alaska's Political and Governmental System," 241). Since 1995, Republicans have controlled the Senate and House. See Table 3.1 for partisanship of state government since statehood. Information accessed on June 30, 2006, at Alaska's State Legislative website at w3.legis.state.ak.us/infodocs/roster/ROSTERALL.pdf and w3.legis.state.ak.us/infodocs/infodocs/htm.

48. Among other unpopular actions, he appointed his daughter Lisa to the US Senate seat he vacated upon taking the governorship; he ended the popular longevity bonus program for seniors in the state, which gave $250 per month to those over 65, as a cost savings measure; he bought a $2.7 million jet for his use and for transporting Alaskan inmates to prisons in other states; and he fired highly respected commission-

er of natural resources Tom Irwin after his disagreements with the governor on gas-line negotiations became public.

49. Matt Volz, "VECO Execs' Donations Rose in Last 2 Years," *Fairbanks Daily News-Miner*, September 6, 2006, p. A-1.

50. Michael Carey, "Alaska GOP Won't Escape Stench of VECO Influence," reprint of *Anchorage Daily News* editorial in the *Fairbanks Daily News-Miner*, October 22, 2006, p. A-5.

51. The data at www.followthemoney.org/database/state_overview.phtml?si= 20061#industries on the top industry contributors was 97 percent complete on November 18, 2007.

52. The data at www.followthemoney.org/database/StateGlance/committee. phtml?si=20061&c=416597 on party contributions was 86 percent complete on August 9, 2007.

53. State of Alaska 2006 general election data available at www.ltgov.state.ak. us/elections.

54. 2006 Subject Year End Summary (lobbying reports filed with the Alaska Public Offices Commission, May 2, 2007), accessed June 25, 2007 at www.state.ak.us/apoc/pdf/2006%20Subject%20Year%20End%20Summary.pdf.

55. Lisa Demer and Sean Cockerham, "Kott Guilty on Three of Four Counts," *Anchorage Daily News*, September 25, 2007, accessed November 2, 2007, at http://community.adn.com/adn/node/111100.

56. Neither had yet been sentenced in November 2007. Nor had Weyhrauch gone to trial. Dan Joling, "Kohring Found Guilty of Corruption: Former Wasilla Lawmaker Convicted in Bribery Case Linked to VECO," *Fairbanks Daily News-Miner*, November 2, 2007, p. A-1.

57. *United States of America v. Bill J. Allen* (2007), Case 3:07-cr-00057-JWS. Factual Basis for Plea (Document 5-2), accessed June 18, 2007, at www.adn.com/static/includes/alaskapolitics/indictments/Allen_plea_agreement_facts.pdf.

58. "Paper Reports Young's VECO Ties Investigated in Federal Probe," *Anchorage Daily News,* July 25, 2007, accessed July 29, 2007, at www.adn.com/news/politics/fbi/story/9162143p-9077780c.html.

59. Frank was a member of the State House of Representatives from 1980 to 1984 and a member of the State Senate from 1984 to 1992.

60. Steve Frank, personal interview, August 21, 2006, Fairbanks.

61. John Davies served five sessions in the Alaska House of Representatives from 1993 to 2002.

62. Stephen Ansolabehere, John M. P. de Figueiredo, and James M. Snyder, professors at Massachusetts Institute of Technology, argue that, considering the volume of federal spending on special interests, it is surprising that these interests spend so little on campaign donations. They argue that most campaign donations are not calculated economic investments aimed at economic returns but instead reflect "consumption," that is, participation in the political process. People give to support their ideological allies and friends and because they can afford this form of political participation. Stephen Ansolabehere, John M. P. de Figueiredo, and James M. Snyder, "Are Campaign Contributions Investment in the Political Marketplace or Individual Consumption? Or 'Why Is There So Little Money in Politics?'" MIT Sloan Working Paper No. 4272-02 (October 2002).

63. John Davies, telephone interview, December 14, 2006.

64. McBeath and Morehouse, "Reforming Alaska's Political and Governmental System," 239.

65. Terrence M. Cole, *Blinded by Riches: The Permanent Funding Problem and*

*the Prudhoe Bay Effect* (Anchorage: Institute of Social and Economic Research, University of Alaska, January 2004), p. 14.

66. Ibid., 29.

67. Institute of Social and Economic Research, *Understanding Alaska: People, Economy, and Resources* (Anchorage: University of Alaska, 2006), p. 7.

68. "Poll: Eskimos Back ANWR Drilling," NewsMax.com, accessed on May 29, 2006, at www.newsmax.com/archives/ic/2005/3/14110729.shtml.

# 4

Petroleum Revenues
and Tax Policy

In the early 1970s, Alaska faced a growing fiscal gap. With construction of the Trans-Alaska Pipeline generating intense spending pressures, and revenues from North Slope production still several years away, the legislature turned to the oil industry to close the deficit. In 1975, it enacted a two mill (0.2 percent) reserves tax that essentially forced the companies to lend the state revenues from production that had not yet occurred. In the late 1990s, the legislature again faced a looming fiscal gap of possibly even greater proportions. Although the state's share of revenues per barrel had dropped to less than it was in the 1970s, the legislature turned instead to a program of cuts in state spending. Taking more from the oil industry had disappeared over the political horizon. Then only seven years later, a conservative Republican-dominated legislature overwhelmingly passed a tax bill that would nearly double production tax collections expected for the next two years.[1] The tax package was pushed by an unpopular, lame-duck governor, in an election year in which the state budget, buoyed by record oil prices, ran a substantial surplus.[2]

How can one explain these three seemingly contradictory actions? Are they simply random events, spawned from political gamesmanship, or do they somehow reflect milestones in the maturing relationship between industry and government? In this chapter, we address these questions by reviewing the history of Alaska's oil revenues and the policies that shaped them. We summarize the different ways that the state collects oil revenues and describe three benchmarks for comparing revenue measures and analyzing changes over time. We then summarize the history of Alaska's state petroleum revenues using the three benchmarks, discussing financial and administrative implications of main events since North Slope oil began to be developed in the 1970s. Next, we review the overall pattern of change and analyze alternative explanations. We conclude with some observations about what the history of Alaska oil revenue policy reveals about the evolution of the overall relationship between the industry and state government.

## ■ Analyzing Fiscal Regimes

Governments own exclusive rights to subsurface resources in nearly every country in the world, except for the United States. In the United States, private landowners may also own underground resources.[3] Alaska state government therefore collects revenue from two distinct roles that it plays with respect to the oil industry. As a resource owner, the state leases its mineral rights and collects payments such as royalties from the lessee. As a sovereign, the state collects taxes from oil and gas production, property, and income. The state carries out its two distinct roles with respect to the oil and gas industry in two state departments: Natural Resources, which administers land management and leasing, and Revenue, which administers taxation. Nevertheless, oil companies generally view the lease and tax payments as a package, often called the *fiscal regime*, that they can compare among operations in different countries. Once established, lease terms are part of a contract and can only be changed by mutual consent. In contrast, the state has a right under its constitution to change taxes at any time.[4]

A "marginal" oil field generates just enough income to pay for the cost of inputs used in production and exploration and yield a competitive return to investors. Most productive oil and gas fields typically generate more income than the marginal field, however. In theory, the government can appropriate this surplus—the so-called *economic rent*—while still leaving adequate incentives for industry to continue searching for more oil and gas.[5] The rent offers a unique revenue base that makes petroleum revenues different from other government revenues. In practice, however, every possible way to collect the economic rent through taxes or lease payments has some adverse effects on industry incentives. There is no perfect mechanism to collect oil revenues; all involve tradeoffs of some kind or another.

Most analyses of petroleum fiscal regimes start with the assumption that the state's primary objective is to collect as much economic rent as possible over the long term. Studies have taken different analytical approaches, however, emphasizing different aspects of the regime. Kenneth Dam's classic comparison of North Sea regimes with the US federal Outer Continental Shelf focused primarily on administrative issues.[6] He favored the arm's-length US auction system over the European negotiated licensing systems as likely to collect rent more efficiently. It is not clear that he would have reached the same conclusion, however, if he had taken another look to consider performance under the upheavals in world oil markets that began shortly after his book was published.

Alexander Kemp analyzed the theoretical performance of a number of fiscal regimes, focusing principally on their financial terms.[7] Kemp also considered two general regime types, which he called auction and special taxes, while acknowledging a third type that mixes financial and administrative issues. Many sovereigns, he noted, particularly third-world states, renegotiated fiscal terms after exploration results became known.[8] Stephen McDonald, in his classic analysis of US federal leasing policy, framed the issue in terms of a debate between competitive and noncompetitive leasing.[9] Steeped in the US tradition of arm's-length transactions between industry and government, he emphasized the superiority of formal auctions, where states lease development rights through competitive bidding, to assigning development rights using lotteries or queues (first-come first-served), on both administrative and financial grounds.

Although these three analysts applied different reference terms to compare fiscal regimes against different criteria, they implicitly share several concepts in common. Together, these concepts provide a rich base from which to discuss the changing petroleum fiscal regime of a jurisdiction such as Alaska.

### Administrative Distance

Dam, McDonald, and Kemp all seem to frame the essential policy question for governments as a choice between some type of auction system and alternatives to it. Starting with such a dichotomy is too simplistic to describe the range of relationships between government and industry in regimes that do not use auctions to capture rent. To span this range, we use the concept of *administrative distance*. Administrative distance is defined as a qualitative measure expressing the degree to which the government acts unilaterally to determine the fiscal regime, rather than negotiating with industry to set its terms.

Governments around the world differ dramatically in their administrative distance from the oil industry. Some countries operate their own oil companies that participate with international firms in joint ventures to develop local reserves or take an equity interest in development projects. At the other extreme are governments, such as most US states, that deal with industry only on an arm's-length basis. Table 4.1 summarizes common administrative procedures related to landowner-industry relations and sovereign-industry relations that we might associate with different degrees of distance.

The classical arm's-length lease auction favored by McDonald typifies distant landowner relations.[10] In this system, the government landowner determines boundaries of tracts to be offered, sets the lease terms and method of bidding, and then holds an auction to sell leases to the highest bidders. The US OCS leasing system operates this way in theory, although industry comments and lobbying may in practice influence lease areas and terms. Negotiated lease terms in many nations outside North America imply a much closer landowner-industry relationship. Competitive solicitation of development proposals where the winning bidder is invited to negotiate an agreement—used at times by the state of Alaska to stimulate economic development—occupies a middle ground.[11]

**Table 4.1    Administrative Distance of Industry-Government Relations**

| Distance of Relationship | Landowner Relations | Sovereign Relations |
|---|---|---|
| High | Competitive lease auctions, state sets lease terms and bid method | State sets tax regime unilaterally |
| Medium | Solicitation of competitive development proposals | Industry participates in drafting proposals for tax changes; legislature may amend before ratification |
| Low | Negotiated development and revenue terms, government participation as equity investor | Negotiated tax terms, negotiated settlement of tax disputes |

Tax policies can also be classified by distance. High-distance taxes are those set unilaterally by governments despite industry opposition, such as the Alaska state tax regime of 1979–1981. Negotiated tax systems would fall into the low-distance category.

Dam and McDonald believed that greater distance would tend to increase the state take, although this has yet to be demonstrated in a comparative study. Dam also suggested that the high distance of the auction system insures against state repudiation, that is, the state unilaterally canceling the leases or changing the terms.[12] However, he noted, as did Kemp, that some states do not hesitate to renegotiate terms as they learn more about potential rents. Obtaining a high take without discouraging development requires that the state gain knowledge of the rents potentially earned. Distance enhances the ability of industry to conceal this information from governments and their constituents.[13]

Advantages of closer industry-government relations include more rapid adaptation to changing economic conditions, less conflict and litigation, and a greater ability to accommodate specific needs of one party or the other. The main disadvantage with closer relations is the loss of transparency. Transparency allows those not party to the negotiations to determine what each side gave up and received, enabling citizens to hold public officials to account for their decisions. That is, there is a tradeoff with administrative distance between flexibility and transparency.

## Government Take

Foremost on the minds of many legislators and industry lobbyists is the amount of revenue that the fiscal regime collects: the *government take*. The state take might best be defined theoretically as the prospective share of long-run economic rent that the fiscal instrument is expected to divert to the government from oil and gas development.[14] Defining expected take prospectively recognizes that governments must set up the fiscal regime to collect future, not past, revenues, knowing that the regime itself imposes a burden that may discourage development. Such a definition of take is impossible to measure, though, given that economic rent can only be assessed after all the oil and gas has been extracted. Lack of publicly available data on exploration, development, and operating costs—required for converting revenue streams into shares of economic rent—challenges even retrospective comparisons of fiscal regimes over time or across jurisdictions.[15]

The difficulty of quantifying costs motivates us to consider a simpler measure of government take. If costs change rather slowly over time, then the ratio of petroleum revenues to wellhead oil and gas production value provides a useful proxy to assess trends in government take in a given regime. While less accurate in theory, this simple measure is easy to compute and easy to understand.

Often the issue of government take is portrayed as a simple tradeoff between revenue to the government and revenue to industry. The way that the government collects its revenue also matters, however. For example, production taxes typically do not allow deductions for costs, while income taxes do. All fiscal instruments create some negative incentives for industry investments. But for any given government take, some instruments have bigger effects than others. As mentioned above, governments adopt fiscal instruments prospectively, based on their expected take—a percentage of an uncertain future tax base. How the fiscal regime shares development risk with industry can affect how the actual take compares to the expected take. This risk-sharing element underlies the third measure for comparing fiscal regimes.

## Risk Sharing

Oil companies face several different types of risk. Only a small fraction of exploration wells find developable oil or gas (exploration risk). Once oil is found, the sizes of reserves and cost of extracting them are uncertain (development risk). Oil and gas prices fluctuate unpredictably (market risk). Finally, governments may change the tax regime or impose unforeseen costly regulations (political risk). The terms *progressive* and *regressive* summarize the degree to which the government shares these risks with the developer through the structure of the fiscal regime.

A progressive petroleum fiscal instrument collects a larger proportion of realized economic rent as rent increases, while a regressive measure collects a larger share of the total economic rent as rent declines.[16] Revenues from a progressive fiscal instrument usually rise by a greater percentage when oil prices rise than the percentage rise in prices. Government revenues from a fiscal regime dominated by regressive measures will be much more stable and predictable in the short run than from a more progressive system. But making payments to the state largely independent of earnings may affect revenues in the long run by adding to the developer's exploration, development, and market risk (which are all very high in the oil business).[17]

Table 4.2 places a number of common petroleum fiscal instruments into categories based on the way that they share financial risks. Progressive lease terms include working interest leases—where the state retains an equity interest in the property—and net profit share leases, where state revenues are based on net earnings from the lease. More progressive taxes include those based on local (ring-fenced) profits, such as Alaska's recently enacted profit-based production tax (PPT), and the separate accounting corporate income tax used from 1979 to 1981.[18] Ad valorem royalties and production taxes are highly regressive when costs change but are more neutral when prices and production rates vary. Taxes and royalties based on constant money units per barrel produced are more regressive, since these revenues do not fluctuate with the price of oil. Highly regressive mechanisms for collecting lease revenue include bonus payments and rental fees, which stay fixed regardless of development outcomes. The most regressive tax instruments are those based on inputs rather than outputs, such as property taxes and tax credits. Because they are assessed on costs, such taxes are often inversely related to the rent; that is, the total take may increase even as rents decline.

A richer classification of fiscal instruments might consider combinations

**Table 4.2   Risk Sharing with Different Lease Payments and Taxes**

| Category | Explanation | Lease Terms | Taxes |
|---|---|---|---|
| Highly regressive | Revenue unrelated or negatively related to production | Bonus bids, rental payments, work commitments | Property tax, reserves tax |
| Moderately regressive | Based on production, ignoring price or cost | Fixed dollar per barrel royalty | Apportioned income tax, fixed dollar per barrel tax |
| Somewhat regressive | Based on gross production value, ignoring cost | Fixed percentage ad valorem royalty[a] | Fixed-rate ad valorem severance tax[a] |
| Neutral | Fixed percentage of net income | Fixed net profit share | Fixed-rate producer profits tax |
| Progressive | Percentage of net income rises as income rises | Variable-rate net profit share | Variable-rate producer profits tax, producer profits tax with investment credit |

*Note:* a. Royalty rates and production tax rates that vary with oil and gas prices may be regressive or progressive, depending on whether the variation in costs (which are not taken into account) matters more or less to investment returns than does the variation in prices.

of administrative distance and risk sharing. Table 4.3 provides examples of such a two-dimensional comparison for common fiscal instruments. Because a regressive regime stabilizes government revenues without reference to industry's ability to pay, governments may face political pressure to change the regime more frequently as conditions in the industry change. As we shall see with the Alaska case, a highly regressive system invites repudiation (high distance) or renegotiation of terms (low distance) if conditions change enough to have a profound effect on profitability. That is, regressive taxes increase political risk to the industry as well as financial risk. On the other hand, progressive measures are often more complex and challenging to administer and modify. The simplest lease revenue measure—the cash bonus bid—is also one of the most regressive. Industry may therefore face a trade-off between simplicity, predictability, and short-term risk on the one hand, and long-term stability of the regime on the other.

## ■ Alaska's Experience

Jack Roderick characterized relations with the oil industry in the era prior to construction of the Trans-Alaska Pipeline as shaped by the "well-established Alaskan attitude that financial interests from 'outside' have had an economic stranglehold on Alaska."[19] After oil started to flow through TAPS, the state took steps to abolish most personal taxes and accept financial dependence on the industry. During this more recent era, in which oil and government cashed in the region's enormous petroleum wealth, new forces began to shape industry-state relations.

**Table 4.3  Examples of Distance and Risk-Sharing Combinations**

| | Administrative Distance | |
|---|---|---|
| Risk Sharing | Near | Far |
| Neutral and progressive | | |
| Landowner relations | Negotiated profit sharing or working interest | Net-profit-share lease auction |
| Sovereign relations | Negotiated income taxes | Legislated separate accounting income tax |
| Regressive | | |
| Landowner relations | Negotiated bonus, drilling, or local hire commitments | Bonus lease auction, work-commitment lease auction, fixed lease rent |
| Sovereign relations | Negotiated tax credits | Property tax, payroll tax |

## Evolution of Alaska's Petroleum Fiscal Regime

Table 4.4 summarizes major changes in Alaska's oil and gas fiscal regime since North Slope oil started to be developed, noting changes that involved large amounts of state revenue. By the time ARCO discovered the Prudhoe Bay field in 1968, oil and gas revenues from Cook Inlet leases already accounted for one-fourth of state general fund revenues. Most of this revenue consisted of bonus and royalty payments from leases on state offshore lands and lease revenues shared with the state from US federal lands.[20] The economic boom caused by construction of TAPS put enormous strain on the state budget. Although ad valorem royalties accounted for the majority of oil revenues at the time, Alaska's treasury gained nothing from the run-up of world oil prices accompanying the Arab oil embargo in 1974. That is because Cook Inlet oil fell into the strictest tier of regulation under the federal price-control program.[21]

The petroleum property tax and the reserves tax were the state's initial solution to the fiscal crisis accompanying the pipeline boom.[22] These early taxes were highly regressive, as they had to be, given that their combined take exceeded 100 percent of total production revenues at the time. Prudhoe Bay, which commenced production in June 1977, fell under less stringent price controls than Cook Inlet.[23] As prices continued to rise in the late 1970s, the highly regressive tax system could not respond to the enormous presumed increase in industry profits. The state could not constitutionally repudiate the lease contracts, so the legislature instead rewrote the tax system.

The dilemma facing the legislature was how to tax the enormous rent projected to flow from Prudhoe Bay without making oil and gas development uneconomic elsewhere, given the constitutional requirement to treat all taxpayers equally. By the time Prudhoe Bay oil started to flow through TAPS in June 1977, the legislature had replaced the old fixed-rate severance tax with a new tax with a variable rate. The key feature of the new severance tax was the Economic Limit Factor—a multiplicative factor in the formula determining the effective tax rate for each oil or gas field. The ELF ranged between zero and one according to a formula—different for oil and gas—based on average daily production per well.[24]

Alaska's variable tax rate confused many outside observers about the effective rate of taxation in the state.[25] Writers often incorrectly referred to the ELF as a tax break. In fact, it was the reverse; the ELF provided a mechanism to tax Prudhoe Bay (and later the Kuparuk field) at a higher rate, without raising taxes on Cook Inlet fields. Under the regulations that implemented the ELF, the tax rate dropped to zero when production fell to 300 barrels per day per well or less.[26] Such an "economic limit" to production rate was originally intended to represent a rate that would match North Slope operating costs. In 1989, the 300-barrel-per-day-per-well economic limit was codified in statute.

**Table 4.4  Major Changes in Alaska's Oil and Gas Fiscal Regime**

| Year | Authority | Brief Description | Administrative Distance | State Take | Risk-Sharing Category |
|---|---|---|---|---|---|
| 1973 | AS 43.56 | Enact property tax | High | Increase | Highly regressive |
| 1975 | AS 43.58 | Reserves tax (temporary) | High | Exceeds 100% | Highly regressive |
| 1977[a] | AS 43.55 | Severance tax with ELF | High | Large increase | Less regressive |
| 1978[a] | AS 43.21 | Separate accounting income tax | High | Large increase | More progressive |
| 1979[a] | AS 38.05 | Expanded lease bidding options | High | Neutral | Options to increase used in major lease sale |
| 1981[a] | AS 43.55; AS 43.20; repeal AS 43.21 | Change income tax and severance tax | High | Decrease | Regressive |
| 1989 | AS 43.55 | Change in ELF | High | Increase | Regressive |
| 1990 | AS 38.05 | Royalty reduction option | Decrease | Decrease | Less regressive |
| 1994 | AS 43.55 | Make hazardous release tax permanent | High | Increase | Regressive |
| 1994 | AS 38.05 | Exploration licensing, credit | Decrease | Decrease | Progressive |
| 1986–2000[a] | Attorney general | Settlement of major tax and royalty disputes | Low | Unknown | Highly regressive |
| 1996 | Ch. 139, SLA 1996 | 1996 Northstar lease renegotiation | Low | Neutral | Change from progressive to regressive |
| 1998[a] | AS 43.82 | Stranded Gas Development Act | Decrease | Decrease | Neutral |
| 2003 | AS 55.025 | Exploration tax credit expanded | Decrease | Decrease | Progressive |
| 2005 | Administrative | Aggregation of small field ELF | High | Increase | Neutral |
| 2006[a] | AS 43.55 | Profit-based Petroleum Production Tax | Moderate | Neutral | Change from regressive to progressive |
| 2007[a] | AS 43.55 | Profit-based Petroleum Production Tax | High | Increase | Progressive |
| 2005–?[a] | Proposed | State investment in natural gas pipeline | Low | Neutral | Progressive |

*Notes:* a. These years had changes that involved large amounts of state revenue. ELF: Economic Limit Factor; AS: Alaska Statutes; SLA: Session Laws of Alaska.

Every oil and gas field paid taxes at a different rate. The effective severance tax rate for Prudhoe Bay was initially about 12 percent. Many Cook Inlet oil fields, on the other hand, continued to operate for years at production rates per well below the limit, paying no severance taxes since the early 1980s.[27]

The year after introducing the ELF-based severance tax, the legislature again raised the state take. It changed the income tax base from company-wide income apportioned to the state, with a formula applied in most other US states, to a tax based on separate accounting of income from operations in Alaska.[28] A primary objective of the separate accounting income tax was to make the state's take more progressive, raising the take at a time of historically high oil prices. Supporters of the measure such as Anchorage Senator Chancy Croft believed that sharing risk with the industry was key to the state getting its fair share.[29] Like most people in and out of the oil business at the time, Alaska legislators heeded the upside risk more than the downside.

It is equally clear, however, that prevailing sentiment at the time was to keep distance high. Attorney General John Havelock recalled Governor Egan saying in 1972 that the state taking an equity interest in TAPS "would be like getting into bed with the oil companies, and that is the last thing he wanted to do."[30] Interestingly, an argument in favor of separate accounting was its ability to provide information about potential rents being generated; the high distance of the state's fiscal regime had kept the state ignorant of its effective take.[31]

With most state revenues now being generated by ad valorem royalties, severance taxes, and the separate accounting income tax, legislators had opted to tie the treasury's fortune to that of the state's oil patch. A new leasing law enacted in 1979, patterned after the federal OCS Act Amendments of 1976, completed the transition to the high-distance, progressive fiscal regime, by providing for royalty bidding and net-profit-share leasing.[32] The new leasing options were used immediately in the Beaufort Sea lease sale, held in December 1979, that contained most of the remaining promising but unleased state acreage on Alaska's North Slope.

The Beaufort Sea lease sale represented the apogee of the high-distance-progressive fiscal regime. Although the statute authorizing net-profit-share leases remained on the books, net profit shares would never again be used as a bid variable in a lease sale and disappeared completely from new leases after 1986. Oil was discovered and eventually brought into production from several North Slope fields containing profit share leases. But the high development costs of these generally "marginal" fields, combined with the generous deductions for capital costs, meant that profit-share payments never constituted more than a tiny fraction of state revenue overall. The progressive nature of the Alaska fiscal regime as a whole, however, made it resistant to repudiation during the run-up of world oil prices in 1979–1981, setting Alaska apart from most other governments in the world at that time.

Despite the separate accounting income tax's value in reducing political risk, industry immediately attacked it, filing suit and mounting an aggressive lobbying campaign to repeal the law. Opponents of separate accounting inadvertently discovered Revenue Commissioner Tom Williams to be an able champion. Williams drafted legislation to replace separate accounting with a new apportionment formula, assuring the legislature that the change would result in only a nominal decline in state take. Instead, the state lost roughly $1 billion over the next five years.[33] The 1981 political compromise included raising the maximum severance tax rate to 15 percent (highest allowed as a deduction from the federal windfall profit tax, in effect at the time) and setting the ELF to 1.0 if calculated as 0.7 or higher. This modification ensured that the effective tax rate on Prudhoe Bay oil would remain at the maximum rate of 15 percent for several more years.

The new income tax not only collected far less revenue, it became quite regressive, thus ironically helping to sustain state revenues during the world oil price crash of 1986. When oil prices rise, refining margins decrease, and vice versa, so that company-wide profits of vertically integrated oil producers fluctuate relatively little with oil prices.[34] The tax change also simplified administration of the petroleum tax system, but there is no evidence that lack of state capacity to audit the separate accounting income tax played any part in the decision to repeal it.

In 1989, the chickens released with the severance tax changes in 1981 were coming home to roost. The ELF for Prudhoe Bay was approaching the 0.7 limit, raising the prospect of a 30 percent drop in severance taxes, which provided half of all state revenues at the time. Doubts about the wisdom of yet another tinkering with the severance tax were erased by the *Exxon Valdez* oil spill that occurred in March of that year. Legislators amended the ELF formula once again, this time adding an exponent based on the overall production rate of the oil field. The 1989 ELF kept tax rates for Prudhoe Bay from falling and raised the tax rate at Kuparuk. Severance tax rates stayed about the same for the third largest field at the time, Endicott, but ended up falling substantially for all other fields that still had a tax liability under the old formula.

The slow initial response of industry to the *Exxon Valdez* oil spill also motivated the legislature to enact a $0.05-per-barrel tax to fill a contingency fund for oil spill and other hazardous materials response. This "temporary surcharge" was made permanent in 1994, at about the same time that declining production rates began to erode the take from the revised severance tax. Because it did not fluctuate with oil prices, the surcharge made the overall regime even more regressive.[35]

The election of Hickel in 1990 ushered in a new chapter in the evolution of Alaska's fiscal regime. While proclaiming Alaska's sovereignty with his "owner state" ideology and suits against the federal government,[36] his administration embarked on a program to decrease the distance of the industry-government relationship. Hickel's attorney general, Charlie Cole, began negotiating settlements to one after another of the tax and royalty accounting disputes that had accumulated over the years. These settlements temporarily increased oil revenues by about one-fifth during the early 1990s. Unlike the settlement of the TAPS tariff dispute several years earlier, no information was ever made public about these settlements beyond the amount of money received.

The trend toward decreased distance continued under the administration of Hickel's successor, Knowles. Oil had been discovered but never developed on state tracts that had been leased with net-profit-sharing bids in the 1979 Beaufort Sea sale. BP acquired these leases, whose terms had expired in 1989, renamed them the Northstar prospect, and asked the state to reissue the leases under a new set of fiscal terms that did not include any net profit shares.[37] The Northstar case offers a striking contrast to the analogous case of the Milne Point and Endicott leases that had expired in the mid-1980s. The state reissued those expired leases only after raising the royalty rates and adding net profit shares to the fiscal terms.

Between 1981 and 2005, the Alaska fiscal regime had become increasingly regressive, but with decreased distance. That combination made it difficult for anyone, either inside or outside state government, to evaluate how the take compared to economic rent. By the beginning of the new century, the state found itself holding considerably less information about the rents actually being generated in its oil patch than it had in 1980. This trend reversed dramatically in 2006.

On August 6, 2006, the Alaska legislature enacted a major change to the state system of taxation for oil and gas, retroactive to April 1 of that year. The new tax, passed after several false starts in the second special session of the year, replaced the ELF-based production taxes on gross wellhead value of oil and gross wellhead value of gas with a single tax on net income earned at the wellhead. The so-called profit-based production tax, or PPT, was quite progressive as initially enacted, and became even more progressive when amended in November 2007.[38] But its enactment did not herald, as discussed below, a reversal of the trend toward reduced administrative distance. The Murkowski administration took steps to consult privately with industry executives as the tax bill was being prepared, leading us to place the change into the "moderate" distance category.[39]

## Analyzing Trends in State Take

Figure 4.1 shows the pattern over time of Alaska state oil and gas lease payments and taxes in constant prices between 1959—the first year of statehood—and 2006, the year the PPT came into effect.[40] Except for the $900 million in bonus bids collected in the 1969 North Slope lease sale, worth about four times that amount in 2006 prices, royalties and production taxes have

**Figure 4.1  Real Alaska State Petroleum Revenues, 1959–2006**

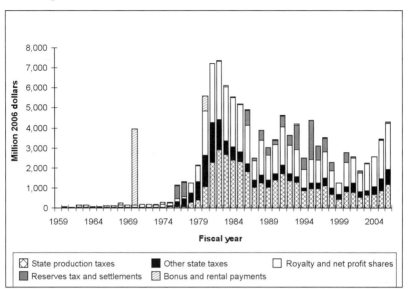

*Source:* Alaska Department of Revenue, Tax Division.

dominated state petroleum revenues. The pattern over time shows a peak in fiscal years 1981 and 1982, followed by a general downward trend until the price spike of the last two years.

Figure 4.2 illustrates the pattern over time of state oil and gas revenues as a percentage of wellhead oil and gas production value.[41] The lower line in the figure shows recurring revenues, defined to include all revenues except bonus and rental payments, the 1976–1977 conservation tax, and tax and royalty settlements, which tend to come sporadically and unpredictably. The upper line adds the nonrecurring revenues converted to an amortized constant dollar amount per barrel during the period, like a mortgage payment.[42] Figure 4.2 shows that the amortized value of these nonrecurring revenues is quite large, $1.48 per barrel for bonus and rental payments (primarily the 1969 bonuses) and about $0.50 per barrel for the nonrecurring tax and royalty revenues.[43]

Figure 4.2 shows a spike in the state take in the 1970s, due to property tax collections just before Prudhoe Bay oil began flowing through TAPS. The ELF-based production tax then stabilized the take at a higher percentage of wellhead value than before. During the 1980s and 1990s, the state take was nearly constant at about 30 percent of wellhead value in recurring revenues and 35–40 percent, considering all petroleum revenues. Total real state revenues (Figure 4.1) first declined in the late 1990s because oil prices fell, then continued to fall because of declining oil production and the production tax's

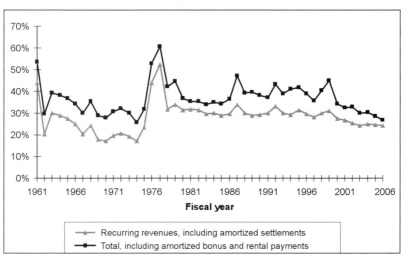

**Figure 4.2   Alaska State Petroleum Revenues as a Percentage of Wellhead Value**

*Source:* Alaska Department of Revenue, Tax Division.

falling ELF. The steep rise in oil prices between 1999 and 2006 masked the impact of the declining take on the state budget.

Alaska has long had a reputation as a high-tax state for oil and gas.[44] While the reputation may have been deserved at one time, Figure 4.3 shows that it had become inaccurate by the 1990s. The figure compares average effective oil and gas severance (production) tax rates in major oil-producing US states.[45] Most states base severance taxes on gross wellhead value. The highest current nominal tax rate for oil is about the same in Louisiana and Montana. But Louisiana taxes gas at a very low rate, and produces lots of gas. The figures for other states are for 1993, because that is the latest year for which comparable data are available. Effective rates have changed little for most states since 1993, but by 2005, Alaska's had dropped by nearly 50 percent, due to the decline in the ELF. Alaska's average 2005 effective tax rate put it in the middle range of US oil states, and the effective rate would have continued to decline under the previous tax structure.[46]

Under the 2006 PPT, Alaska's average effective tax rate would have been comparable to Montana's at high oil prices, but closer to that of Colorado or Kansas at low oil prices (see analysis below). Pedro van Meurs, the Murkowski administration's consultant on fiscal issues for the gas pipeline financing negotiations, developed the initial PPT proposal.[47] Van Meurs analyzed two versions of the tax in his report, prepared before the legislature acted on the bill: one with a 25 percent base rate and one with a 20 percent base

**Figure 4.3   Average Effective Oil and Gas Severance Tax Rates**

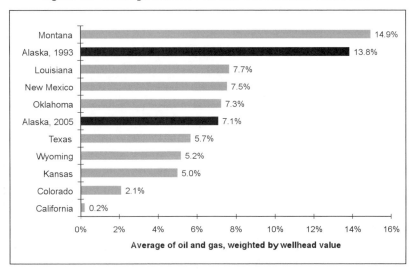

*Source:* Alaska: Alaska Dept. of Revenue, Tax Division, *Revenue Sources Book,* Fall 2005 and unpublished data from the Division. Montana: Montana Department of Revenue, Tax Reform Committee Memo, March 2004. Other States: US DOE Energy Information Administration (EIA), State Energy Severance Taxes, 1985–1993, www.eia.doe.gov/emeu/sevtax/, accessed March 15, 2006. New Mexico includes severance taxes assessed by local governments. Analysis provided by Pete Larson.

rate.[48] He recommended the higher tax rate, but Governor Murkowski, after meeting with executives of Alaska's major oil companies, introduced a bill with a 20 percent rate.[49] The legislature ultimately enacted a 22.5 percent base tax rate, midway between the 20 percent and 25 percent versions.

In his report on the PPT, van Meurs also compared Alaska's fiscal regime to those of nine representative jurisdictions. Table 4.5 shows the results, ranked in order of an index of overall competitiveness. In the table, a lower number indicates a lower government take. When comparing the total government take from Alaska's fiscal regime to that of other nations, one must also add federal taxes to state taxes and lease terms; the US federal government levies a 35 percent tax on corporate income. There are no state taxes on oil and gas produced in federal offshore waters, helping to give the US Gulf of Mexico regime the lowest ranking on government take among those van Meurs analyzed. The comparisons in Table 4.5 suggest that the total state and federal take under the PPT would place Alaska in eighth place among the jurisdictions listed, just ahead of Angola.[50]

Controversy over the PPT's take and the oil companies' influence on the bill did not end with enactment of the legislation. The anticipated skirmishing

**Table 4.5    International Comparison of Selected Petroleum Fiscal Regimes, Ranked by Attractiveness to Industry**

| Fiscal Regime | Overall Competitiveness Ranking | Government Take Ranking |
|---|---|---|
| US Gulf of Mexico | 1 | 1 |
| UK | 2 | 4 |
| Alberta, Oil Sands | 3 | 2 |
| Nigeria | 4 | 3 |
| Angola | 5 | 7 (tie) |
| PPT, 20% | 6 | 7 (tie) |
| Azerbaijan | 7 | 5 |
| PPT, 25% | 8 | 9 |
| Alaska 2005 (ELF) | 9 | 6 |
| Norway | 10 | 11 |
| Russia, Sakhalin | 11 | 10 |

*Source:* Derived from analysis presented in Pedro van Meurs, "Proposal for a Profit Based Production Tax for Alaska," February 14, 2006, pp. 107–118.

*Note:* Fiscal regimes are ranked from most attractive to industry (1) to least attractive (11). The overall competitiveness ranking is based on three financial performance measures in addition to government take.

over the regulations for defining which costs could be deducted from the base for the PPT gave way to the public concern with how the bill itself had been enacted. Indictments of several legislators for bribery and attempted extortion from oil field service firm VECO raised suspicions that the vote on the PPT was tainted. Apparently, during the first of two special sessions called by the governor to address oil and gas issues, leaders of the two legislative chambers had agreed on the parameters of the bill. When it came up for a vote in the House of Representatives, Rep. Weyhrauch of Juneau raised a procedural objection that effectively killed the bill. The bill that died had a base tax rate that was one percentage point higher than that contained in the bill that eventually passed in the second special session. Based on our analysis of the PPT (discussed below), the difference in rates might have added up to $110 million per year at the average wellhead oil price prevailing during state fiscal year 2007 ($55 per barrel). Weyhrauch declined to stand for reelection in 2006 and was subsequently indicted.[51]

New revenue figures from the Department of Revenue showing that the new tax was yielding nearly $1 billion less than had been projected for fiscal year 2007—while the industry was enjoying record high oil prices and profits—added to the unease with the PPT. In essence, tax analysts with the department had based projected state take from the tax on industry costs prevailing during 2002–2005, and had failed to account for the effect of rapidly rising oil prices in 2006 on costs. Higher prices and profits provide oil companies with more cash to spend on drilling and maintenance activities, driving up development and operating costs as companies bid for drilling rigs and services.[52] Because such costs are deductible from the PPT tax base and are positively correlated with oil prices, projections that assume costs are unrelated to prices will underestimate tax revenues at low oil prices and overstate them when prices are high. While the fiscal year 2007 revenue shortfall might not surprise industry economists, it came as an uncomfortable surprise to legislators.[53]

After receiving a report detailing this and other unexpected outcomes of the PPT,[54] Governor Palin called the legislature into special session in October 2007 to review the oil tax regime once again. Democrats in the legislature favored abandoning the PPT and returning to a severance tax based on gross value, but with a higher rate than the old ELF-based tax. Pro-industry Republicans favored keeping the PPT structure and rates. Major oil companies, aware of public anger at the industry over the VECO bribery revelations, stressed the need to keep taxes low enough to make future oil field investments profitable. Governor Palin proposed a compromise tax revision plan, drawn from recommendations of the Department of Revenue staff. Dubbed Alaskans' Clear and Equitable Share (ACES), the governor's proposal combined elements of both views. ACES proposed a tax on gross wellhead value at low oil prices moving to a PPT at relatively high oil prices, although at a somewhat higher tax rate than in the 2006 law.

On November 16, 2007, the last day of a special session overshadowed by the VECO corruption trials, the two legislative houses agreed to a different tax plan. Anxious to demonstrate independence from industry, legislators kept the PPT structure designed by van Meurs largely intact, while reducing some tax credits and raising tax rates substantially. Revenues expected from the 2007 tax in fact still fell a little short of the initial optimistic projections for the 2006 PPT.[55] The revisions largely neutralized the effects of underprediction of costs with oil prices. Although expected tax revenue changed little from what had been (erroneously) forecast in 2006, the government take measured as a fraction of gross value rose substantially (see further analysis below).

### Risk Sharing and the New PPT

Oil taxes generally involve a tradeoff between the share of the rent collected by the government and profits kept by the industry. Higher government takes increase the likelihood of adverse effects on business decisions, but as discussed above, some ways of taking revenue have bigger effects on industry than others per dollar of revenue collected. In Table 4.5, van Meurs ranked some fiscal systems higher for government take than for overall competitiveness, a measure of the relative attractiveness of the jurisdiction to an oil company considering a hypothetical investment.

Two main factors contribute to the disparity in van Meurs's rankings. First, fiscal instruments that defer collection of revenues allow companies to recover investment costs faster, increasing the rate of return. Second, regressive taxes and lease payments, especially those assessed without taking costs or profit into consideration, may make some marginal fields uneconomic to develop that could be profitably developed without the tax or royalty.[56] Viewed prospectively, when a company is considering a development investment, such taxes increase development risks. Alaska's fiscal regime from 1981 until 2006 relied on up-front lease bonuses, property taxes, fixed royalties, and production taxes. This caused it to rank poorly on both the government take and overall competitiveness criteria, even after taking the federal income tax into account. The PPT, with a tax credit for capital expenses and cash-flow deductions for capital and operating costs, fares much better. Consequently, changing to the PPT reduced the relative ranking on government take (meaning more revenue paid to governments) while increasing the overall competitiveness ranking.[57]

Figure 4.4 shows that Alaska has relied historically on regressive lease and tax payments, except for a brief period when it levied the separate accounting income tax.[58] Although Alaska has had net-profit-share leases since 1979, these account for a small fraction of lease revenues.[59] The line in the figure plots the average wellhead oil price, adjusted for inflation. The share of wellhead value collected by the fiscal regime did not rise when oil prices rose; in fact, the figure shows an inverse relationship. The PPT will significantly change this pattern, by replacing about half the "somewhat regressive" revenues with "neutral or progressive" revenues.

The 2006 PPT bill levied a 22.5 percent tax on wellhead value net of pro-

**Figure 4.4    Alaska State Government Take by Progressivity of Revenue Source**

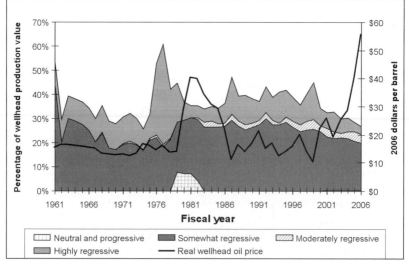

*Source:* Author's estimates.

duction costs and granted oil companies a transferable 20 percent investment tax credit.[60] When a company's net wellhead value exceeded $40 per barrel, the tax rate rose by 0.25 percent per additional dollar earned. For example, the tax rate on net wellhead value of $50 per barrel would be 25 percent. The 2007 amendments raised the base tax rate to 25 percent (the rate initially proposed by van Meurs). It also raised the tax rate by 0.4 percent per additional dollar earned when a company's net wellhead value exceeded $30 per barrel.[61] This would raise the effective tax rate on net wellhead value of $50 per barrel, for example, from 25 percent to 30 percent. The PPT also contains ceiling and floor tax rates that the 2007 law left intact. Additional credits in the 2006 law that reduced effective tax rates during the first six to ten years were eliminated, and other changes limited certain cost deductions.[62]

Figure 4.5 compares how the estimated take under the 2006 and 2007 taxes would vary with Alaska North Slope (ANS) West Coast oil prices, using the investment, operating cost, price, and production assumptions contained in the Department of Revenue's November 2007 analysis of both bills.[63] According to these estimates, the state take under the PPT would exceed the 2005 average effective tax rate at market prices of about $35 per barrel. But

**Figure 4.5   PPT Average Effective Oil Production Tax Rates at Different Oil Prices, 2009 Projected Production Rates and Costs**

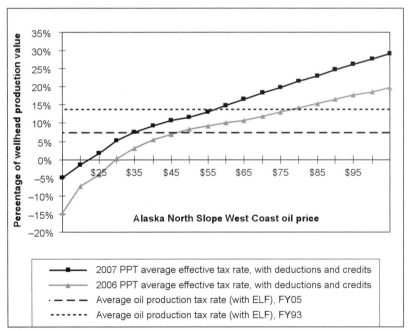

*Source:* Author's estimates.

oil prices would have to remain above $55 per barrel to keep the state take from the PPT higher than the 1993 average effective rate of 13 percent. If history is a guide, oil prices are likely to average much less over the coming decades than they did in 2006. In only nine out of the past forty-five years has the real wellhead price averaged more than $25 per barrel. At real world oil prices below $22, the PPT would lose money.[64] Oil prices stayed below that threshold nearly 30 percent of the time during the past forty-five years, including during two years out of the past ten.

The DOR analysis underlying the projected effects of the PPT in Figure 4.5 is based on oil production costs and investment assumptions known at the time, all of which could change. It assumes that operating costs, adjusted for inflation, will rise by 3 percent, and capital costs will rise by 2 percent, for each 10 percent rise in oil prices. North Slope gas sales and heavy oil development could change the pattern in ways that are difficult to predict. Nevertheless, the replacement of the ELF-based severance tax with the PPT represents a shift to a qualitatively different fiscal regime.

### Explaining the Pattern of Change

The broad pattern that emerges from Table 4.4 and Figure 4.4 describes the evolution during the 1980s and 1990s of a relatively progressive and administratively distant fiscal regime, enacted at the beginning of the North Slope era, into a regressive system with much lower distance. The replacement of the regressive severance taxes with the progressive PPT in 2006 interrupted the prolonged period of incremental change.

A number of plausible hypotheses might be advanced to explain this pattern of take and risk sharing over time. Looking across the continents, one might suggest that the changes in Alaska might have been driven by changes in world oil markets. Many national fiscal regimes changed during this time period, first raising the government take as prices ballooned, next lowering it after 1986 as prices deflated, then raising it again in the price spiral of 2003–2006. A second hypothesis, also with international analogues, is that the state's evolving fiscal dependence on the industry drives the fiscal regime. When a government has few other sources of revenue, it is more likely to turn to the oil industry to solve budget problems. It will also prefer relatively more regressive revenues because it cannot afford to take budget risks.

Both of these hypotheses may be partly correct. But as it turns out, neither fully explains the Alaska pattern. World oil prices rose rapidly between 1973 and 1981, then fell and began fluctuating after 1986. The largest tax reduction in Alaska history occurred in 1981, when oil profits peaked and industry could most afford a high government take. Not only did the legislature reduce the take in 1981, it made the regime more regressive at a time when few experts foresaw much downside risk to oil development, and the state could easily afford to share the risk. Furthermore, in 1989, the state raised the take shortly after oil prices crashed, the opposite of what the oil-market hypothesis would predict.[65]

Perhaps most telling is what did not occur. In the late 1990s, the state was running a substantial general fund deficit, with deficits projected to increase.[66] The legislature's only change to the fiscal regime was to pass the Stranded Gas Development Act. This law authorized the state to negotiate a separate fiscal regime for North Slope natural gas, potentially reducing the state take, in order to encourage construction of a transportation system to bring it to market.[67]

Then in 1999, the state's two largest oil field operators, BP and ARCO, proposed merging. BP's acquisition would have effectively created a monopoly on North Slope operations, and the companies badly needed the state's support to win regulatory approval. If there ever was a time for the state to turn to the industry for money, now was the time. Instead, Alaska's Democratic governor, Knowles, chose to negotiate a settlement agreement with BP executives that required relatively minor concessions, such as a continued commitment to Alaska hire.[68] The state turned largely to other, nontax sources of revenue to finance its deficit.[69] Such a turn of events could hardly have been imagined twenty years earlier. BP's acquisition, if proposed then, would have likely been countered with aggressive litigation from the executive branch, along with a credible threat from the legislative branch to raise industry taxes.

Neither oil-price shifts nor revenue needs fully explain the pattern of change in the state's take and risk sharing. Instead, the pattern appears to be associated with the steadily decreasing distance in the state-industry relationship. The reduction in distance was an important strategic step, which the oil companies used to gain support and influence among elected state officials. The gradual change toward a regressive system, followed by the shift in 2006 to a more progressive regime, largely followed industry goals. The main advantage for industry of the turn toward less distance and reliance on regressive fiscal instruments is that it kept information about the industry's ability to pay private.[70]

### The 2006 PPT: An Anomaly?

In this context, how does one explain enactment of the PPT? First, although the tax bill appeared to be a unilateral move by the state, the idea of changing Alaska's production tax actually originated from industry. During 2005, the state was deeply engaged in negotiations with the three large North Slope leaseholders—BP, ConocoPhillips, and Exxon—over an agreement for the state to participate in financing a $20 billion to $30 billion North Slope natural gas pipeline. Governor Murkowski dearly wanted an accord. Industry executives, concerned that the declining state take and the state's structural budget deficit might push a future legislature to increase taxes, requested that the production tax be revised first, to reduce political risk for financing the gas pipeline.

The tax revision was quite progressive.[71] Oil companies, while lobbying to keep the expected take low, did not oppose its progressive terms. Why, then, would industry favor a return to progressive taxation even as oil prices reached historic highs? The most likely answer lies in the changing economic parameters of Alaska oil. By 2006, Prudhoe Bay production had fallen from the 1980s level of 1.5 million barrels per day to only 340,000 barrels per day. Kuparuk, the second most productive field, had declined by 60 percent from its 1990 rate.[72] The economic rents to be realized from Alaska North Slope oil development were running out, and the industry now had more to gain from revealing its long-run economic vulnerability than from obscuring its short-run profits.

Although the legislature had never addressed the state's general fund deficit, the government in 2006 found itself in a very different position financially from that of the early years in the era of North Slope oil. For the decade preceding the 1975 tax increase, petroleum revenues accounted for between one-fourth and one-half of state revenues, not counting fiscal year 1970 when North Slope lease bonuses contributed over $900 million.[73] For two decades after the 1975 taxes took effect, oil financed the majority of all state expenditures, and personal taxes all but disappeared. By 1998, oil revenues again constituted less than 40 percent of all state revenues, with income from state savings accounts of nearly $50,000 per resident greatly exceeding oil revenues.[74] More recent data and revenue projections suggest that reliance on oil revenues will continue to decrease, and that the increased share of petroleum revenues may be short-lived.[75]

When the 1981 tax reductions were being considered, Alaska had little savings and was still deeply in debt. Current petroleum revenues financed as much as 90 percent of unrestricted general fund expenditures.[76] By 1989, the state had accumulated large savings in the Permanent Fund and was beginning to generate reserve accounts from budget surpluses, gradually becoming less financially dependent on current oil revenues. The legislature elected to place large one-time settlements of tax and royalty disputes into the Constitutional Budget Reserve (CBR) account. By the end of the 1990s, investment earnings from the CBR and a Permanent Fund with more than $20 billion in assets were overtaking oil revenues.[77] With billions of dollars of cash in the bank, the state could have afforded to share oil development risks via a more progressive fiscal regime a decade earlier than it did. Yet it chose not to, because, as the Northstar lease renegotiation case illustrates, industry was strongly opposed.

## ▨ Concluding Observations

At the beginning of the North Slope era, Alaska's government found itself in debt, with few options to raise large amounts of revenue besides raising oil taxes. The main challenge of state fiscal policy became how to tax the wealth of Prudhoe Bay without taxing anyone else. Three decades later, the state's focus has changed. With large savings accounts to buffer revenue fluctuations, but declining oil production and revenues from existing developments, the challenge of the state's petroleum fiscal policy has become how to promote oil field investment without further reducing long-run revenues. The legislature's view has changed, from seeing the petroleum industry in Alaska as the first and only call for revenues, to seeing it also as an engine of economic activity.

For industry, the main challenge in the early North Slope years was to hang on to as much of the rent windfall as possible. Now that the windfall has largely been liquidated and distributed to stockholders and governments, the main challenge has become how to finance the investments needed to stay in business in Alaska. This realignment of interests has helped push the relationship between the state and the oil industry from a more confrontational stance toward one of accommodation, negotiation, and bargaining. The antagonistic attitude toward large corporate interests, characteristic of the 1970s and earlier, never died. But the power of that attitude to shape the state's oil revenue policy appears to have faded, even in the face of a public corruption scandal involving industry interests.[78]

The maturing of the oil industry from a geologic and economic standpoint seems associated with a maturing administrative relationship, as each side gained more confidence that its needs could be met. Alaska state agencies have developed a much stronger institutional capacity for analysis and bargaining with the oil industry. However, starting with the large tax and royalty settlements in the 1980s, and continuing with the Murkowski administration's negotiations over North Slope gas pipeline financing, there has been a significant loss of transparency. Alaskans, aside from the few officials involved in the negotiations, will never know what their public servants left on the table to achieve these agreements. Governor Palin—a political outsider campaigning for more openness in government—beat Murkowski in the 2006 primary election in part due to the public distrust of the closed-door talks. But in the quest for an agreement, the PPT was passed and became law, and it was affirmed the following year by a legislature and governor determined to distance themselves from the 2007 VECO corruption scandal. The PPT returns to a more progressive tax system that aligns state oil taxes closely with industry earnings, heralding a new chapter for Alaska's petroleum fiscal regime.

## ▨ Notes

1. Revenue projections are from Fiscal Note Number 4 (Corrected), SCS CSHB 3001(NGD), State of Alaska, 2006 Legislative Session, published August 9, 2006.

2. While world oil prices were actually slightly higher in 1981 than in the summer of 2006, after adjusting for inflation, Alaska wellhead prices—the relevant base for most Alaska state revenues—exceeded those of 1981.

3. Alaska Native regional corporations, for example, own mineral rights to lands granted to village and regional corporations under the Alaska Native Claims Settlement Act. The state of Alaska, however, retained subsurface ownership when it disposed of the lands it acquired at statehood, which generally parallels the situation in other countries.

4. Alaska Constitution, Article 9, Section 1. Taxing Power, states, "The power of taxation shall never be surrendered. This power shall not be suspended or contracted away, except as provided in this article."

5. Economic rent is defined as the value of production minus the cost of capital, labor, and materials used in production.

6. Kenneth W. Dam, *Oil Resources: Who Gets What How?* (Chicago: University of Chicago Press, 1976).

7. Alexander Kemp, *Petroleum Rent Collection Around the World* (Halifax: The Institute for Research on Public Policy, 1987); and Alexander Kemp, "Development Risks and Petroleum Fiscal Systems: A Comparative Study of the U.K., Norway, Denmark, and the Netherlands," *The Energy Journal* 13, no. 3 (1992): 17–39.

8. Kemp, *Petroleum Rent Collection*, p. xxxviii.

9. Stephen L. McDonald, *The Leasing of Federal Lands for Fossil Fuels Production* (Baltimore: The Johns Hopkins Press for Resources for the Future, 1979).

10. Ibid.

11. See Chapter 7.

12. Dam, *Oil Resources*, 175.

13. Matthew Berman, "Caveat Emptor: Negotiated Fiscal Regimes," *Journal of Petroleum Finance and Development* 2, no. 1 (1997): 25–43, elaborates this point.

14. See Kemp, *Petroleum Rent Collection*.

15. Field operating costs, development capital costs, and exploration costs for new fields are difficult enough to estimate after development occurs. For example, Matthew Berman, Eric Myers, William Nebesky, Karen White, and Teresa Hull, *Alaska Petroleum Revenues: The Influence of Federal Policy* (Anchorage: Institute of Social and Economic Research, October 1984), and Kemp, *Petroleum Rent Collection,* made estimates for the early years of Alaska North Slope production based on publicly available data. Even industry analysts with access to proprietary data can only provide rough guesses of expected rent in advance of development, and these estimates often turn out later to have been wildly inaccurate.

16. A progressive instrument may be defined formally as the elasticity of government take with respect to the revenue base. (*Elasticity* denotes the percentage change in take divided by the percentage change in the base.) The base for oil and gas revenues is not income but rather economic rent—or more precisely, the deviation of economic rent from the expected level. The terms *progressive* and *regressive* are often popularly associated with other more imprecise measures of the oil revenue base, such as oil price, production level, and net income. Variations in these other measures are often, but not always, correlated with variations in economic rent.

17. See Kemp, "Development Risks."

18. Alaska Statutes sec. 43.21. The notion of "ring fencing" refers to limiting the geographic scope of the revenue base. The profitability of a company's Alaska operations may have little influence on state income tax payments if based on a company's worldwide income; hence the attractiveness of ring-fencing by limiting the tax base to income from Alaska operations.

19. Jack Roderick, *Crude Dreams: A Personal History of Oil and Politics in Alaska* (Fairbanks: Epicenter Press, 1997), p. 13.

20. The US federal government shared 90 percent of its one-eighth royalty share from onshore oil and gas leases on federal lands with the state of Alaska. The state leased its lands with a bonus-bid auction and a one-eighth royalty.

21. See Berman et al., *Alaska Petroleum Revenues.*

22. Alaska Statutes sec. 43.56 and sec. 43.58, respectively.

23. Berman et al., *Alaska Petroleum Revenues.*

24. See Alaska Department of Revenue, Oil and Gas Audit Division, *Revenue Sources Book: Forecast and Historical Data* (Fall 2006), for a technical discussion of the ELF-based tax.

25. For example, see Peter Mieszkowski and Eric Toder, "Taxation of Energy Resources." In Charles E. McLure Jr. and Peter Mieszkowski, eds., *Fiscal Federalism and the Taxation of Natural Resources* (Lexington, MA: D. C. Heath and Co., 1983), pp. 65–92.

26. For comparison, a "stripper well," the definition of marginal production in other US states, produces less than 10 barrels per day. Most onshore oil production in other US states would pay zero tax under the ELF.

27. While the ELF was initially constructed to prevent severance taxes from encouraging early shutdown of producing fields, it also potentially set low tax rates for new fields. For example, if the giant West Sak field had been brought into full commercial production under the regime, it would likely never have had to pay any severance tax under the ELF formula, since production from the heavy oil giant would never have reached 300 barrels per day per well.

28. Alaska Statutes sec. 43.21.

29. Compare Jack Roderick's account of Senator Croft's pursuit of a right-of-way leasing bill that would share risk from TAPS revenues (Roderick, *Crude Dreams,* 347–353).

30. Ibid., 351. At the time, Egan favored 100 percent state ownership of TAPS.

31. John Strohmeyer, *Extreme Conditions: Big Oil and the Transformation of Alaska* (New York: Simon and Schuster, 1993), pp. 209–211.

32. Alaska Statutes sec. 38.05.180.

33. Author's estimate, based on the reported change in corporate income taxes between 1979–1981 and 1983–1986 and a recalculation of Prudhoe Bay severance tax revenues. After leaving office with the retirement of Governor Hammond in 1982, Williams obtained a job as a tax analyst in BP's Anchorage headquarters, where he has worked ever since.

34. The revised income tax apportions company-wide income to Alaska based on the shares of company oil and gas production, sales plus pipeline tariffs, and assets occurring in the state. The formula applied by other states uses employment, sales, and assets.

35. Alaska Statutes sec. 200, sec. 201, and sec. 300.

36. See discussion of the owner state concept in Chapter 6.

37. It is unlikely that BP's objective in this interchange would have been to save money. The state's analysis showed that the government take would decrease by perhaps $9 million if development had proceeded without delay. Because the net profit share terms allowed previously incurred costs to accumulate interest at a high rate, any delay would have reduced the state's share. After agreeing to the change in terms, field development was actually delayed by as much as two years due to an unrelated environmental dispute. Consequently, BP will almost certainly pay more under the new

terms. Instead, BP's probable objective was to conceal information about true profits from development.

38. Alaska's PPT has several unique features that distinguish it from other taxes on profits or net income. As with net profit shares in the state's leases, capital costs are fully deductible from the PPT and do not have to be depreciated or amortized over a number of years as they do for income taxes. The PPT also allows oil companies to deduct exploration and development costs in the year that they are made (cash-flow accounting) against any income earned from oil and gas production in the state (except from Cook Inlet fields, which are treated separately). Profit share leases only allow capital cost deductions from earnings from that particular lease. The PPT also contains a tradable 20 percent credit for exploration and development costs, in addition to the full deduction. That way a company can get credit for a portion of exploration or development costs even if it has no Alaska earnings. See Alaska Statutes sec. 43.55.011.

39. See Richard Richtmyer and Wesley Loy, "Governor Puts Forth Oil-Tax Reform Plan Package: Murkowski Also Says BP and Exxon Will Join Conoco on Gas Line Contract," *Anchorage Daily News*, February 22, 2006; and the discussion that follows in this chapter of the controversy over the PPT.

40. Although the 2006 PPT was retroactive to April 1 of that year, oil companies had until early 2007 to make all their retroactive payments. Consequently, the figures for fiscal year 2006, which ended on June 30, largely reflect the previous tax regime.

41. Comparing trends in state revenues as a percentage of wellhead value ignores the effect of trends in costs and federal taxes on industry profits. It also overstates the true percentage take from the wellhead somewhat because income and property taxes collected on the Trans-Alaska Pipeline are included in the numerator but not in the denominator. Taxes collected on pipelines, especially income taxes, vary over the years and would be difficult to separate out from taxes collected at the wellhead.

42. That is, the nonrecurring revenues are expressed as the constant real dollar amount per barrel, adjusted for remaining reserves in currently known fields, that has the same value, with interest, as the stream of nonrecurring revenues invested at the same interest rate. The interest rate used for the calculation is a 10 percent real annual rate, reflecting the high risk involved. This is the same rate used in the analysis of the PPT prepared for the Alaska Department of Revenue: Pedro van Meurs, "Proposal for a Profit Based Production Tax for Alaska," manuscript, February 14, 2006.

43. Although the reserves tax and the tax and royalty settlements collectively totaled several billion dollars and were much larger, even after adjusting for inflation, than the bonus bids, they were collected much more recently and therefore do not carry nearly as much interest as do the bonus bids, resulting in a lower amortized value per barrel.

44. See Mieszkowski and Toder, "Taxation of Energy Resources."

45. The oil and gas industry pays other taxes besides severance taxes, but these are ignored because other industries generally pay them, too, and they are not specific to oil and gas.

46. Official state revenue projections showed the oil ELF, and therefore the oil severance tax, declining by about one-third over the next seven years (Alaska Department of Revenue, Oil and Gas Audit Division, *Revenue Sources Book* [Fall 2005], p. 14).

47. Chapter 6 contains a discussion of the gas pipeline financing issue.

48. Van Meurs, "Proposal for a Profit Based Production Tax."

49. Richtmyer and Loy, "Governor Puts Forth Oil-Tax Reform."

50. Van Meurs projected an increase in government take with the switch to the PPT, while we have projected that the 2006 tax was revenue-neutral in Table 4.4. The

discrepancy is due to the apparently incorrect assumption by van Meurs that oil-field costs will remain the same as they were historically, despite higher real oil prices (see further discussion in this chapter). Also, although production tax revenue is likely to increase substantially in the short run under the PPT, the take in the long run might well be lower, if its incentives work to increase exploration and bring more marginal fields into production.

51. US Department of Justice, "Three Current and Former Alaska State Legislators Indicted on Public Corruption Charges," May 4, 2007 (www.usdoj.gov/opa/pr/2007/May/07_crm_330.html); Pat Forgey, "Indictment: Weyhrauch Sought Work with VECO: VECO Corp. Acknowledges It's the Company Named in Indictment," *Juneau Empire*, May 6, 2007. Two other legislative proponents of lower oil taxes in the 2006 legislature—former House Speaker Pete Kott and Representative Vic Kohring—were also indicted, and later convicted, for taking bribes from VECO.

52. See "Econ One: Industry Costs Up," *Petroleum News*, vol. 12, no. 45 (November 11, 2007). Nationally, drilling costs rose 34 percent between 2003 and 2005 during the run-up of oil prices, after adjusting for general price inflation. (US Energy Information Administration, based on the 2005 Joint Association Survey on Drilling Costs (www.eia.doe.gov/emeu/aer/txt/ptb0408.html). Drilling costs were deflated using the gross domestic product implicit price deflator. Over the past two decades, drilling costs from the Joint Association Survey are highly correlated with oil prices. Statistical analysis shows that on average, a 10 percent change in oil prices was positively associated with a 3 percent change in drilling costs.

53. The April 2006 to March 2007 tax reconciliation payments generated $805 million more under the PPT than projected by DOR for the old tax, which was $89 million less than expected even after adjusting for forecast discrepancies for the old tax. Of this total, DOR analysts could explain $50 million in higher expenditures, leaving about $30 million to reconcile in audits (letter from Patrick Galvin, commissioner of the Alaska Department of Revenue, to Governor Sarah Palin, April 30, 2007). Given that the PPT was effective retroactively to April 1, 2006, these figures represent a 15-month period, during which oil prices fluctuated substantially. Therefore, it is difficult to determine an accurate estimate of the state take for Fiscal Year 2007.

54. The difference between projected and realized costs and revenues is detailed in "Petroleum Profits Tax (PPT) Implementation Status Report," Alaska Department of Revenue, August 3, 2007.

55. The official revenue forecast available to the legislature when they debated the 2006 PPT—Fiscal Note Number 4 (Corrected), SCS CSHB 3001 (NGD), published August 9, 2006, State of Alaska, 2006 Legislative Session—projected that revenues under the bill would be about $2.4 billion at oil prices of $60 per barrel. The forecast for the 2007 PPT, with revised cost assumptions—Fiscal Note Number 10, SCS CSHB 2001 (FIN), State of Alaska, 2008 Legislative Session—projected $2.2 billion for Fiscal Year 2008, and $2.0 billion for the next five years. Adjusting for the lower oil production assumptions in the more recent projection, the two forecasts project very similar government revenues per barrel.

56. Another problem with royalties and taxes based on production rather than net income is that they may lead to premature abandonment of oil and gas fields. This was the original rationale for the ELF. While the ELF does eliminate tax incentives for premature abandonment by lowering the tax rate to zero as production rates decline, it poorly addresses the much bigger problem of investment in new high-cost fields.

57. One should keep in mind that van Meurs intentionally drafted the PPT so that it would rank high for government take and low for effects on competitiveness.

58. Alaska's Separate Accounting Corporate Income Tax (Alaska Statutes sec.

43.21) defined the tax base as net income earned in Alaska. This is sometimes called a "ring-fenced" income tax. In contrast, most state income taxes apply to a fraction of total company income that is apportioned to the state based on a formula that does not include income earned in that state. The separate accounting tax was repealed in 1981 under intense industry lobbying and litigation pressure.

59. Net profit share leases became controversial in 1996 when BP insisted on renegotiating lease terms for its Northstar prospect to eliminate net profit shares, some of which ranged as high as 90 percent, before developing the field (see Table 4.4). However, BP and several other companies have been producing oil from several North Slope fields with smaller net profit shares, generally 30 percent, for many years without conflict or controversy.

60. The first $0.30 per barrel of capital costs may not be deducted or taken as a tax credit. Additional tax credits are allowed for some exploration investments.

61. The 0.4 percent marginal tax rate applied to net value between $30 and $90 per barrel. Above $92.50, the marginal tax rate dropped to 0.1 percent, with a ceiling of 75 percent of net value, including the 25 percent base rate (Alaska Statutes 44.55.011).

62. So-called "transition credits" were restricted in the 2007 law to companies not producing oil in 2006. The 2007 law limited pipeline transportation deductions to "reasonable cost" instead of the TAPS tariff settlement method. In fiscal year 2008, the difference was expected to be $2.76 vs. $5.28. The 2007 law allowed only one-half of capital credits to be taken in the first year, with the balance carried over to the next year. Operating cost deductions were frozen at 2006 levels, except for inflation, until 2010. (HB2001, transmitted to the governor, November 16, 2007.)

63. Fiscal Note Number 10, SCS CSHB 2001 (FIN), State of Alaska, 2008 Legislative Session, published November 15, 2007. The fiscal notes estimate state revenues only during the first few years after implementation and include the effects of a number of transition features with near-term expiration dates. Most ANS oil is sold on the US West Coast. The wellhead price is lower than the market price by the amount charged for transportation from the lease to the point of sale. For Alaska oil, this differential has varied somewhat over time but is currently about $6 per barrel.

64. The PPT allows losses and unused tax credits to be carried forward indefinitely and sold to firms with tax liability. In years when no company has a positive tax liability, the industry would essentially be loaning money to the state, which would have to pay it back as soon as the industry returned to profitability.

65. The 1989 severance tax change changed the ELF formula in a way that raised the take only slightly for the current year, but prevented a large percentage decrease predicted in future years. The bill likely passed only because of the momentary backlash against the industry following the *Exxon Valdez* oil spill, which occurred while the bill was being debated.

66. See Alaska Department of Revenue, Oil and Gas Audit Division, *Revenue Sources Book: Forecast and Historical Data* (Spring 1999).

67. The Stranded Gas Act (Alaska Statutes sec. 43.82) is discussed in the context of North Slope gas development in Chapter 6.

68. State of Alaska, BP, and ARCO, "Charter for Development of the Alaskan North Slope," December 2, 1999 (www.gov.state.ak.us/bparco/FinalCharter1202. html). Although Alaska agreed not to object to the merger, the state of California continued to oppose it. In order to satisfy California's concerns about market power on the US West Coast, the Federal Trade Commission required BP to sell ARCO's entire Alaska operation to a third company (Phillips Petroleum), before allowing the merger to proceed.

69. See Scott Goldsmith, Linda Leask, and Mary Killorin, "Alaska's Budget: Where the Money Came From and Went 1990–2002," *ISER Fiscal Policy Papers*, no. 13 (May 2003).

70. As discussed in Chapter 3, the trend toward reduced distance coincided with the increased importance of money in state elections and the prominent role of the major oil companies and their suppliers and contractors in campaign finance. Around 1980, ARCO began to move management personnel for its Alaska operations from company headquarters to Anchorage. It brought over 1,000 highly paid, politically active employees to the state and told them which candidates to support. BP followed suit and moved headquarters staff to Anchorage several years later. Both companies aggressively developed agent-client relationships with oil field service companies, insecure of their position with respect to the two dominant firms. One might wonder whether the BP-ARCO merger itself was made possible precisely because of the change in the distance of the state's fiscal relationship. An aggressive, no-compromise lawsuit from the state would likely have caused BP to walk away from the merger rather than have to turn over corporate financial records in a discovery proceeding. ARCO employees laid off after the merger might wonder if the truncation of their careers was a by-product of their company's political education campaign.

71. Van Meurs, "Proposal for a Profit Based Production Tax."

72. Alaska Department of Revenue, Oil and Gas Audit Division, *Revenue Sources Book,* 2006.

73. Ibid.

74. Scott Goldsmith, "From Oil to Assets: Managing Alaska's New Wealth," *ISER Fiscal Policy Papers*, no. 10 (June 1998), pp. 1–8.

75. Alaska Department of Revenue, Oil and Gas Audit Division, *Revenue Sources Book,* 2007.

76. Ibid.

77. Goldsmith, "From Oil to Assets."

78. As noted above, the legislature in the 2007 special session maintained the PPT tax structure favored by industry, raising rates to recover no more revenue than state projections had inaccurately forecast they would have received under the previous law. In 2006, members of the Democratic legislative minority, led by gubernatorial candidate Eric Croft, son of Chancy Croft, grew impatient with the slow progress of pipeline talks (see Chapter 6) and drafted a ballot initiative to impose a reserves tax on natural gas. Industry regarded the initiative as punitive and campaigned vigorously against it. The initiative failed at the polls in November 2006.

# 5

## Oil Supply, Budgets, and Expenditures

The Richfield Oil Company's discovery of marketable quantities of oil on the Kenai Peninsula in the 1950s and production at the Swanson River fields were used as evidence of sufficient economic development in arguments before the US Congress to grant Alaska statehood (see Chapter 2 for a detailed account). The state's largest working oil patch, however, is Prudhoe Bay on the North Slope. State geologists surveyed this region shortly after statehood and claimed it as part of the statehood land grant entitlement (part of the 103.5 million acres allocated to the state from the federal public domain). In 1968, Atlantic-Richfield Company announced the discovery of America's largest petroleum reservoir, with an estimated recoverable volume of 12 billion barrels (now known to contain nearly 16 billion barrels). The discovery caused a rush of oil companies to bid for oil and gas leases, which netted the state treasury $900 million in 1969, the largest single-year earnings from lease sales in the history of the state. During the 1980s and 1990s, Alaska supplied about 21 percent of the oil produced in the United States. Alaska Department of Revenue data show Alaska crude oil production peaking at 738.14 million barrels in 1988 and declining to 270.5 million barrels in 2006. Even with an obsolescing oil patch, however, Alaska still accounted for 19.2 percent of domestic production in 2000, and more than 14.5 percent in 2006 (see Table 5.1).[1]

Energy resources have figured prominently in the economic development of several American states. But only Alaska has depended on a single natural resource for its survival during more than half its statehood years. Furthermore, the price of petroleum is set by international markets, which have been highly volatile since the OPEC oil embargo of 1973. Alaska fiscal policymaking, therefore, has been more turbulent than that of most states. State revenues were some 75 percent dependent on oil severance taxes and royalties during the period 1977–1999, and each dollar change in the price of oil causes revenues to fluctuate by $100 million to $150 million. Disruptions were particularly severe at the close of the Iran-Iraq War in 1986, when oil prices dived below $10 per barrel, and in 1998–1999, when inflation-adjusted prices reached their lowest level since before the 1973 global shock.

Developments in the early twenty-first century continue to demonstrate the direct link between volatile oil markets and Alaska's fiscal situation. In fiscal year (FY) 2006, as a result of an average price of $43.40 a barrel for Alaska North Slope (ANS) crude on spot markets during FY 2005, oil revenues contributed almost $3.7 billion to the state budget—a staggering 88 percent of unrestricted general fund revenues. Continued high prices in FY 2006 (averaging $60.80 for ANS crude) have led to even higher projections for FY 2007. But the state Department of Revenue, under the assumption that oil prices peaked in mid-2005 and that North Slope production will continue to decline, projected a steadily shrinking revenue base beginning in FY 2008 (see Table 5.2 below).[2] These assumptions were disproved as oil prices reached $99.16 a barrel in late November 2007. Nevertheless, these developments did not fundamentally challenge the gloomy long-term scenario based on declining production and state lawmakers reacted by attempting to capture more of the windfall with a revised tax regime.[3]

Through the lens of fiscal policy, we continue our examination of how the state has grown and prospered from its relationship with volatile global ener-

### Table 5.1  Production of Crude Oil (millions of barrels)

|          | 2000    | 2001    | 2002    | 2003    | 2004    | 2005    | 2006    |
|----------|---------|---------|---------|---------|---------|---------|---------|
| Alaska   | 355.2   | 351.4   | 359.3   | 355.6   | 332.5   | 315.4   | 270.5   |
| US total | 1,850   | 2,117.5 | 2,097.1 | 2,073.4 | 1,983.3 | 1,890.1 | 1,862.2 |
| Imports  | 3,319.8 | 3,404.9 | 3,336.2 | 3,527.7 | 3,692.1 | 3,695.9 | 3,693.1 |

*Source:* Compiled by the authors from data provided by the US Energy Information Administration, "Annual Crude Oil Production," available at http://tonto.eia.doe.gov/dnav/pet/pet_crd_crpdn_adc_mbbl_a.htm, and "US Crude Oil Imports from All Countries," available at http://tonto.eia.doe.gov/dnav/pet/hist/mcrimus1A.htm.

### Table 5.2  Unrestricted General Fund Revenues (in $ millions by fiscal year)

|                                            | 2006    | 2007[a]  | 2008[a]  |
|--------------------------------------------|---------|----------|----------|
| Oil revenue                                | 3,699.2 | 4,324.7  | 2,967.2  |
| Other (excluding federal and investment)   | 447.9   | 531.6    | 484.3    |
| Investment earnings                        | 53.3    | 123.9    | 96.1     |
| Total                                      | 4,200.4 | 4,980.2  | 3,547.6  |

*Source:* Compiled by the authors from data published in the Alaska Department of Revenue, Tax Division, *Spring 2007 Revenue Sources Book,* pp. 4–5.

*Note:* a. These are forecast figures.

gy markets. We also wish to strike a note of concern. The diversification strategies discussed in Chapter 4 (as well as further below and in Chapters 6 and 7) have been remarkably successful in generating income from the reinvestment of oil revenues and providing a legislative savings account to deal with fiscal emergencies and exigencies. These strategies have done little, however, to de-link the state's revenue streams from global oil markets, and in the case of the Permanent Fund, have added the additional variable of global equities markets to the fiscal mix.[4] In Chapter 4, we showed that attempts by the state to increase its leverage with oil multinationals by renegotiating taxes and royalties have met with only limited success and in some cases have had unintended consequences. As a result, the state's legislature and executive resort to fiscal belt-tightening during times of low crude-oil prices and continue to find it hard not to be profligate when prices are high.

In this chapter we elaborate on the complex and indirect relationships of state politics to global oil markets, variations in available in-state reserves, and the capacity of state government to make effective fiscal policy. The argument of the chapter unfolds in two sections. First, we evaluate the relationship between global oil price volatility and Alaska fiscal policy responses, focusing on the two primary oil price shocks to Alaska—in 1986 and 1998–1999—and the dramatic rise in world market prices in 2005–2007. This part of our discussion includes tactics selected by executives and legislators to address both short- and long-term oil price declines, and schemes for taking advantage of price surges. Second, we analyze the politics of the Alaska fiscal policy process: interbranch competition and cooperation, partisan changes, interest group pressures, and the impact of political pressure on agency budget shares.[5] A related topic—the impact of multinational oil corporations on Alaska's fiscal policy regime—will also be discussed to show how market volatility drives the executive and legislature to renegotiate its bargain with Big Oil. Along the way, we extend the discussion of revenues begun in Chapter 4 by including some additional observations on attempts by the state to stabilize its revenue sources and to reduce its expenditures in order to decrease the uncertainties that oil dependency creates for short- and long-term budgetary commitments.

## ▩ Strategies to Reduce Natural Resource Dependence

Alaska policymakers have not been blind to the limits of oil-based development strategies and have attempted to use the state's oil wealth as an engine for economic diversification. (In Chapter 6, we discuss the royalty-in-kind program—an attempt to use oil earnings to capitalize industrial projects.) In general, the state's fiscal policies have focused on three tactics: (1) state subsidies to new and existing areas of production and services;[6] (2) deposits from oil earnings into savings accounts that turn excess oil revenues into income for the resident population and a hedge against budget deficits; and (3) increased federal revenue flows, mainly in the form of military expenditures.[7] Of the three, only the second and third have had significant impact, and only the second is subject to *state* fiscal policy. Therefore, we concentrate on this second approach in this section of the chapter and consider the third approach later in our analysis.

By creating the two savings accounts noted in the previous chapter, the Permanent Fund and the Constitutional Budget Reserve, the state has mitigated some of the more onerous effects of its dependence on natural resource exports. The story is complex, however, and we leave a detailed chronological treatment to Chapter 7. For present purposes, we offer a few observations on the PF and CBR as responses to the impact of fluctuations in oil earnings on state spending.

The first major oil-related impact on the state budget was the $900 million windfall from the bonus lease sale of 1969. The spending that followed found support among rural residents who pointed to the unmet needs of the state in schools, other public construction, and services. More conservative critics, however, saw it as a spree that signaled the dangers of giving legislators unrestricted access to the revenues the state would surely receive when the Trans-Alaska Pipeline came online.

A 1976 amendment to the state constitution established the Alaska Permanent Fund. Although the amendment did not specify any purpose for the PF other than to produce income, its framers clearly sought to remove some of the new oil dollars from the grasp of the state legislature and to use the earnings to support state government when North Slope oil was depleted. The latter purpose, however, appears neither in the constitutional amendment nor in statute. Separate legislation established a Permanent Fund Corporation—directed by gubernatorial appointees who are confirmed by the legislature—with broad policymaking power concerning PF investments.

Statutes developed in 1980 commit one-half of annual fund income to the dividend program (discussed below) and require a sufficient portion of the balance to be deposited to the PF principal in order to offset the effects of inflation. Any remaining earnings were to be deposited into an earnings reserve account, available for future dividends and inflation-proofing.[8] Inflation-proofing and direct legislative appropriation have increased the corpus of the PF materially over the years. To date, no legislature has applied fund earnings to the support of general fund programs of state government.

The creation of a reserve fund from government-owned natural resources is hardly unique. Alaska has other reserve funds, such as the CBR and the mental health trust fund. The state of Texas has a mineral trust fund used to support the University of Texas. The Alberta Heritage Fund is often compared to the Alaska PF because it was created from the province's oil wealth. A number of Middle Eastern nations with oil wealth have created reserve funds. But

Alaska's Permanent Fund differs from those in two respects: its large size—over $40.1 billion by mid-2007—and its conservative management principle. Unlike other reserve funds the PF is an endowment trust and employs the "prudent investor" rule. Reacting to the state's poor experience with development grants and loans, the state legislature adopted the "prudent investor" approach in the Permanent Fund Management Act of 1980, despite considerable pressure to use the fund to stimulate economic growth and infrastructure—the route followed by the Alberta Heritage Fund.[9]

From the perspective of US state politics, the most unusual aspect of the state's savings strategy is the Alaska Permanent Fund Dividend program (created in 1980). Advocates argued that dividends would be the most efficient way to deliver the benefits of petroleum development equally to all state citizens, would discourage government inefficiency and bureaucratic growth, and would create a popular constituency with a vested interest in protecting the fund from legislative raids.[10] As indicated, this argument has since been extended to protection of earnings as well.

A resident qualifying for every dividend since the PFD's first distribution in 1982 would have received a total of $27,536.41 as of 2007. In FY 1999 the fund distributed $973 million in revenue to state residents. By 2005, that amount had decreased to $558.8 million, but it recovered to $725.36 million in 2006. We have no way of calculating the effects of these payouts on government spending or other aspects of fiscal policy, but the PFDs have had significant effects on individual state residents and on the economy of the state as a whole. A study by the University of Alaska–Anchorage's Institute for Social and Economic Research (ISER) showed that the PFDs had a different distributional effect than if the same amount of money were spent on daily government operations, capital spending, or loan subsidies. ISER concluded that the PFD produced more statewide personal income, employment, and population growth than would alternative government expenditures, because it is paid directly to the entire state population instead of to a small number of well-paid state employees serving different target groups with special programs.[11]

Finally, the PFDs have become wildly popular in Alaska and have achieved the aim of the program's creators: to build loyalty for the Permanent Fund *and* protect the inflation-proofing and earnings reserve, which serve to increase the amount of annual dividends. Furthermore, the same year the legislature enacted the dividend program it abolished the state individual income tax, making Alaskans the least-taxed citizens in the nation. Local property and sales taxes also were reduced as state government increased revenue sharing and other aid to local governments.

Alaska entered an era of declining oil production and generally lower oil prices without the capacity to tax its citizens' incomes and with severe restrictions on its ability to use its savings accounts to pay for government services. One result is that in times of low oil prices the onus frequently falls on boroughs and cities. Nevertheless, the PFD seems destined to remain the main engine of income diversification derived from oil revenues.

In 2003, Governor Murkowski attempted to move public and legislative sentiment toward a rethinking of the fund's role in Alaskan fiscal policy. The governor called for a conference of fifty-five Alaskan leaders—the "Conference of Alaskans"—which he charged with the task of making recommendations that could be the basis for ballot propositions on the fund for the 2004 general election. He attempted to limit the conferees' deliberations to the fund, asking them not to consider new taxes. Instead, the conference adopted four main proposals to

1. embed the Permanent Fund Dividend in the state constitution,
2. consider the reinstatement of the state income tax,
3. seek voter approval of the percent-of-market-value proposal to stabilize dividends,[12] and
4. maintain a minimum amount ($1 billion) in the Constitutional Budget Reserve as a state rainy day fund.

One response to the conference was a populist outcry from a group calling itself the "People's Conference," who claimed the elite nature of the conferees blinded them to the effects that an income tax would have on Alaska's poor. None of the conference proposals was adopted by the legislature.[13]

Thus, the PF affects the state's capacity to spend in four important ways. First, it limits the amount of oil revenues that can be deposited in the general fund to be disbursed through the regular budgetary and appropriations processes. Second, through prudent investments, it has a multiplier effect on the oil earnings deposited in it, and it creates a substantial savings account, albeit one that is difficult to access. Third, through the dividend program it provides direct payments to individuals that may serve to mute demands for increased expenditures on state services. Finally, without state income or sales taxes, very little of the annual dividend payments can be recaptured as general fund revenue.

## ■ Oil Price Volatility and Fiscal Policy Responses

The pattern of the last twenty-five years in Alaska has been one of crisis and recovery associated with events in the global and national political economies that affect energy markets. As shown in Chapter 4, the reactions of state policymakers have not always been in lockstep with changes in the market or fluctuations in the state's oil supply. Instead the state has tried to optimize its advantages and minimize its vulnerabilities to market shifts, and typically, that has been as far as it went. State executives and legislatures have shown only a limited propensity for seeking long-term solutions. Politically, especially as expressed by changes in fiscal policy, the responses usually have been episodic and epiphenomenal rather than strategic and structural. Where we see policy change, it is mainly in the form of adjustments to received fiscal challenges, and it takes the form of attempts to modify the fiscal relationship of the state to the oil multinationals. The most significant and effective changes have been the state's innovative methods for accumulating excess oil revenues when prices are high and restraining the legislature from spending windfall revenues when prices are low.

## Crisis and Response

Low oil prices wreaked havoc on Alaska's fiscal policy regime after the early 1980s, and they stimulated state policymakers to reduce expenditures and dip into available reserves. From an inflation-adjusted rate of $7.3 billion, general fund unrestricted revenue (about 75 percent of which came from petroleum rents) fell to under $2 billion in 1998. In 1998, the Alaska Department of Revenue predicted that oil revenues (including production and corporate taxes, and gross royalties) would decline from $1,518.4 million in 1998 to $1,042.4 million in 1999, and it projected a nearly 63 percent decline by 2020.[14] By 1999, Alaskan political leaders were taking seriously the possible need to reinstate the income tax.

In the mid-1980s, changes in oil markets made revenue-stream problems unavoidable. General fund unrestricted revenues fell to just over $5 billion in 1985 and to under $2 billion in 1988. Significantly, Alaska North Slope crude real-market prices collapsed from $43.15 per barrel in 1985 to $16.03 in 1998 and $12.82 in 1999.[15]

Several variables contribute to oil price swings. Demand factors are both seasonal and economic. Warm winter temperatures reduce demand for heating oil in consuming states and nations and lead to oil gluts. So too do recessions in Europe and the United States, which were episodic occurrences in the 1980s. The recessions suffered by most East and Southeast Asian nations after the 1997 financial crises sharply lowered demand for oil and reduced prices.

Supply factors probably have been even more significant in causing oil price volatility for most of the period under examination here. OPEC, a formidable cartel throughout most of the 1970s, gradually lost its ability to control global oil production in the 1980s and 1990s. The development of new oil fields in Alaska and the North Sea increased the number of oil market players that were outside OPEC and not subject to its production controls. The major OPEC price broker, Saudi Arabia, lost its incentive to support high oil prices by limiting supply when such action damaged Saudi investments in Europe and the United States. Unstable regimes in OPEC members with large populations and endemic poverty, such as Nigeria and Venezuela, became heavily dependent on oil revenues for their economic and political survival, giving them strong incentives to cheat by increasing production over agreed-upon ceilings. A related factor influencing supply was the reentrance of Iran to full production after the end of the Iran-Iraq War and the 1998 agreement by Western nations to allow Iraq to resume oil production and sales.

Earlier, when oil prices peaked in the late 1970s and early 1980s, Alaska's governor and legislature had no reason to curb state spending. Before he left office, however, Governor Hammond insisted that the legislature propose a constitutional amendment to institute a state spending cap, and voters adopted it in 1982. In exchange for lawmakers' approval of the limit, Hammond agreed to the legislature's $1.8 billion capital budget that year. In the 1982 election, he told voters the limit "may be our last chance to control the juggernaut which otherwise will likely crush us into bankruptcy."[16]

As a number of analysts had predicted, however, the spending limit had virtually no effect. Its drafters in the legislature and governor's office set a ceiling of $2.5 billion on appropriations. They also provided for raising the ceiling in response to population growth and inflation, and they allowed for various exceptions to the ceiling. By the time the limit was to take effect in 1984, revenues had already fallen nearly to the level of the ceiling; soon after, they dropped below it.

The spending limit was intended to apply to the operating budget, not to capital expenditures, and capital spending increased precipitously in the early 1980s. From an average annual capital budget of about $130 million in the 1970s, it soared to $1.4 billion in 1981 and peaked at more than $1.8 billion the following year. In just two years, the legislature had committed $7,000 in capital projects for every person in Alaska. Just as suddenly, when oil prices dropped after 1982, capital spending fell sharply.[17] Operating budgets grew at a more even pace, doubling from $1.3 billion in the late 1970s to $2.5 billion in the mid-1980s. As the capital budget took the brunt of the oil price decline of the 1980s, the operating budget leveled off at about $2.3 billion (general fund) at the end of the decade and remained near that level for most of the 1990s.

Still, even this moderated level of general expenditures made Alaska by far the highest per capita spender among the states in the late 1980s, according to the Advisory Commission on Intergovernmental Relations (ACIR). Taking into account relative population size, levels of service demand, and labor costs, ACIR calculated that Alaska spent over three times more than its allotted, "representative" share of state expenditures in 1987.[18]

A second, somewhat more desperate attempt to curb spending occurred in the context of Alaska's first oil price shock in 1985–1986. Oil prices plummeted to the lowest level in the state's history as an oil state, falling below $10 per barrel (which prompted the state's senior US senator, Ted Stevens, to remark that perhaps the state should turn off the pipeline). Governor Sheffield

(1982–1986) felt forced to impound 10 percent of all agency appropriations, including those for pass-through programs such as school funding. The Fairbanks North Star Borough mayor, assembly, and school board took the state to court, contending that fund impoundment was unconstitutional because it violated the separation of powers as well as the legislature's authority to make appropriations. The superior court upheld this position, but the legislature enacted the impoundment in its next session, rendering the issue moot before an appeal could reach the state supreme court.

This oil price shock was the worst the state had experienced. By the mid-1980s, it was harder to cut capital spending and reduce the new loan programs and generous operating budgets. As the budget required deeper cuts, however, widespread losses of jobs, incomes, businesses, and property occurred. Both the cities of Anchorage and Fairbanks, Alaska's first- and second-largest, saw reductions of 50 percent in the value of housing and business facilities. Alaska suffered an economic collapse, as did the other major oil-producing states at about the same time.

True to historical patterns, net population varied directly with the oil economy. Forty thousand more people left Alaska than came to the state during the recession, which lasted until the end of the decade. The transience accompanying the 1980s boom was more extensive and more volatile than that of the pipeline boom of the 1970s. During the first half of the decade, the population grew by more than 75,000, nearly a fifth of Alaska's 1980 population.[19] More than half that number left the state in the late 1980s.

Beyond the Sheffield impoundment, state government mostly muddled through its budget crises. Much nonessential spending could readily be cut. In addition, oil revenues often came in above conservative state projections, and various surplus funds were available to patch up annual budgets. But another crisis loomed on the horizon—one the state could not count on muddling through: a further drop in revenues. According to state projections in the mid-1990s, oil production would decline by 5 to 8 percent a year during the 1990s until total production was cut in half by the year 2000. During the 1990s, oil production from the huge reservoir at Prudhoe Bay dropped precipitously. Figure 5.1 shows the accuracy of those projections, forecasts production for the coming decade, and compares North Slope production to Cook Inlet and total state production.

Reactions to the late-1980s recession brought two changes to the fiscal policy process. Leaders won voter approval to establish a Constitutional Budget Reserve, which cushioned the state temporarily against further downturns in both oil prices and production. Analysts and political leaders also began to outline options meant to provide a "safe landing" for the state's fiscal regime.

The CBR was the second dedicated fund created under Article IX of the Alaska Constitution. Governor Steve Cowper (1986–1990) proposed and cam-

**Figure 5.1    Alaska Crude Oil Production**

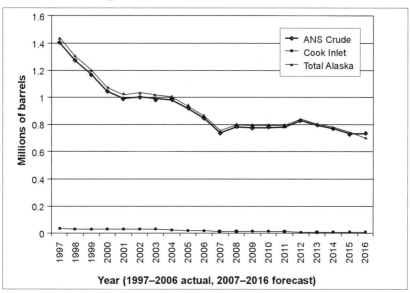

Year (1997–2006 actual, 2007–2016 forecast)

paigned for a second rainy day fund for the state, to be used when oil revenues declined in the 1990s. Moreover, extensive litigation in which the state had been engaged with oil companies over back taxes, transportation charges, and other issues was beginning to bear fruit. Many policymakers, seeing that the appropriation limit had failed, feared that if one-time oil tax and other litigation settlements were deposited directly into the general fund, they would be quickly spent. Thus, in 1990, the legislature passed a constitutional amendment, which the voters approved that November.

Aggressive litigation by the administration of Governor Hickel (1990–1994) brought billions of dollars into the CBR, and lawmakers felt pressured to spend it as oil revenues continued to decline. However, two provisions of the amendment restricted access. Moneys could be spent from the CBR only when revenues of the current fiscal year were lower than the previous year, and then no more could be spent totally than had been spent in the previous fiscal year. A second provision required a three-fourths majority before moneys could be appropriated.[20]

Table 5.3 indicates the status of the CBR as of spring 2007 and shows its importance as a rainy day fund during the most recent fiscal crisis in 2002–2003 (discussed further later in this chapter). The size of the CBR—which at its zenith reached $3.559 billion—the strictures requiring cooperation of legislature and executive to gain access to it, and the requirement that the legislature repay the fund when it is able, were buffers for the hard budget times

**Table 5.3    Constitutional Budget Reserve Fund Summary (in $ millions by fiscal year)**

|                                     | FY 2002 | FY 2003 | FY 2004 | FY 2005 | FY 2006 | FY 2007 |
|-------------------------------------|---------|---------|---------|---------|---------|---------|
| Beginning balance                   | 3,110.1 | 2,466.9 | 2,093.6 | 2,155.1 | 2,235.7 | 2,268.0 |
| Budget percentage funded from CBR   | N/A     | 20%     | 0.5%    | 0.01%   | 0%      | 0%      |
| Ending balance                      | 2,466.9 | 2,093.5 | 2,155.1 | 2,235.7 | 2,423.7 | 2,250.0 |

*Source:* Compiled by the authors from data provided by the Alaska Department of Revenue, and Alaska Office of Management and Budget, Missions and Measures, and State of Alaska Department of Revenue, *Spring 2007 Revenue Sources Book,* p. 63.
*Note:* CBR: Constitutional Budget Reserve.

Alaska encountered in the 1990s and again in the early 2000s. The legislature has used the CBR to balance the budget in ten of the last fifteen fiscal years (typically drawing increments of $100 million several times during a fiscal year), with most of this activity clustered in the period from FY 1998 to early in FY 2004. For example, data provided by the state Department of Revenue shows eight separate draws ranging from $50 million to 200 million each during FY 1999.[21] The rise in oil prices that began in 2003 has allowed the state to deposit about $5.8 billion into the reserve fund, generating another $1.9 billion in earnings from CBR investments. Since late in calendar year 2003, no CBR withdrawals have been needed to balance the state's budget.[22]

As oil prices fluctuate and North Slope production declines, the state may come to depend more on the CBR in the near future. Over the longer run, however, the prospects are not good and cannot be improved through fiscal policy alone. The state's Department of Revenue offers two projections for the future of the CBR fund (CBRF). Given declining oil production and revenues, if the legislature deposits all expected budget surpluses in the CBRF, then the fund will be depleted by May 2015. If none of the surpluses are deposited in the CBRF, it will run out in October 2014.[23]

Coinciding developments also helped to expand the duration of North Slope oil revenues. Oil companies continued their exploration and brought online reservoirs once considered marginal. Technological changes in oil drilling (for example, directional drilling, which allowed exploitation of nearshore deposits to a distance of four miles; reduction in the size of gravel pads; and improvement in seismic data) cut exploration and production costs by nearly two-thirds, making it feasible for companies to develop small fields, in the range of 100 million to 350 million barrels of oil, which previously could not be exploited profitably. Production from the smaller fields thus mitigated by a factor of 10–15 percent the reduction of revenue as the Prudhoe Bay and Kuparuk fields were being depleted.

Policy analysts predicted a future budget crash from the first day oil flowed through the Trans-Alaska Pipeline. State government walked into a fiscal trap when it followed a policy of unsustainable spending; it was spending nonrecurring revenues from a nonrenewable resource with an unstable price, and it spent most of the revenues available.[24] There was a pattern to the spending: the oil money was treated as a common property resource. A common property resource is one that everyone has access to and can use but that no one person has the responsibility or incentive to protect or conserve.

ISER economist Scott Goldsmith made the first systematic critique of state fiscal policy response in his series "Safe Landing: A Fiscal Strategy for the 1990s."[25] Goldsmith and other ISER economists pointed to the decline of Prudhoe Bay production and the necessity of both curbing growth in state expenditures and finding new, recurring revenues to fund state government—including capping the PFD and assessing income or statewide sales taxes. Indeed, there were obvious major discrepancies between Alaska's tax capacity (high) and its tax effort (low) in the areas of personal income taxes, sales taxes, and corporate income taxes. In his first budget message, Governor Hickel used part of Goldsmith's argument, calling for a 5 percent across-the-board reduction in state agency expenditures, which was reduced after confrontation and negotiation with the legislature to a 2 percent cut.

The first formal political critique of state fiscal policy responses was initiated in the Knowles administration (1994–2002). In March 1995, his fourth month as governor, Democrat Knowles gained support from the legislature's Republican leadership to form a joint executive-legislative fiscal planning commission to recommend ways to close the fiscal gap. Its fifteen members included present and former legislators and commissioners, and several business leaders, representing both political parties. The commission issued its report in October 1995, noting that the state was spending $524 million more than it would take in during FY 1996, and that the gap would grow to $1.3 billion annually by the year 2005. It recommended a combination of spending cuts, revenue increases, and changes in the state's Permanent Fund to balance the budget in three years. Spending cuts were relatively modest but with compounding would reduce the operating budget by $300 million.

Proposals to increase revenues were more dramatic. They included raising tobacco,[26] alcohol, and gasoline taxes and increasing taxes on fisheries and other resources. More unpopular was a proposal to reconstitute the PF as an endowment to partially replace declining oil revenues, while boosting the earning power of the PF. The most controversial recommendation was to cap the PFD by reducing the total amount spent for the program by $50 million a year for three years. Significantly, the commission did not recommend immediate reinstitution of the state income tax, postponing a decision on increased personal taxation for two years.[27]

The commission's recommendations reflected a political compromise. The compromise offered little that was new, reduced government size minimally, and increased taxes where opposition would be least. The response to the recommendations was lukewarm and divided along partisan and interest lines. Republicans sought deeper cuts in agency budgets; former governor Hammond (the chief architect of the PFD) urged an income tax before dividends were touched. Even Governor Knowles indicated that he would prefer an income tax to any alteration of the dividend program.

Thus, by the time that the second oil price shock hit Alaska in 1998–1999, the public was familiar with the different strategies to reach fiscal balance. This crisis was more serious than the oil price decline of 1985–1986. Oil prices slid to $9.50 a barrel, which, adjusted for inflation, was lower than the pre-OPEC embargo oil price of 1973. Most experts saw oil prices staying low for three years because of a complex of factors producing weak demand and oversupply. However, few of the facets of the late-1980s recession reappeared. The housing market did not crash. Employment remained high. Few Alaskans moved out of the state. Although the state faced a budget deficit of $1.2 billion and legislators worried about the need for draconian measures to close the fiscal gap, there was little concern in the state capital about the ability to fund the FY 2000 budget. The oil price shock did, however, prompt the governor to lay on the table in January 1999 a proposal to reinstate the income tax, the first since the income tax was eliminated in 1980. He paired this proposal with a plan to divert some $4 billion from the PF's earning reserve over a three-year period. The diverted earnings would be placed into the CBR, to cover the fiscal gap while oil prices remained low, where it was hoped they would generate sufficient revenues to balance the budget in the years beyond.

Then, the Republican-controlled house unveiled its long-awaited solution to the 1999–2000 fiscal gap. After the legislature unanimously rejected the governor's call for an income tax, the house majority suggested capping PFDs at $1,000 for the next three years. Excess earnings would be used to balance the budget and fund growth of just under 1.5 percent in public safety, education, and transportation over the next twenty years. The proposal allowed for no growth in any other agencies. Strong negative reactions from the commissioners of public safety and health, the president of the state university system, and some liberal Democrats followed the announcement.[28]

Apparently, then, in the fourteen-year period beginning in 1986 the state's fiscal policy regime changed in ways that allowed government to mitigate adverse impacts of the lowest oil prices since production began. Credit goes, in part, to the creation of the CBR and other budget reserve funds, which could be used to balance budgets. But most of the answer lies in the pattern of reducing agency general fund appropriations and increasing both program receipts and federal dollars.

Table 5.4 presents information on state budgets from FY 1986 through FY 2005. It allows us to compare the general fund budget with both federal funds and the other funds[29] actually expended in the budget years.

Table 5.4    **Actual Expenditures by Source, 1986–2005 (in $ millions by fiscal year)**

| Budget Year | General Fund | Federal Funds | Other Funds | Total |
|---|---|---|---|---|
| 1986 | $1,994.12 | $232.90 | $288.94 | $2,515.96 |
| 1987 | 1,837.74 | 251.01 | 306.29 | 2,395.05 |
| 1988 | 2,018.55 | 291.11 | 321.15 | 2,630.82 |
| 1989 | 2,138.86 | 324.24 | 361.31 | 2,824.41 |
| 1990 | 2,103.18 | 363.88 | 400.31 | 2,867.37 |
| 1991 | 2,373.08 | 426.89 | 442.43 | 3,242.40 |
| 1992 | 2,192.79 | 466.07 | 804.99 | 3,463.86 |
| 1993 | 2,197.47 | 537.36 | 860.05 | 3,594.89 |
| 1994 | 2,249.49 | 561.85 | 834.22 | 3,645.55 |
| 1995 | 2,200.02 | 652.70 | 831.65 | 3,684.37 |
| 1996 | 2,207.21 | 643.74 | 832.73 | 3,698.53 |
| 1997 | 2,192.91 | 665.70 | 838.85 | 3,697.47 |
| 1998 | 2,130.83 | 717.03 | 880.47 | 3,728.34 |
| 1999[a] | 2,159.39 | 864.71 | 1,001.32 | 4,025.42 |
| 2000 | 1,984.10 | 1,837.10 | 781.40 | 4,602.60 |
| 2001 | 2,105.10 | 1,825.80 | 1,007.70 | 4,938.60 |
| 2002 | 2,290.00 | 1,164.00 | 1,234.00 | 4,668.00 |
| 2003 | 1,539.50 | 2,321.90 | 1,018.10 | 4,879.50 |
| 2004 | 2,187.92 | 1,497.32 | 2,728.24 | 6,413.48 |
| 2005 | 2,312.32 | 1,566.04 | 2,228.87 | 6,107.24 |

*Source:* Compiled by authors from data supplied by the Alaska Legislative Finance Division.
*Note:* a. Only authorized expenditure statistics were available for fiscal year 1999.

These data illustrate a steady growth in the Alaska state budget (general fund), with the exception of two years. During the first oil price shock, the Sheffield administration impounded 10 percent of agency appropriations, an amount nearly reflected in the budget changes from FY 1986 to FY 1987. Second, in FY 1997 total state expenditures declined only $1 million from the previous fiscal year. The decline in general fund expenditures in FY 1997 was greater, some $15 million, but increases in federal and other funds moderated the reduction. There were other years in which the general fund was reduced from the previous year's level: FY 1990, FY 1992, FY 1995, and FY 1998. In each of these four years, however, growth in federal and/or other funds compensated for the general fund reduction.

However, the growth in the state budget lagged considerably behind inflation over this time period. Using the Anchorage consumer price index (CPI) as the measure of inflation statewide, with 1982–1984 pegged at a value of 100, in our base year of FY 1986 the Anchorage CPI stood at about 105. The CPI for 1999 is 150. Thus, prices have increased by 45 percent over the fourteen-year study period.[30] The state's total expenditures in FY 1986, in 1999 inflation-adjusted dollars, are $3,648 million; compared with FY 1999 expenditures of $4,025 million. Spending over the fourteen-year period increased by only $377 million for an annual average of *less than 1 percent.*

We gain a better sense of the magnitude of fiscal reductions in Alaska by considering fund sources separately. The general fund budget of the state attracts most public and legislative attention, as it is the amount most directly under legislative control. The growth in actual general fund moneys from FY 1986 to FY 1999 was only $165 million. On an inflation-adjusted basis, the general fund of the state over this fourteen-year period *declined* by $732 million, or *2 percent* annually.

However, both federal and other funds increased, more than making up the difference. In FY 1986, federal funds were 9 percent of total state expenditures; by 1999, they composed over 21 percent. During the fourteen-year period, on an inflation-adjusted basis, federal funds increased by over 250 percent. The growth in other funds—including, for example, tuition at the state university system, drivers' license and vehicle registration fees, permit charges, and the like—increased equally dramatically. In FY 1986, other funds were 11 percent of total state expenditures; by 1999, they composed 25 percent. Significantly, federal and other funds now make up 46 percent of total state expenditures in Alaska, compared to one out of five dollars in FY 1986. (Recent trends in federal funding are discussed further in this chapter.)

In short, what fiscal policymakers did over this fourteen-year period of declining oil prices and oil production was to hold the general fund budget steady, with reductions in some years. When considered against inflationary price increases, that represents a gradual annual reduction at an average rate of 2 percent.[31] However, policymakers were able to increase user fees, program receipts, and other state charges, which were low on a comparative state basis in FY 1986. And they attracted more federal moneys to Alaska, assisted by the state's veteran congressional delegation, led by Senator Stevens, who chaired the US Senate Appropriations Committee from 1997 to 2001. The capability of the state to increase federal and other funds without increasing general fund expenditures enabled it to survive in difficult fiscal times without touching its huge savings account (either the principal of the PF, the amount needed to finance growing PFDs, inflation-proofing, or the earnings reserve). As mentioned, during this period the state did spend down many of its other reserves.

## A New Boom

In 2002, a convergence of factors set off a spike in world oil prices that was to reach unprecedented heights. Increasing tensions in the Middle East, leading to the US invasion of Iraq in March 2003, were already having an effect. In addition, oil-producing countries in Latin America, led by Venezuela's populist president Hugo Chavez, were becoming increasingly assertive in the use of their own energy supplies for political as well as economic purposes. Several incidents in the oil-producing regions of Nigeria added to a climate of uncertainty about the political future of that tenuous democracy, and in September 2005, Hurricane Katrina disrupted oil supplies and refinery production in the Gulf of Mexico. The effect on nominal prices, along with the scenario for the near future created at that time by the Alaska state Department of Revenue, is illustrated in Figure 5.2. The effects on Alaska's fiscal policy were complex.

Suspicion of and ill will toward oil multinationals increased. Particularly in the aftermath of the Hurricane Katrina tragedy, oil companies were perceived to be taking undue advantage of adversity at home and abroad. This impression was deepened for many when ExxonMobil, one of the three major oil corporations still operating in Alaska, posted record profits at the end of 2005. Meanwhile soaring gasoline and home heating oil prices combined with the Murkowski administration's elimination of funding for municipal revenue sharing to create a financial calamity for Alaska's remote native villages.[32] In Alaska the stage was set for renegotiating the basic structure of the state's fiscal relationship with the oil industry. The beleaguered Democratic minority in the state legislature saw an opportunity to take a populist stance against Big Oil, including pressuring the governor—whose administration was already

**Figure 5.2    Alaska North Slope Crude Oil Price History and Forecast**

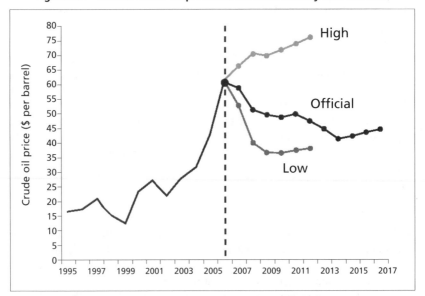

*Source:* Alaska Department of Revenue–Tax Division, *Spring 2007 Revenue Source Book,* State of Alaska, p. 31.

seen as ethically challenged due to a series of scandals concerning conflicts of interest and the firing of the state's commissioner of natural resources—to extract more rents from the state's shrinking oil patch.

Some of the specific effects of the resultant policy changes are discussed in the following pages, but generally speaking, the policy responses to these fortuitous changes in the world oil markets served to deepen the state's commitment to oil and gas as the foundation of its fiscal stability.

## ▉ The Politics of the Alaska Fiscal Policy Process

Executives and legislatures have alternated in exercising leadership over the Alaska budget process. Until the oil boom years, the legislature reacted to the recommendations of the executive, making few adjustments to the operating budgets and only minor alterations to the modest capital budgets. The flood of oil revenues in the late 1970s and early 1980s geometrically increased available revenues, far exceeding agency requirements. Legislators pursuing large capital budgets, in part to ameliorate the post-pipeline recession, became aggressive in seeking control of the budget process. From 1979 until the middle of the Sheffield administration in 1984, the multibillion-dollar capital budget was cut up into "equal thirds." The governor, House, and Senate independently drew up essentially veto-proof project lists.

There were significant budget battles between executive and legislature from FY 1986 to FY 1999. In FY 1987, Governor Sheffield impounded 10 percent of agency appropriations after the legislature had adjourned. Beginning with the Sheffield administration, governors used their line-item veto powers to curb legislative budget initiatives that did not fit into their plans or to punish political opponents.[33] In FY 1992, Governor Hickel sought 5 percent across-the-board reductions in agency budgets. Then, in FY 1996, the large Republican majority of the legislature sought to reduce the budget request of Governor Knowles by 5 percent.

One indication of the rivalry between executive and legislature is the difference between the governor's budget request and the legislature's authorization. Table 5.5 compares these figures for the general fund budgets from FY 1986 through FY 2004.

This is not the complete story of executive-legislative budget rivalry, as it excludes federal and other funds. (In two of the eighteen years, there were significant legislative-executive differences over the use of these funding sources.[34]) Nevertheless, Table 5.5 illustrates how the legislature addressed the governor's request, and the margin between its resolution and the governor's numbers indicates the significance of rivalry between the two branches.

In five of the seventeen years for which we have data, legislatures authorized more than the governor requested. The first three of these years were in

**Table 5.5    Governor's Request and Authorized Expenditures, 1986–2004 (in $ thousands by fiscal year)**

| Budget Year | Governor's Request | Legislature's Authorization |
|---|---|---|
| 1986 | $2,373,943.8 | $2,026,394.4 |
| 1987 | 1,975,374.8 | 2,022,552.7 |
| 1988 | 1,560,037.1 | 1,861,365.6 |
| 1989 | 1,958.943.8 | 2,131,479.8 |
| 1990 | 2,211,694.8 | 2,173,105.2 |
| 1991 | 2,290,558.8 | 2,188,110.1 |
| 1992 | 2,220,019.5 | 2,204,521.5 |
| 1993 | 2,313,478.0 | 2,173,696.9 |
| 1994 | 2,223,726.1 | 2,239,490.4 |
| 1995 | 2,243,156.9 | 2,221,833.2 |
| 1996 | 2,297,958.2 | 2,218,067.7 |
| 1997 | 2,225,214.9 | 2,207,215.1 |
| 1998 | 2,229,717.0 | 2,137,535.5 |
| 1999 | 2,231,623.2 | 2,159,385.1 |
| 2000 | N/A | 2,177,511.9 |
| 2001 | 2,247,878.1 | 2,137,541.0 |
| 2002 | 2,296,848.9 | 2,286,756.7 |
| 2003 | 2,432,219.4 | 2,291,682.5 |
| 2004 | 2,188,223.4 | 2,319,100.0 |

*Source:* Compiled by the authors from data provided by the Alaska Legislative Finance Division, February 25, 1999, and State of Alaska Office of Management and Budget, *Alaska Budget Information, AY 2001–2004.*

the Cowper administration (1986–1990)[35]; the fourth was the FY 1994 budget, authorized during the third year of the Hickel administration. The fifth was in the middle of the Murkowski administration (2002–2006) as legislators asserted themselves against an increasingly unpopular governor. In all other years, the legislature reduced the governors' budget requests. However, the gap between legislative action and the governor's request varied by more than 1 percent in only two years: FY 1986 and FY 1988. In two years of the Cowper administration (FY 1987 and FY 1990), two years of the Hickel administration (FY 1992 and FY 1994), and all five years of the Knowles administration, the difference between legislative authorization and the governor's request was less than $100 million, a small amount in a general fund budget exceeding $2 billion.

The progression in the statistics is also informative, for as oil prices and productivity fell, budget discipline seemed to infect both branches of state government. During these years, participants and commentators reported budget battles between executive and legislature, but the resulting general fund appropriations display more cooperation than competition, even when, as in the Knowles administration, a Democratic governor confronted a Republican legislature. Of course, given declining oil revenues and the inability to tap the state's Permanent Fund and related reserves, interbranch differences over relatively small amounts became hot disputes.

Interbranch competition was no greater a determinant of budget priorities than partisanship, which intensified in the legislatures of the 1990s. Until consolidation of the Alaska Republican Party in the 1990s,[36] Alaska's legislative parties had little ideological unity, as demonstrated by the large number of legislative coalitions. For example, in the eighteen legislative sessions up to the 1994 elections, nine Senates and eight Houses were headed by coalitions based more on urban/rural fault lines than on ideological or partisan affinities, and although the 2007 House had a Republican majority, the Senate organized a bipartisan majority caucus with key committee chairs distributed among moderate and conservative legislators of both parties.

The 1994 election was a watershed event in Alaska politics as it was nationally. Benefiting from the strong Republican bias of the 1990–1992 reapportionment, Republicans gained solid majorities in both House and Senate; the first such occurrence since the late 1960s and only the second since statehood. Republicans increased their strength in both the 1996 and 1998 elections, attaining veto-proof, three-fourths majorities in both houses.

In the nineteenth legislature (1995–1996), Republican leaders announced a "Contract with Alaska," which emphasized budget reform, welfare reform, and a comprehensive crime package. The chief part of their conservative strategy was to reduce the state's operating budget by $250 million over five years.[37] In the clearest partisan division in recent Alaska history, Republican leaders insisted that the state's operating budget be reduced by 10 percent. Democrats and the Democratic governor recommended reductions closer to 2 percent.

The nineteenth through the twenty-first legislatures illuminated the combined effects of partisan and interbranch rivalries, as Democratic governor Knowles faced a relatively united Republican legislature, where the Democratic minority lacked the votes to have its budget amendments considered. This was a period of sustained budget reductions, but the dollar amounts cut were no greater than from 1990 to 1994 when Governor Hickel, elected on the Alaska Independence Party ticket (but a Republican), faced legislative coalitions.

In 2006, Sarah Palin won the Republican Party nomination and the governor's office on a platform of ethics reform, fiscal conservatism, and a minimalist view of the responsibilities of state government. Alaska's youngest and first woman governor enjoys a Republican majority in the house but faces a Senate majority coalition consisting of one faction of a divided Republican delegation and the entire Democratic membership. Interestingly, Senate majority and minority leaders are both Republicans.

Overall, Governor Palin's operating budget request was larger than the last budget of the Murkowski administration, but her capital budget request of about $3.9 billion was some $400 million smaller than that for FY 2007.

Notable items in the operating budget request were $37 million to fund the Longevity Bonus (a senior citizen benefit defunded by the Murkowski administration and later eliminated by the legislature from the Palin budget proposal as well), about $48 million in revenue-sharing funds for municipalities (another popular program that had its funding eliminated by Murkowski), and $463 million to assist communities and municipalities with their retirement costs. The capital budget included barely enough to qualify the state for federal matching funds, mainly for school construction and infrastructure.

An additional difference from FY 2007 was a promise by the new governor to deposit surplus revenues in both the state's CBR and PF. The governor also announced at the beginning of the legislative session that she had instructed her commissioners to each find 10 percent in savings from their agency budgets through greater efficiencies. By early March, Governor Palin's departmental review had produced nearly 10 percent in savings, amounting to approximately $124 million. Her critics called it "smoke and mirrors," claiming that the cuts were "not real . . . but rather are based on switching funding sources, using this year's surplus for next year's spending, and hopes of finding undetermined, money-saving solutions to long-term, costly problems."[38]

In deference to an overwhelmingly popular new governor, the legislative response to the budget was positive but reserved. Early in the legislative session, the governor also requested a supplemental budget for FY 2007 of $85 million. The supplemental budget request received little attention from the legislature, as it was quite small compared to previous Murkowski administration supplemental requests. Also, the legislature was preoccupied with what was to be the centerpiece of the governor's legislative initiatives, the Alaska Gasline Inducement Act (discussed in Chapters 2 and 6), during most of the second half of the legislative session.

The legislature concluded the regular session by adopting the governor's operating budget request nearly intact and making only cosmetic changes to the supplemental request. However, legislators objected to the small size of the capital budget request, and they enlarged it significantly. By the end of the session, this budget was $1.8 billion, including $534 million of state funds (a giant leap over the governor's request of $181 million).[39] The governor responded after the regular session had adjourned by using her line-item veto authority to remove some $231 million in spending from the capital budget. The cuts affected projects throughout the state, including deferred maintenance on schools and other public buildings. The Senate majority and officials of local governments protested but took no substantive actions. Linda Anderson, a lobbyist for the Fairbanks North Star Borough, commented that the governor had changed the budgetary process by undercutting the role of the legislature. Fairbanks Democratic representative David Guttenberg predicted a future of more contentious relations between the governor and legislators over budgetary matters.[40]

## Interest Groups, Lobbying, and the Budget

Oil wealth brought about two changes in interest group politics in Alaska. First, the number of interests seeking a legislative hearing increased greatly, from approximately 200 registered lobbying groups and individuals in 1975 to 500 in 1985. Second, the interests themselves underwent a transformation. State agencies, local governments, the state university system, and school districts all hired lobbyists or government relations specialists. On a per-capita basis, more registered lobbyists operated in Alaska than in any other state. The decline in state revenues after 1986 did not reduce the number of interests represented in the capital. It only increased the pressure exerted by groups on the political system.

Chapter 3 shows the oil and gas industry influencing fiscal policy in two ways. First, it carefully tracks oil legislation, seeking to reduce taxation to make its existing Alaska operations more profitable and seeking tax breaks for new oil-field developments. Until the creation of the PPT (described in Chapter 4 and later in this chapter), the most controversial recent case concerned the Northstar lease, which BP purchased from Amerada Hess in 1994. BP sought to change unfavorable lease terms that stipulated that it give the state nine-tenths of the profits it made on the 130-million-barrel field. Late in the 1996 legislative session, Governor Knowles introduced legislation allowing BP to pay the state only a 20 percent royalty, with supplemental royalties due when oil prices increased. Critics complained about the loss of revenue to the state, but BP countered that it would not develop this "marginal" field unless the state improved the lease terms.[41] Then BP launched a $100,000 campaign to win support, with full-page newspaper ads and glossy letters to all Alaskans. The bill passed the legislature (controlled by Republicans who had gained the lion's share of oil industry campaign contributions) with little opposition, and the governor signed it. More recently, the industry has funded campaigns to influence legislative and public opinion on new oil tax and royalty regimes and competing plans for a pipeline to carry North Slope natural gas to market.

Second, the oil industry participates in broad business coalitions, such as Commonwealth North and the Alaska Resource Development Council. Although these coalitions have not attempted to influence campaigns directly, they have focused attention on fiscal policy, often utilizing full-page newspaper ads, elaborately produced television advertisements, and direct mail to urge reductions in the state's operating budget, reductions in industry-related taxes and royalties, and state and federal support for the development of new oil and gas prospects.

Labor associations, such as the Alliance, which represents oil field service employees, sometimes join industry in supporting oil development issues. Labor unions, especially public sector unions, have lobbied the legislature increasingly to protect employee salaries and benefits. For example, in the first half of the nineteenth legislature, the Republican majority declined to ratify contracts negotiated by the Hickel administration, claiming they were too costly. The Knowles administration negotiated better terms for the state, but the contracts still contained cost-of-living increases of 1.5 percent and merit increases of 2–3 percent for one-third of the state's 17,000 workforce. The state public employee association needed to vigorously lobby both executive and legislature in order to have these contracts funded.

The intergovernmental lobby, which represents state and local government employees and those who benefit from the funding of public institutions, has been particularly active in defense of the state's foundation formula for the funding of kindergarten through twelfth-grade (K–12) education. In 1999, at $967 million, this was the single largest appropriation in the budget, accounting for 24 percent of total expenditures. During the period of oil price and production declines, the foundation formula has taken no cuts, although the formula has not been increased sufficiently to offset erosion by inflation.

## Funding State Agencies

In an era of cutback budgeting, interest groups have focused on protecting appropriations. Although lobbying has been intense, few have been successful in enlarging budget shares. Only four agencies changed their budget shares by more than 1 percent between FY 1986 and FY 1999: administration, community and regional affairs, health and social services, and revenue. The Department of Administration increased its budget share from 5.3 to 6.4 percent over the fourteen-year period, which is attributable primarily to housing in this department a series of commissions and state benefit programs that formerly had been independent. The Department of Community and Regional Affairs (DCRA) sustained a loss in budget share from 7.7 percent to 4 percent. This loss in budget share is explained by reductions in state revenue sharing and assistance to local governments, moneys that were passed through DCRA to boroughs and cities. On the other hand, the Health and Social Services (HSS) budget share increased from 13.3 percent to 23.3 percent. Much of the increase represented federal dollars trapped by aggressive state bureaucrats in order to reduce state contributions to Medicaid and the former Aid to Families with Dependent Children (now Temporary Assistance for Needy Families) programs. Also, the Democratic Knowles administration sought relatively greater increases in funding for children and family services than had previous administrations. Finally, the Revenue Department increased its budget share from 1.7 to 3.6 percent, which can be attributed to its new responsibilities for collection of user charges, permit fees, and the like. The large change in both DCRA and HSS reflected the politics of the fiscal policy process. The intergovernmental lobby of local governments was successful in blocking much larger cuts to municipalities sought by both governors and legislators, who thought that mayors and assemblies could easily increase local tax rates and reduce the state's burden. Also, legislatures in the 1990s increasingly sought federal dollars to pay for federally mandated functions and had a strong congressional delegation to aid in this campaign.[42]

Restricted federal funds make important contributions to particular state agencies, including the three resource agencies—Department of Natural Resources (DNR), Department of Environmental Conservation (DEC), Alaska Department of Fish and Game (ADFG)—and the University of Alaska. The DEC and ADFG are probably the least popular state agencies, as they write and implement regulations restricting the activities of miners, loggers, fishermen, oil companies, and the average resident who seeks to use natural resources for recreation, subsistence, and profit. The Hickel administration and Republican-majority legislatures in the 1990s curbed general fund appropriations to these agencies, insisting that they increase or institute user fees and charge for the services of processing permit applications. In the case of the DEC, general fund allocations declined by 55 percent. Some critics allege that the environmental regulatory functions of all three resource agencies have been impaired by budget cuts.[43] (Chapter 8 provides a detailed discussion of environmental regulations.)

The University of Alaska is the state's comprehensive university system. Although its spending authority increased from $253 million in FY 1986 to $442 million in FY 1999, virtually 90 percent of the increase is accounted for by rises in student tuition, student and other user fees, and federal and private grants and contracts. State general funding remained flat for a decade, while inflation and other direct costs eroded the university's funding basis. Lack of support from both governors and legislatures for increased university funding was the primary impetus for unionization of senior college faculty in 1996, and for the university regents to hire a new president in 1998 to marshal government support for the beleaguered system of higher education. The university system had its funding increased regularly for each academic year from 2000 through 2007, although much of that increase is included in the capital rather than operating budget of the state. Some of the increase has gone to essential maintenance deferred during the lean years. Increased funding, however, has also been accompanied by substantial tuition increases for university students.[44]

Thus, for most of the period under examination, the politics of Alaska's fiscal policy process—including the effects of changing oil revenues and relations with the federal government—are manifest in the ways that individual state agencies are funded.

## Recent Trends in Federal Funding

As we have seen, federal funding provides an important source of revenue in several key areas, and the state has regularly benefited from high levels of federal support. For example, in FY 2004 (the last year for which data is available) the federal government spent a total of $8.4 billion in the state, or $13,000 for each resident, making Alaska first in the nation on a per-capita basis. By comparison, the nearest western state was New Mexico with approximately $11,500 per capita, and the national average was slightly less than $8,000 per capita. Alaska also continues to be a net gainer in the flow of federal dollars, having received $1.87 in federal spending for every $1 paid by Alaskans in federal taxes in 2004.[45]

In real terms, federal spending in the state more than doubled between 1982 and 2002,[46] and in FY 2006, federal funding accounted for 19 percent of the state's total revenues. Virtually all federal funds are "restricted," i.e., appropriated by the US Congress for specific purposes. Thirty-eight percent of 2004 federal funding came in the form of grants, many of which require matching funds (a total of $501.1 million for FY 2007). Therefore, state fiscal policy can be directly affected by decisions made at the federal level. Federal funding has been important for transportation projects, medical care (principally through Medicaid matching funds), and education (both K–12 and university). Federal defense spending is also an important element of the state's economy, as the state houses several major military installations. In 2004, 20 percent of federal spending in Alaska (more than $2.52 billion) came from the US Department of Defense. Also, 20 percent of federal spending in Alaska ($1.728 billion) was for wages and salaries. In 2002, for example, ISER estimated that about 96,000 Alaska jobs (1 in 3) depended on federal spending, attributable in large part to the numerous military personnel stationed in the state (accounting for 38,000 military and civilian jobs in 2002).[47] Recent trends and events, however, have caused concern among state lawmakers and demonstrate the uncertainties that come from dependence on policy decisions made in Washington, DC.

The state Office of Management and Budget forecasts nearly $3 billion in federal receipts for Alaska in FY 2007, up from $1.97 billion in 2006, but only $2.48 billion for FY 2008.[48] Historically and to the present, Alaska has enjoyed high levels of federal spending due to its strategic location and geography. For example, World War II brought Alaska its only highway link to the "lower 48"; the state hosts two installations of the new missile defense system; and Alaska contains more national parks and federal land than any other state. But continued success in securing a large share of federal funding also depends on the capabilities of the state's congressional delegation to influence a wide array of national policy decisions. Recently, Alaska's reputation as the recipient of federal "pork" has received unfavorable national and international attention, including allegations of waste and corruption.[49]

Senator Stevens was first appointed to fill a vacant US Senate seat in 1968 and has served continuously since then. In 2007, Stevens became the longest-serving Republican in US Senate history. He has used his seniority, key com-

mittee positions, and considerable earmarking skills to secure numerous federally funded projects and programs for the state. His success over the years
earned him the moniker "Uncle Ted," a name that carries different implications for supporters and opponents. In 2006 alone, Alaska received $1.05 bil-
lion in earmarks, an average of $1,667 per resident, the highest amount in the
nation.[50]

The state's sole member of the House of Representative, Republican Don
Young, has served in that position since 1973, making him the third ranking
house Republican and the seventh ranking member overall.[51] In 2005, he generated much controversy for his aggressive defense of an earmarked project
that became known as the "bridge to nowhere." Young, as chair of the House
Transportation and Infrastructure Committee, engineered three earmarks
(totaling $320 million) to a highway appropriations bill to fund construction
of a bridge linking the southeast Alaska city of Ketchikan (population 8,900)
to Gravina Island (population 50 and the location of the city's airport). The
action came in for withering criticism from Young's fellow Republicans in the
House and Senate as well as congressional Democrats.[52]

This increased awareness and criticism of federal funding for Alaska
appeared against a background of mounting federal deficits and lurid accounts
of high-profile corruption scandals involving legislators and lobbyists both in
Washington, DC, and Juneau. In addition, congressional elections in 2006
gave Democrats majorities in both the US House and Senate, thus depriving
the Alaska delegation of its powerful committee and subcommittee chairs. At
this point, we can only speculate on the long-term effects of these developments. Young remains the ranking member of the House Transportation and
Infrastructure Committee. Stevens is the most senior member of both the
Senate Commerce Committee and the Defense Appropriations Subcommittee.
And Lisa Murkowski (the state's junior senator) is ranking member of the
Subcommittee on Water and Power and sits on the Health, Education, Labor,
and Pension Committee. It is likely, therefore, that the changes in the US
Congress will reduce but not eliminate the ability of the delegation to bring
home federal dollars.[53]

## A Regime Change for State Oil Taxes

For those who believed that additional fiscal restraint would be the key to the
long-term stability of Alaska's oil economy, the general elections of 2002 were
a hopeful event, despite the fact that gross budgetary data indicate that change
of party in the governor's mansion makes little difference. In the US Senate,
Republican Frank Murkowski had established a strong record of support for
resource and infrastructural development, and fiscal and social conservatism.
As governor he would have an advantage not enjoyed by his immediate predecessor—dominant majorities in both houses of the legislature. In 2003, the

governor cut or defunded some popular programs, including the Longevity Bonus for the state's senior citizens and municipal revenue sharing. The governor also exercised the line-item veto several times. In the end, the legislature treated his budget requests similarly to those of his Democratic predecessor, and in 2004 the legislature actually authorized almost $139 million more than the governor requested. However, as we noted in Chapter 4, the Murkowski administration did usher in an important change in Alaska's fiscal regime: the end of the ELF and its replacement by a profit-based oil production tax.

Dramatic increases in oil prices, and the resulting windfall profits for oil companies, sparked angry debate over Alaska's "fair share" of its resources in 2005. The existing tax system, based on the ELF, had long been the subject of criticism by watchdogs of the industry. The ELF system based taxes on the gross value of specific oil properties, with base rates of 12.5 percent and 15 percent depending on the age of the field, and the possibility of substantial reductions (even total exemption) for fields considered marginal. By calculating individual rates for each field, ELF created a fragmented system that critics felt operated to the advantage of oil companies, especially as prices increased. In January 2005, Governor Murkowski and the Department of Revenue took the first step toward dismantling ELF by aggregating seven fields in Prudhoe Bay, arguing that they were actually being operated as a single unit and that at then current oil prices the so-called satellite fields could not be considered marginal.[54] Shortly thereafter, the executive entered into negotiations with the major oil multinationals to establish a new tax regime that ostensibly would capture more of current and future earnings for the state.

The new system was ratified by a special session of the state legislature in August 2006. The state described the PPT as "a significant departure from the prior production tax system, based on the ELF." Under the PPT, profits were taxed at a rate of 22.5 percent. The tax rate also increased by 0.5 percent for every dollar the production value of a barrel of oil exceeded $40.[55] But controversy swirled around the PPT. Industry critics, including key Democrats in the legislature, expressed reservations about the new formula on four counts: (1) Many in the state did not trust oil MNCs to fairly and accurately report earnings, fearing, for example, that companies would resort to transfer pricing schemes to hide profits.[56] (2) While the tax liability reduction provisions of ELF were unpopular with industry critics, the production tax principle was not. Critics of the Murkowski administration and the industry expressed dislike for a system that relied on market-driven measures of oil company profitability rather than the quantitative depletion of Alaska's shrinking reserves. (3) Governor Murkowski came in for severe criticism for the way the PPT negotiations were conducted, even from members of his own party. The administration was seen as secretive, overly compliant to industry demands, and unethical in its treatment of competing interests and dissenting viewpoints. (4) In the aftermath of the 2006 Prudhoe Bay pipeline leak (see

Chapter 8), the legislature continued to debate whether companies should be allowed to deduct expenses for repairs and cleanups that may have resulted from their own negligence.

We will never know what the long-term fiscal impact of PPT would have been. Structurally, PPT tied state revenues to the profitability of oil companies, and the Department of Revenue projected significant gains for the state under *prevailing* market conditions. But revenues from PPT did not meet expectations and oil prices and oil company profits continued to rise. In the special session called by the governor in fall 2007, the legislature raised the rate of taxation on oil company profits and closed some loopholes in the Murkowski plan but did not change the basic underlying principle of a profit-based tax. Not surprisingly, the response of the oil MNCs was negative, including threats to curtail and even withdraw their investments.

In the meantime continued high prices and the new tax rates led the governor to predict a $1.6 billion budget surplus for FY 2008. Noting that oil prices will not stay at record highs forever, the governor asked for public input on how this latest windfall should be "saved and invested" in her FY 2009 budget proposal.[57] A survey posted on the state's website invited Alaskans to prioritize among the CBRF, PF, Public Education Fund (K–12), state and municipal employee retirement funds, an alternative energy fund, transportation and infrastructure, workforce development, public health and safety, and resource development.[58]

It is too soon to tell if the latest revision of the tax regime will significantly diminish the power of oil MNCs to determine the value of the state's resources, but absent a more developed diversification strategy it can at best buy the state a little more time. And although the governor's electronic solicitation of direct public input on the disposition of new revenues is a novelty in Alaska state politics, state budgetary politics will continue to be a contest among the governor, agencies, legislators, local governments, and interest groups vying to claim their pieces of what is expected to be a shrinking pie.

## ◼ Conclusion

The question with which we began this chapter was how and to what extent Alaska has used fiscal policy to stabilize its political economy. Here and in Chapter 4 we have presented the historical dimensions of this problem, examining the way the state has used particular fiscal policy instruments to extract rents from the activities of oil companies operating within its borders. Boom-and-bust cycles typified the exploitation and development of resources, well before oil was discovered at Prudhoe Bay in 1968. The magnitude of the North Slope oil patch, however, seemed to promise a more stable future for the Alaska political economy.

Alaskans tried to use part of their new oil wealth in the 1970s and 1980s to diversify the economy, but most of these ventures failed to create sustained, renewable resource development. The greatest success achieved by the state was in the establishment of the PF in 1976, with its conservative management following the "prudent investor" rule, its protection through inflation-proofing, and its enlargement through deposits of excess earnings into the corpus of the fund. Then, in the same year that the legislature eliminated the state income tax, it created the PFD program, possibly the most popular program in any state's history. PFDs helped stabilize the economy through their multiplier effects. They provided a new source of individual income and thereby created a deep loyalty to the PF itself, making it very difficult for future policymakers to dedicate fund earnings toward an original purpose—support of state government services.

Oil taxes and royalties have provided about 75 percent of state general fund revenues from 1977 through 1999 and have increased in importance during recent boom years, but the state's take has come to depend increasingly on the price of oil, which is set on volatile international markets. We have focused on the fiscal policy responses to declining global oil prices from the mid-1980s through the end of the century and to the depletion of the Prudhoe Bay reservoir. The state's first oil price shock came in 1986 and produced a recession lasting the rest of the 1980s. No precautionary device prevented disruptions from this shock—neither the 1982 constitutional amendment limiting appropriations nor the billions in reserves.

Alaska's second oil price shock arrived in 1998–1999, when oil prices declined to a level below that in 1973 before the OPEC oil embargo. This was a more serious shock as measured by its impact on state revenues, and far less oil remained in the giant Prudhoe Bay and Kuparak reservoirs, but the reaction in Alaska was moderated. We attribute this change in atmosphere to the somewhat greater diversification of the Alaska economy, to spending down some state reserves, to judicious use of the CBRF, and to transformations in the funding sources of Alaska's budget (especially increases in federal funds and user charges and fees). As a result, state appropriations on an inflation-adjusted basis declined by about 2 percent annually. Of equal importance, federal and other funds increased over the fourteen-year period by about 250 percent. The state budget, which plays a larger role in Alaska than in the other states, had cushioned the impact of short-term changes in oil prices. By the end of the twentieth century, however, it was evident to most Alaska policymakers that the PF was the only sure buffer against long-term changes in oil prices and supplies, and discussions about tapping the fund have now begun.

Finally, we have looked at recent responses to soaring oil prices and profits. We find the state taking new measures to extract additional oil rents per barrel, with an eye toward sustaining the fiscal benefits of a shrinking oil patch. But we also find that recommendations for further diversification of revenue sources, even the relatively modest ones coming out of the 2003 "Conference of Alaskans," have been largely swept aside in favor of new strategies to extract oil rents and a move to greater exploitation of the state's natural gas reserves.

We also asked about the ways in which the politics of fiscal policymaking have influenced budget outcomes. We found evidence of changes resulting from interbranch competition, from partisan conflict, and from interest-group activity. But we did not find evidence that any of the major actors in the political competition over state fiscal policy have been or are likely in the near future to promote structural change away from dependence on extractive industries. In short, petroleum dependency is likely to remain the defining condition of Alaska's economic and political life for the foreseeable future.

## ■ Notes

1. Data on imports is included to help gauge the overall contribution of Alaska production to the domestic energy supply.

2. The state projects that by 2013 oil revenue will fall below $3 billion annually and decline to just under $2.15 billion in 2016.

3. The $99.16 price is for a barrel of West Texas Intermediate crude on the international spot market (see US Energy Information Agency, "Spot Prices," available at http://tonto.eia.doe.gov/dnav/pet/pet_pri_spt_s1_d.htm.

4. In March 2007, the PF posted a single-day net loss of $630 million when the Dow Jones Industrial Average fell 416.02 points. By July 13, 2007, the PF had more than recovered, reaching $40.155 billion as the Dow neared 13,900. See Eric Lidji, "Permanent Fund Tops $40 Billion," *Fairbanks Daily News-Miner*, July 14, 2007, p. A-1.

5. Much of this analysis is drawn from Jerry McBeath's reports on Alaska's fiscal policymaking in *Proceedings of the Roundtable on State and Local Budgeting*, Center for Public Policy and Administration, University of Utah, 1992 through 2007.

6. For example, during the peak years of global oil prices, the Hammond administration (1974–1982) implemented spending plans to diversify the economy. Governor Hammond popularized the concept of developing "renewable resources" to counter the state's dependence on nonrenewable petroleum deposits. He championed the development of Alaska's agriculture, tourism, and industry. With substantial state support, tourism has become a vibrant and politically powerful industry, and by 1999 had become the second-largest primary employer in the state. Cruise ships and planes transport nearly three-quarters of a million visitors to Alaska annually. However, tourism-related jobs are generally low-wage and seasonal, and they account for only about 5 percent of the state's total employment and wages.

7. Alaska's development has been aided by strategic interests dating from World War II and extending through the Cold War to the present, including not just military bases and ancillary services, but the construction during World War II of the Alaska-Canada Highway. Continued high levels of federal expenditure have been protected by a powerful and senior congressional delegation that until January 2006 held critical committee chairs in both the House and Senate.

8. Gordon S. Harrison, "The Economics and Politics of the Alaska Permanent

Fund Dividend Program." In Clive S. Thomas, ed., *Alaska Public Policy Issues* (Juneau: Denali Press, 1999), pp. 3–4.

9. Ibid., p. 3.

10. Gerald A. McBeath and Thomas A. Morehouse, *Alaska Politics and Government* (Lincoln: University of Nebraska Press, 1994), p. 64.

11. Harrison, "The Economics and Politics," p. 8.

12. Percent of market value (POMV, also known as "the 5 percent solution") would limit spending from the earnings of the fund to an amount equal to the expected rate of annual earnings minus the projected annual rate of inflation. As proposed by the state Permanent Fund Corporation this would amount to 8 percent – 3 percent = 5 percent. See Alaska Permanent Fund Corporation, "An Overview of POMV: The 5% Solution," available at www.apfc.org/iceimages/pomv/POMV_Overview_3_04.pdf.

13. Amy Lovecraft and Jerry McBeath, "Alaska." In Carl Mott, ed., *Proceedings: Roundtable on State Budgeting in the 13 Western States* (Salt Lake City: University of Utah, 2005).

14. Alaska Department of Revenue, *Fall 1998 Revenue Sources Book: Forecast and Historical Data* (Juneau: Oil and Gas Audit Division, 1998), p. 37.

15. Ibid., p. 35, 38.

16. *Anchorage Daily News*, October 29, 1982.

17. McBeath and Morehouse, *Alaska Politics and Government*, 62.

18. Robert W. Rafuse Jr., *Representative Expenditures: Addressing the Neglected Dimension of Fiscal Capacity*, Information Report M-174 (Washington, DC: Advisory Commission on Intergovernmental Relations, 1990), p. viii.

19. McBeath and Morehouse, *Alaska Politics and Government*, 63.

20. Gerald A. McBeath, *The Alaska State Constitution: A Reference Guide* (Westport, CT: Greenwood Press, 1997), p. 178.

21. James M. McKnight, Alaska State Department of Revenue, personal communication, August 9, 2007.

22. Alaska Department of Revenue, *Spring 2007 Revenue Sources Book*, p. 17.

23. Ibid., 17–18.

24. McBeath and Morehouse, *Alaska Politics and Government*, 57.

25. Oliver Scott Goldsmith, "Safe Landing: A Fiscal Strategy for the 1990s," *ISER Fiscal Policy Papers,* no. 7 (Anchorage: Institute of Social and Economic Research, University of Alaska, July 1992).

26. The increase in cigarette taxes to $1 per pack was the only recommendation of the commission adopted by the legislature (in 1997). Because Republican leaders had pledged "no new taxes," revenues went into a special educational fund, focused on preventing teen smoking.

27. Alaska, The Long Range Financial Planning Commission, "The State Long Range Financial Planning Commission Report" (October 1995).

28. *Fairbanks Daily News-Miner*, May 9, 1999.

29. These include a variety of taxes levied by the state, such as those on estate transfers, tobacco, motor fuels, alcoholic beverages, insurance premiums, charitable gaming, and electrical and telephone services; taxes and fees related to fishing, hunting, and mining; fees for drivers' licenses, vehicle registration, hunting, fishing, and other regulated activities; fees charged for various government programs and services; royalties from coal and other mining activities; receipts from fines and forfeitures; and payments from settlements. These revenues are divided between restricted and unrestricted funds depending on their sources and the governing statutes. See Alaska Department of Revenue, *Spring 2007 Revenue Sources Book*, 41–52.

30. Scott Goldsmith, personal communication, March 6, 1999.

31. Obviously, such reductions had an impact on the quantity and quality of state government services, but that is a story beyond the scope of this book.

32. Associated Press, "Exxon Mobil Posts Record Profit of $10.7 Billion: Fourth Quarter Earnings Top Targets for World's Largest Oil Company," January 30, 2006; downloaded from www.msnbc.msn.com/id/11098458/.

33. Alaska has one of the strongest executives, providing a true balance to the legislature. The governor's term begins one month before the legislature convenes; the governor may call a special session of the legislature at any time and force it to deal with his or her agenda; the veto powers of the office are stronger than those in most states, because they allow the governor to "strike or reduce" appropriations.

34. In FY 1986, the governor's request included $548.6 million in other funds, while the legislature authorized only $350.9 million. In FY 1992, the governor's request included $571.3 million in other funds, while the legislature authorized a larger amount, $771.2 million.

35. Alaskans who expected Governor Cowper to increase state appropriations as one means of countering the recession in the late 1980s were shocked to hear him state in his inaugural address that "all bets are off."

36. See Gerald A. McBeath, "Transformation of the Alaska Blanket Primary System," *Comparative State Politics* 15, no. 4 (1994): 25–42.

37. *Anchorage Daily News*, February 24, 1995.

38. Sabra Ayres, "100 Days in Charge Are Sweet for Palin," *Anchorage Daily News*, March 13, 2007; "Budget Cuts Not So Easy: Some Are Real, Some Are Hopeful," *Anchorage Daily News*, March 12, 2007.

39. Jerry McBeath, "Alaska's FY 08 Budget Plan," unpublished manuscript (Fairbanks: University of Alaska, 2007).

40. Stefan Milkowski, "Palin Rewrites Budget Process with Vetoes," *Fairbanks Daily News-Miner*, July 8, 2007, p. B-1-2.

41. *Fairbanks Daily News-Miner*, July 11, 1996.

42. Data supplied by Alaska Legislative Finance Division, February 25, 1999.

43. McBeath, et al., *Natural Resource Issues and Policies on Alaska's North Slope* (Anchorage: Department of Natural Resources, July 1981).

44. Whether credit for increased funding should be assigned to the leadership of the new university president, Mark Hamilton, or to the recovery and dramatic rise in oil prices in 2000 is a subject of some disagreement. The best we can say is that the two coincided.

45. Alaska Department of Revenue, *Spring 2007 Revenue Sources Book*, 55.

46. Scott Goldsmith and Eric Larson, "What Does $7.6 Billion in Federal Money Mean to Alaska?" *UA Research Summary,* no. 2 (Anchorage: Institute of Social and Economic Research, University of Alaska, November 2003), p. 1.

47. Alaska Department of Revenue, *Spring 2007 Revenue Sources Book*, 56; Goldsmith and Larson, "What Does $7.6 Billion in Federal Money Mean?" 2.

48. Alaska Department of Revenue, *Spring 2007 Revenue Sources Book*, 54.

49. "Political Corruption: Investigating Alaska," *The Economist*, August 4, 2007, p. 25.

50. *Anchorage Daily News,* December 5, 2006.

51. Biographical data posted on Representative Young's official website can be accessed at http://donyoung.house.gov/bio.htm.

52. Ronald D. Utt, "The Bridge to Nowhere: A National Embarrassment," Heritage Foundation webmemo #889, October 20, 2005, available at www.heritage.org/Research/Budget/wm889.cfm; and Shailagh Murray, "For a Senate

Foe of Pork Barrel Spending, Two Bridges Too Far," *Washington Post*, October 21, 2005, p. A8.

53. For example, early in the first session of the new Congress, Ted Stevens's name was linked to some $209 million in Department of Defense earmarks for Alaska (*Fairbanks Daily News-Miner*, March 8, 2007).

54. Alaska Department of Revenue, *Fall 2006 Revenue Sources Book*, pp. 33–34.

55. Ibid., 31.

56. "Transfer pricing" schemes are a ploy used to reduce tax liability by inflating the costs of intrafirm trade. Companies overstate the prices that divisions charge each other for intermediate goods and services thus increasing the paper costs of production and decreasing reportable profits.

57. "Governor Wants Input on What to Do with Predicted $1.6 Billion Budget Surplus," *Fairbanks Daily News-Miner,* November 22, 2007, B-2.

58. See http://www.surveymonkey.com/s.aspx?sm=SdLawkgxb2H6o7oAkmv 2ZA_3d_3d.

# 6

## Economic Development and State Ownership of Oil and Gas

When Alaska became a state, it, like other remote regions, possessed few options for economic development besides export of natural resources.[1] For the most part, state interests have coincided with federal and private interests in developing Alaska's natural resources over the past half century, masking the state's economic dependence on decisions made in remote political and financial centers. But a perceived conflict has emerged with outside interests, increasingly MNCs, when development of public resources has not advanced at the pace or in the direction that Alaskans believed that it should. The current struggle to win a firm commitment to construct a pipeline to bring North Slope natural gas to market represents the most recent in a long history of such cases.[2]

The urge to regulate development in the public interest clashes with Alaskans' frontier ethics of individualism and free enterprise. The resolution of the contradiction lies in a populist notion of the "owner state," in which the state acts as an agent or active proprietor of the people's resources.[3] Consistent with the ideology of limited government, the owner state generally exercises its authority through setting policy for the disposition of state-owned oil and gas and other resources, rather than by developing the resources itself. The state has three primary mechanisms for articulating its client-agent relationship for its petroleum resources: leasing mineral rights for exploration and development, conservation regulation of oil and gas production, and disposition of the retained royalty share.[4] In this chapter, we focus mainly on the third mechanism available to the owner state: disposition of the royalty share. Alaska's history of attempts to stimulate economic development using royalty oil and gas illustrates how a politically mature, natural resource–dependent state attempts to deal with MNCs to address local political and social concerns, under conditions of severe economic uncertainty. This history provides a precedent for understanding the current policy debate over the North Slope natural gas pipeline.

We start by providing the economic and regulatory context: summarizing the state's economic development problem and the role that control of state petroleum resources could play. Next, we review the history of the state's policy and programs for the disposition of its royalty oil and gas. Then, we describe the industrial facilities built to process royalty oil and gas, economic benefits resulting from the program, and impacts on state revenues. We also discuss oil and gas dispositions that failed to achieve their promise. We then evaluate the contribution of state policy to the pattern of successes and failures. We conclude with a discussion of implications for economic development policy for Alaska generally, and for the gas pipeline project in particular.

## ■ Petroleum and Alaska Economic Development

The United States is one of the few nations in the world in which petroleum and other subsurface resources may be privately owned. In most of the nation, the history of oil and gas development describes struggles among private owners.[5] Two factors made Alaska an exception to this rule. First, the federal government awarded the state a 102-million-acre land entitlement, including subsurface rights, when it entered the union in 1959. Second, Alaska's long coastline entitled the state to a vast offshore estate within three miles of land, derived from the 1953 Submerged Lands Act, that settled intergovernmental disputes with coastal states over offshore mineral rights. The geology was fortuitous, rewarding the state handsomely with oil and gas resources from both onshore and offshore entitlements.

The new state adopted a progressive set of policies with respect to managing petroleum resources, including competitive leasing.[6] Once resources were leased to oil companies, however, the Alaska Department of Natural Resources (DNR) adopted a permissive policy about extending leases beyond the statutory ten-year expiration date, as long as the company drilled a well or filed joint plans to drill with neighboring leases. In fact, only once in forty years has the DNR refused an oil company's request to renew a set of leases. As a lame-duck governor, Murkowski terminated the leases for the Point Thompson field after a long dispute with ExxonMobil over missed development deadlines.[7] The Alaska Oil and Gas Conservation Commission (AOGCC) was given broad statutory authority to regulate oil and gas drilling and production to prevent "waste" in lease operations.[8] AOGCC has expected producers holding leases over the same oil or gas field to operate jointly with pooled financial interests (unitization). It can compel unitization to settle disputes over property rights, but it has never invoked that authority.[9] However, threats to compel unitization may have served as the catalyst needed to bring Prudhoe Bay leaseholders into agreement on unit operations, both before oil began flowing through the TAPS, and more recently with respect to Prudhoe Bay gas.[10]

## Objectives and Constraints of Economic Development

At the time Alaska entered the union, oil and gas resources in the Cook Inlet region were seen as key to the new state's economic viability.[11] Discovery of the largest field in North America at Prudhoe Bay in 1968 entrenched and enhanced Alaska's status as a petroleum state. The oil and gas industry provided new high-paying jobs, but many of these were held by nonresident workers.[12] "Downstream" vertical integration in the form of petroleum refining and petrochemical industries provided a logical opportunity for increasing resident employment and other economic benefits from oil and gas production. Downstream development does not break the link to world energy markets, so it does not really make the state economy less dependent on petroleum. Nevertheless, it provides a direct opportunity to increase value added in the state from the state's resource endowment.

Alaska economists have defined three objectives for regional industrial development. New industry can (1) increase jobs and personal income, (2) expand the state and local tax base, and (3) increase the share of economic activity retained in the region (increase the economic multiplier).[13] To these one might add a fourth objective: providing benefits to regional consumers. Consumers benefit from development that reduces the cost of living or the cost of doing business, or that provides products and services that were not previously available locally. This objective was particularly relevant in Alaska during the 1960s and 1970s, when the high costs posed significant barriers to economic development and diversification.

Two key factors that determine how expansion of different industries might differently achieve the development objectives are (1) whether wages in the industry are relatively low or high, and (2) the relative capital intensity.[14] Oil and gas processing industries are capital intensive, meaning they provide relatively few jobs as a percentage of value added, but those jobs are highly skilled and pay high wages.[15] Consequently, one would expect that petroleum processing would provide relatively few permanent jobs, but relatively more enhancement to the property tax base and per-capita income.

The geology and economics that allow large quantities of oil and gas to be produced in Alaska do not guarantee that petroleum processing in the state will be feasible. Alaska has long faced significantly higher construction costs relative to the nation as a whole. In addition, its remote location makes relative transportation costs of raw materials and manufactured products a key factor in economic viability. Crude oil is very inexpensively moved around the globe by tanker. Natural gas, because of its lower value per volume and the expense to liquefy for marine transport, is relatively expensive to move long distances. Refined products and petrochemicals are typically more expensive to move than crude oil but less expensive to move than natural gas over long distances.[16] As a result, transportation economics disfavor Alaska locations for export petroleum refineries and oil-based petrochemical plants, but might favor refineries to serve in-state needs. Transportation economics favor converting Alaska gas to petrochemicals in-state, if anywhere.[17]

## Import Substitution vs. Export-Led Growth

Traditional economic wisdom holds that the path to economic development in less-developed regions is through increased exports. This maxim definitely applies to resource development in remote regions, where exporting minerals to world markets provides the most obvious opportunity for growth. Alaska's traditional "basic" industries such as fisheries, tourism, mining, and forest products, as well as oil and gas, exemplify trade-dependent exports. In the early years of statehood, however, federal civilian and military government employment provided the largest source of basic industry employment. Federal government employment is an export industry in the sense that the demand for the services is determined by forces external to the state—i.e., the US Congress.

Figure 6.1 illustrates the shares of Alaska employment by major industry in 1965 and compares 1965 total employment and employment shares to those in 2001. In 1965, the federal government was by far Alaska's largest employ-

**Figure 6.1    Alaska Employment, 1965 vs. 2001**

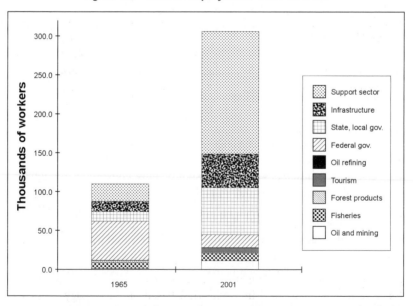

*Source:* Institute for Social and Economic Research, Man in the Arctic Program Database.

er, employing 50,000 civilian and military workers, nearly one in two Alaskan workers. All resource industries and tourism combined employed only about 11,000 workers, or 10 percent of the total. The budget shares for 2001 contrast sharply with those of 1965. One obvious difference is the decline in federal government employment (largely due to military staff cutbacks) and the growth in oil and gas and state employment. But the growth in support sector employment accounts for the biggest change by far. This sector, composed primarily of trade and services, grew sevenfold. The growth largely occurred through import substitution: replacement of imported services by locally produced services.

Import substitution also provides an alternative to export-led growth in the manufacturing sector. A 1988 study found that nearly all manufacturing industries present in Alaska in the 1980s directly served either a basic industry or final consumer demand. That is, Alaska produced relatively few inputs to other industries. In contrast, the majority of manufacturing industries nationally produced such intermediate goods. Another finding was that a much higher share of Alaska industries than US industries had high transport costs: 60 percent vs. 30 percent.[18] These findings suggest that successful Alaska manufactures be favored by a location that is either close to consumers or near a key input with very high transport costs.[19]

Another geographic feature of the Alaska economy—Alaska's remoteness and sparse population density—requires that the state burn a lot more fuel per capita in transportation than other states. Its basic industries other than oil— fishing, tourism, logging, mining, and aviation—all rely on refined petroleum products as essential production inputs. Energy Information Administration (EIA) 2001 data show that Alaska consumes more than three times as much energy per capita as the US average, 30 percent more per capita than the next most energy-intensive state (Wyoming). Even without an industrial base using petroleum as feedstock for petrochemicals, Alaska consumes nearly three and a half times as much petroleum products per capita as the nation, and nearly 40 percent more than the next highest state (Louisiana). Still, the total amount, about 140,000 barrels per day, is relatively small.[20]

## Economies of Scale

The relatively small size of the Alaska economy can discourage production for local use if there are economies of scale in manufacturing. Petroleum refining and petrochemical manufacturing, like most chemical process industries and nearly all forms of oil and gas transportation, have substantial economies of scale.[21] F. M. Scherer and his colleagues compiled information on minimum efficient scales (MES), the smallest size plant that achieves competitive costs, for a variety of manufacturing industries, based on technology available in 1967. They reported an MES for petroleum refining of 1.9 percent of production.[22] Based on EIA historical consumption data, the MES would require a throughput of roughly 230,000 barrels per day (b/d), substantially more than current Alaska consumption and nearly eight times consumption in 1965.

Scherer et al. also computed the cost disadvantage for plants operating less than the MES. For petroleum refining, a plant with a capacity of one-third the MES in 1967 (approximately 70,000 b/d) faced a cost disadvantage of 4.8 percent relative to an MES plant.[23] For an Alaskan refinery at a scale appropriate for serving the local market in the late 1960s, the projected cost disadvantage might be closer to 10 percent. Even configured to maximize recovery of fuels that have large Alaskan demand, a local refinery would have to find a market for some products outside the state. The combination of economies of scale, process limits on the product mix in refinery runs, and the small size of Alaska's product markets suggest that a refinery producing for the local market could face significant cost disadvantages that might not be offset by higher transportation costs for competitors' imported products.

## Royalty-in-Kind (RIK) Program

Alaska's narrow economic base provided the state with few options for raising revenue besides oil. Because industry costs were so high in the state, only the richest and largest deposits could be profitably exploited, and relatively few jobs were needed to extract their reserves.[24] Alaska's sparse population also meant that fuel demands for transportation were high; and its remoteness guaranteed that fuel would be expensive. From the early years, state officials looked toward developing an in-state petroleum processing industry to create more jobs in the state and to reduce fuel costs. This created a dilemma. The state might stimulate economic development by giving away its natural resources to sponsors of projects that promised attractive economic benefits. Yet it could not afford to dissipate the potential rent without losing its principal revenue source.

The state of Alaska attempted to resolve the dilemma by leasing its state-owned oil lands competitively, while retaining the option to dispose of its royalty share—the share retained by the landowner of oil and gas produced from leased lands—in kind to prospective industrial developers. Although many states and the federal government have RIK programs, Alaska has been uniquely aggressive in pursuing this option. Since 1969, Alaska has executed more than thirty RIK sales involving more than 800 million barrels of oil, or just over half of all state royalty oil.

### Evolution of the Program

The intellectual roots of the state's development policy toward oil and gas were well established before the oil wealth was realized, however. In his keynote address to the Alaska Constitutional Convention (November 8, 1955), E. L. Bartlett reflected prevailing views when he said,

> The financial welfare of the future state and the well-being of its present and unborn citizens depend upon the wise administration and oversight of these developmental activities. Two very real dangers are present. The first, and most obvious, danger is that of exploitation under the thin guise of development. The taking of Alaska's mineral resources without leaving some reasonable return for the support of Alaska government and the use of all the people in Alaska will mean a betrayal in the administration of the people's wealth. The second danger is that outside interests, determined to stifle any development in Alaska which might compete with their activities elsewhere, will attempt to acquire great areas of Alaska's public lands in order *not* to develop them until . . . they see fit [emphasis in original].[25]

Delegates clearly had Bartlett's ideas in mind when they drafted Article VIII of the Alaska Constitution. Section 1 reads, "It is the policy of the State to encourage the settlement of its land and the development of its resources by making them available for maximum use consistent with the public interest." And Section 2 reads, "The legislature shall provide for the utilization, development, and conservation of all natural resources belonging to the state, including land and waters for the maximum benefit of its people."[26] As a consensus document, the language is suitably vague. To some Alaskans, state ownership of petroleum and other resources gave the government the opportunity to push aggressively for specific utilization and development projects that were deemed in the public interest. This perspective is closely aligned with the owner state model of governance mentioned earlier. To others, the public interest was better served with the state's taking a more passive stewardship role, leaving development decisions to private initiative and market forces.

Alaska's RIK program resembles production-sharing contracts popular in the developing world in the sense that they reserve a share of the state's oil and gas to the state landowner for disposal to promote economic development. However, Alaska, like the federal government and other US states, never considered creating a state oil company or entering the oil production business. The practice since statehood has been to lease lands competitively to private developers in arm's-length transactions. The state retains a royalty share from its leases.[27] Alaska law permits the DNR to take its royalty oil and gas in kind or in value (that is, letting the oil companies market it on behalf of the state). Many Alaskans favored taking the state's royalty share in kind, and making it available to specific projects that would provide additional private-sector jobs and possibly stimulate additional development. Jack Roderick, commissioner of natural resources for Alaska's first governor, Egan, reported that the governor saw a dual role for royalty-in-kind disposals: job creation and reduced costs for Alaskans.[28]

In this regard, Alaska differed from other states and the federal government, where the primary purpose of a royalty-in-kind option was to maximize revenue. Like production-sharing contracts in developing countries, Alaska's choice to dispose of royalties in kind for any purpose other than revenue maximization subjected the program to charges of political favoritism and, potentially, corruption. This is exactly what transpired the first time that the commissioner of natural resources entered into a royalty-in-kind contract during the first term of Governor Hickel, who followed Egan.

In February 1969, Commissioner Kelley negotiated a deal to sell up to 15,000 barrels per day of Cook Inlet royalty oil for eight years—at that time all the state's royalty oil—to a company called Alaska Oil and Refining Company. The company, which appeared to have been created entirely for the purpose of purchasing the royalty oil, promised to build a refinery in Alaska and pay the state the same price for its oil as the producers received for theirs (the so-called in-value price). Suspicions deepened when the company merged five months later with Tesoro, an independent refining company. Tesoro did immediately begin construction of a refinery to process the oil in Nikiski, north of Kenai, but the lack of transparency in the negotiations leading to the sale rankled legislators and created lingering doubts about whether the public interest had been served.[29]

The euphoria over the $900 million brought in by the 1969 North Slope oil lease sale soon diverted public attention from the Tesoro case. But legislative debate about the propriety of the 1969 royalty disposal continued, spilling over into the larger question of the appropriate state role in TAPS and other projects involving North Slope oil and gas. According to Roderick, things came to a head in a September 1973 special legislative session called by Governor Egan (elected again after Hickel resigned) to address these issues. Roderick called this a pivotal time in Alaska's political history, one of two times when the relationship between the state and the oil industry changed in a significant way.[30] Legislators dropped a proposal for a 20 percent equity ownership in TAPS and a right-of-way leasing law that could set tariffs and raised severance taxes instead. The following year, the legislature rewrote the statutes governing royalty-in-kind disposals, in a bid to ensure transparency of negotiations for future sales of royalty oil and gas from Prudhoe Bay.

The 1974 statute set criteria and standards for the commissioner of natural resources to meet in royalty-in-kind disposals.[31] RIK disposals must be competitive, unless the state's "best interest" required that they be noncompetitive, and earn at least as much as if the oil were taken in-value. In-state domestic and industrial needs had priority over export sales of royalty-in-kind oil and gas.[32] The statute defined the constitutionally required "maximum benefits" to the state in terms of cash, effects on the economy, benefits of in-state processing, provision of products to benefit in-state consumers, and specific criteria related to local economic development benefits.[33] The 1974 statute also created a commission called the Royalty Oil and Gas Development Advisory Board (ROGDAB), which would hold public hearings on proposed sales, review benefit claims against the statutory criteria, and recommend to the legislature whether to ratify contracts.[34]

The changed climate favoring transparency was evident in the way that Governor Hammond, who succeeded Egan, announced the next proposed royalty-in-kind sale: a proposal to sell Prudhoe Bay royalty gas in support of an "All-Alaska Pipeline."[35] In a statewide radio address, the governor carefully articulated the reasons for his best-interest finding. The rationale included how delivery of gas to tidewater improved the chances of using the gas for industrial purposes in Alaska, an assurance that royalty gas in kind removed in Alaska would not be subject to federal regulation, and a negotiated "takeback" provision if a need developed for in-state use of the gas.[36] By the time Hammond left office in 1982, his administration had institutionalized royalty disposals so much that his deputy commissioner, Geoffrey Haynes, found it necessary to write a thick handbook explaining the process for the incoming administration.[37]

## Summary of Disposals

Between 1969 and 2003, about 57 percent of all Alaska state royalty oil was taken in kind. Relatively little gas was taken in kind, however, despite several attempts.[38] Figure 6.2 shows the distribution over time of state royalty oil and the disposals by purchaser. Oil production began in 1958 on federal lands in the Cook Inlet region, and production commenced in 1966 on state-leased lands generating royalties for potential disposal in kind. State royalties dramatically increased with completion of TAPS in 1977. By 2004, two in-state refiners—Tesoro and Mapco (later Williams and now Flint Hills)—had each purchased about 40 percent of royalty-in-kind oil. Chevron (also an in-state refiner) purchased another 10 percent. Two percent was sold to Golden Valley Electric Association—the Fairbanks area electric utility—for turbine fuel.[39] Altogether, 94 percent of royalty-in-kind oil was sold to promote in-state use, with the remainder sold in competitive auctions. Not all royalty disposals, as we shall see below, successfully served their intended purpose.

## ▓ Evaluation of Royalty-in-Kind Dispositions

Answers to four main questions are needed in order to evaluate the success or failure of Alaska's RIK program. The first and most obvious question is, what facilities were constructed related to the program? A second question would be, what facilities were proposed and supported with RIK disposals, but never completed? Third is the question of how much it cost the taxpayers: how much

**Figure 6.2    Disposition of Alaska Royalty Oil**

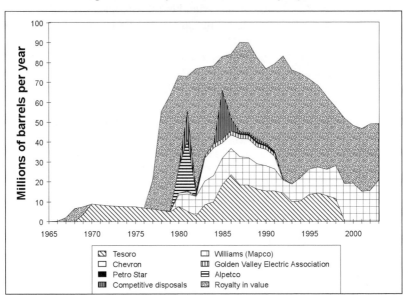

Tesoro
Chevron
Petro Star
Competitive disposals
Williams (Mapco)
Golden Valley Electric Association
Alpetco
Royalty in value

*Sources:* 1969–1978, M. Berman et al., *Alaska Petroleum Revenues: The Influence of Federal Policy* (Anchorage: Institute of Social and Economic Research, 1984); 1979–2003, Alaska Division of Oil and Gas Annual Reports.

more revenue might the state have received if it had sold all oil competitively? Finally, to what extent might RIK oil and gas contracts have been necessary to get the facilities built and make their operations successful?

## Facilities Constructed

When Alaska entered the union in 1959, no oil and gas processing facilities existed anywhere in the state. All petroleum products were imported from the lower forty-eight states or abroad, and there was no natural gas distribution system.[40] Table 6.1 summarizes Alaska oil and gas processing facilities constructed between 1959 and 2004. The table shows that many of the early Cook Inlet facilities were constructed without the benefit of any state royalty oil or gas by or in joint ventures with Cook Inlet producers. Chevron constructed the first modern oil refinery in Alaska in 1963 before the RIK program commenced, although the company did purchase some royalty oil later.[41]

Other Cook Inlet facilities constructed in the early years, in addition to the Tesoro refinery mentioned above, were the Phillips-Marathon liquefied natural gas (LNG) plant and an ammonia-urea fertilizer plant, using natural gas as feedstock. The Collier Chemical Company, later merged into Unocal, built the

**Table 6.1   Alaska Oil and Gas Processing Facilities Constructed**

| Owner | Location | Start | Feedstock | Capacity | Royalty-in-Kind | Products | Destination | Status (as of October 2007) |
|---|---|---|---|---|---|---|---|---|
| ConocoPhillips | Prudhoe Bay | 1975? | Crude oil | 14,000 b/d | No | Diesel | Prudhoe Bay | Operating |
| ConocoPhillips | Kuparuk | 1981 | Crude oil | 14,000 b/d | No | Diesel | Kuparuk | Operating |
| Flint Hills (Williams/Mapco) | North Pole | 1977 | Crude oil | 220,000 b/d | Yes | Gasoline | Alaska | Operating |
| | | | | | | Jet fuel | Alaska | |
| | | | | | | Diesel | Alaska | |
| | | | | | | Gas oil | Alaska | |
| | | | | | | Asphalt | Alaska | |
| | | | | | | Residual | Returned to TAPS | |
| Petro Star | North Pole | 1985 | Crude oil | 15,000 b/d | Yes | Kerosene | Alaska | Operating |
| | | | | | | Jet fuel | Alaska | |
| | | | | | | Diesel | Alaska | |
| | | | | | | Residual | Returned to TAPS | |
| Petro Star | Valdez | 1992 | Crude oil | 46,000 b/d | Option, not exercised | Jet fuel | Operating | |
| | | | | | | Diesel | | |
| | | | | | | Residual | Returned to TAPS | |
| Tesoro | Nikiski | 1969 | Crude oil | 72,000 b/d | Yes | Gasoline | Alaska | Operating |
| | | | | | | Jet fuel | Alaska | |
| | | | | | | Diesel | Alaska | |
| | | | | | | Fuel oil | Export | |
| | | | | | | Asphalt | Alaska | |
| | | | | | | Propane | Alaska | |
| | | | | | | Sulfur | Lower 48 | |
| | | | | | | Residual | Lower 48, export | |
| Chevron | Nikiski | 1963 | Crude oil | 18,000 b/d | Initially no, later yes | Naphtha | Lower 48 | Closed in 1991 |
| | | | | | | Jet fuel | Alaska | |
| | | | | | | Diesel | Alaska | |
| | | | | | | Fuel oil | Lower 48 | |
| | | | | | | Asphalt | Alaska | |
| Conoco Phillips-Marathon | Nikiski | 1969 | Natural gas | 235,000 Mcf/d | No | Liquefied natural gas | Japan | Operating |
| Agrium (Unocal/Collier) | Nikiski | 1969 | Natural gas | 160,000 Mcf/d | No | Ammonia, urea | Export | Closing in 2008 |

*Note:* TAPS is the Trans-Alaska Pipeline System; b/d is barrels per day; Mcf/d is millions of cubic feet per day.

fertilizer plant to serve Pacific Rim demand. Unocal sold the plant to Agrium in 2000. After North Slope oil started flowing through TAPS, two oil refineries were built near Fairbanks and a third was constructed in Valdez. All three take oil from TAPS, refine it into products for Alaska markets, and return the residual back to the TAPS oil stream. They pay a fee, called a Quality Bank adjustment, for reducing the quality of the oil stream. Earth Resources (later Mapco), a partnership involving the Doyon regional native corporation, built the largest of these refineries. The Mapco refinery, eventually sold to Williams and then to Flint Hills, was expanded several times over the years. Arctic Slope Regional Corporation, another Alaska Native regional corporation, owns an interest in Petro Star, the operator of the other two TAPS refineries.

In 2003, the six major facilities listed in Table 6.1 that were operating at that time employed 685 workers on an average annual basis.[42] Agrium was the largest employer, with nearly 40 percent of the total, followed by Tesoro. The jobs generated a payroll of roughly $550 million annually (precise figures are proprietary). In addition to high-paying jobs, the facilities also contributed to the local property tax base. Although Alaska has no state property tax for oil and gas processing facilities, all these plants are located in the Kenai Peninsula Borough, the Fairbanks North Star Borough, and the city of Valdez and pay property taxes to support schools and other local government activities. The total assessed value about equals the annual payroll. Tax rates vary by jurisdiction, but the plants have probably allowed the boroughs to reduce their overall tax rates somewhat for other taxpayers.

## Facilities Proposed but Not Constructed

Table 6.2 summarizes Alaska oil and gas transportation and processing facilities that were proposed, and supported by royalty-in-kind disposals, but never constructed. All four were massive undertakings conceived during the national energy crisis in the late 1970s. None of the four could meet a market test after oil and gas wellhead prices were deregulated early in the next decade.

Alaska Petrochemical Company (Alpetco) was the winning bidder in the first solicitation for offers to purchase royalty-in-kind oil from Prudhoe Bay. Alpetco—a partnership of Alaska Interstate (later Enstar) (60 percent), Alaska Consolidated Shipping (itself a consortium of Native corporations and the shipping company Seatrain) (20 percent), and Barbour Oil (20 percent)—proposed to build a world-scale oil-based petrochemical plant (see Table 6.2). The plant, to be located at tidewater in southcentral Alaska, would produce up to 2.1 million pounds per year of polyethylene, polypropylene, styrene, and similar products. It would cost an estimated $1.5 billion to build and require an additional $400 million of working capital, ultimately generating a $2.3 billion tax base. Construction would require 3,500 to 4,000 temporary workers, while operations would generate 2,000 permanent jobs.[43] In 1978, the state agreed to

**Table 6.2   Proposed Alaska Oil and Gas Facilities (not constructed, but receiving royalty-in-kind contracts or options)**

| Owner | Location | Start | Feedstock | Capacity | Royalty-in-Kind | Products | Destination |
|---|---|---|---|---|---|---|---|
| El Paso Natural Gas | Prudhoe Bay to Valdez | 1978 | Natural gas | 2 billion cf/d | Option, not exercised | Liquefied natural gas | Lower 48 |
| Alaska Petrochemical Co. (Alpetco) | Valdez | 1977 | Crude oil | 150,000 b/d | Yes, renegotiated | Polyethylene | Lower 48, export |
| | | | | | | Polypropylene | Lower 48, export |
| | | | | | | Styrene | Lower 48, export |
| Alpetco | Valdez | 1980 | Crude oil | 100,000 b/d | Yes, terminated | Naphtha | Lower 48, export |
| | | | | | | Olefins | Lower 48, export |
| Dow-Shell | Valdez | 1982 | Natural gas liquids | 210,000 b/d | Option, not exercised | Ethylene | Lower 48, export |
| | | | | | | Polyethylene | Lower 48, export |
| | | | | | | Ethylene glycol | Lower 48, export |

*Note:* cf/d is cubic feet per day; b/d is barrels per day.

sell up to 150,000 b/d of royalty oil for twenty-seven years to support the project. After review by the ROGDAB, the legislature approved the contract, with minor amendments.[44]

In early 1980, US oil markets were deregulated, rapidly changing the market outlook for Alaska oil.[45] That May, the parties agreed to Alpetco's request to amend the contract. By then, the project's sponsor had changed to the Alaska Oil Company, whose major partner was Charter Oil, a Caribbean refiner. Alpetco's new partnership proposed a 100,000 b/d refinery in Valdez to produce naphtha and olefins for further processing elsewhere. Alpetco would receive 75,000 b/d beginning July 18, 1980, until the refinery was operational. At that point, the volume would rise to 100,000 b/d. The market outlook continued to deteriorate for Alpetco's project. One year later, the company abandoned the refinery project, and its contract was terminated in January 1982.

As mentioned above, the state entered into a contract to sell Prudhoe Bay royalty gas to a consortium including El Paso Natural Gas, the sponsor of the All-Alaska gas pipeline project. When the federal government selected the Alaska Natural Gas Transportation System (ANGTS) as the preferred route for the project, a second proposal emerged for a natural gas liquids (NGLs) pipeline following the route El Paso had proposed. After reviewing proposals from several contenders, the state selected a consortium headed by Dow Chemical and calling itself the Dow-Shell Group to perform a detailed feasibility study of the project. As outlined by the proposers, the project would manufacture 210,000 b/d of ethane and liquefied petroleum gases (LPGs)—propane, butane, etc.—into petrochemicals for export. The project entailed a complex of four interrelated facilities costing roughly $7 billion, including

- a $1 billion plant on the North Slope to extract NGLs from produced gas;
- a 20-inch pipeline from Prudhoe Bay to Valdez or Cook Inlet, costing $2.3 billion;
- a $175 million fractionation plant to separate ethane from the LPGs; and
- a petrochemical plant using 90,000 b/d of ethane feedstock, costing $3.5 billion.[46]

The petrochemical infrastructure would develop in two phases. In phase 1, the plant would have the capacity to produce up to 4 million pounds per year of ethylene, polyethylene, and ethylene glycol. In phase 2, capacity would expand to produce another 3.5 million pounds of derivative products. Peak construction employment would top 11,000, while 3,500 permanent workers would be needed for operations in phase 1, and 6,800 in phase 2.

In addition to a commitment from the state to sell its entire royalty share of NGLs, Dow-Shell had obtained a right of first refusal from ARCO, and an agreement to negotiate in good faith with Sohio. Exxon, the other major North Slope owner, refused to negotiate with Dow-Shell and instead pursued its own feasibility study. Dow-Shell Group's detailed feasibility study concluded that crude oil prices would have to remain at $38 (in 1981 prices) to make the NGL pipeline feasible.[47] Shortly after releasing the feasibility study, world oil prices started to decline. Dow-Shell backed out of the project in 1982, citing adverse market trends.

The first North Slope royalty-in-kind solicitations and the Alpetco and Dow-Shell bids spawned much debate among Alaskans about whether petrochemical development at this scale was appropriate for the state. Although construction never began for the new petrochemical facilities, the official deliberations created a litany of engineering and market feasibility studies. Mostly funded by the state, the state's urgent need to understand the parameters and implications of the industry spread a windfall to engineering firms and other consultants in the state and around the nation.

Since the Alpetco and Dow-Shell episode, state officials have been more cautious about approving royalty oil and gas sales other than for in-state refining. Several gas and NGL offers have been made in recent years. Agrium requested Cook Inlet royalty gas at a low price, but the state balked when other gas purchasers objected. Williams once expressed interest in buying North Slope NGLs for a petrochemical plant but backed out before making a formal offer when it determined that transportation costs made it infeasible to ship ethylene or polyethylene to the Japanese market.[48] The state continues to get expressions of interest, some more credible than others. The state has not kept a comprehensive record of denied requests. According to Kevin Banks, manager of the program for DNR, most smaller traders lose interest as soon as they see the bureaucratic process involved in obtaining a "best-interest" finding that is required to complete a sale.[49]

## How Much Did RIK Disposals Cost the State?

By statute, the state must earn at least as much from a RIK disposal as it would earn if the oil had been taken in value, the default method. No one has ever challenged a sale on the grounds that it failed to achieve this statutory requirement. So leaving aside the administrative cost of the analyses leading to the requisite "best-interest" findings, one could argue that the burden of proof would be on detractors to prove that the program has cost the state anything at all. In truth, however, the question is not so easy to answer.

Most royalty-in-kind disposals involved contracts with a pricing provision that specifies that the purchaser will pay the royalty-in-value price, or a slight premium above it. While this should in principle have guaranteed that the state not lose money on RIK sales, the state and producers have been in litigation over some aspect or another of in-value royalty accounting for more than twenty-five years.[50] Various aspects of the lawsuit have been settled out of court, but often not until years after the royalty sales. Limitations of contracts and the passage of time have made it difficult, if not impossible, for the state to collect retroactive payments from all past royalty purchasers when it receives an in-value settlement from producers. The state must negotiate a separate settlement for each contract (assuming that the firm that held the contract is still in business). The price in the most recent contract with Williams (acquired by Flint Hills) is not directly tied to the in-value price. A full and accurate retrospective accounting of the RIK program would be a monumental undertaking.[51]

Arguably, however, the correct test should not be based on in-value prices but on whether the state *expected* to receive at least as much over the long term from its RIK sales as it could have *expected* to have received from the *best opportunity available at the time*. Unfortunately, there are also many reasons why the comparison of expected sales receipts to the opportunity cost would be difficult to make over the years. First, most RIK disposals are long-term contracts. Available market indicators for oil and gas reflect short-term, or spot, prices. The spot market is extremely volatile and often diverges substantially from long-term conditions.[52]

Second, both spot and long-term markets for Alaska oil have been replete with market distortions that cause Alaska oil prices to diverge from what free, competitive markets would have signaled. These distortions arose from federal regulation, combined with imperfect competition. Between 1974 and 1980, the federal government controlled wellhead oil prices throughout the nation. Cook Inlet and North Slope oil had different regulatory statuses and traded at very different prices.[53] When Congress authorized TAPS in 1973, it prohibited exports of Alaska oil. This created a surplus of oil on the US West Coast that kept prices for Alaska oil from rising as fast after deregulation as they did elsewhere. Shipping between US ports was subject to the Merchant Marine Act of 1920 (Jones Act), which required that products move in US-built tankers operated by US crews. This increased shipping costs substantially and further depressed Alaska wellhead prices. In addition, the major Alaska oil producers enjoyed significant market power in West Coast markets. These firms sold most of their Alaska oil to their own refineries at artificial transfer prices. They used their market power to divert some of their oil through the Panama Canal to the US Gulf Coast, at an apparent loss, in order to relieve downward pressure on West Coast prices.[54]

Alpetco had proposed its refining and petrochemical project in the midst of these distortions. Refined products, unlike crude oil, could be exported in foreign vessels at unregulated competitive prices. Export refinery economics were therefore built on a structure of market distortions created by the wellhead price regulation, the export ban on crude oil, imperfect competition in the West Coast markets, the lack of transparency in netback prices, and the Jones

Act. When just one of the pillars of this structure gave way—wellhead price regulation—the project started to unravel.

The history of Alaska natural gas markets is likewise convoluted. Cook Inlet gas was mostly developed during the era of federal wellhead price regulation. Regulated prices were based on historical cost, without reference to current supply-and-demand conditions. During the late 1970s, acute gas shortages developed in the lower forty-eight states, leading to passage in 1978 of the Natural Gas Policy Act (NGPA). NGPA further extended regulation to allocate gas to preferential uses. Alaska won an exemption from some aspects of NGPA, allowing it to continue to process natural gas into fertilizer and LNG for export, as well as to burn gas to generate electric power, activities curtailed elsewhere in the nation. It was in this environment that the NGL-based petrochemical project appeared. Petrochemicals manufactured from NGLs were exempt from price regulation. If exported, they could also avoid the Jones Act shipping-cost penalty. The phased deregulation of natural gas in the 1980s allowed US natural gas supplies to begin shifting toward higher-valued uses, causing Dow-Shell to lose interest in its Alaska petrochemical project.

The array of distortions in oil and gas markets makes it extremely difficult to determine ex post facto whether the state's expected revenues from RIK sales matched or exceeded the expected revenues from the best alternative option. It would have been unreasonable to expect that the state could have made this determination at the time. It remains unclear whether the program made any significant difference in the royalty revenues that would otherwise have been received. The slight premium over in-value prices must be balanced against the costs of administration, including those incurred with the failed contracts.

## Role of RIK Contracts

If the net cost of the program was small, one must ask, then, whether the program produced any significant economic benefits for the state and for society? If so, were the RIK contracts important to the success of projects that generated these benefits? Arguably, the wages and taxes paid were just reallocations of economic activity and did not consist of true benefits. Alaska is an open economy, with net migration balancing local labor markets relatively quickly with national markets. Workers constructing and operating Alaska oil and gas processing plants probably would not have moved to Alaska if these plants had not been built. Once here, they need more local government services, which the larger tax base provides. The local economy is larger, but economic well-being has improved relatively little.

Do Alaska consumers benefit from import substitution? Figure 6.3 shows the approximate distribution of products produced. These percentages varied over time depending on market conditions, and the exact distribution at any

**Figure 6.3    Approximate Alaska Refinery Product Percentages**

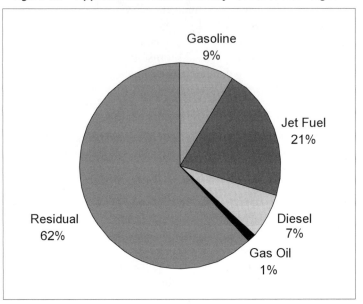

*Source:* Estimated from Alaska Division of Oil and Gas Annual Reports and data provided by the refining companies.

given time is proprietary. However, the figure gives a snapshot of the approximate product mix. The largest share of production is residual oil, which is all exported from the state into competitive world markets. Three products—jet fuel, gasoline, and number 2 diesel—dominate the output of Alaska refineries marketed within the state.

Figure 6.4 compares price differentials over time calculated from EIA data for distillate fuels (diesel), jet fuel, and motor gasoline. The $0.05 to $0.10 premium in the 1970s largely reflects the transportation cost differential. After 1980, competition between Mapco and Tesoro appears to have periodically given Alaska consumers diesel price savings of up to $0.20 per gallon. Substantial gasoline price savings also appeared in 1991 and again after 1998. Jet fuel prices have also been drifting down since 1991, at a time when Alaska refineries have continued to raise jet fuel production, suggesting a benefit from competition of a few cents per gallon. The price differentials in Figure 6.4 show no huge savings but do suggest that Alaska consumers and businesses likely benefited measurably from the competition among Alaska refineries.

If RIK contracts did not involve a subsidy, then were they really needed for the success of the projects they supported? RIK contracts at fair mar-

**Figure 6.4 Alaska-Washington Price Differentials for Selected Petroleum Products, 1970–2000**

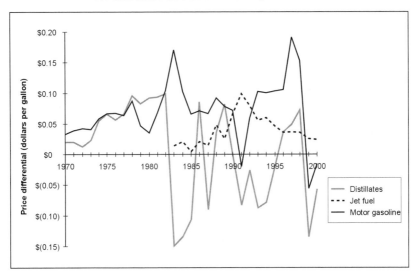

*Source:* Energy Information Administration, total energy consumption, transportation sector.

ket value provided two direct benefits to the purchasers. First, the long-term contracts provided an element of security from the volatility of spot oil markets. Large integrated oil producers enjoyed this advantage, and the state's contracts helped level the playing field for independent refiners like Tesoro and Mapco. The security from spot-market fluctuations played a significant role in financing refinery expansion. For example, in 1992, Petro Star obtained an option to buy RIK oil to start a refinery in Valdez. After it was able to obtain financing, the company decided it did not need the oil and elected not to exercise its option.[55] Second, the contracts provided independent refiners with diversification of supplies: in particular, a source outside major oil company control. The major North Slope producers have a vested interest in reducing competition in the West Coast market, which includes Alaska. Once it was clear that the new refineries were going to be built, however, the producers appeared to have been willing to sell them oil at competitive prices.

If RIK contracts have these advantages, then why has the state not elected to take more of their oil and gas in kind? In general, according to DNR staff, the refiners have not asked for more oil.[56] They pay a slight premium for long-term contracts and appear comfortable with buying the rest of their needs from the producers.

## ◼ Conclusions:
## Lessons for the North Slope Gas Pipeline

Alaska's RIK program fostered the development of a local refining industry that employed relatively few workers but contributed significantly to local tax bases. Competition from Alaska refiners appears to have provided benefits to Alaska consumers and businesses. In-state refining has not only made a direct value-added contribution to the economy, but has also presumably made an indirect contribution to diversification, by substituting in-state-manufactured fuel for imported fuel with at least some reduction in price. The state's dependence on royalty revenues has muted political pressure to give away the state's resources to project sponsors promising economic benefits. Distribution of PFDs derived from royalty income gives citizens a direct stake in the tradeoff between development and revenues. The PFD program will likely protect the transparency that the RIK program has enjoyed since the 1974 legislative amendments.[57]

As oil production declined, Alaska's economic development issue of the day shifted away from petroleum processing toward obtaining a firm commitment to construct a pipeline to bring natural gas from Prudhoe Bay and other North Slope fields to market. The project remains elusive after more than thirty years, despite a Congressional offer of $16 billion in federal loan guarantees and directed policy initiatives from the past three successive governors.[58] The primary reason that the project lies fallow is most likely its enormous cost and high risk. North Slope gas producers (shippers) would have to guarantee enough gasline revenue over three decades to pay for unlimited cost overruns, selling gas into a highly volatile market. Despite the risky economics, many observers, including legislators, DNR analysts, and members of the public believe that the project would move forward were it not for Big Oil's need for total control and its indifference to Alaska. The perception that the state must act to overcome industry dithering or equivocating echoes Bartlett's second danger: that the MNCs are determined to prevent the gas resources they leased from the state from being developed in competition with their gas prospects elsewhere.[59]

The Alaska Gasline Inducement Act (AGIA) proposed by Governor Sarah Palin represents the most recent of a series of attempts to forge a state policy with respect to the North Slope gas pipeline. Like its predecessors, AGIA proposed state-directed development to achieve political goals. The history of state-directed development of its royalty oil and gas provides insight into the struggle over gasline policy and prospects for AGIA's success. The successes and failures of the RIK program suggest four lessons for development policy for Alaska.

The first lesson is an affirmation of the benefits of transparency. Alaska was very fortunate to have avoided the potential economic disaster that would have occurred if it had embarked on either of the massive proposed petrochemical development schemes. Because cautious state officials had built milestones that Alpetco and Dow-Shell had to meet before they received additional help, both companies withdrew from their contracts early before they could inflict serious losses on the state.

The second lesson is that projects relying on free market forces are more likely to succeed in the long run than projects built around regulatory policies or economic distortions. Market distortions are inherently arbitrary and ephemeral. They can change rapidly due to national policy shifts or other factors unrelated to either global supply and demand or Alaska conditions. The political risk of relying on these incentives only compounds the inherent economic risks that all new development projects face.

A third lesson to draw from Alaska's RIK program is that import substitution is as effective as exports for providing economic benefits. In some cases, import substitution can be preferable, as in the case of Alaska fuels, where it might reduce the cost of a critical imported input to a broad range of industrial activities.

The final lesson is that projects that can start at a small scale and expand gradually over time are more likely to succeed than ones that require a huge, risky up-front investment. Alaska's main refineries all started relatively small but made a series of upgrades over the years to keep pace with market opportunities. Today, the combined capacities of the two largest refineries substantially exceed the proposed size of Alpetco's export refinery. But unlike Alpetco, which had to raise $1.5 billion at one time, Tesoro and Mapco and its successors had two decades over which to raise a comparable sum.

These four lessons directly apply to state policies toward the North Slope pipeline, including AGIA. The pipeline already has two strikes against it. First, it has to operate on a huge scale to be viable. Second, it relies on export of gas, as in-state use could only account for a small fraction of the volume of 4.3 billion cubic feet per day considered optimal for economic feasibility.[60] The history of Alaska's management of its royalty oil suggests that for the project to proceed, state policy must rely on market forces rather than regulatory distortions and adhere to a transparent decision process. The main previous federal gas pipeline policy initiative, the ANGTS developed under the Carter administration, failed the former criterion. Governor Murkowski's attempt to negotiate a gas pipeline contract directly with the producers struck out on the latter.

AGIA called for an open competition, ending November 30, 2007, for an exclusive license to build the pipeline, in exchange for a potential $500 million state subsidy and a commitment from the state on transportation of its royalty gas. The history of Alaska's royalty oil and gas development policy suggests that AGIA's greater reliance on market forces and improved transparency make it more likely to succeed than previous policy initiatives. It remains to be seen whether the $500 million to defray permitting costs and good relations with the state that AGIA offers the winning bidder will be sufficient to overcome the financial risk.

## ▓ Notes

Large portions of this chapter are adapted from Matthew Berman, "Economic Development Through State Ownership of Oil and Gas: Evaluating Alaska's Royalty-in-Kind Program," *International Journal of Global Energy Issues* 26, no. 1–2 (2006): 83–103.

1. See Thomas Morehouse and Lee Huskey, "Development in Remote Regions: What Do We Know?" *Arctic* 45, no. 2 (June 1992).

2. Frustration with federal control of fisheries and national forests played a prominent role in the drive for statehood. See Richard Cooley, *Politics and Conservation: The Decline of Alaska Salmon* (New York: Harper & Row, 1963), and Lawrence Rakestraw, *A History of the U.S. Forest Service in Alaska* (Juneau: US Department of Agriculture, Forest Service, Alaska Region, 2002).

3. The term *owner state* is attributed to former governor Wally Hickel (Walter J. Hickel, *Crisis in the Commons: The Alaska Solution* [Oakland: ICS Press, 2002]). Hickel served as governor of Alaska from 1966 to 1969, and again from 1990 to 1994, and also as US secretary of the interior, 1969–1970.

4. The state also has the ability to invest a portion of savings derived from oil and gas revenues in development projects, which may or may not include petroleum industry projects. Chapter 7 addresses this type of investment in the context of overall management of petroleum-derived wealth.

5. The issue of the so-called split estate (surface tenure vs. subsurface rights) is discussed extensively in W. F. Lovejoy and P. T. Homan, *Economic Aspects of Oil Conservation Regulation* (Baltimore: Johns Hopkins Press for Resources for the Future, 1967); and Stephen L. McDonald, *Petroleum Conservation in the United States* (Baltimore: Johns Hopkins Press for Resources for the Future, 1971).

6. Sec. 38.05.180 of Alaska statutes describes the five-year plan for oil and gas lease sales, and the various lease terms (see also the discussion in Chapter 4).

7. The Murkowski administration hailed the decision, but ExxonMobil challenged it. See Wesley Loy, "Point Thompson Action Likely to Go to Court," *Anchorage Daily News*, December 4, 2006. Two previous administrations extended leases with changed terms. Under Jay Hammond's administration, expiring leases for the Duck Island Unit were renewed, but only after the DNR insisted on a higher state take. The Endicott oil field was developed several years later around the leases in question. During Tony Knowles' administration, BP offered to develop leases at the Northstar prospect only if the state changed the lease terms to eliminate net profit shares. The administration agreed but required a local hire provision and a higher royalty rate. The decision was affirmed by the state supreme court after a legal challenge (*Baxley vs. Alaska Dep't. of Natural Resources* [5/15/98], 958 P 2d 422).

8. Alaska Statutes sec. 31.05.095. Waste is not precisely defined but has generally been viewed as physical loss of oil or gas.

9. Alaska Statues sec. 31.05.100(c) provides for compulsory unitization if producers cannot agree. Sec. 31.05.110(b) allows AOGCC to set rules for operating oil fields if it determines that producers are allowing waste to occur.

10. See Bruce Melzer, "The Common Good Oil and Gas Don't Mix. And Neither

Do the Financial Interests of Those Who Own Mainly One or the Other, Yet Share America's Largest Oil Field," *Anchorage Daily News*, April 18, 1996. AOGCC has also consistently held to a policy of requiring reinjection of natural gas produced from oil wells at Prudhoe Bay and other fields, despite rising costs as the oil becomes increasingly depleted.

11. See George Rogers, *The Future of Alaska: Economic Consequences of Statehood* (Baltimore: Johns Hopkins Press for Resources for the Future, 1962); and the discussion in Chapter 2.

12. Although major oil companies made a concerted effort to move employees to Alaska, nonresident workers still represent 28 percent of oil industry employees. Neal Fried and Brigitta Windisch-Cole, "The Oil Industry," *Alaska Economic Trends* 23, no. 9 (September 2003): 3–12.

13. David Kresge, Daniel Seiver, Oliver S. Goldsmith, and Michael Scott, *Regions and Resources: Strategies for Development* (Cambridge: MIT Press, 1984), p. 192.

14. Kresge et al., *Regions and Resources,* 198–199.

15. See Arlon Tussing and Lois Kramer, *Hydrocarbon Processing: A Primer for Alaska* (Anchorage: Institute of Social and Economic Research, 1981).

16. These basic facts led Tussing and Kramer to postulate three axioms for location of petroleum processing facilities based on the transportation economics of oil and gas: (1) petroleum refineries tend to be located near their markets; (2) naphtha- and gas-oil–based petrochemical plants tend to be located near refineries; and (3) natural-gas–based petrochemical plants tend to be located near raw-materials sources (Tussing and Kramer, *Hydrocarbon Processing,* 114).

17. Ibid., 115.

18. Bradford Tuck, Lee Huskey, Dona Lehr, and Eric Larson, *Alaska Economic Growth and Change: Opportunities for Import Substitution* (Anchorage: Institute of Social and Economic Research, 1988). The authors defined a high-transportation-cost industry as one for which more than 3 percent of total costs typically paid for transportation.

19. Tuck et al., *Alaska Economic Growth,* III.B.4–III.B.5.

20. Figures from Energy Information Administration, *State Energy Data 2001: Consumption* (no date), available from www.eia.doe.gov/emeu/states/_use_multistate.html.

21. Tussing and Kramer, *Hydrocarbon Processing.*

22. F. M. Scherer, Alan Beckenstein, Erich Kaufer, and R. D. Murphy, *The Economics of Multi-Plant Operation: An International Comparisons Study* (Cambridge: Harvard University Press, 1975), p. 80.

23. Scherer et al., *Economics of Multi-Plant Operation,* 91.

24. For example, data from the Alaska Department of Labor and the Texas Department of Labor show that Texas, which produces only a little more oil than Alaska, has seven times as many jobs in oil and gas extraction, as measured in October 2006.

25. Quoted in Victor Fischer, *Alaska's Constitutional Convention* (Fairbanks: University of Alaska Press, 1975), p. 131.

26. Gordon Harrison, *Alaska's Constitution: A Citizen's Guide,* 4th ed. (Juneau: Alaska Legislative Affairs Agency, 2002), p. 129.

27. See Stephen L. McDonald, *The Leasing of Federal Lands for Fossil Fuels Production* (Baltimore: Johns Hopkins Press for Resources for the Future, 1979), for a discussion of the benefits of competitive leasing to private oil companies. In 1979, Alaska's oil and gas leasing law was changed to give the state the option of net profit

share leases that do not include a royalty share. However, that provision was used only one time—in the 1979 Beaufort Sea sale—and has not been used since. According to a former petroleum economist with the Department of Natural Resources, one reason that the state did not use its net-profit-share lease option is that these leases do not provide the state with royalty oil for disposition (Ed Phillips, personal communication, May 24, 1986).

28. Jack Roderick, *Crude Dreams: A Personal History of Oil and Politics in Alaska* (Fairbanks: Epicenter Press, 1997), p. 401.

29. Ibid., 248–249.

30. Ibid., 367. The other time was in 1981, when the legislature bowed to oil company pressure to revise its tax code (see Chapter 4).

31. Alaska Statutes sec. 38.05.183.

32. Alaska Statutes sec. 38.05.183(c) and sec. 38.05.183(d), respectively.

33. Alaska Statutes sec. 38.05.183(e).

34. Alaska Statutes sec. 38.06.

35. The purchasers of the proposed contract were Tenneco (50 percent share), Southern Natural Gas Co. (25 percent), and El Paso Natural Gas Co. (the pipeline sponsor, 25 percent). The contract was approved but never implemented, because El Paso did not receive federal certification for the project.

36. Jay Hammond, "Alaska's Royalty Gas: A Statewide Radio Address," Alaska Office of the Governor, Juneau, November 12, 1976.

37. Geoffrey Haynes, *Review of Alaska Royalty Oil* (Juneau: Alaska Department of Natural Resources, 1983).

38. The state sold 10.4 billion cubic feet—about one-half of one year's worth of Cook Inlet royalty gas—to the local gas distributor, Alaska Pipeline Company (Enstar), from 1977 to 1984 (Alaska Division of Oil and Gas, *Alaska Oil and Gas Report, December 2004* [Anchorage: Alaska Department of Natural Resources, 2004], p. 5-1). In addition, several natural gas pipeline companies and Dow-Shell acquired options to purchase large quantities of North Slope natural gas and gas liquids but never exercised them. This project is discussed further in the next section.

39. GVEA never took physical custody of the oil but swapped the crude oil in exchange for refined turbine fuel from Mapco (Alaska Division of Oil and Gas, *Alaska Oil and Gas Report*, 5-2).

40. A small oil refinery had been in operation in Katalla in the early part of the twentieth century but burned down in the 1930s (Rakestraw, *History of the U.S. Forest Service*).

41. Faced with the need to make large expenditures to convert the refinery from Cook Inlet oil feedstock to North Slope feedstock as Cook Inlet production declined, Chevron closed and dismantled the plant in 1991, after twenty-seven years in operation.

42. This summary of economic benefits leaves out information for the two small North Slope refineries, built by Arco Alaska (now ConocoPhillips) to serve oil field operations. Figures for employment and assessed value for these refineries are relatively small and not separately reported from those of the oil production operations.

43. Alaska Petrochemical Company, *Preliminary Proposal to Purchase Alaska State Royalty Crude and to Construct a Petrochemical Refinery Complex in Alaska* (Houston: 1977).

44. Haynes, *Review of Alaska Royalty Oil*.

45. Congress had prohibited export of North Slope crude oil, but not of products manufactured from it. The export ban, combined with the crude oil price controls and allocation rules in effect during the 1970s and other factors discussed below, caused a

wide gap to open between the price of refined products manufactured on the US West Coast from North Slope oil and the product prices in foreign markets such as Japan. This gave Alpetco a much higher margin (the difference between product price and feedstock cost) than West Coast refineries. Deregulation reduced the differential but did not eliminate it.

46. The Dow-Shell Group, *Petrochemical Development for Alaska: A Proposal* (Midland, MI: Dow Chemical, 1980).

47. The Dow-Shell Group, *Alaska Petrochemical Industry Feasibility Study: A Report to the State of Alaska* (Midland, MI: Dow Chemical, 1981).

48. The state has also recently tried to use its royalty gas as leverage to shape the course of negotiations over a North Slope natural-gas pipeline. Anadarko and Encana were awarded contracts for the option to take up to 70 percent of the state's North Slope gas royalty share, giving them a right to claim capacity of a common pipeline carrier. The idea was to force the main North Slope producers to increase the design capacity of the pipeline to encourage gas exploration.

49. Kevin Banks, Division of Oil and Gas, Alaska Department of Natural Resources, personal communication, August 5, 2004.

50. *State v. Amerada Hess, et al.,* 1JU-77-847 Civ. (Superior Court, First Judicial District). For a summary of the history of the case, see Office of Management and Budget, "Use of the Amerada Hess Settlement to Fund Capital Projects," March 8, 2005, available from (www.gov.state.ak.us/omb/06_OMB/AmeradaHess.pdf.

51. DNR staff did at one time attempt to construct a retrospective analysis of in-kind vs. in-value sales prices for royalty oil. However, this analysis was never published, due to doubts among agency staff about its accuracy (Kevin Banks, personal communication, August 5, 2004).

52. The outcomes of the state's few competitive short-term disposals illustrate the difficulty of comparing the two markets at any given time. The state sold about 6 percent of its oil in competitive sales, totaling about 50 million barrels. In the first North Slope competitive sale, held in 1981 at a time when the state believed that the in-value price was below the true market value, the average premium of winning bidders was $2.57 above in-value. All purchasers in this contract ended up losing money. When it came time to start taking the oil several months later, prices had slid, sending one firm into bankruptcy and causing another to default (Haynes, *Review of Alaska Royalty Oil*). Over the life of the one-year contracts, we estimate that the state had received less than $1.82 on average above in-value, not counting substantial legal costs to settle with the largest purchaser. In a desire to avoid repeating this experience in the next competitive sale (1985), the state allowed purchasers an option of early termination. Only three of seven contracts in that sale lasted the full year. The state also offered up to 4,000 barrels a day in competitive sales of Cook Inlet oil for export, beginning in 1987, with a Taiwanese company picking up the contract. In 1991, after the eruption of Mt. Redoubt temporarily shut down operations at the Cook Inlet westside oil terminal, the company claimed force majeure and backed out of the contract.

53. In 1980, when Congress deregulated oil prices, it passed the Windfall Profits Tax. This tax had a variable rate depending on the previous regulatory status of the oil. Cook Inlet oil was taxed at the highest rate (90 percent of the difference between the market and the previous regulated price). State royalty oil was exempt from taxation. The tax was phased out when the oil market collapsed in 1986.

54. Still another regulatory artifact that affects in-value as well as RIK oil prices relates to price adjustments for oil of differing characteristics. TAPS ships oil commingled from several different fields with varying chemical properties. Fields producing lower-quality oil pay a fee into a Quality Bank, which pays out to fields producing

higher-quality oil. Alaska refineries at North Pole and Valdez also pay into the Quality Bank when they discharge their residual oil back into TAPS. The Quality Bank charges, like other aspects of royalty pricing, reflect a legal settlement that mediates conflicting interests over a variety of issues. (See Chapter 2.)

55. Alaska Division of Oil and Gas, *Alaska Oil and Gas Report,* 5-2.

56. Kevin Banks, personal communication, February 15, 2005.

57. See Chapter 7.

58. See Chapter 2. Beginning with Tony Knowles, each successive governor has attempted to make the gasline a legacy. Knowles's approach was the 1998 Alaska Stranded Gas Development Act (Alaska Statutes sec. 43.82). The Stranded Gas Act created a mechanism for negotiating lower state and local taxes and royalties. The Murkowski administration negotiated directly with producers to obtain a development contract in 2006, posed as an amendment to the Stranded Gas Act. However, the legislature failed to ratify Murkowski's contract, largely because it was negotiated in secret and because it fixed oil as well as gas taxes for decades, a likely unconstitutional restriction on future legislatures. In addition to the administrations' initiatives, an initiative creating an Alaska Gas Port Authority with authority to sell bonds to develop the project passed in 2004, and a ballot measure that would impose a reserves tax on producers that failed to commit gas to the project failed at the polls in November 2006, under heavy negative industry pressure.

59. Specific reasons that DNR analysts give for the gas pipeline delay include (1) Exxon wants federal policy with respect to importing liquefied natural gas (LNG) changed; (2) different companies have different objectives with respect to gas development and cannot agree to a schedule; (3) MNCs require a much higher rate of return before proceeding to develop a project that can be deferred, compared to one that has a "develop it or lose it" contract provision; (4) MNCs believe that the state will become increasingly desperate for gas pipeline development and could get a better deal in the future; and (5) bringing Alaska gas to market would reduce prices in the lower forty-eight states, hurting existing sales from the same companies (Anthony Scott, Division of Oil and Gas, Alaska Department of Natural Resources, personal communication, July 26, 2007).

60. William Nebesky, Division of Oil and Gas, Alaska Department of Natural Resources, personal communication, July 26, 2007.

# 7

# Managing the Wealth

Although several other US states have oil and gas bonanzas, only Alaska has developed a comprehensive system to preserve part of its natural resource wealth for posterity.[1] This chapter examines the way Alaska has managed the wealth derived from oil and gas production, beyond the fiscal policy decisions reflected in annual budgets. It also considers the extent to which the state's investment strategy has reduced its dependence on multinational oil companies and made it less vulnerable to volatile world markets and the depletion of Prudhoe Bay.

Chapter 5 summarized the history of the Permanent Fund and Permanent Fund Dividend program in the context of state fiscal policies. This chapter recounts and analyzes in detail the development of these programs and the issues surrounding them. We begin with a discussion of the creation of the PF, the state's premier trust account. We consider the motivations explaining policymakers' decision to recommend the establishment of the PF, adopted by voters in the November 1976 elections. We also treat the early decisions of the executive and legislature to form the Alaska Permanent Fund Corporation (APFC) and the conservative investment rules guiding the PF's growth. In this section, we also discuss some other funds developed by the legislature.

Then, the chapter describes the development of the PFD program, which surely is the most popular program of any state government. The PFD program has paid out more than $14 billion to Alaskans since 1982. It has had a large impact on personal finances of Alaskans, growth of the state's economy, and the direction of fiscal policy in the state.

Next we turn to the record in growth of state wealth, from the first deposits into the PF in 1977, to 2007, when the value of the fund reached $40 billion. We treat additions to the fund by the legislature, which have nearly doubled the amount which constitutionally must be deposited into the PF. In the next section, we compare the concept of the PF with other investment funds. The PF inspired regional and municipal governments throughout

Alaska to create their own trust funds. We briefly discuss the largest regional fund, that of the North Slope Borough, and three smaller funds elsewhere in the state. Then we compare the PF with trust funds established by other nations, with a special focus on the Alberta Heritage Fund and the Norwegian Petroleum Fund.

In the last section, we consider attempts to allocate income of the PF, from the 1980s to the present, including an examination of the proposal to embed inflation-proofing of the fund in the Alaska Constitution. The chapter concludes with the continuing question: What, beyond distributing dividends, is the purpose of the PF?

## ■ Creation of the Permanent Fund

As discussed in Chapter 2, the first stream of oil wealth flowed from the Swanson River field in the Kenai Peninsula starting in 1955. This oil and gas development became increasingly important in the funding of state programs, but it was dwarfed by the colossal discovery well sunk at Prudhoe Bay in January 1968. When news of the discovery spread, oil companies pounced on the opportunity to buy state oil and gas leases. The first opportunity after the Prudhoe Bay discovery was the September 1969 state oil/gas lease sale.

This lease sale was the most productive to that point in Alaska history: oil companies paid the state over $900 million in bonuses. The immediate question was what to do with lease proceeds, but the sale was the catalyst to the formation of the PF. The state legislature appropriated funding to consider whether the lease sale proceeds should be saved or spent and invited the Brookings Institution to conduct seminars on this issue.[2]

### The Idea of a Permanent Fund

The idea of a permanent fund to protect some of Alaska's oil wealth into posterity slowly gathered support. Robert Krantz, an investment banker from Kidder, Peabody & Co., appeared before the state Chamber of Commerce convention in October 1969 and recommended the creation of a "perpetual and permanent capital fund for the continuing development of Alaska."[3] He compared the pressures to spend available capital in the home and business world with the even stronger pressures in government, which necessitated the protection of state wealth.

Within a year, Governor Keith Miller introduced legislation to establish a resources permanent fund. This legislation passed the Senate but failed in the House. Discussion of the bill introduced important issues that helped define the nature of the PF. Miller's proposal was for a nondedicated fund into which the legislature would appropriate revenues, and this raised the issue of the fund's permanence. Also, Miller's proposal appeared to entrust management of the fund solely to the legislature, raising the separation-of-power issue— lack of executive involvement as well as partisan advantage in the legislature.[4]

Meanwhile, within three years of the 1969 bonus lease sale, the legislature had appropriated nearly all of the state's $900 million windfall. Critics alleged that legislators had "wasted" the proceeds, but Alaska had hundreds of unmet needs at the time—for schools, roads, harbors, airports, public safety, and salary increases for state employees, among others. Nothing prohibited the legislature from spending to meet state needs, which prompted concern for a dedicated fund in which to store oil revenues.

## Amending the State Constitution

Alaska has a "model" constitution, written at a time of reform in state governing documents nationwide. Article IX of the Alaska Constitution had a provision prohibiting the dedication of public revenues to specific purposes, because the framers believed that dedicated funds hobbled state legislatures in their work to serve public needs.[5] Nearly twenty years after the crafting of the state constitution, the common perception was that this ban limited the state's ability to preserve its wealth into the future.

In 1975 and 1976, both the legislature and Republican governor Jay Hammond made plans to create a state permanent fund. The legislature passed an act establishing a permanent fund, proposing to allocate 50 percent of mineral lease bonuses to the corpus of the fund.[6] The act provided for investments into the fund as state surplus funds accumulated, and investment earnings could be reinvested, used to pay for administrative costs, or appropriated for any other capital or operating budget purpose.[7] This was the first legislative act creating any kind of dedicated fund.

Governor Hammond expressed sympathy for the legislature's intent, but vetoed the legislation because it violated the constitutional prohibition against dedicated funds and, in his view, allocated too large a portion (50 percent) to the fund. He called for an amendment to the state constitution, and in the following year's legislative session, he introduced his bill to accomplish that.[8] Hammond proposed that only 10 percent of mineral lease bonuses be deposited in the fund. The legislature raised the cap to 25 percent, and the bill passed each house with large majorities.[9]

In the November 1976 elections, voters decided on this amendment to the state constitution:

> Section 15. *Alaska Permanent Fund.* At least twenty-five percent of all mineral lease rentals, royalties, royalty sale proceeds, federal mineral revenue sharing payments and bonuses received by the state shall be placed in a permanent fund, the principal of which shall be used only for those income producing investments specifically designated by law as eligible

for permanent fund investments. All income from the permanent fund
shall be deposited in the General Fund unless otherwise provided by law.

Voters approved this constitutional amendment by a 2 to 1 margin, and in retrospect, it is the most significant change of constitution in the state's history.
During the limited public debate about creation of the fund, many ideas for its
use were discussed. The closest approach to a policy statement was a paper
issued by the state Department of Revenue. It reasoned that the fund could
save money for the future, control spending by government, assist in the economic diversification of the state, share revenue with local governments, even
assist capital construction in communities, pay for services, and aid community businesses.[10] However, the constitutional and statutory language is silent
about its objectives. Simply, it is a "permanent" fund whose principal must
remain untouched except to produce income, and that income is available in
the state's general fund for the legislature to appropriate as it wishes.

## Management of the Fund

In the next four years, policymakers explored several options to focus the PF.
The governor expanded the State Investment Advisory Committee and asked
it to consider organizational structure and investment possibilities for the PF.[11]
The immediate management issue was resolved by having the commissioner
of revenue invest the PF conservatively. The House of Representatives established the Special Committee on the Permanent Fund, chaired by Rep. Clark
Gruening, which held hearings statewide. The legislature hired consultants, as
did the executive, to provide advice on management structure and fund purposes.

The management issue was whether the PF should be under the control of
an executive department, such as Revenue. This was the sentiment of the
Alaska Senate Special Committee on the Permanent Fund. The House dis-
agreed, believing that the management should be independent of the state government in order to insulate decisionmaking from politics while retaining
accountability.[12] The legislature ultimately, in 1980, adopted the House view,
and created the APFC as a government corporation with six trustees. Four
trustees were to be public members, appointed by the governor to staggered,
four-year terms. The fifth trustee is the sitting commissioner of revenue, and
the sixth is another cabinet member selected by the governor.

Policymakers did not specify the purposes of the fund, beyond those mentioned constitutionally, but they did reach consensus on the strategy of PF
investments. Although there was then (as there remains today) support for
investment in Alaska businesses and use of the PF as a state development
bank, the majority of policymakers (and nearly all consultants) believed the PF
should be a savings account, not an in-state development fund, and that it

should follow the "Prudent Man Rule" (meaning the avoidance of speculative and risky investments), which too was adopted into statute.[13]

By 1980, then, Alaska had a PF directed toward the safe accumulation of wealth, protected by a board of appointed officials, independent of both executive and legislature. Effectively the PF had two parts, one holding the untouchable principal, and the second containing undistributed income, since 1986 called the "earnings reserve account."

## Other Alaska State Funds

A factor conditioning executive and legislative acceptance of the Prudent Man Rule and an independent state corporation was creation of other funds, more clearly directed to state development needs. None of these funds was constitutionally protected, and in some cases ambiguous statutory language barely protected them from the charge of violating the Article IX prohibition against dedicated funds. In 2007, the seven state public corporations (excluding the Permanent Fund) had combined total assets of $9.3 billion, most of which has been employed in building physical infrastructure or making investments.[14]

Large development funds included the Alaska Renewable Resources Corporation, the Alaska Science and Technology Commission, the Alaska Housing Finance Corporation, and the Alaska Industrial Development and Export Authority. The Alaska Renewable Resources Corporation represents the checkered history of several development efforts. It was established in 1978 to expand the fishing, timber, and other renewable resource industries into new kinds of in-state production and processing through subsidized loans. However, bankrupt enterprises and loan defaults soon overwhelmed the program, and the legislature abolished it in 1982.[15]

Governor Cowper proposed the Alaska Science and Technology Commission in 1988, to spur the economy through applied research and development. This fund made grants from the income of its investments, but unlike the PF had no formal earnings reserve account. When the fund experienced large losses in 2001–2002, at a time of state budget deficits, the legislature declined to deposit additional funds and closed it down.

The Alaska Housing Finance Corporation (AHFC) has an old pedigree. It began in the territorial era (1949) as the Alaska Housing Authority to manage federal urban renewal funds in Alaska. In 1959, at statehood, the housing authority became the major source of housing assistance, including both rental and home-ownership programs. It bonded for government office space and continued urban renewal programs, which accelerated after the 1964 earthquake. In 1971, the legislature transformed the authority into a public corporation with the mission to provide affordable housing through offering financing at below-market rates. Initially, assistance was for low- and middle-income residents, but in the 1980s, these restrictions were lifted. This mission has been enlarged over the years to include community planning and development, technical assistance, tax credits, weatherization programs, and the like. AHFC sells bonds to provide funding for its programs. (Like all the state's public corporations, initially the legislature capitalized it.) By mid-2006, its net assets were $1.99 billion, and in FY 2007, it transferred $80.6 million as a "dividend" to the state's general fund. Total transfers to the state through FY 2006 were greater than $1.5 billion.[16]

The Alaska Industrial Development and Export Authority (AIDEA) was established in 1981. Its mission is to develop infrastructure to advance private enterprise in regions throughout the state, such as roads, ports, airports, utilities, and facilities for tourism destinations. All facilities projects are supposed to produce sufficient revenues to repay AIDEA's investment. Examples of its investments include the port and road for the Red Dog Mine, the Skagway ore terminal, the marine center dock in Unalaska, an aircraft maintenance facility for Federal Express in Anchorage, the Alaska Seafood Center (Anchorage), the Snettisham hydroelectric project near Juneau, and the Healy clean coal project.[17] Its largest program is providing loans to develop, refine, or enhance Alaska business enterprises. It is a partner of the US Export-Import Bank in providing loans for export transactions. Also, it has rural development initiatives and small business economic development programs. Finally, AIDEA acts as a conduit for issues of taxable as well as tax-exempt bonds. In mid-2006, AIDEA's net assets were $856 million, and in FY 2007, it transferred $16.6 million to the state's general fund. Since establishment of its dividend program in 1996, AIDEA has produced $204 million in contributions to the state treasury.[18]

Five additional corporations spread the developmental reach of the state in other directions: in transportation (Alaska Railroad), post-secondary education (Alaska Student Loan Corporation [ASLC]), energy management (Alaska Energy Authority), local government assistance (Alaska Municipal Bond Bank Authority [AMBBA]), and even into space (Alaska Aerospace Development Corporation).

As mentioned, some development funds went bankrupt, illustrating the high risk of investment in Alaska's private sector. Yet the funds satisfied constituent pressures for development assistance, which otherwise likely would have hammered the Permanent Fund. Dave Rose, the Alaska Permanent Fund Corporation's first executive director, made this point in a 1997 interview:

> One of the reasons I think the subject (using the PF as a development bank) has not been revisited is because we built other institutions in Alaska to take the pressure off the Permanent Fund and off the retirement funds so that they would not be in the development area. That is one of the reasons we have a very strong Alaska Industrial Development and Export Authority; why we have a very strong Alaska Housing Finance Corporation; why we have a Bond Bank; and why we still have vestiges of the

energy organization now vested in AIDEA. All of these, to some degree, served as blockers.[19]

Finally, four of the profitable corporations (AHFC, AIDEA, ASLC, and AMBBA) returned dividends to the state, depicting a possible scenario for the earnings reserve account of the PF.

The state's only other constitutionally protected fund is the Constitutional Budget Reserve, established by voters in 1990 at the end of the Cowper administration. This fund was designed to receive money the state expected to win in litigation over oil taxes and royalties, and it was to be used only in case of significant decreases in state revenues.[20] As noted in Chapter 5 and summarized in Figure 7.1, the CBR has buffered the state during its nearly two-decade period of declining oil production, during more than half of which oil prices were low. In the view of some commentators, the CBR, with a balance of $2.7 billion in FY 2007 (from a high of $5 billion, deposited over several years), has played a role intended for the PF itself—to protect basic state services when natural resource revenues decline.

## ■ Permanent Fund Dividends

Even before the establishment of the PF, Governor Hammond had recommended a cash distribution of PF income to residents of the state. His propos-

**Figure 7.1  Constitutional Budget Reserve History, April 1991 to May 2007**

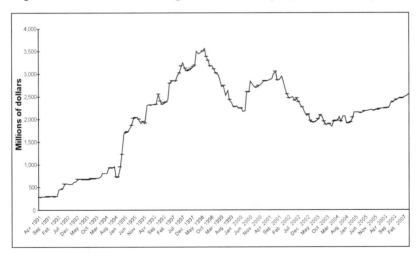

*Source:* Alaska Legislative Finance Division.
*Notes:* CBRF Subaccount starts July 2000. Withdrawals from the CBRF occur when the general fund sufficiency balance slips below $100 million.

al, called Alaska Inc., would have made payments to registered voters of one share for every five years of residency, based on a 50 percent payout annually of the PF's annual income.[21] Although introduced to the legislature in 1977, the bill did not emerge from either of the houses.

Governor Hammond's proposal gradually gained support from legislators, in the context of discussions mentioned above to find an appropriate management structure and to decide whether the fund should be prudently managed or used as a development portfolio. In a 1980 memo to Rep. Hugh Malone, Hammond wrote that a dividend program would "provide benefits to all Alaskans from the earnings of their resource wealth"; it could "confine benefits to Alaskans" and "would equitably impact both rich and poor." It would "retain the taxpayers' one remaining tie with, and consequent concern for, government growth: How much it costs them." At the same time, it would "maximize favorable impact upon the state's economy by keeping a far larger portion of the money to fund the programs here in Alaska."[22]

The program adopted by the legislature in 1980 embodied two of these arguments. First, dividends were considered the most efficient way to deliver the benefits of petroleum development equally to all state citizens. Second, advocates argued that dividends would create a popular constituency with a vested interest in protecting the fund from raids on its principal.[23] Many proponents of the program also believed that it would provide a way to curb government inefficiency and bureaucratic growth.

The legislation endorsed by Governor Hammond and enacted by the legislature gave every Alaska resident $50 for each year he/she had lived in Alaska since statehood in 1959. This embodied the concept of "durational residency," which had been favored by legislators previously, as seen in the Alaska Pioneers' Homes (nursing homes established in territorial days for seniors who had lived in Alaska for at least 10 years) and the Longevity Bonus (monthly payments to seniors aged 65 or older). Many states have this concept embedded in laws that favor residents over newcomers in tuition charges for state universities, hunting/fishing licenses, and other benefit programs. Supporters clearly hoped that the graduated payments would be less of an incentive for migration to Alaska than an equal payment to each resident, while rewarding long-term residents over newcomers.

Anchorage attorneys Ron and Patricia Zobel (who then had been in the state less than one year) took the state to court, arguing that durational residency violated their rights to equal protection under the Alaska and US Constitutions. The Alaska Supreme Court sided with the state, and the Zobels then appealed to the US Supreme Court. While awaiting the high court's judgment, Governor Hammond urged the legislature to enact "backstop" legislation, to provide for a dividend under an equal distribution formula if the high court ruled against the state. Initially, the legislature was reluctant to act on an unpopular dividend formula, but after the governor threatened to either call legislators into special session or veto funding for preferred projects, they complied.[24] This legislation provided dividends in equal amounts to every six-month resident of the state, and it passed late in the 1982 legislative session. When the US Supreme Court decided in an 8-1 vote that the original durational residency scheme was unconstitutional, Alaska was prepared to distribute checks in the amount of $1,000 to all eligible residents. Thus was born the Alaska PFD program.

From 1982 through 2006, the dividend program has paid out more than $14 billion to eligible Alaskans. (The amount of the annual dividend is determined by adding net income of the PF in the previous five years, multiplying it by 21 percent, dividing by two, and then dividing by the number of eligible applicants.) The healthy size of dividends is a product of both inflation-proofing the PF and adding additional appropriations into it. Had legislators not transferred large amounts from the earnings reserve account into the fund principal, overall PFD distributions would have been less than one-third to one-half what they amounted to. Because the base of distribution is a rolling average of the previous five years, amounts have varied from year to year, as indicated in Table 7.1.

As noted in Chapter 5, an Alaska resident who began collecting dividends in 1982 would have gained a total of $27,536.41 by the distribution in October 2007. The annual PFD distribution typically accounts for about one-quarter of the state's annual budget. The announcement of dividends is greeted with acclaim throughout the state. Instantly, firms announce sales, especially of items such as snowmobiles, cars, and vacation and travel packages.

ISER has conducted several studies of the impact of the PFDs on the Alaska population and economy.[25] ISER's 1984 study showed that for 26 percent of the population, the PFDs brought a 10 to 25 percent increase in family income; it represented greater than a 25 percent rise in family income for 13 percent of the population.[26] Sampling a portion of 1982 and 1983 dividend recipients, this 1984 study found expenditures of 5 to 15 percent for consumer purchases such as plane tickets, home appliances, and similar items; 15 to 25 percent was saved; about 5 percent went to debt reduction; 20 percent to taxes; and between 35 and 55 percent for day-to-day living expenses, including food, housing, and clothing.[27]

ISER's 1989 study of the impact of the PFD on the Alaska economy found a significant multiplier effect, meaning that spending and respending of dividend proceeds probably created around 5,600 jobs in the state (for the previous year, 1988).[28] Indeed, PFDs are now an important driver of the Alaska economy, and they have tended to reduce somewhat the volatility of Alaska's boom-and-bust cycle. The PFD is the primary means (to the present) through which the state's investment strategy has reduced dependence on multinational oil companies.

Political scientist Gordon Harrison notes that the distributive effects of the

**Table 7.1    Annual Per Capita Permanent Fund Dividend**

| Year | Dividend |
|------|----------|
| 1982 | $1,000.00 |
| 1983 | $386.15 |
| 1984 | $331.29 |
| 1985 | $404.00 |
| 1986 | $556.26 |
| 1987 | $708.19 |
| 1988 | $826.93 |
| 1989 | $873.16 |
| 1990 | $952.63 |
| 1991 | $931.34 |
| 1992 | $915.84 |
| 1993 | $949.46 |
| 1994 | $983.90 |
| 1995 | $990.30 |
| 1996 | $1,130.68 |
| 1997 | $1,296.54 |
| 1998 | $1,540.88 |
| 1999 | $1,769.84 |
| 2000 | $1,963.86 |
| 2001 | $1,850.28 |
| 2002 | $1,540.76 |
| 2003 | $1,107.56 |
| 2004 | $919.84 |
| 2005 | $845.76 |
| 2006 | $1,106.96 |
| 2007 | $1,654.00 |

*Source:* Alaska Permanent Fund Corporation, *An Alaskan's Guide to the Permanent Fund,* 11th ed. (2005), p. 29, and authors' compilation.

PFDs are different from those of state spending, as "the money is paid directly to the entire statewide population rather than to a comparatively small number of well-paid state employees who serve various target groups with special programs that would in turn receive most of the benefits if it were appropriated for conventional state activities."[29] In this sense, PFDs have reduced income inequality in the state. Particularly, they have been a boon for poor families in rural Alaska, for whom they constitute a large part of annual income.

A later study, by the Alaska Permanent Fund Corporation itself, suggests that as the PFDs have become a predictable event, a greater portion of them may be saved. In 1994, a sample of respondents indicated that they would be saving half or more of their PFDs in that year.[30] This finding conflicts with what economists call the "permanent income hypothesis"—to wit, that consumers are not likely to strongly react to predictable changes in their income. Perhaps in response to the first PFD of $1,000, an unpredictable event, Alaska residents saved a large portion of their payments. Yet when PFDs appeared annually, and then predictably every October, residents spent most of them.[31] Princeton economist Chang-Tai Hsieh tested the permanent income hypothesis with a sample of Anchorage residents receiving PFDs from 1980 to 2001. He found that "households in Alaska smooth their dividend payments" in a manner consistent with the hypothesis. They did not change their consumption patterns, as they did when receiving an unexpected payment, such as an income tax refund that was difficult to predict.[32]

Little additional research has been conducted on the impact of the PFDs on individuals and families in Alaska. What is abundantly clear, however, is that the dividends have created a powerful constituency in support of the PF itself and opposed to any expenditure of PF earnings that might challenge the annual payout of dividends.

## ■ Growth in State Wealth

### *Increase in Fund Value*

From the first deposits in 1977, the PF has grown enormously (as seen in Figure 7.2). The total unaudited fund value as of July 13, 2007, was $40 billion. In FY 2006, the PF produced an 11 percent return, following a 10.4 percent return in the previous fiscal year, and a 14.2 percent rate of return in FY 2004.[33]

**Figure 7.2   Permanent Fund Historical Returns, 1985–2006**

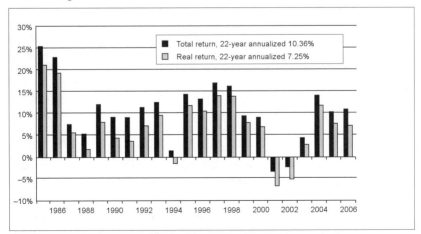

*Source:* Communications Department, Alaska Permanent Fund Corporation.
*Note:* Total return minus inflation equals real return.

At the start, PF moneys were placed only in the most secure investments. Gradually, investment targets were diversified to include foreign stocks and real estate. Amendments in 1982 to the statutes establishing the Permanent Fund required that it be administered in accord with the "Prudent Investor Rule," a legal standard that provides guidelines to investment managers regarding the management of an investment portfolio in a legally satisfactory manner. Alaska statutes delineate the responsibilities of the PF trustees:

> The prudent investor rule as applied to investment activity of the fund means that the corporation shall exercise the judgment and care under the circumstances then prevailing that an institutional investor of ordinary prudence, discretion, and intelligence exercises in the designation and management of large investments entrusted to it, not in regard to speculation, but in regard to the permanent disposition of funds, considering preservation of the purchasing power of the fund over time while maximizing the expected total return from both income and the appreciation of capital.[34]

What this means in practice is that decisions of the trustees are to be judged following four criteria:

- Decisionmaking procedures are based on the best available knowledge, fully transparent, and replicable.
- Assessment of risk is based on the total portfolio as opposed to individual investments.
- The portfolio is to be diversified, both with respect to geography and type of investment.
- Liquidity is required, considering the goals and cash-flow needs of the eventual recipients of the fund.[35]

The six-member Board of Trustees in recent years has followed an investment strategy that is designed to produce an average annual real (inflation-adjusted) rate of return of 5 percent. (In the 22-year period from FY 1985 to FY 2006 [as noted in Figure 7.2], the PF's real rate of return was 7.25 percent. The total annualized return for 23.5 years [to mid-2007] was 10.42 percent; the real rate of return for this period was 7.31 percent.[36]) Trustees have an annual asset allocation target. In 2007, the asset allocation was 26 percent in domestic and nondollar bonds, 54 percent in domestic and international stocks, 10 percent in real estate, and 10 percent in alternative asset classes.[37]

The PF is operated as a savings account, not a standard endowment. Two early trustees, Elmer Rasmuson and George Rogers, persuaded the legislature to adopt the policy of inflation-proofing the PF. Typically this is accomplished by redepositing fund earnings into the principal of the fund. Inflation-proofing the fund has protected its earning power, while limiting the revenues available from the earnings for expenditure.[38]

In testimony before the House Judiciary Committee in 2001, Trustee Gruening stated that only one-third of the value of the PF came from the constitutionally mandated 25 percent of mineral proceeds. Some two-thirds of the fund's value resulted from the legislature's having made deposits from state revenues, including inflation-proofing the fund.[39] Over the history of the PF, some 52 percent of fund earnings have been saved, in the form of inflation-proofing the principal ($9 billion), special legislative appropriations to the principal ($4.2 billion), and retaining the earnings reserve ($1.4 billion). The remaining 48 percent of fund earnings have been spent on PFDs, with the exception of $300 million transferred to the state's general fund (used to pay for administration of the PF).[40]

In 2007, the Alaska Permanent Fund was one of the world's 100 largest investment trusts. It has had an effect on local governments in Alaska and on competing funds globally.

## Alaska's "Baby" Permanent Funds

Alaska's Permanent Fund has inspired some municipalities in the state to adopt their own trust funds. As of 2007, four municipalities have done so: Sitka, the North Slope Borough, Anchorage, and Fairbanks. We discuss each in turn.

The North Slope Borough is the largest and richest regional government in Alaska. It covers about 20 percent of Alaska's land, and includes all of the oil-producing areas of northern Alaska. The depletion of Prudhoe Bay oil will more directly affect this region than any other in the state, as its rate of oil dependence is in excess of 90 percent. In 1984, borough voters approved the establishment of the North Slope Borough Fund to preserve part of borough wealth into the future. By March 31, 2000, the fund's corpus was $482 million; its unaudited value in early July 2007 was $575 million.[41] The North Slope fund has a target rate of return of 8 percent, but in most years has exceeded this. Through charter changes in 1997, 5.5 percent of the rolling average total value of the fund is transferred to the general fund annually. The principal amount of contributions and growth in excess of annual transfers remains in the fund in perpetuity.[42] In 2004, the borough code was further amended to permit transfers to the borough general fund of between 0 and 8 percent. The previous percentage was believed to be too limiting when the borough was facing deficits. In FY 2007, the transfer from the fund to the operating budget amounted to $23.6 million and constituted 9 percent of this budget.[43]

Sitka, an early capital of Alaska during territorial days (and capital of Russian America), was the second unified municipality to establish a permanent fund, the year after that in the North Slope Borough. Sitka had saved millions of dollars when state revenue sharing and municipal assistance grants washed through Alaska's cities and boroughs in the early 1980s. The current value of the Sitka Permanent Fund is $22 million, and it too is protected in the municipal charter. Sitka policymakers attempt to achieve a 9 percent rate of return on the fund. (In 2003–2006, it was closer to 7 percent.) The borough assembly allocates 6 percent of the fund to the municipal general fund (based on a three-year average of fund value), along with small revenues from land leases, and the remainder of all earnings is used to inflation-proof the fund. The assembly also appropriates proceeds from land sales to the fund.[44]

The other two funds—in Anchorage and Fairbanks—were created after privatization of municipal utilities services. In 1998, Anchorage sold the Alaska Telephone Utility and then in 1999 banked $118 million into the city's trust account. The fund is protected in the municipal charter, and to make any change in it requires a vote of the people. In 2007, this account was worth $150 million, and it has established a 5.19 percent real rate of return. The municipal assembly annually appropriates 5 percent to the general fund, based on a five-year average of the fund's value, with the remainder of earnings used to inflation-proof the account.[45]

In 1996, Fairbanks city voters approved the sale of the Municipal Utilities Service to private firms. The selling price was $150 million, which after the deduction of debt left $100 million. The following year, voters established the Fairbanks Permanent Fund with that amount. The Fairbanks fund also is protected in the city charter. The city council annually draws down 4 percent of the fund's value, based on a five-year average of its market value, and deposits this into the operating budget. An additional 0.5 percent is used for capital needs of the city.[46] The Fairbanks fund, like Sitka's, is protected by the "percent of market value" (or POMV) approach, regarded as the most progressive method to insure that inflation does not erode the principal of trust funds.[47] The approach was established through a voter initiative in Fairbanks in 2002. Now totaling $110 million, the Fairbanks fund has reached an average rate of return in the 6 percent range, before adjusting for inflation. Thus with a payout of 4.5 percent annually, it is not fully inflation-proofed, and this poses a future problem for city policymakers.

The four baby funds share two characteristics. Each local government is a "home rule" municipality, governed under a charter, and the trust funds are protected in the charter. They can only be modified by a vote of the people. Second, each fund makes an annual payment into the operating budget of the municipality, based on a 3- to 5-year rolling average of the market value of the account. Two of the funds—in Sitka and Anchorage—are managed conservatively and are effectively inflation-proofed, in that the annual dividend to the operating budget is less than the real rate of return of the fund, and the balance is redeposited into the corpus of the fund. In the case of Fairbanks and the North Slope Borough, there is the potential that the corpus of the funds will be eroded, as a greater amount may be transferred to the jurisdiction's operating budget than the real rate of return of the fund.

## Comparisons of the PF to Other Investment Funds

The superior record of performance of the Alaska Permanent Fund is nearly unmatched, on a global basis. A late-1980s comparative study of Alaska's PF with oil-generated savings accounts in other countries suggests the advantages of the methods and rules adopted to manage Alaska's fund. The report author, political scientist Thomas Stauffer, distinguished Alaska's fund from three groups of funds. The first, "negative savers," including Algeria, Mexico, Venezuela, and Nigeria, spent most of their oil revenues, including windfall profits. The second group, "passive savers," including Saudi Arabia and Libya, saved some of their oil wealth, but did so on an ad hoc basis.[48]

Alaska's PF compared favorably with the third group of countries, which "institutionalized their savings." The five countries in this group as of the late 1980s were Iran, United Arab Emirates, Oman, Kuwait, and briefly Canada's Alberta Province. The funds of Alaska, Oman, and Kuwait were all trust funds. Second, the funds of Alaska and Kuwait were invested mostly outside of the oil-producing region. (Less than 1 percent of PF assets have been invested in Alaska.) In Stauffer's words, this reduced the inflationary impact on the domestic economy of too rapid expenditure of natural resource income, the so-called "Dutch disease."[49]

The circumstances of Alaska's oil wealth have little to do with oil-producing regions of Latin America, the Middle East, and Africa. Alaska is a circumpolar northern state, and its oil development region compares best with other northern regions. Two northern states have investment funds—Canada's Alberta province and the nation-state of Norway—that can be compared reasonably to the Alaska Permanent Fund.

The Alberta Heritage Savings Trust Fund (AHF) is a natural comparative reference point to the Alaska Permanent Fund. It was established in the same year, 1976, and for similar reasons—to save oil wealth and to reduce the volatility of Alberta's nonrenewable-resource-based economy. Yet the purposes, management structure, investments, returns, and prospects of the AHF differ greatly from those of the PF.[50]

Introducing the legislation creating the AHF, Alberta premier Peter Lougheed specified four objectives of the fund: to provide "a future source of revenue," to "reduce the debt load" of the province, to "improve the quality of life in this province," and to "strengthen and diversify the economy."[51] The fund was not constitutionally protected, and it has been managed by the government, not an independent board or corporation.

Initially, the parliament deposited $1.5 billion (Canadian) into the AHF, and from 1976 to 1983, some 30 percent of revenues from oil and natural gas production went to the fund; but then in 1984, these deposits were halved. In 1987, the provincial government ceased making transfers into the fund for ten years. By this cutoff date, the AHF had received C$12 billion, which was its growth peak. Thereafter, the provincial government placed oil and gas revenues in general revenues to pay for current government expenses. No inflation-proofing of the fund was done, and the value of the fund eroded until restructuring occurred in 1997.[52]

At its inception, the AHF was composed of three divisions. An Alberta Investment Division absorbed the lion's share of mineral revenue transfers. Its mission was to make debt or equity investments to diversify Alberta's economy, but most investments were loans to Crown corporations—Alberta Mortgage and Housing Corporation, Alberta Agricultural Development Corporation, Alberta Municipal Financing Corporation, and Alberta Government Telephone. Allan Warrack and Russell Keddie of the University of Alberta's business faculty allege that this division was used "as a political lever—indirectly covering shortfalls in government revenue from ailing Crown corporations."[53] A second branch, the Canada Investments Division, made loans at below-market rates to other provincial governments or government agencies. Until 1982, when lending activity ceased, this division made more than thirty loans to provinces such as Newfoundland, New Brunswick, Manitoba, and Quebec and to government enterprises. The third branch, the Capital Projects Division, invested in projects to bring social and economic benefits to Alberta such as medical research facilities, schools, and transportation and communication projects.[54]

Alberta's investment goals were more diverse than those of the Alaska PF; it did not follow the Prudent Investor Rule; and it invested primarily in-province. Yet, the overall rate of return was above 9 percent. The fund value in 2007 stood at C$16.6 billion, 37 percent of the PF total. The AHF flushed nearly $30 billion through the Alberta economy, created jobs, and addressed a number of social and economic needs.[55]

The restructuring of the AHF in 1997 changed the asset mix to increase returns, making it more like an endowment. An oversight committee as well as a private sector advisory committee increased transparency somewhat, but the AHF remained a Crown corporation and Warrack and Keddie conclude that it remains "a political lever used to implement and reinforce public policy decisions" and that "the direction of the fund is dependent on the desires of the government of the day."[56]

The Petroleum Fund of Norway (in 2006 renamed the Government Pension Fund–Global) presents an interesting contrast to the PF and AHF. Norway's North Sea was a late entry to global oil production, and the Norwegian Petroleum Fund (NPF) was established only in 1990. The motivation behind its establishment was to reduce the inflationary pressures of huge oil revenues on the Norwegian economy, as well as lessen volatility from fluctuating oil prices. Norway's take of oil revenues has been greater than that of either Alaska or Alberta, because a national oil firm, Statoil, earns profits, while the state collects both corporate taxes and exploration license fees from multinational oil firms.[57]

It was the Norwegian Parliament that established the NPF in 1990, and like the AHF, it lacks constitutional protection. The parliament left the fund under government control. The Ministry of Finance has delegated operational control to Norges Bank Investment Management, a division of the Norwegian Central Bank. Parliament also loosely allocated to the fund whatever budget surplus remained each year after funding Norway's expansive welfare state and clearing government deficits. For example, in 2004, transfers from the fund to finance the budget deficit were $11 billion (or about 10 percent of expenditures).[58] Given the government's concern with reducing pressure on the domestic economy, it is understandable that the NPF has invested substantially in foreign assets. At least half of its portfolio (split 40-60 into investments in equities and fixed-income instruments) is in bonds, stocks, and derivatives, with most investments in Europe but a substantial number in the United States.[59]

Rognvaldur Hannesson, an economist with the Norwegian School of Economics and Business Administration, objects to the NPF's guidelines, which do not focus on the Prudent Investor Rule.[60] Yet the fund outpaces both the AHF and PF—and in fact most global investment funds. It is Europe's largest public fund; in 2007, the fund totaled 1.908 trillion Norwegian krone (US$389 billion). In 2006, it earned a cumulative return of 7.9 percent, and experts expect it to double by 2010.[61] If the funds were divided equally among residents, in 2007, each Norwegian would receive $78,000 compared to $28,000 for each Alaskan and $4,500 for each Albertan.

This comparison emphasizes the different decisions made in the attempt to reduce price volatility and address depletion of nonrenewable resources. A first difference is the "permanence" of the investment funds. We have focused on constitutional protection, which has greater meaning in separation of power systems with independent judiciaries than in parliamentary states. Both the AHF and NPF could be erased by a new party coalition in parliament breaking links with the past.

A second difference across cases is the management structure. Only the PF has a hands-off relationship between fund managers and government. The AHF management is little different from a government department, which prompts critics to allege that investments have been made on political grounds. The NPF is subject to the same criticism, as observers worry about using fund earnings to cover large budget gaps.

Investment strategies of the funds differ too. In most of its history, the AHF has resembled a development bank and invested most of its resources in Alberta. Both the PF and NPF resemble endowments and invest mainly outside their political jurisdictions. The PF has the clearest mission to increase wealth. Hannesson notes that the PF has "demonstrated the usefulness of the investment fund approach as a device for turning non-renewable resource wealth into a permanent wealth."[62] In Norway, while the NPF is not managed as a pension fund, the money is to be used for pensions in the future, to finance Norway's pay-as-you-go retirement system. These investment strategies obviously have affected the size of the funds, with both Alaska and Norway outperforming Alberta.

The objectives of the funds reflect differences in political culture among the three jurisdictions. The Canadian political culture emphasizes collectivism and is supportive of (in fact, appears deferential to) government direction. Norway is a modern welfare state with a social responsibility ethic. Alaskans, on the other hand, prize individualism and are ambivalent about government.

Alaska has the only oil-generated trust that consistently issues dividends to residents (the AHF has issued small dividends on occasion), and many believe that this is what has protected the PF against legislative raids during times of low oil prices and economic downturns in the state. Unlike most of the other political jurisdictions, Alaska's procedures for fund management are transparent, and this is directly related to the democratic character of American state systems. Also, the legislature has been under constant pressure to preserve the dividends.

## ▓ Attempts to Allocate Income from the Permanent Fund

For twenty years, attempts to allocate the income of the PF have occupied public discourse. Each administration has proposed ways to use fund earnings to benefit the public broadly, but with pronounced differences of emphasis.

### Proposals to Allocate the Earnings Reserve

Efforts to allocate the earnings reserve of the PF began in the Cowper administration (1986–1990). The governor proposed the creation of an education endowment, which would have placed earnings from the fund into an endowment dedicated to K–12 schooling. The proposal gained enthusiastic support from the state's education community, but many Alaskans (including the most vocal at public hearings held statewide on the issue) feared "raids" on the fund and a quick diminution of PFDs. The governor's proposal died in the legislature.

Governor Hickel did not introduce legislation to divert fund earnings into normal or exceptional state government programs. During his last term in office (1990–1994), however, he did question the purpose of the PF. On several occasions, he suggested that part of the fund earnings be used for community construction and other local projects statewide. He believed that a "community dividend" (without specifying how it would be paid and by whom) would make lasting improvements to cities and towns, whereas the PFDs led to consumption without permanent benefits.

During the Knowles administration (1994–2002), the state's political environment was polarized. The new Democratic governor confronted a Republican legislature at a time when Prudhoe Bay oil had passed the production high point and oil prices remained low. In 1996, for the first time, PF earnings exceeded oil/gas revenues to the state. Knowles emphasized the necessity of long-range fiscal planning, frequently addressed the press on fiscal issues, and convened a long-range bipartisan fiscal-policy task force to develop a plan. This combined executive-legislative task force considered tax increases, spending cuts, and use of fund earnings to pay for government services. However, none of the task force proposals gained legislative approval.

In 1997 and 1998, the Alaska Humanities Forum held a large statewide conference and conducted 100 town hall meetings in 41 communities on the PF called "The Role of the Permanent Fund in Alaska's Future: The Principles and Interests Project." Participants in the town meetings had the opportunity to offer their opinions on the use of the PF earnings reserve and other public policy questions, as indicated in Table 7.2.

Respondents were not a random or representative sample of Alaskans. Nevertheless their answers are instructive. Only a small minority believed in cashing out the PF. About one-third believed that no part of earnings should be used except to protect the PF principal and maximize dividends. Presented with four proposed uses of the earnings reserve, only one-fourth supported investment in the private sector. Some 46 percent supported using earnings to

**Table 7.2   Alaskans' Opinions on the Permanent Fund**

| "How do you feel about these approaches to using Alaska's public wealth in the permanent fund?" | Percentage Agreeing |
|---|---|
| a. Put all permanent fund earnings back into the fund to provide maximum growth of dividends, *even if* this means continued cuts to the state budget to match decreasing oil revenues. | 35 |
| b. Use the permanent fund or fund earnings to create endowments for public programs, such as education, arts, etc., *even if* this means future dividend checks would not grow as fast. | 56 |
| c. Use the permanent fund or fund earnings to invest in commercial and industrial projects in Alaska, *even if* this means future dividend checks would stay the same or get smaller. | 26 |
| d. Distribute some permanent fund earnings to communities to build infrastructure, *even if* this means future dividend checks would not grow as fast. | 53 |
| e. Use some permanent fund earnings to increase the current level of state services, as determined by elected representatives, *even if* this means future dividend checks would not grow as fast. | 46 |
| f. Give each Alaskan here today their share now, either $38,000 lump sum or stock shares in the permanent fund, *even if* this means future Alaskans (unborn children or people who move here later) would not receive any benefits. | 13 |

*Source:* Adapted by the authors from Alaska Permanent Fund Corporation, *Alaskans Speak Out on Public Policy Choices, Trustees' Papers,* Vol. 6 (Juneau: 1999), p. 55.

increase state services. Only two options gained majority support: building infrastructure in communities (53 percent) and creating endowments for public programs (56 percent). These responses show lack of consensus on the use of fund earnings.

The pivotal year in the campaign to use fund earnings for government services was 1999. A much-studied proposal would have appropriated a portion (the figure mentioned most often was 5 percent) of PF earnings to the general fund, and it seemed to enjoy legislative support. However, few legislators were willing to make the decision, which under law they were empowered to make, and the Republican leadership proposed an advisory statewide ballot proposition on the issue. Opposition quickly formed to the proposal, with conservatives calling it yet another attempted raid on the PF. However, many of those inclined to support the plan believed the measure was too restrictive and would not have much of an impact on long-term budget sustainability. Led by the state's largest newspaper, the *Anchorage Daily News,* the coalition of die-hard and ad hoc opponents publicized negative commentary. The "no" votes on the statewide proposition totaled 83 percent of the electorate. This vote has made it very difficult to consider allocation of fund earnings to support government services.

From 2002 to 2006, Alaska had a Republican governor (Murkowski) and a Republican legislature and efforts continued to use fund earnings for public programs. Although the governor had campaigned to respect the PF and PFDs, shortly upon taking office he suggested that the PF could be used to leverage economic development.[63] Also, he called a "conference of all Alaskans" in 2003 to consider fiscal issues among others. Conference delegates reworked the 1999 proposal and adopted it, but this did not emerge from either house of the state legislature during the governor's tenure. A creative approach—to use some PF earnings to pay interest on bonds to finance large capital projects in the state—did issue from the state Senate in the second-to-last year of the governor's tenure, but the House declined to adopt it.

## Constitutional Protection of Inflation-Proofing

Although the PF amendment to the state constitution prohibits expenditure of the fund principal, there is no similar prohibition of spending from the earnings reserve account. This may be appropriated by the legislature for any lawful purpose. As mentioned, these earnings have grown significantly since the mid-1980s. The PF trustees state their "greatest fear for the future is not the markets, it's overspending. As Alaska's public leaders begin to contemplate the use of Fund earnings for more than just the dividend program, the Trustees are mindful that the Fund is not as well protected as it could be."[64]

The PF trustees have urged the legislature to adopt another constitutional amendment, which would enshrine the POMV approach into the state's basic law:

> The Trustees believe that the sustainable yield for the Fund is five percent each year. They have proposed amending Alaska's constitution to limit withdrawals from the Fund to no more than five percent of the Fund's average total value for the previous five years. Because the Trustees' investment goal is a five percent annual return after inflation, limiting spending to five percent of the Fund would still allow it to grow at the rate of inflation.[65]

The trustees' proposal would limit withdrawal to a maximum of 5 percent of the PF's value. This 5 percent would provide a cushion to pay dividends and leave a residual amount (estimated in 2003 dollars to reach $175 million to $300 million) to appropriate if the legislature voted to do so.[66]

From FY 2004 to FY 2007, the PF's annual return has been over 10 percent, but financial markets inevitably will decline at several points in the future. If markets decline when low prices reduce the state's oil revenues, POMV would insure normal growth of the PF.

The legislature has considered the trustees' POMV proposal but has yet to adopt it. In 2003, at a time of low oil prices, the state Senate conducted votes on several versions of the proposal. As a proposed constitutional amendment, a two-thirds vote was necessary, but legislative supporters were unable to attain even a majority. Most legislators feared opposition from the public if they were to permanently assign any part of the PF's undistributed income. They feared that the public would accuse them of "raiding the fund," which would mean certain death to reelection prospects.[67] This issue has not been revisited since the 2005–2007 surge in oil prices produced large surpluses for the state.

Thus, in 2007, the PF was used to make money, which pays for annual PFDs, inflation-proofing, and small management expenses. There is no consensus about other uses of the PF at present in Alaska, and because of high oil prices in 2005–2007, there has been no pressing need to divert earnings to specified public purposes.

## ■ Conclusions

The Alaska Permanent Fund is one of the most successful fiscal institutions of any US state, and one of the most successful public investment funds worldwide. It was established by amendment to the state constitution in 1976, and in 2007 was valued at $40 billion. Several factors explain the growth of the fund and in turn the wealth of the state. First, the PF amendment required the state to deposit 25 percent of mineral revenues into the fund, and it did so at a time when oil prices were relatively high.

Second, since 1982, fund managers have followed the Prudent Investor Rule. They were averse to risky investments, and they diversified the fund—

both in domestic and foreign stocks, bonds, and real estate. Their procedures were transparent. Third, the legislature increased the value of the fund by voluntarily depositing additional funds in it. State statute requires inflation-proofing of the fund, and 52 percent of the earnings of the PF have been redeposited into its corpus.

Under the leadership of a populist governor, Hammond, the legislature established the Permanent Fund Dividend program in 1982. Over the history of this program, each Alaska resident (present in the state since 1982) has drawn $27,536.41 from PF earnings. This has provided a solid constituency in support of the PF and in opposition to any attempt to "raid the fund."

Although PFDs go to rich and poor Alaskans, they are of the greatest benefit to Alaska's lower middle class and poor population (many of whom live in remote villages in rural Alaska). The dividends have a strongly positive impact on the state's economy, and this impact reduces the state's dependence on the multinational oil industry. The annual October distribution of PFDs is nearly as popular as Christmas throughout Alaska, and firms large and small gear advertising campaigns to capture this largesse.

The popularity of the PFDs has made it very difficult for policymakers to enact legislation to spend earnings of the PF. In 1999, voters by a margin of 83 percent opposed using even "a portion of the permanent fund to help balance the budget." Lawmakers justifiably fear a backlash at the polls if they support using fund earnings for education, infrastructure such as roads and airports, or assistance to Alaska's struggling municipalities. To many Alaskans, however, reinstituting an income tax or assessing a state sales tax does not make sense when the state is distributing cash annually in the form of PFDs.

In 1996, for the first time, net income from the PF surpassed state oil revenues. It seems likely that the Alaska Permanent Fund will be in place when Alaska's oil and gas resources are depleted and multinational firms have left the state. It will, however, take a large fiscal crisis for Alaskans willingly to allocate a portion of fund earnings to pay for government services. For these reasons, then, the purpose of the PF is to save Alaska's oil wealth into posterity and to distribute part of the earnings from that wealth to every eligible Alaskan.

### ■ Notes

1. Wyoming, Montana, and Texas have natural resource funds, but none of these can be considered a "permanent" fund.

2. Joan Kason, "The Creation of the Alaska Permanent Fund: A Short History." In *The Early History of the Alaska Permanent Fund: The Trustee Papers,* Vol. 5 (Juneau: Alaska Permanent Fund Corporation, 1997), p. 13.

3. Quoted in ibid., 14.

4. Ibid.

5. See Gerald A. McBeath, *The Alaska State Constitution: A Reference Guide*

(Westport, CT: Greenwood Press, 1997), pp. 175–176; and Gordon Harrison, *Alaska's Constitution: A Citizen's Guide* (Juneau: Alaska Legislative Affairs Agency, 2002), pp. 149–151.

6. The legislative vehicle was Committee Substitute for House Bill 324 amended Senate.

7. Kason, "The Creation of the Alaska Permanent Fund," 15.

8. Sponsor Substitute for House Joint Resolution 39.

9. Kason, "The Creation of the Alaska Permanent Fund," 15.

10. Ibid., 16.

11. Ibid.

12. Ibid., 20

13. Rural Research Agency, "Alaska's Permanent Fund: Legislative History, Intent, and Operations." In *The Trustee Papers*, Vol. 5 (Juneau: Alaska Permanent Fund Corporation, 1997), pp. 47, 55–56.

14. Alaska Department of Revenue, *Spring 2007 Revenue Sources Book* (Juneau: Oil and Gas Audit Division, 2007), p. 74; also see Institute of Social and Economic Research, "The Alaska Citizen's Guide to the Budget: 6. State Assets," Anchorage (2002), accessed December 12, 2006, at http://citizensguide.uaa.alaska.edu/6.STATE_assets/6.State_Assets.htm.

15. Gerald A. McBeath and Thomas A. Morehouse, *Alaska Politics and Government* (Lincoln: University of Nebraska Press, 1994), p. 67.

16. See Alaska Housing Finance Corporation, *2006 Annual Report* (Anchorage: 2007), p. 3.

17. Alaska Industrial Development and Export Authority, *2006 Annual Report* (Anchorage: 2007), p. 4.

18. Ibid., 18ff.

19. Quoted in Alaska Permanent Fund Corporation, *Changes to the Investment World During the Permanent Fund's First Two Decades. Trustees' Papers,* Vol. 4 (Juneau: 1997), p. 30.

20. McBeath and Morehouse, *Alaska Politics and Government,* 128.

21. Kason, "The Creation of the Alaska Permanent Fund," 17.

22. Quoted in ibid., 20–21.

23. McBeath and Morehouse, *Alaska Politics and Government,* 64.

24. Clifford J. Groh and Gregg Erickson, "The Permanent Fund Dividend Program: Alaska's 'Nobel Experiment.'" In *The Early History of the Alaska Permanent Fund: The Trustee Papers*, Vol. 5 (Juneau: Alaska Permanent Fund Corporation, 1997), p. 31.

25. This section follows Gordon S. Harrison, "The Economics and Politics of the Alaska Permanent Fund Dividend Program." In Clive S. Thomas, ed., *Alaska Public Policy Issues* (Juneau: Denali Press, 1999), pp. 85–86.

26. Ibid., 85.

27. Ibid.

28. Ibid., 86.

29. Ibid.

30. Ibid.

31. I thank Scott Goldsmith for this observation.

32. Chang-Tai Hsieh, "Do Consumers React to Anticipated Income Changes? Evidence from the Alaska Permanent Fund," *The American Economic Review* 93, no. 1 (March 2003): 404. See also, Martin Browning and M. Dolores Collado, "The Response of Expenditures to Anticipated Income Change: Panel Data Estimates," *The American Economic Review* 91, no. 3 (June 2001): 681–692.

33. Alaska Permanent Fund Corporation, *2006 Annual Report* (Juneau: 2006), p. 19.

34. Alaska Statute sec. 37.13.120(a).

35. Rural Research Agency, "Alaska's Permanent Fund: Legislative History, Intent, and Operations." Reprinted in *The Early History of the Alaska Permanent Fund: The Trustee Papers,* vol. 5 (Juneau: Alaska Permanent Fund Corporation, 1997), p. 56.

36. Laura Achee, APFC Communications Director, personal communication, August 14, 2007, and Alaska Permanent Fund Corporation, *2007 Annual Report* (Juneau: 2007), p. 25.

37. See http://www.apfc.org/ accessed on November 25, 2007.

38. Ibid., 54–55.

39. Alaska Permanent Fund Corporation, "Making the Case for Complete and Protected Inflation-Proofing," *The Trustees' Papers*, Vol. 7 (Juneau: 2001), p. 4.

40. Alaska Permanent Fund Corporation, *An Alaskan's Guide to the Permanent Fund*, 11th ed. (Juneau: 2005), p. 31.

41. John Ames, Director, Department of Administration and Finance, North Slope Borough, personal interview, July 18, 2007.

42. North Slope Borough, "Financial Summary" (Barrow, AK: Department of Administration and Finance, June 15–16, 2000), p. 9.

43. North Slope Borough, "FY 2006–2007 Operating Budget, Revenue Summary," p. A-7.

44. David Wolf, city finance manager, Sitka, personal interviews, December 13, 2006; July 18, 2007; and August 10, 2007.

45. Dan Moore, treasurer, Municipality of Anchorage, personal interviews, December 13, 2006; July 18, 2007; and August 10, 2007.

46. Pat Cole, Fairbanks city manager, personal interviews, December 13, 2006; July 23, 2007.

47. Bert Wagoner, Alaska Permanent Capital Management, Anchorage, personal interview, December 13, 2006.

48. Alaska Permanent Fund Corporation, *Wealth Management—A Comparison of the Alaska Permanent Fund and Other Oil-Generated Savings Accounts Around the World. Trustees' Papers*, Vol. 3 (Juneau: 1988), pp. 4–5.

49. Ibid., 10.

50. See Peter Smith, "The Politics of Plenty: Investing Natural Resource Revenues in Alberta and Alaska," *Canadian Public Policy* 17 (1991): 139–154, for a comparison of both funds from 1976 to 1989.

51. Quoted in Glen Mumey and Joseph Ostermann, "Alberta Heritage Fund: Measuring Value and Achievement," *Canadian Public Policy* 16, no. 1 (1990): 30.

52. Allan Warrack and Russell Keddie, "Alberta Heritage Fund vs. Alaska Permanent Fund: A Comparative Analysis," Alaska Permanent Fund Corporation, unpublished papers, no date, p. 4, 6.

53. Ibid., 3.

54. Ibid., 3.

55. See "Heritage Fund Historical Timeline," accessed July 18, 2007, from www.finance.gov.ab.ca/business/ahstf/history.html.

56. Warrack and Keddie, "Alberta Heritage Fund vs. Alaska Permanent Fund," 7.

57. Yet Klapp argues that domestic opposition to Statoil from shipowners and fishermen "limited the ultimate share the state itself could get from bargaining with the MNCs." See Merrie Klapp, "The State—Landlord or Entrepreneur?" *International Organization* 36, no. 3 (1982): 605.

58. Alan Cowell, "Is Norway's Oil Pool Deep Enough? Aging Baby Boomers Loom over a Fund Financed by Petroleum," *New York Times*, January 1, 2005.

59. The NPF follows strict ethical guidelines in making investments. It does not invest in firms making cluster bombs, landmines, nuclear weapons, or related components, which means that General Dynamics, Northrop Grumman, Boeing, and Lockheed Martin are on its blacklist. The NPF made the news in 2007 when it added Wal-Mart Stores to this list (selling off more than $400 million in Wal-Mart shares), stating that the retailer had tolerated child-labor violations by suppliers in LDCs and obstructed unions in the United States. See Mark Landler, "Norway Backs Its Ethics with Its Cash," *New York Times*, May 4, 2007.

60. Rognvaldur Hannesson, *Investing for Sustainability: The Management of Mineral Wealth* (Norwell, MA: Kluwer Academic Publishers, 2001), p. 67.

61. See Mercer Inc., *Norwegian Government Pension Fund–Global: Annual Performance Evaluation Report 2006* (London: Mercer, 2007).

62. Hannesson, *Investing for Sustainability*, 66.

63. Bill McAllister, "Alaska Officials Eye Oil Fund in Budget Crisis," *Anchorage Daily News*, February 6, 2003.

64. Alaska Permanent Fund Corporation, *An Alaskan's Guide to the Permanent Fund*, 44.

65. Ibid., 45.

66. "APFC Analysis of SJR 13." In *Making the Case for Complete and Protected Inflation Proofing*, p. 8.

67. Gene Therriault, Alaska State Senate (and then senate president), personal interview, December 13, 2006.

# 8

## Protecting the Environment

We have noted that oil from Alaska's North Slope has produced about 75 percent of state general fund revenue for thirty years. Pumped through the 800-mile Trans-Alaska Pipeline to Valdez and shipped to refineries in California, the Gulf Coast, and even briefly to East Asia, North Slope crude supplied an average 21 percent of US petroleum production in the 1980s and 1990s. State and federal dependence on the multinational oil corporations that explore, develop, and produce North Slope crude would seem to limit government's ability to regulate oil and gas development in the public interest, notwithstanding the fact that the land and subsurface estate of almost all current North Slope oil-producing regions are owned by the public. This dependence underlies the subject of this chapter. Specifically, we ask the following:

- What is the nature of the regulatory regime protecting Alaska's environmental resources?
- How does the oil industry influence the state's environmental regulatory regime, especially the laws, policies, and the permitting process for establishing, expanding, and monitoring oil fields?
- How does oil and gas development complement and conflict with development and utilization of Alaska's other natural resources—for example, sand and gravel, water and ambient air, and fish and game resources—and the cultural resources of the North Slope's Inupiaq population?

A wealth of data contributes to the answers. Federal, state, and borough regulatory offices bulge with document files describing the interplay of industry and government. Journalistic accounts, consultant reports, interest group manifestos, even some scholarly analyses offer explanations. Of greatest value are the participants in the oil and gas regulatory process—agency officials, political leaders, industry employees, Native community residents, and environmental group representatives—who have freely shared their views. This study takes advantage of all these sources of data, but it is most informed by interviews with the participants.[1]

An advantage to the crafting of this analysis is the existence of a 1981 baseline study.[2] This makes it possible to investigate the change over time of the oil and gas environmental regulatory regime[3] on the North Slope, comparing the early 1980s with the early twenty-first century. The argument unfolds in four parts. First, we present the authorities and agencies for environmental regulation of oil and gas development in Alaska. Second, we summarize the kinds of environmental disturbances—to land, water, and air—that necessitate regulation and the major issues in environmental regulation. Third, we briefly consider environmental issues related to transportation of oil and gas to market. Finally, we analyze the state's role as regulator vis-à-vis the oil industry.

## ▓ The Structure of the Regulatory Regime: Authorities and Agencies for Environmental Regulation

We review the laws and some regulations that authorize government agencies to protect North Slope environmental resources during oil and gas exploration and development. We also consider interest group access and pressures on this system.

### Government Agencies and Their Authority to Mitigate Resource Impacts

All three tiers of government are actively involved in the regulation of oil and gas development on Alaska's North Slope. Federal government agencies act based on public laws, executive orders, and regulations. State government agencies follow state statutes, administrative orders, interagency agreements, and regulations. North Slope Borough agencies rely on delegated authority from the state and on local ordinances.

*Federal agencies, laws, and regulations.* Six agencies spearhead most federal activity on the North Slope. The Fish and Wildlife Service (FWS) of the Department of the Interior administers three public laws. The Fish and Wildlife Coordination Act of 1934 (as amended) authorizes the agency to review federally licensed water-resource development projects and to attach protective conditions on US Army Corps of Engineers' permits in navigable waters. The Endangered Species Act of 1973 authorizes FWS to control and prohibit the taking of threatened or endangered species.[4] Amendments to this act in 1994 prohibited the harassing,[5] catching, and killing of marine mammals (primarily polar bears and bowhead whales). As a result, FWS issues letters of authorization for the incidental take of marine mammals (polar bears and Pacific walrus), called Incidental Harassment Authorization (IHA). Finally, the Migratory Bird Treaty Act of 1918 gives FWS authority to control disturbances of bird habitat.

The National Marine Fisheries Service (NMFS; since 2004 called NOAA-Fisheries) of the US Department of Commerce is a mirror image of the FWS and shares authority with it under the Endangered Species Act. NMFS is the primary federal agency regulating the marine environment of the 200-mile exclusive economic zone of the United States. It enforces the Marine Mammal Protection Act, which protects nearshore and offshore marine resources. NMFS issues IHAs (for whales, sea lions, and seals) and may require industry to sign plans of cooperation with the Alaska Eskimo Whaling Commission and the North Slope Borough. NMFS also has new authority to monitor endangered fish habitats and Steller sea lion recovery plans.

The second Interior Department agency with regulatory authority is the Minerals Management Service (MMS). The federal government's Outer Continental Shelf (OCS) program off the North Slope began in 1976, selling leases valued at $3.5 billion, but only two leases have proceeded toward development—Northstar and Liberty (put on hold by BP in January 2002). (See Figure 2.2 for locations.) MMS approves development and production plans, approves pipeline applications, and issues permits to drill. It has approval authority in dredging and is the permitting agency for operations on islands. The Oil Pollution Act of 1990 increased the financial obligations of the oil and gas industry. Under the act, MMS monitors whether companies have sufficient contingency funds to compensate for environmental damage resulting from work in the OCS and on state-submerged lands.[6]

A third Interior agency, the Bureau of Land Management (BLM) operates with authority allocated by the Outer Continental Shelf Lands Act Amendments of 1978. This legislation gives BLM the responsibility to balance orderly energy resource development with protection of human, marine, and coastal environments. BLM is the lead federal agency in the federal-state Joint Pipeline Office (JPO), which monitors the Trans-Alaska Pipeline corridor, discussed below.

The Environmental Protection Agency (EPA) has major powers under the National Environmental Policy Act of 1969. NEPA requires federal agencies to prepare a detailed EIS for all major federal actions significantly affecting the quality of the human environment.[7] Under the Federal Water Pollution Control Act (commonly called the Clean Water Act [CWA] of 1972), EPA is authorized to issue National Pollution Discharge Elimination System (NPDES) permits for discharges into navigable waters. This permit process is established largely on the basis of industry self-monitoring, with heavy penalties for infractions. Under NPDES, state and federal regulators provide permits to all facilities that discharge wastes into public waterways. NPDES permits require industrial sources of pollution to install the "best practicable pollution control technology."[8]

The Clean Air Act of 1970 as amended in 1977 sets ambient air quality standards, which EPA enforces nationally, and standards for new source performance; it provides authority to issue Prevention of Significant Deterioration (PSD) permits, which are designed to insure that air quality is protected from becoming materially more polluted. The EPA also is affected by the Oil Pollution Act of 1990, which codified the relationships of state and federal agencies as to onshore and offshore oil spills.[9]

The Corps of Engineers (COE) has the oldest authority under the Rivers and Harbors Act of 1899—to issue permits for dredging and filling in navigable waters and wetlands. Because nearly all North Slope lands are considered wetlands (as are most of the other lands in Alaska), all oil and gas development requires COE approval. The second basis of the COE's authority is the CWA, which authorizes COE to issue permits for all projects (called 404 permits) that require placement of fill or dredged material on wetlands. A specific executive order (11990) enhances the COE's protection of wetlands.

Two other federal agencies engage less frequently in North Slope regulation. The National Oceanic and Atmospheric Agency (NOAA, the parent agency of NMFS) has general supervisory responsibility under the Coastal Zone Management Act of 1972 and under the National Historic Preservation Act of 1966. The US Coast Guard has a role under the Rivers and Harbors Act, too, in permitting construction of bridges and causeways. It also approves oil discharge prevention and contingency plans.

*State agencies.* The state of Alaska, through its statutes and regulations, directly affects oil and gas development activities. Three state resource departments are the primary actors: the DNR, the ADFG, and the DEC. The JPO issues pipeline rights-of-way (ROWs) for changes to the pipeline corridor incidental to new oil/gas developments. State resource agencies examine the overall effects of any project. Thus, there is an artificial separation of pipeline from processing in the way state agencies treat projects.

Three divisions within DNR contain most of its regulatory personnel. The Division of Oil and Gas (DOG) both regulates and facilitates oil development. Under Alaska Statute 38, it prepares a five-year leasing schedule and determines whether lease sales are in the state interest. DOG issues lease operations approvals and geophysical exploration permits. The Division of Land (DOL) has joint authority (with the Division of Mining and Water Management [DMWM]) to approve oil company plans of operations and development. It issues miscellaneous land-use permits (to cross tundra, for example) and approves sales of state-owned materials, such as gravel and water. DMWM issues regular and temporary water-use permits, the latter for authorization to use water for ice road construction.

ADFG has broad authority for the protection of fisheries and game resources in Alaska.[10] Under Title 41, the department issues permits regarding anadromous fish and critical habitat. It may require fishways, and it has commenting authority on plans of operations and miscellaneous land-use permits. ADFG also reviews water-use permits issued by DMWM and issues letters of nonobjection to construction and development using state waters. In exercising its wildlife-protection responsibilities, ADFG sometimes defers to the authority of the North Slope Borough under the Alaska Coastal Management Plan (ACMP).[11]

The Department of Environmental Conservation is the state version of the national EPA. Under Title 46 of Alaska Statutes, it issues solid-waste and wastewater facility and disposal permits. Additionally, it issues air quality control (PSD) permits, surface oiling permits, permits for disposal of hazardous substances, and oil discharge permits.[12] DEC is the state's lead agency in oil-spill planning and response, under tough legislation adopted after the *Exxon Valdez* oil-spill disaster of 1989; it approves oil-discharge prevention and contingency plans. Recently, it required applicants to complete a "best available technology" plan as part of its contingency plan review. Perhaps its broadest authority, however, is to issue "certificates of reasonable assurance" for discharge into navigable waters, the section 401 clearance required on all COE permits. This is the second delegation of EPA power to the state.[13]

A relatively new agency, the Division of Governmental Coordination (DGC), was lodged within the Office of Management and Budget in the governor's office until Governor Murkowski transferred it to the Department of Natural Resources in early 2003, where it became the Office of Project Management and Permitting (OPMP). An executive order of Governor Sheffield created the agency in 1984 in an attempt to streamline the state's permitting process. OPMP is the lead agency for large-projects permitting, and it coordinates the consistency review (discussed further on in this chapter) of state action with the Alaska Coastal Management Plan, enacted by the legislature in 1977.

The AOGCC issues permits to drill. AOGCC is an independent regulatory agency placed in the Department of Administration for bookkeeping purposes. Broadly, it regulates oil reservoir management. Regulators witness safety-valve inspections and the plugging in and clearance of exploratory wells. The Division of Parks and Outdoor Recreation (within DNR) has authority under both the National Historic Preservation Act of 1966 and the Alaska Historic Preservation Act of 1971. It reviews permits and checks compliance in the excavation of historical sites, coordinating its work with the History and Culture Department of the North Slope Borough.

*Local agencies.* Title 29 of Alaska statutes gives local governments the authority to adopt zoning ordinances, which restrict development within the jurisdiction of the borough or North Slope villages. The North Slope Borough has used this authority to develop its zoning ordinance, Title 19 of the borough municipal code. By the authority of the ACMP, it has developed the North Slope Borough Coastal Management Program, adopted by the borough assembly in 1984. Two borough departments—planning and wildlife management—implement the borough's zoning code. The borough also comments on state and federal permits. Through the ACMP process, the borough may object to the issuance of a final consistency determination by the state, or request an elevation to the state resource agency directors if it disagrees with a permitting decision.

Other North Slope organizations are involved in the permitting process, too. For example, as part of an agreement with NMFS in July 1997, oil industry operators signed annual "Open Water Conflict Avoidance Agreements" with the Alaska Eskimo Whaling Commission (AEWC) and the Whaling Captains' Associations of Barrow, Kaktovik, and Nuiqsut. The agreement specifies working guidelines and communication procedures for implementation during fall migrations of bowhead whales.[14]

## Government Policies and Permits

Either in laws or regulations, federal, state, and local governments make policy statements concerning the way in which oil and gas development should proceed. Such statements set the tone for the permitting process and influence the drafting of stipulations attached to permits. Alaska has policy statements for each of the four possible types of environmental disturbance—to land, water, air, and noise/activity.

Policy statements on mitigating the effects of disturbances to land surfaces are comprehensive. The state has a mandate to manage land and water resources, as well as minerals, in a manner consistent with the long-term public interest. To minimize adverse effects of oil and gas development on the land surface of the North Slope, the state developed policies concerning permanent facilities, coastal planning, consolidation of material sites, and rehabilitation. During research and exploration phases prior to actual oil and gas development, permanent facilities other than drill site pads normally are not permitted. This includes roads and airstrips.

Generally, the state's policy is that development on state waters be held to a minimum, and that water bodies important to fish and wildlife be protected, expressed most clearly in the ACMP. The ACMP also specifies managing barrier islands and lagoons in a manner that will maintain adequate flows of sediments, detritus, and water. It discourages activities reducing the use of these areas by coastal species. Too, ACMP seeks management of rivers, streams, and lakes so as to protect natural vegetation, water quality, habitat, and natural water flow.

Policies to mitigate the effects of pollution are part of the statutes, as in the following: "It is the policy of the state to conserve, improve, and protect its natural resources and environment and control water, land, and air pollution, in order to enhance the health, safety, and welfare of the people of the state and their overall economic and social well being."[15]

No general policy statement comprehends the mitigation of effects of noise and human/machine activity, but statute assigns responsibility to the Department of Fish and Game. This agency is to "manage, protect, maintain, improve, and extend the fish, game, and aquatic plant resources of the state." Particular attention is paid to avoiding unnecessary disturbance to wildlife and to the protection of endangered species and their habitat, as well as highly productive or critical habitats of other species. Statutes explicitly discourage harassment of wildlife, even if it is the unintended consequence of another activity, and the interruption or alteration of historic migratory routes.

The bias of law, regulation, and policy is to prohibit development activities posing a risk of environmental disturbance, but to allow exceptions, on a case-by-case basis. In the nearly four decades of intensive exploration, development, and production of oil on the North Slope, agencies developed a series of measures through the permitting process, in order to mitigate disturbances to land and water bodies and reduce the risk of pollution.

Initially, agencies attached stipulations to individual permits after review. (At the federal level, these restrictions are called "conditions.")[16] Although each permit is still reviewed individually on a site-specific basis, standard stipulations, often derived from general concurrences,[17] are used to protect against a range of comparable disturbances. For example, a standard stipulation places seasonal and spatial restrictions on such activities as drilling, placement of fill, and construction. Another regulates use of ground contact vehicles for off-road travel. More recently, in several areas, oil companies have incorporated mitigation measures into their operational plans. For example, BP has a routine practice of orienting ice pads and arranging pad layouts in relation to the prevailing wind direction in order to minimize drifting snow that can provide hiding places for polar bears. In other instances, state agencies have required oil companies to submit waste management plans and wildlife response plans as part of their permit applications, which saves costs by having industry regulate itself.

Special stipulations, on the other hand, address a particular concern at a specific stage of development, for a given species or area—for example, restrictions on activity in the nesting region of the peregrine falcon, different start-up times for on-tundra activities depending on the impact or magnitude of the operations, or rerouting ice roads around known grizzly bear dens. Recently, regulatory agencies have added "advisories" to permits, recommending actions such as forming local spill response teams and imposing constraints on drill rig activities to limit toxic emissions.

In general terms, stipulations have had the effect of resolving specific issue disputes related to the use of land and water resources, and for the prevention of pollution. Usually, they involve a close working relationship between the applicant and the agency. Oil and gas development has proceeded, albeit less rapidly than industry might prefer. Major species have been protected, and other resource values have been considered.

### Integrated Management Systems

The issuing of a single permit invariably involves multiple agency review, usually with both state and federal agencies. For these reasons, coordination of the regulatory process is particularly important. Three coordinating systems are used in the regulation of large projects: the coastal-zone consistency determination process, the EIS review, and JPO right-of-way approvals, discussed here.

All of the activities needing a federal permit also require a consistency determination with Alaska's Coastal Management Plan. Typically, the COE will receive application for a 404 permit, which it transmits to interested parties as part of the public notice requirements. The state Office of Project Management and Permitting in the DNR is notified, and it sends copies to interested state agencies, which have thirty days to respond. OPMP collects the comments of state agencies and sends them on to COE. The COE must have the state's consistency determination in order to issue its permit. However, and this point is important to critics of redundancy in the regulatory regime, the consistency determination is submitted separately; it is not formally a part of the federal EIS system.

For large projects that may have major environmental effects, according to NEPA rules an environmental assessment (EA) is undertaken. If an EA finds there would be significant consequences, an EIS is required. This constitutes the broadest examination of issues, and it must consider alternatives, comparing their environmental as well as social and economic impacts. A small number of EISs have been done on the North Slope. The first and most significant was the Trans-Alaska Pipeline EIS, and the second was for the Prudhoe Bay Water Flood Project. Since then, EISs have been required more frequently, as oil and gas development has moved offshore and oil companies propose new technologies not tested for Arctic conditions. Thus, EISs were done for Endicott, Northstar, and Liberty oil field developments. EISs also have been done for federal OCS and NPR-A lease sales.

For most of the North Slope EIS reviews, the COE has been the lead agency. It is typically joined by FWS, EPA, NMFS, and MMS. The state of Alaska has the opportunity to serve as a "cooperating agency,"[18] meaning that it sits at the table with federal regulators, or it may be a "commenting agency," which places it at a distance from the federal government. In the recently completed EIS for the Northstar field, the state declined to be a cooperating agency, both because of the expense and because of the legal limitation on the ability of agencies to work with the oil company in the design process.[19] However, the COE invited the North Slope Borough, with a long-standing concern about OCS development, to sit with the federal team.

The regulatory process has a mechanism for settling interagency disputes as well. By interagency agreement, stipulations to permits or leases can be attached by state agencies other than the issuing agency. If the agencies disagree on a stipulation, they are instructed to hold meetings to work out their differences. If resolution is not achieved (an infrequent occurrence), the dispute can be elevated to division directors, to the commissioner level, and to the governor. Elevations have occurred only on large projects such as development of offshore facilities, pipelines, and causeways where agency missions conflict. A similar resolution mechanism is used at the federal level but has been used even less often than at the state level. Examples are ARCO's construction of a drilling pad at Kuparuk and the inclusion of waters offshore of ANWR in an OCS lease sale. The most recent federal elevation concerned the subsea pipeline location in BP's Northstar project. When conflicts are elevated, decisions may be made rather abruptly. It is therefore usually not in the interest of lower-level officials to have disputes settled over their heads, and elevation is discouraged by the commissioners or secretaries in cases not involving vital state or federal interests.

At the start of the Murkowski administration (2002–2006), the governor made DNR the state's lead agency on all oil/gas development issues. Because the decision was controversial (with other state agencies as well as with environmentalists), it may not be permanent.

## Interest Group Access and Pressures

Three types of interests regularly participate in the oil and gas regulatory process: the oil and gas industry, environmental nongovernmental organizations (NGOs), and Native organizations. Oil companies are involved at each stage. Most of the North Slope exploration, development, and production activity is done by two multinational oil corporations: BP and ConocoPhillips. Through recent mergers and acquisitions, they are the world's third and fifth largest oil firms, respectively. Both BP and ConocoPhillips maintain large environmental-services, regulatory, and government-relations staffs, with headquarters in Anchorage. The world's largest oil company, ExxonMobil, has ownership interests in many North Slope fields, including Prudhoe Bay and Kuparuk; however, in 2007 it operated no major Alaska oil field. With fewer than fifty employees in the state, ExxonMobil has limited contacts with state and federal regulators, but this will change if its leasehold at Point Thompson is developed. A midnight act of the Murkowski administration was to enjoin ExxonMobil for failing to develop this field.

Smaller, national oil companies, such as Marathon, Anadarko, Unocal, and Forest, as well as ANCSA corporations (Cook Inlet Regional Inc. [CIRI] and Arctic Slope Regional Corp. [ASRC]) often are partners of BP and ConocoPhillips or have smaller, independent operations. They are less of a presence in the state's regulatory process. Finally, two trade associations follow state regulations and enter the political process. The Alaska Oil and Gas Association (AOGA) represents eighteen owner and operator companies. It regularly monitors state resource agencies and the state's coastal zone consistency process. Second, the Alliance represents about seventeen to eighteen large oil-field contractors that perform diversified services for the oil companies, including VECO, ANCSA corporations such as Doyon and NANA, and oil-transportation firms such as Crowley Navigation. The Alliance is more active in tracking legislation and participating in election campaigns than in the regulatory process.

Alaska has a large number of environmental NGOs, more than fifty active ones, and there is a division of labor: The Audubon society looks at birds; the Wilderness Society at landscape changes; the Alaska Center for the Environment (with the largest membership at 10,000) works on state lands issues.[20] Many are state branches of national (and a few international) environmental organizations, which have only a token presence in the state. Most active in the monitoring of North Slope oil and gas development have been the Northern Center (located in Fairbanks), Greenpeace, Trustees for Alaska, the Sierra Club, and the National Wildlife Federation. Members of these groups frequently contact agency officials, with a preference for state over federal offices because the former allow easier access. They use Freedom of Information Act (FOIA) authority to review documents in the permitting process. Their representatives speak at public hearings held as part of major projects' review, and they submit comments for the record, with federal commenting opportunities better than those at the state and local levels.

In the 2000 and succeeding elections, the Alaska Conservation Voters, an umbrella group, ranked candidates for state legislative races and provided polling data for them, but it has been much less prominent in campaigns and elections than the oil industry (see Chapter 3). A sister organization, the Alaska Conservation Alliance, brings together forty conservation organizations. It has an oil and gas issues group, which negotiates positions. Groups of environmental organizations have used the federal courts (district and appellate) to influence oil and gas development. For example, Trustees for Alaska, representing several environmental groups, sued the US Army Corps of Engineers over its permitting of Alpine oil field development without requiring an EIS. And Greenpeace sued the US Minerals Management Service for permitting Northstar development on two grounds: that it paid insufficient attention to cumulative effects and that it lacked a detailed trajectory analysis for oil spills. Although neither suit was successful, both affected oil industry and agency operations.

Native organizations are less active participants as interest groups, largely because many of their interests are incorporated in the governmental regulatory process. The North Slope Borough has regulatory authority and participates with other governmental agencies in major projects and permitting reviews. The AEWC and Whaling Captains, as mentioned, are quasi-governments in bowhead whale monitoring. Only when the borough's position diverges from tribal interests have other Alaska Native groups become active, seen for example in the objection of the Inupiat Community of the Arctic Slope, a regional Native organization, to development in the OCS at Northstar, and Gwitch'in opposition to the opening of ANWR for oil and gas development.

## ◼ Environmental Issues in Oil and Gas Development on Alaska's North Slope

### *Pattern of Development*

North Slope oil development faced conditions common in the Arctic: a relatively pristine environment, easily degraded by industrial activities; Native populations still engaged in subsistence hunting and fishing, which supplied the majority of their daily caloric intake; and inclement climatic conditions that challenged oil production technology. This focused attention on instituting the least intrusive method of development—creation of an industrial enclave remote from population centers and a regulatory regime highly protective of environmental values.

Prudhoe Bay is a super-giant oil field, the largest in the United States. From the discovery well in 1968 until the mid-1980s, only Prudhoe Bay and the adjacent Kuparuk field (the nation's second-largest) produced oil (see Chapter 2). Then the pattern changed, with a proliferation of oil-field developments, for three reasons. First, the prospect of declining Prudhoe Bay oil production gave both the oil industry and the state an incentive to spur development of new sources of petroleum. Second, the established infrastructure lowered production costs. Also, technological developments in the oil industry made it possible for the oil industry to profitably develop reservoirs once considered marginal, as production costs dropped to one-fourth of those in the late 1960s.

The technological changes also have had environmentally benign effects. Five specific changes bear mention (also see discussion in Chapter 2). First, directional (extended reach) drilling changed the way the oil industry taps distant petroleum accumulations. From a single pad, operators have access to a larger area, to a distance of four miles. Second, exploration and production footprints have been reduced by more than 80 percent through closer spacing of wellheads and construction of smaller pads. Third, drilling efficiency has increased because of the acquisition of advanced seismic data and interpretation. Fourth, disturbances to tundra declined as industry created roadless developments and used winter ice roads (leaving little trace after breakup) instead of gravel roads. Finally, industry increasingly has reinjected drilling mud and other industrial waste into wells instead of disposing of it in surface reserve pits.

Nevertheless, oil development still presents a risk to critical habitats and gravel, water, and cultural resources that engage the regulatory regime. In its operation over a generation, the regulatory system—its information requirements, its handling of emerging issues such as cumulative impacts and climate change, the sufficiency of authority, redundancy and delay, as well as the failure of reform—has become an issue as well.

## Habitat Protection

Physical disturbances to the North Slope environment become issues when they affect resources of value to humans—fish, game, and other biological resources used in subsistence pursuits. As industrial activity on the North Slope has increased, so has pollution of air, land, and water. Arctic haze from Prudhoe Bay and newer production facilities may increase incidence of respiratory diseases. There is great potential for damage from catastrophic pollution, such as oil-well blowouts and pipeline ruptures, because present technology for cleanup of large oil spills in the Arctic is untested, particularly in offshore areas. Noise and activity have the effect of displacing fish and game species from their habitats. The disturbances caused by noise and human activity also may interfere with critical life stages, such as caribou calving and rearing of seal pups, and they may cause stress that influences the long-term productivity of the species. Finally, human activity attracts curious animals; feeding of animals encourages their dependence and later poor survival in the natural environment.

## Gravel and Water Resources

Gravel, and to a far lesser extent sand, are essential industrial resources on the North Slope, necessary in most phases of oil and gas development and production. Gravel currently is a plentiful resource in the North Slope region, but convenient and environmentally acceptable sources of fill are in short supply. Industry prefers to take gravel from streams, rivers, and floodplains where it is most easily mined. (Such an extraction site also leaves little visible scar on the terrain.) The Alaska Department of Fish and Game objects to this because of the dangers of siltation and formation of fish traps and the potential damage to overwintering fish. The North Slope Borough also has opposed extraction of gravel from riverbeds. This issue was resolved partially by the development of gravel extraction sites in inactive areas of streambeds. The Division of Lands, which has the authority to allocate state gravel, planned upland as well as riverbed gravel sites through multiple-use agreements among users. Use of upland sites has the added advantage of creating reservoirs for water use. However, development of multiple-use pits has made it necessary to build roads to more distant exploratory sites in some cases, increasing the use of this nonrenewable resource, and consolidation increases traffic on these roads. Proximity to gravel is an even more pressing issue in near- and offshore oil exploration and development. The recycling of gravel reduced this environmental disturbance somewhat in the 1990s and early twenty-first century.

Water is as critical a resource as gravel in the major phases of oil and gas development. The freshwater supply requirements for field support facilities in Prudhoe Bay in 1981 were over one million gallons a day; in the early twenty-first century, they are more than twice that amount. There is a sharp decrease in availability of freshwater during winter months, with the minimum supply at the time when ice cover is thickest, in April and May. In development of the Prudhoe Bay field, freshwater was drawn from deep pools of the Sagavanirktok River, which were eventually pumped dry. These pools were overwintering habitat for fish populations, and water removal resulted in some mortality. Since the early 1980s, alternative sources of freshwater supply have been preferred, such as large-scale reservoirs; however, these only introduce different environmental disturbances.[21]

## Cultural Resources

For industry and most government agencies, archaeological artifacts and historical and cultural sites are less important resources to protect; for Native residents of the North Slope, they rank next in importance only to protection of subsistence resources. In the North Slope oil region, there are important traditional burial grounds (located along the coast) and remains of traditional structures such as sod houses and whaling and fishing camps.[22] Farther inland, there are a larger number of historical sites. Cross Island is a national natural landmark. Rivers, lakes, and the coastal floodplain have been used traditionally by the North Slope Inupiaq, and these areas are today the sites of significant remains and artifacts of historic, archaeological, and cultural value. Disturbances in or near water bodies that have been used traditionally, particularly equipment crossings, vehicle and equipment operations in water, and gravel mining, may damage or destroy these resources. Grave sites and remains of cellars have been covered with gravel and destroyed by bulldozing.

## Sufficiency of Information

Information is vitally important to effective mitigation of environmental disturbances.[23] Both ecological baseline data and information on impacts to biological species are essential. Information requirements are influenced by

NEPA standards, which call for the best available information. Ecological baseline data include habitat descriptions, species inventories, species ecology and behavior, and physical and ecological processes data. However, baseline data are incomplete. For example, data are lacking on fish overwintering sites and migration routes, on the flora and fauna of the oil development region, and on relationships among marine mammals, birds, fish, and the benthic environment. Data on patterns of ice gouging and ocean currents (open water and full pack ice) also are insufficient. These data limitations are particularly troublesome in an era of rapid Arctic climate change.

Presently, biological impacts data are still insufficient to predict the exact impact of numerous proposed activities that might disturb the North Slope physical environment and in turn influence species habitats. For example, the long-term impact of noise and activity disturbances on caribou calving is still unclear. There are findings indicating that caribou cows avoid areas of noise and human or machine activity. There are also data indicating that the size of the central Arctic herd has fluctuated.[24] Existing data, however, do not show a cause-and-effect relationship between noise and activity disturbances and calving. The ambiguity of information in this area is at least partly responsible for the tension produced when state resource agencies stipulate seasonal restrictions on oil company activity near calving areas. A similar question is whether causeways on the North Slope have affected fish habitat by altering the salinity and circulation of sea water,[25] or how near-shore oil exploration will affect the spectacled eider, an endangered species.

Knowledge gaps or incomplete information are especially problematic when technology is untested in Arctic conditions (such as the subsea pipeline used for Northstar oil development) or thought to be inadequate or nonexistent, as in, for example, a methodology to clean up oil spills in the Beaufort Sea (under the sea ice, or in white-out, ice fog, and blizzard conditions). This makes the assessment of risks of spills or breaks due to ice keels and strudel scours (caused by melting freshwater penetrating shore-fast ice and scouring holes in the sea floor) hard to ascertain.

An additional area in which information is insufficient is the economic cost associated with effective mitigation of environmental disturbances. For example, government agencies prefer backhauling to on-site disposal of noninjectable drilling wastes when exploratory wells are drilled, but this has uncertain cost implications. Also uncertain is the environmental benefit derived from costly industry mitigations. For example, in 1993, the EPA insisted that ARCO change the direction of a planned roadway from east-west to north-south to accommodate a pair of nesting swans. The EPA argued that the birds used the same nesting site each year and if it were destroyed, they would become confused. Faced with denial of a wetlands permit, ARCO changed its plan, adding $700,000 to project costs for the sake of a noncritical habitat.

## Measurement of Change

Associated with questions about the sufficiency of information to make sound regulatory decisions is the issue of whether existing measurements capture the impacts important to residents. These measurement questions concern traditional ecological knowledge (TEK), the cumulative impacts of oil and gas development, and changes associated with climate warming.[26] TEK is not a formal requirement of the federal EIS process or state permit review, but the North Slope Borough has inserted it in many of its stipulations, and agencies have responded. The COE devoted a section of the multivolume Northstar EIS to traditional knowledge concerns. Oil companies increasingly consult with village residents to determine, for example, break-up conditions in the Colville river delta. Yet use of TEK is not universal and its measurement remains inexact. Said one DNR regulator:

> The problem is that it is anecdotal . . . . We are trying to give it greater weight. If there is no scientific basis for it, or how to refute it, then that's dicey. Take the case of bowhead whales traveling under ice. The Natives have said for years that whales traveled under solid ice. The experts said no. Finally, they observed whales traveling under solid ice and breaking thin ice. So that was proven to be correct.[27]

Both ecological baseline and biological impact data are needed in order to determine the range and extent of cumulative impacts[28] on the North Slope oil development region.[29] This is a typical (and long-standing) complaint of environmental organizations. For example, in their joint scoping comments for BP's Liberty development project, seven environmental groups opined, "No comprehensive review of the cumulative impacts of oil development in the American Arctic has ever been completed."[30] Nor are there sectoral analyses of cumulative effects, for example of the effects of air emissions on human health, comprehensive offshore sediment monitoring, or number of spills and contaminated sites. Given that data are gathered to answer specific questions on permit applications, such cumulative data seem unlikely to be aggregated. Both environmental NGOs and Native groups object to the metaphor of the North Slope as a "vacant hotel," with room available for species disturbed by oil and gas activity. Notwithstanding thirty years of studies on North Slope species, costing in excess of $100 million, knowledge gaps remain.[31] The National Research Council's *Cumulative Environmental Effects of Oil and Gas Activities on Alaska's North Slope* addresses only some of these information gaps.[32]

Finally, environmental organizations have pointed to the impact that oil and gas development has on climate change through production of hydrocarbons for eventual combustion and the issue of greenhouse gas emissions from production facilities themselves. Increasingly, they have raised questions about specific effects of climate change—for example, erosion from rising sea levels, gouging, and strudel scour from sea ice changes—on new production facilities and pipelines. The Northstar EIS was the first to acknowledge climate change effects, but until 2004–2005, few government regulators took it seriously in their evaluation of lease approvals or production plans.

## Sufficiency of Regulatory Authority

A problem in any regulatory regime is the sufficiency of agency authority and the lack in clarity of statutes and regulations. This element is strongly influenced by the age of institutions and applies to state and local agencies more than federal ones. ADFG, for example, lacks explicit statutory authority to regulate impacts on species other than anadromous fish. Yet this agency's mission is to protect general wildlife values in the state, to manage fish and game for the maximum economic benefit of the people of Alaska. Statutes, regulations, and policies frequently are unclear as to which agency has the authority to mitigate a given disturbance (or decide that no mitigation is necessary). DEC, for example, has ample authority to prevent and control pollution, but the extent to which this can apply to generalized effects of disturbances, such as sedimentation of streams, seems unclear. Too, DEC's authority to regulate spill prevention and response plans has been challenged.[33] The extent to which DOG's authority as guardian of the state's proprietary interest in oil and gas leases extends to surface uses of land is also unclear. Even DOL's authority to issue ice-road construction permits has been challenged in court.[34]

Finally, the authority of agencies to issue stipulations may be at issue—among other government agencies and within the context of the ACMP. Both agency staff and oil industry directors have objected to the forest of stipulations attached to permits. Some simply repeat the agency's statutory authority. Others sometimes are derived from general concurrences that are inapplicable or unnecessary for the specific project under review—for example, conditions for crossing open water and streams at riffles when the oil company proposed crossing streams that were frozen solid, or the authority of DEC to impose procedures on mud and cuttings that its own solid-waste regulations define as being exempt from its regulatory authority. The most recent regulatory authority, that of the North Slope Borough, is least established and most controversial.

## Redundancy and Delay

The roles and ranking of agencies in the state's decisionmaking process are also ambiguous, and the process is highly duplicative.[35] (The federal side of the regulatory regime is clearer, because the lead agency role was established earlier and fewer primary agencies are involved.) Too, each permitting program is jealous of its regulatory turf and has no incentive to cooperate with others. Making the system even more complex is the North Slope Borough's role under the ACMP. State agencies, such as DOG, object to the borough's permitting authority. For example, when the North Slope Borough denied a 1998 permit for a Beaufort Sea seismic survey, DOG asked the governor to override, but under the ACMP this recourse was not possible.

The interagency review process leads to delays in issuing permits. Resource agencies have specified periods in which to respond, but they may elect to delay their comments; in this case, unless the situation calls for immediate action, the process is prolonged. There are several explanations for delay. It is a product of both the complex interrelationships of agencies (state, federal, and local), staffing, and information requirements. The resource agencies (excepting DNR) are connected to sister federal agencies with which they often coordinate reviews; they also lack staff to review permits (discussed below). In addition, state agencies often lack information to evaluate the impacts of the proposed activity, which makes reliance on other agencies and sources necessary, delaying the agencies' responses. Also, permit applications are often vague regarding details of planned operations, necessitating further contacts with the applicants. And the industry may change its plan during permit review, as BP did after its initial submission of the Northstar EIS. Although the changes reduced environmental disturbances (such as eliminating some wastewater discharge), they doubled the length of the review process, which normally takes sixteen to eighteen months.

A major and consistent complaint of industry has been that many actions an operator seeks to take must be approved by three discrete government levels—local, state, and federal. Furthermore, agencies of more than one governmental level may be involved in the determination of any given government's permit process. The objection is that this places industry in a position of double and on occasion triple jeopardy, and time-sensitive projects are held hostage; it delays the application process unnecessarily, and it is redundant and produces inconsistent stipulations or conditions.

All three levels of government are involved in assessing industry plans of operation for leased lands on the North Slope. The borough, through its zoning ordinance, claims authority to approve plans, and oil companies have complied with this request, irrespective of the ambiguity of the borough's authority. The state has authority to regulate operations on state-owned lands, both as landlord and regulator. But operations in navigable waters and on wetlands and tidelands may require COE 404 permits and EPA (DEC) 401 certification, and through these federal requirements, the COE has become a major actor in the regulatory process. The federal permitting system differs from the state system in two respects. First, it requires public notice, which extends the time period for review and involves more interests. Thus, state resource agencies, the borough, industry, environmental NGOs, and other interest groups may review and comment on the federal permits. Second, the COE is a large, elaborate bureaucratic organization, and interests—environmental and developmental—have multiple, formalized access points to its permitting process.

The overall intergovernmental process tends to be duplicative in two respects. Industry may need to file numerous applications for one project—i.e., COE, DOG, DEC, ADFG, and AOGCC. Second, a particular state agency, such as ADFG, may have as many as three opportunities to comment on the same project—e.g., review of a lease operations application, a Title 41 anadromous fish protection permit, and a COE permit. Reducing this influence was a motivation behind the 2003 transfer of ADFG's Habitat Division to DNR. However, this redundancy is a characteristic of the system, and of intergovernmental systems by definition. As Martin Landau observes, the utility of complex layering is the greater control it provides over private sector activities. Yet, the process does produce inconsistent results, in that industry may be required to follow stipulations flowing from one regulatory process that are different from those of another (or not even required by it).

## Attempts to Reform the Process

These concerns have led to several suggestions for reform of the state's regulatory regime. In 1981, the National Petroleum Council urged radical change in the system.[36] Shortly thereafter, DEC developed a master permit system, which would allow an applicant to process several permits simultaneously, by use of the "one window" or clearinghouse approach. Industry, however, preferred to keep track of each permit rather than lose sight of them in what appeared to be a master permit process in name only. Most reform efforts focus on the comprehensive permit systems, such as the coastal-zone consistency review.

DNR officials repeatedly have tried to impose discipline on other state agencies involved in the consistency process. In 1978, the commissioner of natural resources sought to give authority to the concept of DOG's leading role. Some twenty years later, DNR proposed to eliminate DGC from the process, giving DNR the lead role, much as it currently has in issuing permits for large-scale mining projects. This proposal emerged in the state legislature in 1998 and linked the elimination of DGC with changes to the ACMP. The proposal received strong support from the AOGA, but opposition of local governments to changes in powers of coastal zone councils and planning authority blocked the proposal and reduced the chance for serious consideration of streamlining changes to the permitting process.

AOGA's criticism summarized the position the oil industry has taken on the state's regulatory regime: "The current complexity and overlap of various permitting processes, the differing information requirements, uncertainty in permitting schedules and the potential for substantial delays due to jurisdictional and other issues clearly demand that state government and the regulated community find a different way of doing business."[37] However, unlike the tenor of the National Petroleum Council report of 1981, which sought the elimination of any state regulation, AOGA proposed neither eliminating the system nor curbing the authority of state and federal agencies to mitigate environmental disturbances of oil and gas development. Instead, it sought streamlining: making the process more efficient through an enforceable schedule, defining agency and public-input (meaning environmental organizations) roles and timelines for input, and increasing accountability (by eliminating DGC and replacing it with DNR as the lead agency). Although the 1998 state legislature failed to adopt AOGA's recommendations, they were reintroduced in 1999 but not enacted. The most significant reform along these lines was the Murkowski administration's drive in 2003 to move ADFG's Habitat Division to DNR and transfer DGC (relabeled OPMP) to DNR. In 2007, DNR is the de facto lead agency for all major project reviews.[38] However, newly elected Governor Palin responded to criticism of environmentalists by suggesting it might be advisable to return the Habitat Division to ADFG.[39]

To the present, several informal changes have taken place in the regulatory process that reduce delay and aid effective mitigation. Operators and agencies bargain freely about proposed plans, and interagency coordination can be accelerated by verbal authorizations. The most significant change has been the movement of mitigation to the pre-permitting stage. ARCO inaugurated this change in 1979; it held annual meetings for interested agencies to review upcoming plans of operations. This made industry and government sensitive to conflicting issues and values and, in the opinion of industry, has contributed to a reduction in delay.

The COE has adopted this method in the preparation of EIS reviews. It conducts scoping meetings with industry and affected interests, especially those of Native communities. Scoping focuses the EIS review on issues brought up by federal, state, or local agencies or in community meetings. BP followed ARCO's lead by sending scientists and other staff to Native villages on the North Slope before filing its permit applications.

For small projects and many large onshore activities, the permitting process has become routine and is not at all controversial. For large projects, the regulatory regime has not been made noticeably more efficient by reforms, and it still appears cumbersome and slow. An underlying issue is whether it can be otherwise, and whether industry can ever be truly satisfied with it. The question, however, is whether the regulatory process contributes to effective mitigation of environmental disturbances, and there seems to be evidence that it does.

## ◼ Environmental Issues Related to Transportation of Oil and Gas to Market

All of the oil produced on the Alaska North Slope (and potentially most of the gas) is transported to market in TAPS, the chief artery of which is the 48-inch warm-oil pipeline traveling 800 miles from Prudhoe Bay to Valdez. (See Figure 2.1 for location.) This section discusses the elements of TAPS, regulation of the pipeline, oil transport security issues, and the TAPS renewal.

## The Trans-Alaska Pipeline System

TAPS crosses seven large physiographic provinces and diverse land forms, ranging from the tundra-covered coastal plain of the North Slope to spruce-fir forests of the interior, and finally to the western hemlock and Sitka spruce forests of the Prince William Sound coastal areas. The line traverses three major mountain ranges. The highest elevation is Atigun Pass in the Brooks Range (4,739 feet), followed by Isabel Pass (3,420 feet) in the Alaska Range, and Thompson Pass (2,812 feet) in the Chugach Mountains. Much of the topography along the route is influenced by past and present glaciation. This has produced steep slide slopes in mountains and valleys bisected by streams and braided rivers carrying large sediment loads.

TAPS is a complex industrial system, consisting of the pipeline itself, pump stations, bridges and access roads, and the Valdez marine terminal, as well as a telecommunications network, workpads, and a gas line.[40] About half of the pipeline is buried, mostly in areas with stable permafrost soils (either insulated or refrigerated and insulated in some areas of unstable soils). To prevent thawing of permafrost, the other half of the pipeline is above ground and mounted on approximately 78,000 vertical support members (VSMs). The pipeline crosses over and under hundreds of rivers, streams, and other water bodies. To protect the pipeline from erosive migration of rivers, banks are fortified. More than 100 valves control oil flow along the pipeline; check valves at or near slopes turn on automatically if oil flow reverses. Too, pressure changes and flow fluctuation can be monitored internally in the pipeline.

Upon TAPS completion in 1977, eleven pump stations pushed Prudhoe Bay oil through the pipeline. With the noticeable decline of production by the mid-1990s, Alyeska closed four of these stations temporarily. Pump stations include valves, pipe, tanks, and control equipment to relieve excessive pressures on the pipeline when shut down. Nearly 300 access roads connect state roads to the pipeline, material sites, disposal sites, and the pump stations.

Located on the southern shore of Port Valdez, the Valdez marine terminal occupies a thousand-acre facility. It stores petroleum and loads oil onto tankers for shipment to market. It also houses the operations control center for TAPS. Currently a fleet of twenty-six tankers (three with double hulls and thirteen with double sides) serves the terminal, but these numbers will change because the Oil Pollution Act of 1990 requires that the fleet consist entirely of double-hulled tankers by 2014.[41]

Since 1970, TAPS has been managed for the owner oil companies by Alyeska. Ownership has changed over the years consequent to mergers and acquisitions of oil companies. In 2007, the six owner companies were BP Pipeline (Alaska) (46.9 percent share); ConocoPhillips Trans Alaska (26.8 percent); ExxonMobil Pipeline Company (20.3 percent); Koch Alaska Pipeline Company (3.1 percent); Amerada Hess Pipeline Corporation (1.5 percent); and Unocal Pipeline Company (1.4 percent).[42]

### Pipeline Regulation

A State Pipeline Coordinator oversaw construction of the TAPS from January 1974 through 1977, supported by a state-federal joint fish and wildlife advisory team. The state disbanded the State Pipeline Coordinator in 1977, returning permitting activities to state resource agencies.[43] In 1979, the US Department of the Interior delegated its pipeline oversight authority to the BLM's Alaska state office, in its special projects office. This loosely coordinated system conducted oversight in the 1980s.[44]

Problems in the detection of corrosion in pipeline sections, and then the *Exxon Valdez* oil spill, focused public attention on TAPS oversight, which led to the formation of the JPO in 1990. Initially, it included four agencies and under forty employees, but by 2007, it had expanded to eleven agencies and nearly a hundred employees. The JPO oversees activity along the pipeline corridor and issues ROWs for new common carrier pipelines. Its authority is based on the federal pipeline lease and the state grant. It is jointly headed by a federal representative of the BLM and a state DNR representative. JPO staff believe it is the most successful coordinating agency of the three major project review processes (the others being EIS and coastal-zone management), which they attribute to its focus on the pipeline corridor, colocation of federal and state regulatory agency offices, sufficiency of finance, and a long history of operation.[45]

### Pipeline Security Issues

Pipeline operation after twenty-five years occasioned concern with integrity of the pipeline itself, localized spills, and safety of tanker transport from the marine terminal. During construction of TAPS, attention focused on flawed welds of many pipe sections. Corrosion problems in the Atigun Pass section led to rerouting and some replacement. However, corrosion problems have been a more serious concern at Prudhoe Bay than along the pipeline route itself.[46] Hydrological changes as well as permafrost melting have affected 6,000 VSMs and about 200 "wobbling" VSMs are on a watch list.

Between 1977 and 1999, 4,283 spills were recorded along the pipeline and at the Valdez marine terminal. Most of the spills were contained in a lined area or cleaned up within about a year. No direct spills to surface water (outside Prince William Sound) have been documented. Of the total spills, only eighty-seven required management under Alyeska's contaminated site management program, less than 1 percent of the total number of spills.[47] The next most recent spill happened in 2001 when a Livengood resident who had "always wanted to shoot a hole in the pipeline" did so. His blast released 285,600 gallons of oil into the environment, with residual contamination of groundwater.

The largest oil spill occurred in Prince William Sound. On March 24, 1989, the *Exxon Valdez* went off course and ran aground on Bligh Reef. Carrying over 1.25 million barrels of crude, more than 10 million gallons spilled into the sound. Although most of the floating oil was removed by skimmers, left the coastal area, evaporated, or was degraded, residues remained in bays, coastal areas, or in bottom sediment into the twenty-first century.[48]

Oil pollution legislation at the federal and the state level was the reaction to the *Exxon Valdez* catastrophe. In addition to the requirement of double-hulled tankers, significant improvements were made in spill prevention and response capability for Prince William Sound. This included the creation of Alyeska's Ship Escort/Response Vessel System, which provides escort vessels for transit of tankers through the Valdez Narrows.[49] Legislation and regulations also increased the amount of spill response equipment, drills, and training exercises. Finally, the Oil Pollution Act of 1990 required formation of the Prince William Sound Regional Citizens Advisory Council to improve spill prevention and response readiness; in 2002–2003, critics of pipeline security urged that a similar advisory council be formed to monitor TAPS itself.[50]

Alyeska's operation of TAPS has been criticized on several fronts in addition to the safety issues represented above. Up to the mid-1990s, the corporation failed to employ and train Alaska Natives, whose workforce percentage dropped to less than 5 percent, requiring extensive recruitment and training. Critics of Alyeska also charged that it harassed employees, particularly whistle-blowers. The JPO's oversight role has also come under frequent criticism, including congressional direction that it provide comprehensive oversight of TAPS, which shifted the emphasis of JPO from response to prevention.[51]

## TAPS Renewal in 2004

The original federal grant for the primary ROW was issued in 1974 (with the state lease following shortly thereafter). Because the federal Mineral Leasing Act limits ROWs to no more than thirty years, the federal grant expired in January 2004. Owner companies requested a renewal of the ROW, and to BLM this constituted a major federal action under NEPA, requiring an EIS. In 2001, BLM conducted a scoping analysis, which indicated a range of concerns.

Foremost among the scoping comments were security issues. Commenters questioned whether TAPS could operate at design capacity for an additional thirty years and recommended that attention be paid to metal fatigue, corrosion, changes in pipeline design and construction criteria, and climate change.[52]

Second were concerns about ecosystem effects from pipeline operation: air quality, wildlife and aquatic habitat, water quality, potential catastrophic incidents, noise, and impacts on cultural resources. Native employment opportunities, use of Native lands, damages to subsistence as well as more general socioeconomic effects on Native Alaskans were among the comments, as well as the Native Alaskan role in the TAPS regulatory process. A few comments addressed oversight and regulatory requirements.

BLM issued its draft environmental impact statement in July 2002. It considered three alternatives: (1) renewal of the TAPS federal grant for thirty years, (2) renewal for less than thirty years, and (3) nonrenewal, the "no-action" alternative.[53] Given the necessity of pipeline transportation for the fiscal health of the state, federal and state agencies supported BLM's recommendation that the grant (and state lease) be renewed for thirty years, subject to several conditions.[54]

### The 2006 North Slope Oil Spill

In early March 2006, an oil field worker on the North Slope noticed a major spill from a hole in a feeder line of the Prudhoe Bay complex that had been leaking undetected for two weeks. The spill grew to 267,000 gallons of crude oil, the largest ever on-land oil spill in Alaska.[55] BP, the owner of most Prudhoe Bay oil and operator of the North Slope oil facilities, had to shut down the pipeline temporarily to replace the defective pipe. Corrosion in the twenty-nine-year-old pipes was the cause of the spill, but BP claimed the pipeline was safe to operate without major repairs.

Alaska's pipeline watchdogs have been consistently critical of the pipeline operation by BP and Alyeska, the TAPS manager. The oil spill occasioned Congress to investigate, and federal inspectors began a criminal investigation of BP's management.[56] They ordered BP to conduct tests for corrosion in the pipeline, and in early August 2006, BP announced that it had discovered sixteen anomalies in twelve locations of a transit line on the eastern side of the field. Some 16 miles of pipeline needed to be replaced or bypassed, and for this reason the company began a shutdown of transit lines delivering 400,000 barrels of oil a day (about 2.6 percent of US supply, and 8 percent of domestic production). The oil company said it was "surprised" to find severe corrosion; it had not used mechanical pigs to clean out the pipeline in fourteen years, because it had not "believed it to be necessary."[57]

The partial shutdown of the pipeline lasted five months, and this news instantly sent oil prices up $2 per barrel. Revenue Commissioner Bill Corbus said the state would lose $6.4 million a day in lost royalties and taxes throughout this period.[58] The state was implicated in pipeline maintenance issues when an engineering firm reported it had warned BP four years previously about prospects of corrosion damage, but state oversight was inadequate.[59]

The issue turned partisan when former officials of the Knowles administration (1994–2002) contended they had asked for twenty-seven new state inspector positions, which the Republican-dominated legislature had declined to fund.

In response to the spill, Governor Murkowski issued Administrative Order 229, which created the Lease Monitoring and Engineering Integrity Coordinating Office in DNR's Division of Oil and Gas. Its purpose is to improve interagency coordination and oversight of all oil and gas production, processing, transportation, and storage facilities on state-owned land.[60] DEC adopted new regulations extending requirements for leak detection and oversight to previously unregulated pipelines. Simultaneously, the US Department of Transportation Office of Pipeline Safety similarly extended its regulatory requirements for pipelines.[61]

## ■ Impact of the Oil Industry on Alaska's Regulatory Regime

Participants in the North Slope regulatory regime interviewed for this chapter were nearly unanimous that regulations had become more comprehensive and complex since 1981. Most also thought the process was redundant, time-consuming, cumbersome, and inefficient. Yet with the exception of environmental NGOs (particularly concerned about enforcement of regulations, knowledge gaps, lack of cumulative impact analysis, and climate change), most thought the regulatory regime was effective in accomplishing its objective: to mitigate disturbances to the land, water, air, and species of the North Slope.

This finding would seem to establish the null hypothesis: that multinational oil companies have had no adverse impact on Alaska's regulatory regime. However, such a conclusion would be unwarranted, because the participants have changed their attitudes toward and relationships with one another. They have established professional working relationships, notwithstanding large differences of interest. Once confrontational in its dealings with federal, state, and local regulatory agencies, the early-twenty-first-century oil industry in Alaska is now generally cooperative because cooperation with regulators is "good business."[62] What explains the improvement in relationships? Has the regulatory regime changed in more subtle ways? If so, whose interests benefit from these changes? In this final section, we consider these questions by focusing on regulatory and statutory changes, the impact of state revenue declines on the regulatory process, and the nature of "compliance partnership," the model toward which Alaska's regulatory regime may be moving.

It is important to note that there has been a national trend toward partnerships and private-sector self-regulation in environmental policy, as well as increased use of market-based incentives and mechanisms, since the Reagan administration in 1981. This is the broad context in which Alaska developments unfolded.[63]

## Changes in Alaska Statutes and Regulations

Much of the legal basis for regulation of oil and gas development in Alaska was established after passage of the National Environmental Policy Act of 1969. Because Alaska was then a new and relatively progressive state, its environmental statutes and regulations reflected the best of what was available in the United States. Some participants in the regulatory process say that Alaska's water-quality laws are among the most stringent in the nation,[64] and the air-quality program is "tougher than California's."[65]

An expansion in regulatory authority followed the environmental catastrophe of *Exxon Valdez* in 1989. At both the federal and state level, new laws and regulations were developed to prevent and to mitigate oil spills. This is a clear case of events driving the regulatory process. In Alaska, legislators of both parties sought to insure that Alaska would experience no other comparable environmental disaster. *Exxon Valdez* temporarily registered on the Alaska public consciousness as the Santa Barbara oil spill did on the California psyche. Conservative legislators toned down derisive remarks toward environmental safeguards, and they moderated their campaigns for growth with qualifications on the need for protection of the environment.

Since 1989, one cannot detect an organized effort on the part of conservative political leaders, who customarily are most hostile to environmental regulations, to weaken the North Slope regulatory regime. This is curious, given the election to the governorship in 1990 of the strongest advocate of unlimited growth in the state's history (Hickel), the large majority in the state legislature attained by Republican conservatives in the 1994 election, and election of Hickel's one-time protégé, Murkowski, to the governorship in 2002.

Changes to the regulatory regime have occurred at the periphery and not the core. For example, the transformation of the state's oil and gas leasing system in 1997 to an areawide program (instead of leasing individual blocks) was supported not only by industry but also by state regulators, who tired of lease applications being tied up in court. This change did not seriously affect the state's ability to manage leases in the interest of environmental security once leases were sold, but it did affect the ability of the state to study and stipulate mitigation measures in advance.

## Impact of Revenue Reductions

Policy analysts who examine oil industry behavior in state arenas tend to find that industry reaction to regulation correlates inversely with its financial situation. Oil multinationals object most strenuously to regulation when the bottom line is endangered and future profits least secure. A few respondents to our study in 1999 believed that industry would assail regulations zealously if oil prices remained low (they did not). Yet, at the time ARCO/Phillips and BP announced large-scale layoffs in early 1999 and then again in 2002, declining oil industry profits had not lessened the companies' payments in support of the regulatory regime, or increased its opposition.

Because of the depletion of Prudhoe Bay oil, the state has experienced more serious revenue downturns (even with the state revenue spikes when oil prices peaked in 2005–2007) than the oil companies, and these have affected those agencies regulating the oil and gas industry. Perhaps reductions in state staffing and the ability to enforce regulations have made oil industry opposition less necessary.

Starting in the 1990s, state resource agencies complained that they had insufficient staff to insure that proposed industrial activities would be investigated to limit potentially adverse impacts and monitored carefully to conform to the stipulations on permits. Most monitoring of oil and gas exploration, development, and production activity is done from the Fairbanks district and Anchorage statewide offices of state resource agencies, but no officer in any of the three state resource agencies is continuously stationed on the North Slope. (AOGCC has one resident representative on the North Slope to inspect wells and drilling rigs and conduct meter tests.) Only two positions in the Fairbanks district office of the Division of Lands, which manages all state lands north of the Alaska Range, are charged with monitoring plans of operations and miscellaneous land-use permits, the most numerous categories of permits. Travel funds allocated to these positions allow only a dozen week-long monitoring trips annually.[66] ADFG's field presence on the North Slope has increased; however, that operation is now primarily funded by oil companies. A northern regional oil-spill response supervisor of DEC said in 2001, "We have too few people to do an adequate job. . . . We can only concentrate on one (oil spill) or the other, or skim along the top."[67]

Budgets of state resource agencies have suffered as a consequence of state general fund reductions (see Chapter 5). DEC, for example, sustained a 50 to 55 percent reduction to its general fund budget over a five-year period. Its total budget increased because of a rise in federal grants and program receipts, but these moneys were earmarked,[68] thus reducing the flexibility of the regulatory branch. General fund appropriations (which pay for monitoring staff) to DEC declined over a decade and were replaced by program receipts and specific federal grants. An EPA regulatory officer who had worked closely with DEC said, "They have been underfunded so long, and have lost so many people, the agency's memory is gone. . . . We find ourselves dealing with what DEC is told to do by the governor."[69]

The general fund budgets for DNR and ADFG also were cut repeatedly. A DOL regulator said, "When I started working for DNR in 1981, we had seventy-two people in the office; in 1992 we had thirty-two; now there are eighteen of us."[70] An experienced ADFG official discussed the impact of budget changes: "It has steadily gotten smaller since 1985–1986. The first new biologist we've hired was last year. From 1984 to 1999, there were no hires. The work load, however, is the same or larger. There is more oil and gas stuff now on the North Slope than I've ever seen."[71]

The development in state agencies of high service fees and encouragement of "partnerships" with the private sector required cooperative attitudes in dealing with Big Oil. The success of conservative Republicans in forming a nearly veto-proof majority in the state legislature from 1995 to 2006 merely accelerated a trend evident in previous years.

State fiscal problems were the sufficient condition for changes to Alaska's North Slope regulatory regime. In the eyes of most government participants in the regime, any source of revenue allowing regulation of environmental disturbances to continue was preferable to the absence of regulation. That the revenue source was multinational corporations was regrettable, but necessary.

## The Alaska Compliance Partnership

As Alaska's North Slope oil and gas regulatory regime has matured, it has come to resemble a "compliance partnership." There are strongly cooperative relationships between the oil industry, state and local regulators, and their political supervisors. In 2007, it was uncertain whether very high oil-company profits from Alaska operations, oil and gas corporations' reluctance to produce gas, and the large North Slope oil spill—and consequent lowering of the normally high public evaluation of energy multinationals—will significantly affect public policy. The concept of compliance partnership is more familiar to regulators in the oil patch outside Alaska, where oil-producing lands are privately owned and not managed in the public trust. Compliance partnership refers to a halfway house, a regulatory process that is neither wholly in the public interest nor completely a captive of private interests. We search for evidence of its development by reviewing the changes in the timing of the regulatory process, its funding, and results.

Throughout, we have mentioned the increased complexity of the Alaska North Slope regulatory regime. One way in which the process has become more complex is by the establishment of a pre-permitting stage and involvement of more participants. Taking the initiative in these developments have been Alaska's oil companies. Their incentive is to reduce costs of new projects and limit opposition to new oil exploration by cultivating relationships with those who will be directly affected by development and those making decisions on their permit applications.

In the 1980s, there was no defined pre-permit phase to the regulatory process; oil company activities have created this new stage. As mentioned, the federal EIS process now has a scoping phase, in which oil-company representatives visit local communities that will be affected by development. They provide small incentives to attend and then explain simply what they propose to develop. A highlight of these presentations is the focus on new jobs that will be created for residents, increases in both state and local tax revenues, and environmentally benign effects of development (and if not, the opportunity for benefits to flow from disaster, as villagers become paid members of spill response teams). Perhaps the most obvious case of such influence is Nuiqsut. This Inupiat village had long opposed Beaufort Sea OCS development, and its residents resolutely opposed ARCO's (now ConocoPhillips) development of the Alpine field. However, Nuiqsut has a subsistence economy with few permanent jobs. Moreover, it lacks an inexpensive supply of energy. A critical element in winning Nuiqsut's acceptance of oil development was the oil company promise to run a natural gas pipeline to the village to meet its energy needs for at least twenty years.

Another way in which the process has become more complex and cumbersome is through the cultivation of positive relations by oil companies with regulators and opposing interest groups, especially environmentalists. Alaska's major oil companies conduct seminars on their present and future operations on the North Slope. The companies hire staff who are sensitive environmentally, knowledgeable, and polished in their interactions with other participants.

The funding of the North Slope regulatory regime has changed significantly in thirty years. At the onset, regulatory agencies were wholly funded by the state or federal government. Presently, nearly one-third of the funding for state regulators is supplied by the oil companies. This funding influences both the knowledge base used in making environmental decisions, the ability to conduct monitoring studies, and the attitudes of personnel themselves.

First, much of the data-gathering on the environmental effects of oil and gas development is paid for by the oil companies. Without this contribution, companies would not be able to supply the information needed to gain approval of development plans. Much of the research contracted for by oil companies may be good science, providing essential data for regulative decisionmaking. Yet, oil company payment for research may taint the quality of the research product; evaluators cannot know the extent to which researchers were motivated by their desire to satisfy those who paid or to gain future research contracts. Increasingly, oil companies have funded agencies themselves to do research studies through reimbursable-services agreements. The mechanism does not eliminate the conflict between the oil companies' proprietorial interest and that of the public.

Second, the ability of two state agencies to conduct any North Slope monitoring at all is dependent on oil-company logistical support. Agency fees have increased to the level that oil companies now pay indirectly for the personnel who regulate them. We lack evidence demonstrating that fee payers control the regulations under which they are assessed, and some regulators see no problem with this arrangement.[72] Yet, the institutional independence of agencies appears to have been compromised in their relations with the regulated.

In 1996, a branch of one of the resource agencies wrote this plaintive letter to an oil company: "The decrease of state funds makes it difficult. . . to review permit action requests. (We suggest that) we enter into a cooperative agreement with your company to fund the necessary work on reviewing your company's permit action requests." The practice of asking business to pay for regulation is increasingly prevalent in the United States and other postindustrial democracies. However, the ability of governments to regulate in the public interest is likely to be impaired when agencies depend on payment from the regulated.

Third, attitudes of participants in the regulatory process have changed. The most frequent comment of government participants was that relationships had become "professional." Contacts were frequent and harmonious. It is in the area of attitudes that political changes—both at the state administrative and legislative levels—probably have the greatest impact. We have mentioned legislative changes that were apparently more responsive to the needs of the oil and gas industry than at previous times. Administrative changes are more pronounced. During his 1994 campaign for the governorship, Democrat Knowles said he would create jobs for Alaskans if elected. Upon taking office and consistently, Governor Knowles talked about the "Partnership with Industry," a phrase he balanced with "Doing it Right," presumably by which he meant sensitivity to environmental and social values. In 2002, Murkowski campaigned to make Alaska even more open for energy development.

These values influenced appointments to the executive branch during the Knowles and Murkowski administrations, appointments particularly in DEC and DNR that were accommodative to industry's concerns. As one participant observed, "Why should the oil industry object to state regulation when BP and ARCO have such good access to commissioners?" Prodevelopment values also influenced agencies' enforcement of regulations, which surfaced in controversial reassignments and a resignation from DEC in early 2002. The commissioner reassigned the supervisor of DEC's program to prevent and respond to North Slope oil spills as well as her assistant, because they were reluctant to allow oil companies to drill when the tundra had begun to thaw.[73] At the request of some DEC employees, Public Employees for Environmental Responsibility, a Washington, DC–based government worker advocacy group, conducted a mail survey of DEC workers. Some 52 percent of the 31 percent of the agency employees who responded agreed that DEC often placed more weight on economic development than resource protection; more than half said regulators had been reassigned for doing their jobs "too well" on controversial projects; 71 percent said the agency did not have sufficient resources to do its job.[74] This was within a Democratic administration. Control over appointments (and information from departments) in the Republican Murkowski administration insured that negative comments about the oil industry did not surface. It was for this reason among others that the governor fired his commissioner of natural resources in 2005.

The last area to examine is results. Have increasingly cooperative relationships between industry and government affected the public interest adversely by sacrificing environmental values? We lack sufficient information to fully test this hypothesis, but the large 2006 oil spill on the Alaska North Slope is a telling indicator of significant lapses—both in industrial self-regulation and in inspection by the state and federal governments.

## ▨ Conclusions

The Alaska North Slope is one of the frontiers of oil and gas development globally. Since discovery of oil at Prudhoe Bay in 1968, the question has been whether energy development can occur in this vast region of great beauty without sacrificing environmental values. To protect those values, governments at the federal, state, and local level established a regulatory regime. They applied it to multinational oil corporations, requiring them to seek the permission of government for small as well as large-scale projects. Until 2006, no major environmental disaster occurred on the North Slope or along the pipeline route. The oil industry touted its experience and behavior in the clean development of oil and gas,[75] but the North Slope regulatory regime also could be given credit. The largest North Slope spill of 2006, however, casts serious doubt on the regime's overall effectiveness.

The regulatory regime is composed of authorities, institutions, and officers. Laws, such as the National Environmental Policy Act and the Endangered Species Act, form its core, but the public laws, state statutes, and local ordinances that protect environmental values are not self-enforcing. Institutions of government at the local, state, and federal level are responsible for the administration of law, and they have done so through the development of policies, general regulations, and specific permits. The way in which oil and gas development occurs is most influenced by the stipulations and conditions in the permitting process that government officials apply to oil industry plans of operations.

The regulatory regime is complex and redundant. It involves the resource departments of the federal, state, and local government, each with its own mission and goals and intent upon protecting the public interest through the exercise of authority. Sometimes agencies' authority and missions conflict—both at the same level of government and across levels. This is to be expected because the environmental values embedded in the regulatory regime are diverse, and each tier of government has found unique ways to protect them.

Although complex, the regime is not unmanageable. Over the years, government managers have developed three different systems to coordinate regulation. The Joint Pipeline Office brings together nearly a dozen federal and state agencies with missions relevant to the maintenance and safe operation of the pipeline corridor. The EIS process for large-scale projects also coordinates intergovernmental activities in environmental assessment. Finally, the state of Alaska's coastal zone management program, administered by the Office of Project Management and Permitting in DNR, is designed to insure that the actions of industry are consistent with the objectives of coastal communities, but since 2003, the objectivity of this program has been challenged.

The oil and gas regulatory regime, like any other regime, operates in the absence of certain knowledge. For this reason, those who seek to develop oil and gas fields are required to jump through many hoops and repeat many actions. Repetition and redundancy in the process are an important way of dealing with the uncertainty of knowledge and the lack of exact data.[76]

In our examination of the regulatory regime, we asked the extent to which it had been "captured" by the oil industry. We found a few parts of the legal environment that had been changed by industry. However, the political environment, particularly at the level of state government, has been strongly influenced, for Alaska remains highly dependent on the sale of energy products for its survival. This need has brought government into a relationship with industry that emphasizes cooperation, where industry increasingly is asked to regulate itself and government is expected to observe silently. This development appears to be at the edge of the national trend in increased use of voluntary and market-based mechanisms as well as industry self-regulation in environmental protection policy.

The "compliance partnership" satisfies the interests of industry and underfunded government agencies. As industry supplies much of the information required to make environmental decisions, and as it increasingly pays for much of the costs of regulation, however, compliance partnership may not satisfy the public interest in environmental protection on Alaska's North Slope. The events of 2006 showed the limits of that partnership and the impacts on government of dependence on the industry.

## ▨ Notes

A paper on which this chapter is based was presented to the Thirty-Eighth Annual Meeting of the Western Regional Science Association, Ojai, California, February 22, 1999.

1. We conducted 105 interviews with federal, state, and local agency officials, as well as with oil industry representatives and representatives of Native and environmental organizations, during the period 1998–2002. Endnotes are used to attribute specific quotations or paraphrases only.

2. Gerald A. McBeath, Thomas A. Morehouse, John Barkdull, and Linda Leask, *Natural Resource Issues and Policies on Alaska's North Slope* (Anchorage: Department of Natural Resources, July 1981).

3. The chapter focuses on environmental regulation, with specific reference to the Alaska North Slope. It pays less attention to two other types of regulation: (1) the state and federal roles as landowners, manifest in the oil and gas leasing program, and (2) conservation regulation to prevent the waste of oil and gas resources.

4. As of April 2007, the federally listed threatened or endangered species in Alaska included (managed by US FWS) the short-tailed albatross, Eskimo curlew, Aleutian shield fern, spectacled eider, Steller's eider, northern sea otter; (and, managed by NMFS) the Steller sea lion, blue whale, bowhead whale, fin whale, humpback whale, North Pacific right whale, sperm whale, sei whale, leatherback sea turtle, Steller sea lion, loggerhead sea turtle, and green sea turtle. See http://Alaska.fws.gov/fisheries/endangered/ accessed November 25, 2007.

5. Harassment is defined broadly as activities or conduct disrupting the animals' normal behavior or causing a significant change in their activity, whether intentional or through negligence.

6. Jeff Walker, Minerals Management Service, US Department of the Interior, interview, February 1, 1999, and October 12, 2000.

7. Council on Environmental Quality (CEQ) regulations implementing NEPA require federal agencies to follow both the "letter and spirit" of the law. Agencies are required to prepare an Environmental Assessment (EA) to determine whether an EIS needs to be prepared. The federal action under NEPA includes "new and continuing activities, including project . . . entirely or partly . . . regulated by federal agencies," and projects include "actions approved by permit." (CEQ, 1996)

8. Mark A. Eisner, Jeff Worsham, and Evan Ringquist, *Contemporary Regulatory Policy* (Boulder, CO: Lynne Rienner Publishers, 2000), p. 140.

9. Al Ewing, US Environmental Protection Agency, interview, February 4, 1999.

10. Overall standards refer to eight habitats: offshore areas; estuaries; wetlands and tide flats; rocky islands and sea cliffs; barrier islands and lagoons; exposed high-energy coasts; rivers, streams, and lakes; and important upland habitat.

11. Early in 2003, the Murkowski administration moved the Habitat Division of ADFG to the Department of Natural Resources in order to streamline permitting work. The transfer was controversial with environmentalists. Shortly after her election to the governorship in 2006, Palin indicated she might reverse this action.

12. Federal-state regulatory duplication is reduced by the EPA's full delegation of the air program to DEC, with federal oversight. The state once sought delegation of hazardous waste controls but declined to assume the authority because of funding requirements.

13. Ted Moore, Division of Spill Prevention and Response, DEC, interview, February 10, 1999.

14. Jeanne Hanson, National Marine Fisheries Service, interview, February 1, 1999, and June 6, 2000.

15. Alaska Statute sec. 46.03.010.

16. The stipulations or conditions are based on regulations and follow a standard of reasonableness. They are supposed to be related to the agency's regulatory authority, reasonably enforceable, and practical.

17. For nearly a decade, the state has used an expedited permit review for its consistency review, which entails A, B, and C lists for permits. The A list is for projects that are categorically consistent and make no significant impact on the coastal zone. No stipulations are required. The B list includes routine activities, and standard stipula-

tions, based on fifty general concurrences statewide, are applied to them. C-list projects—including all the large oil and gas development and production plans—undergo a full review.

18. The cooperating agency is required to identify additional information it needs to comment and make more specific comments on the draft EIS. If it objects or has reservations based on environmental impacts, the agency must identify the mitigation measures necessary for the project to proceed.

19. Cooperating agencies cannot have direct contact with the applicant. Alvin Ott, Department of Fish and Game, interview, January 28, 1999.

20. Sara Chapell, Regional Representative, Sierra Club, Anchorage, interview, April 6, 2001.

21. The sufficiency of North Slope water resources is an issue of contention. In its petition to the circuit court to overturn the MMS's approval of the Northstar production plan, Greenpeace argued that at the current rate of use, water sources in the vicinity of Prudhoe Bay would be depleted within ten years. The state's division of water resources, however, sees no shortage: "I'm not aware that there is a water availability issue on the North Slope. There's just one big watershed there; it is not like the removal of water from the area" (Kellie Westphal, Natural Resources Manager, DNR, Anchorage, interview, October 13, 2000).

22. See Jon M. Nielson, *Beaufort Sea Study—Historic and Subsistence Site Inventory: A Preliminary Cultural Resource Assessment* (Barrow: North Slope Borough, 1977).

23. See Nicholas E. Flanders, Rex V. Brown, Yelena Andre'eva, and Oleg Larichev, "Justifying Public Decisions in Arctic Oil and Gas Development: American and Russian Approaches," *Arctic* 51, no. 3 (September 1998): 275–278.

24. Raymond D. Cameron, Kenneth R. Whitten, Walter T. Smith, and Daniel D. Roby, "Caribou Distribution and Group Composition Associated with Construction of the Trans-Alaska Pipeline," *The Canadian Field Naturalist* (1993): 155–163. A state survey released in 2001, however, indicated that the central arctic caribou herd was at its largest point since scientists began tracking it twenty-three years previously. The herd had swelled to 27,000, a 35 percent increase since the previous measurement in 1997. See *Fairbanks Daily News-Miner*, January 15, 2001.

25. Ray Tyson, "Causeway Compromise," *Alaska Business Monthly* (March 1991).

26. See Jerry McBeath and Carl E. Shepro, "The Effects of Environmental Change on an Arctic Native Community: Evaluation Using Local Cultural Perceptions," *The American Indian Quarterly* 31, no. 1 (Winter 2007): 44–65.

27. Matt Rader, DGC representative, DNR, Oil and Gas Division, Anchorage, interview, October 14, 2000.

28. Cumulative impacts result when the effects of an action are added to or interact with other effects in a specific place and time. Incremental effects accumulate when additional disturbances occur in an area before the resource can rebound fully from the effect of the first disturbance. The concept of cumulative impacts includes direct, indirect, secondary, and interrelated effects from other actions occurring simultaneously. See National Research Council, *Cumulative Environmental Effects of Oil and Gas Activities on Alaska's North Slope* (Washington, DC: The National Academies Press, 2003), p. 2.

29. D. A. Walker, P. J. Webber, E. F. Binndian, K. R. Everrett, N. D. Lederer, E. A. Northstrang, and M. D. Walker, "Cumulative Effects of Oil Fields on Northern Alaskan Landscapes," *Science* 238 (1996): 757–759.

30. Scoping comments of Greenpeace, Trustees for Alaska, Northern Alaska Environmental Center, Alaska Community Action on Toxics, Alaska Forum for

Environmental Responsibility, Alaska Center for the Environment, and Sierra Club for BP's Liberty development project, in letter to Fred King, Liberty EIS Coordinator, Minerals Management Service, April 9, 1997.

31.  The federal cumulative impacts criterion has been evaluated in 2001–2002 by an advisory panel to the National Research Council. In the state, however, there is no law comparable to NEPA. Said one environmental lawyer: "State agencies are not obligated to consider cumulative impacts, even in the coastal consistency process. The North Slope Borough coastal management plan does require cumulative impacts analysis, but it has never rejected a project under this authority" (Michael Frank, Trustees for Alaska, Anchorage, interview, July 20, 2000).

32.  National Research Council, *Cumulative Environmental Effects of Oil and Gas Activities on Alaska's North Slope* (Washington, DC: 2003).

33.  Phillips dropped its plans to develop an offshore exploration well at the McCovey Prospect, twelve miles north of Prudhoe Bay, because of a DEC stipulation. In its announcement, the company complained that the agency lacked authority under statute to stop the project: "In our opinion, the proposed stipulations go far beyond any interpretation to date of what could be viewed as 'reasonable terms and conditions' that ADEC may attach to plans it approves (under statute)," (*Anchorage Daily News*, June 1, 2001).

34.  Greenpeace sued over the winter 1997–1998 construction of an ice road, claiming that DOL had no authority to issue the permit under an existing permit for off-road construction. The agency had contended that the ice road had minor environmental impacts and the decision fell within its discretion. Leon Lynch, Natural Resources Specialist, DOL, DNR, Fairbanks, interview, June 16, 2000.

35.  An internal memo of DNR sought to eliminate multiple decisions on the same issue. It argued, "Currently, an activity within the coastal zone that requires a DNR permit may be subject to five appeals/elevations *of the same issue!* The initial consistency determination may be elevated to DC through the coastal zone consistency process, and then appealed again to the Coastal Policy Council. DNR's decision may also be separately appealed to DNR Division Directors, then to the DNR Commissioner. Following those two reviews, the appellant can ask for reconsideration by the DNR Commissioner. Where agency jurisdiction overlaps, they can separately appeal the same or similar issue to another agency through that agency's permit." (DNR, "The Permitting Practices Act," 1996.)

36.  National Petroleum Council, Committee on Arctic Oil and Gas Resources, *Report of the Exploration Task Group* (1981).

37.  Judy Brady, Executive Director, AOGA, "Detailed Comments on SB 186," February 19, 1998. Reflecting on DGC's proposed new regulations for the Coastal Policy Council, Brady remarked, "The process is so convoluted, there's no consistent way to work through it. It is completely subjective. We are trying to come up with changes in regulations and laws to make it more consistent. Now, we are the same place as we were in the 1960s." (Interview, August 29, 2002.)

38.  A compromise in 2003–2004 also separated DEC's consistency review process from that of other agencies, because it had such long time frames. Steve Schmitz, DOG natural resource specialist, personal interview, August 3, 2007.

39.  Critics said moving the Habitat Division to DNR compromised environmental protection. ADFG seeks the return of the division, while DNR wants it to remain. See transition reports of DNR, ADFG, and DEC, November and December 2006.

40.  See US Department of the Interior, Bureau of Land Management, *Draft Environmental Impact Statement: Renewal of the Trans-Alaska Pipeline System Right-of-Way* (Washington, DC: 2002), pp. 1.7–1.9.

41.  Ibid., 3.1–3.21.

42. Ibid., 1.1.

43. The state's authority to monitor pipeline integrity lies in Alaska Statute sec. 38.35.225, which specifies police and regulatory powers to protect lands and the public from contamination.

44. Ibid., 3.1–3.2.

45. According to Jerry Brossia, Director, JPO, federal-state cooperation on pipeline matters began in 1974 by terms of an agreement between Interior Secretary Rogers Morton and Governor Bill Egan, which provided for joint monitoring of pipeline construction and maintenance. When industry sought to construct a Northwest Alaska gas pipeline in 1978, expenditure of $80 million on government oversight without a result renewed attention to improving coordination. This experience led to nomination, through presidential executive order in 1979, of a federal inspector. During this period, permits were issued to extend TAPS to Kuparuk, Endicott, Point MacIntyre, and Milne, and authorization of 1,400 miles of gathering lines. The JPO today is most influenced by the *Exxon Valdez* disaster and problems of the aging pipeline. Governor Cowper sought to strengthen the office to review and improve oil spill plans and to correct massive corrosion problems on the pipeline. Providing coordination for the gasline project (then spearheaded by Yukon Pacific) was an objective as well. JPO includes a core group of eleven government agencies and offers a one-stop agency to the oil and gas industry. It is financed primarily by Alyeska representing the consortium of oil companies, which pays $1.4 million annually in order to have permits issued expeditiously. (Jerry Brossia, interviews, January 27, 1998, and July 21, 2000.)

46. See "Corroding Pipelines Show Prudhoe Bay's Age," *Fairbanks Daily News-Miner,* April 23, 2001. Prudhoe Bay BP workers complained about maintenance problems and violations, including pressure valves and fire-suppression systems at oil processing centers that had not been inspected on schedule. Their complaints reached Rep. John Dingell (D-Michigan) and Rep. George Miller (D-California), who pressured BP to investigate complaints and remedy safety and maintenance problems. See also *Fairbanks Daily News-Miner*, July 18, 2001.

47. BLM, *Draft Environmental Impact Statement*, 3.7–3.14.

48. A large number of scientific studies and reports document the extensive restoration activities. See, for example, P. G. Well, J. N. Butler, and J. S. Hughes, eds., *Exxon Valdez Oil Spill: Fate and Effects in Alaskan Waters* (Philadelphia: ASTM, 1995). Also see the *Exxon Valdez* Oil Spill Trustee Council website at www.evostc.state.ak.us.

49. BLM, *Draft Environmental Impact Statement*, 3.1–3.21.

50. For example, Walter Parker and Stan Stephens, "Oil Pipeline Oversight Needed," *Fairbanks Daily News-Miner,* July 3, 2002.

51. BLM, *Draft Environmental Impact Statement*, 3.1–3.3.

52. Joint Pipeline Office, *Summary of Public Scoping Comments: Trans-Alaska Pipeline System Right-of-Way Renewal Environmental Impact Statement* (Anchorage: November 2001), p. 3.

53. BLM, *Draft Environmental Impact Statement*, ES-2.

54. See Jerry McBeath, "Oil Transportation Infrastructure: The Trans-Alaska Pipeline System and the Challenge of Environmental Change." In M. Ruth, ed., *Smart Growth and Climate Change: Regional Development, Infrastructure and Adaptation* (Northampton, MA: Edward Elgar, 2006), pp. 129–152.

55. *Anchorage Daily News,* March 11, 2006.

56. *Fairbanks Daily News-Miner*, April 7, 2006.

57. Ibid., August 8, 2006.

58. Ibid., August 9, 2006.

59. Ibid., August 26, 2006. Also see Richard Fineberg, "Evidence Mounts from

Alaska and Elsewhere: BP's North Slope Problems Should Have Been No Surprise to Public Officials or Monitors," September 3, 2006, available from www.fineberg research.com (accessed January 26, 2007).

60. Report of the Alaska Department of Natural Resources Transition Team, December 19, 2006.

61. Report of the Alaska Department of Environmental Conservation's Transition Team, December 19, 2006.

62. Peter Hanley, BP Exploration (Alaska) Inc., interviews, February 8, 1999, and December 19, 2000.

63. Walter A. Rosenbaum, *Environmental Politics and Policy*, 5th ed. (Washington, DC: CQ Press, 2002).

64. Brad Fristoe, Department of Environmental Conservation, interviews, January 27, 1999, and June 20, 2000.

65. Mark Major, ARCO Alaska Inc., interview, January 28, 1999.

66. Gary Schultz, Division of Land, interviews, February 5, 1999, and June 16, 2000.

67. *Fairbanks Daily News-Miner,* August 19, 2001. These comments were repeated by all DEC personnel interviewed. For example, an environmental specialist said, "We do less in the field than we want and there's much less equipment, travel, training than we need to do our jobs." Ted Moore, Division of Spill Prevention and Response, Industry Preparedness and Pipeline Program, DEC, Anchorage, interview, June 6, 2000.

68. Title 5 is completely funded by fees. Oil companies pay five cents per barrel into the Superfund program.

69. Ted Rockwell, EPA, Anchorage, interview, July 21, 2000.

70. Gary Schulz, Natural Resource Specialist, DOL, DNR, Fairbanks, interview, June 16, 2000.

71. Al Ott, Supervisor, Habitat Division, ADFG, Fairbanks, interview, June 21, 2000.

72. An ADFG respondent stated, "Without industry support, we would have no field presence at all. We need people in the field to do a good job on permits. I don't view industry paying for our research and travel as a conflict. The statutes allow us to do that." Personal interview with Al Ott, ADFG, Fairbanks, June 21, 2000.

73. *Anchorage Daily News*, March 6, 2002.

74. *Fairbanks Daily News-Miner,* March 1, 2002. Neither BP nor Phillips responded to reports of the survey. However, the Knowles administration pointed to the low response rate and said "half of those had pretty good positive things to say about the agency." The commissioner, Michelle Brown, who had made several controversial reassignments, charged the survey agency with bias and said, "The vast majority of DEC employees are very active problem-solvers looking for real environmental improvement." In the continuing controversy over DEC enforcement of regulations, a group of four environmental organizations sued the agency, alleging permits had been illegally granted to the oil industry based on a set of inadequate assumptions about oil spills. See *Fairbanks Daily News-Miner*, July 12, 2002.

75. A recent glossy BP oil development manual emphasizes that "the industry on the North Slope operates in a safe and environmentally careful manner." See BP Exploration (Alaska) Inc., *Environmental Performance on Alaska's North Slope* (Anchorage: February 1998), p. iii.

76. For the classic argument for the value of redundancy in the context of public administration, see Martin Landau, "Redundance, Rationality, and the Problem of Duplication and Overlap," *Public Administration Review* 29 (July–August 1969): 346–358.

# 9

## Conclusion

We conclude this study by examining three topics. First, we summarize the similarities and differences between Alaska and other oil-producing regions of the world. Second, we address the question of Alaska's dependency, by considering six important oil industry–state relationships. Finally, we suggest the relevance of Alaska's story to other oil-producing regions.

### ▓ Alaska Compared to Other Oil-Producing Regions

In his recent study of Alaska history entitled *Alaska: An American Colony*, historian Stephen Haycox comments,

> Alaska is an economic colony and increasingly a political and social one as well. Its cultures and livelihood are characterized by dependence on forces outside the territory and largely outside the control of its residents. Despite protestations, mythologies, and even intimations of independence, this former *and present* colony is likely to remain dependent well into the future.[1] (emphasis added)

The Haycox perspective echoes Jeannette Nichols's and other historians' traditional "neglect thesis" of Alaska history, which holds that the federal government neglected Alaska, thereby exposing the region's resources to corporate exploitation and making it an economic colony.[2] While recognizing exploitation and colonization, revisionist interpretations like those of William Wilson, Claus-M. Naske, and Terrence Cole present evidence that Alaska was not neglected by the federal government, and that even if it were, its remote location and small population would have justified some degree of neglect.[3] Our question is whether contemporary Alaska remains an "American colony," and we believe that this view can no longer be sustained.

Part of the current mythology of politics in Alaska is the state's alleged "quasi-colonial" status, seen in the Alaska stories reflecting conflict of settlers, transients, and Alaska Natives with outside forces, including both multinational corporations and the federal government. Indeed, there are several similarities between Alaska and oil-producing regions in the Third World. Alaska, like Saudi Arabia and Nigeria, has a "one crop" economy, lacking significant economic diversification even fifty years after statehood. Alaska, like the oil fields in Indonesia and Russia, is remote and isolated from both national and global centers of power. Like most other oil-producing regions, Alaska has an underdeveloped infrastructure. There are no roads in many rural areas, and the number of roads connecting Alaska cities is small. The human infrastructure of sanitary water systems and mechanized waste removal in a third of Native villages is lacking or primitive. Finally, Alaska is relatively easily penetrated by external forces, such as national and multinational corporations with investment plans able to discount the high costs of doing business in the distant North.

The differences between Alaska and other oil-producing regions, however, make a strong argument against use of the colonial label. Alaska, unlike most of the other oil-producing regions of the world, has a large variety of natural resources, both renewable and nonrenewable. Although it continues to have a boom-and-bust economy, the central points of the economy have changed since acquisition by Russia in the 1740s—from fur-bearing animals, to gold mining, salmon fishery, timber harvesting, and up to the contemporary oil and gas boom. Fur-bearing animals are now less abundant but also are little demanded in the twenty-first-century marketplace. Not only does the state still hold large quantities of gold but also other scarce minerals such as nickel and molybdenum. The fate of the salmon fishery rises and falls with climate cycles and changing demand for wild as opposed to farmed products, but the offshore fishery of the state is the world's richest. Coal resources are among the world's largest, and the low sulfur content of most Alaska coal makes it less of an environmental pollutant than coal from many other regions. Timber resources remain relatively abundant, and the state hosts much of North America's remaining old-growth forests. Finally, although the state's first and second largest oil fields—Prudhoe Bay and Kuparuk—are approaching depletion within two decades, undeveloped oil resources in ANWR and NPR-A are estimated to be huge, and North Slope natural gas resources alone, waiting to be exploited, amount to more than 38 trillion cubic feet, greater than those of any other US or contemporary Canadian region.

The key point is who benefits from development of these resources. Here, the political differences between Alaska and the other oil-producing regions are equally striking. Alaska is part of the world's richest and strongest nation-state, and this state has a powerful administrative capability. The United States enshrines the rule of law in all government operations, and its political processes are relatively transparent. The state of Alaska mirrors these national attributes, and it has the political-legal authority and administrative capacity to capture significant benefits from its resources and to regulate their development. As a result of oil development, the state is quite rich, with the highest per-capita spending (in both state and federal dollars) of any US state. In addition to a Permanent Fund containing $40 billion in mid-2007, a first for any US government, it has rainy-day and development accounts totaling another $10 billion. The wealth of the state is sufficient to award each resident an annual PF dividend that cumulatively reached $27,536.41 per resident by October 2007.

## ▨ The Question of Dependency

Notwithstanding Alaska's position in a rich and powerful nation-state and the state's political-administrative capacity and resource and capital wealth, there remain colonial aspects to the state's relationship to its environment and particularly to multinational oil and gas companies. It is difficult to answer the question of the state's dependency unequivocally because the nature of the state's relationship varies by changing in-state, national, and global conditions and over time as well. We can, however, approach an answer by exploring state–oil industry relationships through six important dimensions.

### *The State as Owner of Hydrocarbon Resources*

Former governor Hickel repeatedly has called Alaska an "owner state" as one means to indicate what in his view is the unfulfilled potential of Alaska as a resource treasure trove. Indeed, the Prudhoe Bay bonanza took place on state-owned lands, the oil and gas reserves of which were leased to multinational oil companies. As noted in Chapters 2 and 4, on two occasions the state has considered exercising its ownership powers through direct participation in the oil and gas business. Although the state has never contemplated exploring for or producing oil and gas or marketing Alaska oil and gas in US or global markets—for example, through a specially chartered state corporation—it has considered part ownership in the system transporting oil and gas to markets.

In the early 1970s, before approval of the routing of TAPS, Governor Egan proposed that the state participate in construction of the pipeline from Prudhoe Bay to Valdez. This was at a time when the state was impoverished and, to balance budgets, it needed to assess reserve taxes on anticipated oil production once the pipeline was completed. The state's bonding authority was limited, raising the question of how the state would finance an ownership interest in the pipeline. A second question was how the state would absorb risk of construction problems or pipeline failure. The governor seemed halfhearted in his pursuit of the idea, which did not gain support from the state legislature, and the proposal was stillborn.

In the 2005–2006 negotiations of the Murkowski administration with natural gas producers, the governor proposed a state minority ownership interest in a natural gas pipeline from Prudhoe Bay to the contiguous forty-eight states. More than three decades after the Egan administration, Alaska was a rich state and could easily fund its 20 percent interest through direct appropriations from surpluses (indeed the Murkowski administration deposited $600 million in a reserve fund for this purpose in the FY 2007 budget) and revenue bonds. Many legislators were cool to this proposal, however, pointing out that the state's stake would not qualify it for control over natural gas transportation charges, while the state might become liable for major risks encountered in pipeline construction. Perhaps of equal importance was the public perception—as expressed by voters in the 2006 Republican gubernatorial primary—that Governor Murkowski had not effectively applied all of the leverage that the state derives from its ownership of the resource in his negotiations with the oil and gas producers.

The new Palin administration reversed the state's approach to the gas producers. She declined to operate under the Stranded Gas Development Act and instead proposed the Alaska Gasline Inducement Act. Rejecting the concept of state partial ownership, she proposed state assistance of up to $500 million in permitting and other preconstruction work. A large majority in both houses of the Alaska legislature approved this plan. Legislators liked its transparency, firm requirements for meeting deadlines on pipeline construction, and its "must haves"—the pipeline company would need to provide for expansion of pipeline capacity as new gas resources (many from independent producers) came online. It would need to provide gas for in-state use and agree to a project labor agreement. In mid-2007, the state opened its request for pipeline construction proposals, but the three gas producers found the terms too rigid and objected to lack of long-term guarantees on taxation. It remains uncertain whether they would agree to market their gas in a line built and owned by other companies.

The state has not taken an ownership interest in the oil and gas transportation business, and thus we cannot know if this would improve its leverage with the industry. The state's decision to lease oil and gas resources to multinational corporations is one expression of its powers of ownership. A second is that state statutes empower the Alaska Oil and Gas Conservation Commission to protect the state's ownership interest. The most recent example is the state's suit against ExxonMobil for this corporation's failure to develop gas from the Point Thompson field, which contains nearly 7 trillion cubic feet of gas. A third expression, noted in Chapter 6, is the state's disposition of its retained royalty share of oil and gas resources. Overall, the state has the capacity to exercise greater leverage over the oil industry than it has done to date. In other words, as an "owner state," Alaska potentially can equal the influence of the oil industry and is not dependent on it.

## The State as Sovereign

The state of Alaska has sovereign powers of taxation over oil industry operations in Alaska, and the profits derived from those operations, through corporate income taxes, severance taxes, and licenses and fees. Chapter 4 indicated the difficulty in determining, across the thirty-year history of oil production from Prudhoe Bay and other North Slope sites, if the state's "take" has been low, high, or average. The supposition, for which there appears to be supporting evidence, is that in most years, the state legislature has been reluctant to tax to the plausible limit for fear of an oil industry "investment strike"—that the industry would leave the state or decline to continue and expand investment to explore for and develop new sources of oil and gas. This supposition suggests that the legislature and executive have *anticipated* adverse oil industry reactions to prospects of increased taxation, and that they have been satisfied with lower tax revenue than possible, a reflection of the dependency argument.

Counter evidence is found in four episodes of increased taxation. The first was the legislature's adoption of "separate accounting" from 1979 to 1981, as explained in Chapters 4 and 5. The separate accounting system did significantly increase the state's take; it was the product of the "sunshine boys," populist reformers who dominated the State House of Representatives until the legislative coup of 1981, a coup that was supported (if not initiated) by the oil industry. Yet, at the recommendation of Governor Hammond, the legislature repealed separate accounting in the belief (which proved unfounded) that the courts would sustain legal challenges by the oil industry.

The second instance was the legislature's modification of the economic limit factor after the *Exxon Valdez* oil spill of March 1989. Public outrage over the massive oil spill in Prince William Sound fortified legislative critics of the oil industry. The third instance was the legislature's adoption of the petroleum profits tax in the second special session of the 2006 legislature. The new tax, which significantly increased the state's revenues (under conditions of high oil prices), was motivated by the impending application of the ELF to the large Kuparuk field, by outrage over very high gasoline prices (and correspondingly high oil company profits), as well as by the 267,000-barrel oil spill on the North Slope, the largest on-land spill in the history of Alaska petroleum production. That a conservative Republican governor, Murkowski, proposed the tax and then insisted that the legislature enact it was a factor of importance as well. Then, little over one year later, Governor Palin called lawmakers into a thirty-day special session to revisit the PPT. She claimed the tax rate had not produced as much revenue as expected and alleged that the process of enacting it was corrupted by VECO (see Chapters 3 and 4).

Meeting less than three months after convictions of two legislators on bribery and corruption charges, and while a third legislator was tried and convicted, the governor proposed raising the PPT to 25 percent, applying a surtax on net operating profits when oil prices exceeded $30/barrel, restricting tax credits, and expanding auditing, reporting, and penalty provisions to strengthen state power. Hearings demonstrated strong opposition from oil companies and their employees, but by the close of the session, two-thirds majorities of each house endorsed Palin's request (which is likely to increase state revenues by $1.6 billion for fiscal year 2008).[4]

Changing partisan patterns in the executive and legislature have bearing on petroleum revenue policy, as do exogenous factors such as serious environmental disturbances. The four tax increases are evidence that the state's taxation policy is not fully hostage to the oil industry.

## The State as Regulator

The third dimension of state power expresses the state's share of full regulatory powers over oil field personnel health and safety and environmental protection on the North Slope, the United State's largest oil province. Chapter 8 exhaustively treated the North Slope oil and gas environmental protection regime, composed of federal, state, and local elements. While federal elements are invariant across US oil regions (and are considered tougher than oil environmental regulations of most nation-states), states vary in their degree of environmental rigor. Alaska modeled its statutes on those of California in the early 1970s, then considered the toughest in the United States.

In the course of oil development on the North Slope, the state refined its regulations and added staff to primary resource regulatory agencies—the Departments of Natural Resources, Environmental Conservation, and Fish and Game. Further strengthening of federal and state law followed environmental crises, most notably the *Exxon Valdez* oil spill of 1989 and the 2006 North Slope oil spill. Throughout the early period (1977 to about 1991), the relationship of both state and federal agencies with the oil industry was distant. As explained in Chapter 8, the distant relationship also bred conflict, creating an adversarial government-to-business connection.

In the 1990s and early twenty-first century, the state's role as regulator of oil and gas development changed. The second Hickel administration from 1990 to 1994 was a near replay of the first (1966–1969) in its emphasis on rapid development of the state's resources, particularly oil and gas. Moreover, the governor intervened in the regulatory process, threatening to fire employees of Fish and Game and DEC who raised environmental objections to granting permits for oil development projects. The next, Democratic administration of Knowles (1994–2002) ironically continued this emphasis. Knowles campaigned for "jobs and kids" in both the 1994 and 1998 state elections, and by the end of his administration he had garnered significant support from the oil industry (support that he held in his 2006 gubernatorial race against

Republican Palin). It was during his administration that environmental critics complained about the weakening of state environmental protection efforts through eliminating or failing to fill empty positions in DNR, DEC, and ADFG. Finally, the Murkowski administration (2002–2006) strengthened the pro-oil development emphasis of the Knowles administration. Following Knowles, Governor Murkowski claimed that the state would simplify regulations affecting the oil industry. Going one step beyond Knowles, Murkowski moved the Habitat Division (which enforces Title 41, the state's important habitat protection power) from the Department of Fish and Game to the Department of Natural Resources (where it is called the Office of Habitat Management and Permitting).

What explains this reversal in the state's regulatory role? Clearly partisan factors are of limited influence, as both Republican and Democratic governors favored the narrowing of distance between the state and the oil industry.[5] We suggest that four alternate factors were more important. First, national environmental policy changed after the Reagan administration, and governments began to encourage public sector–industry partnerships and use of market-based mechanisms, while reducing command-and-control methods. Second, both the state and the oil industry had matured during their negotiations of many years. Both government and industry representatives whom we interviewed remarked that close ties made relationships more efficient, and they had become used to dealing with one another.

Third, oil production from Prudhoe Bay began to decline in 1989, making state officials increasingly aware of the need to spur investment into new oil and gas exploratory efforts. This prompted more laissez-faire attitudes on the part of state officials. Fourth and simultaneous with the decline in oil production, oil prices were relatively low, particularly from the mid-1990s through 2004. Indeed, on ten occasions in the fifteen years from 1992 to 2007, the state needed to borrow money from the CBR to balance the budget. Royalties and severance taxes from oil production were insufficient alone to pay for costs of state government services.

Near the end of his term in office, Governor Murkowski had negotiated with the three multinational firms owning leases to most of Alaska's North Slope oil and natural gas—ExxonMobil, BP, and ConocoPhillips. That agreement resulted in the PPT, an increase in the state's take from oil production when oil prices are high. The oil companies had asked for certainty in the state's petroleum taxation regime and supported the governor's proposal. Company officials blanched when legislators increased the take from 20 to 22.5 percent (yet legislators also increased oil company credits), but they ultimately accepted the legislation. (As noted above, in November 2007, legislators increased the take again.)

This was a clear benefit to the state's close bargaining relationship with the oil industry. The cost, however, was the natural gas pipeline proposal, which not only pledged a state ownership interest in the line, without accounting for liability, but also would have frozen taxes on state gas through the lifetime of the contract (thirty-five years), without guaranteeing that the companies would build the line, provide Alaskans easy access to the gas, or affirmatively hire Alaskans for pipeline jobs. The governor's chief consultant, Pedro van Meurs, while supporting the contract proposal, pointed out that the taxation provisions were flawed: "This is a degree of fiscal stability that is normally reserved for highly corrupt and completely unreliable states. . . . There is absolutely no need to treat Alaska as a banana republic in order to secure the gas line."[6]

Thus, as a regulator, the state reduced its distance from oil companies, and the companies in turn more than met the state halfway. The close relationship brought benefits to the state, but there were costs as well—not only in the Murkowski natural gas contract proposal but also in monitoring of TAPS, as indicated in Chapter 8.

The state's powers as owner, sovereign, and regulator give it significant opportunities for leverage with the multinational oil industry. What our research reveals, however, is the reluctance of the state to exercise its full powers, most often because it is *apprehensive* that the oil industry will reduce its investment in Alaska. To complete this analysis, we turn to the powers and resources of the oil industry.

## The Oil Industry as Resource Developer

As mentioned, Alaska's political leaders have never debated publicly whether the state should explore for and produce its own oil and gas resources. Nor have political leaders ever publicly discussed selling Alaska's oil and gas resources to markets in the contiguous forty-eight states. As Chapter 6 makes clear, the state consistently has settled for royalty shares of oil, a part of which has been sold to in-state refineries to meet local needs. Thus, we conclude that the only interest displayed by the state in the oil and gas business has been transportation of product to market, and this interest became serious only in the context of development of the Alaska natural gas pipeline. These attitudes of state leaders reflect a traditional American indisposition to intervention in oil and gas energy markets. After all, no American state government has ever explored for, produced, or marketed that state's oil and gas resources.

Instead, the state reflexively turned to international oil and gas corporations. Since oil began flowing through TAPS, Alaska has negotiated primarily with just three multinational oil corporations (or the predecessors, which they absorbed): ExxonMobil, BP, and ConocoPhillips. In 2007, these were the world's second, fourth, and ninth largest corporations, respectively (and the world's first, third, and fifth largest oil/gas-producing firms). The capitalization required to produce oil and gas in a remote region such as Alaska and market the resource is huge, and these corporations are among the world's richest firms. In 2007, ExxonMobil had assets of $219 billion; BP, $217 billion; and ConocoPhillips, $113 billion.[7]

These companies are the source of the expensive technology needed to explore for, produce, and transport oil and gas to markets, and as the technology has improved, it has become more expensive. Too, oil company assets have become increasingly concentrated through the international wave of mergers and acquisitions in the 1990s. The most familiar name in Alaska oil business, Atlantic Richfield (later ARCO), disappeared when it was acquired by BP in 1999. While a number of smaller oil firms do business in Alaska, such as Anadarko, the role of small firms and independents has been eclipsed by multinationals.

We noted in both Chapters 5 and 7 that the wealth of Alaska has increased dramatically since statehood, as represented in the Permanent Fund and reserve funds totaling more than $40 billion (not including the value of sub-surface resources owned by the state). The state's credit rating has improved as well, and for these two reasons, in the twenty-first century the state could participate in gas pipeline construction, but under the Palin administration it has declined to do so. Still, however, the tradable assets of multinational corporations dwarf those of the richest state government in the United States.

## Oil Corporations as Free Agents

Although multinational corporations in Alaska are chartered as public corporations and required to act in the public interest, they are not place-bound. Each of the multinationals has large investments in other parts of the United States and the world. For example, only 33 percent of ExxonMobil's operations are in North and South America. If ExxonMobil, BP, and ConocoPhillips find their operations in Alaska to be unprofitable, they are free to move and invest elsewhere.

The oil industry does not hesitate to flaunt its free agency. As discussed in more detail below, the industry spends millions of dollars for full-page newspaper ads and ninety-second TV spots in which it makes veiled threats that if state terms of doing business become unacceptable, it will transfer operations to other places.

As noted throughout this volume, state policymakers have been reluctant to take on Big Oil. Only environmental crises and rare periods of public outrage (as in 1989–1990 and 2006–2007) have emboldened leaders to cry out for a rebalancing of the state's relationship with the industry.

## Oil Industry as Policy Advocate

The final strength of the oil industry in Alaska is in its role as policy advocate, a role protected by the Alaska and federal constitutions. The industry has been successful in cultivating both the public and leaders through three means: campaign contributions and activity, media advertising, and lobbying. Through mobilization of its resources in the state, industry has reduced and often eliminated conflict with government and the public.

As noted in Chapter 3, since the late 1980s, the oil industry has donated more money to election and issue campaigns than any other group in Alaska, including all unions. Typically, the industry prefers to support Republican candidates, who are more likely to support development goals than Democrats; yet the industry has a record of supporting incumbents whether Republican or Democrat, particularly if they hold leadership positions. In close races, oil industry contributions may be a factor in determining outcomes, although several candidates receiving large oil industry donations in close races have lost. The industry also makes large contributions in noncompetitive races as a means to fortify its access to decisionmakers.

In addition, the oil industry is the most consistent advertiser of policy positions in the state's newspapers and television channels. Invariably, these ads emphasize the need to develop Alaska's oil and/or gas resources and the industry's commitment to the Alaska workforce by featuring employees who sing corporate praises. Many of the ads also are self-consciously multicultural and multiethnic, portraying the industry's interests as complementary to those of the state's indigenous and minority populations. Oil companies have been assiduous in their contributions to community groups and charitable organizations. These contributions are mentioned in industry advertising. In fact, during the mid-2006 PPT debate, a full-page newspaper ad purchased by ConocoPhillips argued that if legislators significantly increased oil profits taxes, the industry would no longer be able to make charitable contributions in Alaska.

Finally, the oil industry has been the state's most effective lobbyist, before both the executive and legislative branches. The companies select lobbyists carefully and prefer to tap former legislators or members of the executive branch. Jerry Reinwand, a former chief-of-staff for Governor Hammond, carries several oil company accounts. Within months of leaving the state senate, Republican Sean Parnell was retained as government relations director for ConocoPhillips. (In the 2006 elections, Parnell was elected lieutenant governor of Alaska.) Second generation Republican legislator Mark Hanley (once chair of the House Finance Committee) is government relations director and chief lobbyist for Anadarko Petroleum.

As noted in an earlier study, the small size of the Alaska legislature works to the advantage of the industry.[8] The Alaska Senate has only twenty members, and the industry need convince only ten in order to stop adverse action. Historically, lobbyists have played roles in the organization of power in the Senate. While public outrage in response to environmental disasters or, in 2006–2007, very high company profits have been an obstacle to oil industry lobbying, many of the regulatory and tax issues concerning the industry receive little public or media attention and are subject to the persuasive influence of lobbyists.

Of course, Alaska is a democratic state with mostly transparent disclosure laws on campaign contributions and lobbying. Enforcement of the rules, however, has been problematic. The campaign and lobbying watchdog agency is the Alaska Public Offices Commission, and it has been subject to attacks from both governors and legislators. In his second term (1990–1994), Governor Hickel proposed to eliminate funding for APOC, arguing that it was the responsibility of newspapers, not a state agency, to monitor campaign contributions. While perhaps no legislature is truly friendly toward an agency dedicated to "follow the money" in election campaigns, the Republican-dominated legislature from 1995 to 2006 cut positions at APOC, while liberalizing both donation rules (reversed by voters in 2006) and lobbying restrictions.

As mentioned in Chapter 3, scandals concerning donations of VECO executives to six legislators (members of the "Corrupt Bastards Club") were a factor in the 2006 state elections and the election of a reformist, Republican governor. In announcing plans for the state's FY 2008 budget, she asked the legislature to add investigative staff to APOC (but only one). It is noteworthy that the Federal Bureau of Investigation and not the state attorney general brought indictments against the legislators. To her credit, the state's new governor asked legislators to conduct a major overhaul of ethics statutes for the executive and legislature, which they did in the 2007 session.

What this review of oil industry relationships suggests is that corporate resources, free agency, and policy advocacy protect private interests quite well during "normal" times. When the public and its representatives are aroused and the media attentive, however, the state has exercised its authority as owner, sovereign, and regulator and set limits to industry action.

Also, one should not forget the importance of differing relationships over time based on changes in interests. As the oil industry matures and state political institutions become more capable, the relationship between the two evolves to address the changing needs of both parties. In the 1970s, the main dynamic could be described as a contest over division of the rent windfall from Prudhoe Bay. By 2000, much of the rent windfall had been realized (and allocated or spent), and the dynamic had shifted to focus on encouraging industry to continue making large financial investments in Alaska instead of elsewhere. In this latter dynamic, the interests of local industry leaders and state leaders are more closely aligned, which has promoted greater cooperation and less conflict.

## ▨ Relevance of Alaska's Story

We believe that this narrative of the multinational oil industry in Alaska is relevant to other oil-producing regions of the world. Space does not permit our presenting an exhaustive list of the lessons from Alaska's experience, and we focus on just four system characteristics: transparency of government operations, populism, state administrative capacity, and civil society. Each characteristic is potentially variable over time, which frustrates the analyst's wish to make tidy judgments about state-industry relationships.

## Transparency

Alaska is a democratic polity, and its laws provide public access to information on campaign contributions, lobbying contracts, business comments to administrative agencies, and personal finances of public officials. It is possible to know who influences the state's oil taxation and policy regime. It is possible to trace the relationship of state decisionmakers to business firms. It is possible to ascertain the comments and responses of public officials to oil exploration, production, and transportation proposals. This transparency has been effective in maintaining public trust and legitimacy in the industry-government relationship, and this transparency is facilitated because of Alaska's relatively small population with its unusually easy access to public officials.

The primary exception to transparency has been the state's Stranded Gas Development Act. This allowed the governor to negotiate with the producers behind closed doors and to release the proposed contract only when he chose to do so. Public (and legislative) outcry over these secret negotiations in 2005–2006 led Governor Palin to seek a new authority for negotiations with potential pipeline builders that were transparent to the public. The Alaska Gasline Inducement Act was the result.

Availability of information and free access to it does not mean that potential conflicts with the law will be revealed automatically. This requires a vigilant public and press, and monitoring of information by agencies both public and private. Recent ethics scandals in Alaska are less a problem of transparency than lack of public and private scrutiny of government operations.

## Populism

Populism is an important element of the Alaska political culture, and it shows its force in relations between the people and their government and between government and industry. As noted in Chapters 5 and 7, the creation of the PFD gave each Alaskan an interest in protecting the PF against "raids," which would lessen the amount available to each in future years. This powerful constituency has made it very difficult for the legislature to allocate PF earnings to government purposes, and perhaps to develop a long-range fiscal plan involving taxation of the citizenry. Thus, the PFDs have become an important constraint on government action.

The PFDs may, however, strengthen the position of the state government.

Most Alaskans now believe that they are owners and entitled to a share of the state's resource wealth. This gives the Alaska public an interest in forming the best bargain with those corporations that would exploit Alaska's wealth. In view of this, a number of commentators urged the Iraqi government to adopt an oil dividend plan to strengthen public involvement and stability in the society. In short, Alaska populism may fortify state government in its negotiations with multinational corporations and assign a watchdog role to the citizenry in state-industry relations.

### State Administrative Capacity

In the territorial era and early into statehood, the Alaska state bureaucracy was a poor match for international oil companies. As the state gained oil wealth, the bureaucracy professionalized. Agencies required applicants with stronger educational and experience qualifications, and they paid them higher salaries. In some of the state agencies, salaries (including benefits and pension plans) competed with industry salaries. This development led to greater equalization of information and expertise on oil and gas issues between the state's resource agencies and members of the industry. The effect is mixed. A better-paid, more influential state bureaucracy facilitates a revolving door for officials moving between government and industry, while the professionalization of its bureaucracy gives the state more autonomy from external forces.

In Chapter 8, we noted that there were lapses, perhaps serious, in the capability of at least one of the state's resource agencies (DEC) in the late 1990s, after continued budget cutting from the Republican legislature. This impaired state monitoring of environmental policy compliance by industry. While state administrative capacity was temporarily impaired, federal capacity was not.

### Civil Society

By civil society, we mean the network of nongovernmental organizations and formal and informal social groups and networks in the state. If the groups collectively are robust, they are a powerful constraint on authoritarian and corrupt tendencies of rulers. Because they are plural, and each reflects a slightly different version of the public interest, collectively they enrich public discourse and may in fact defend the interest of the state against external forces.

The size and robustness of civil society varies by population size and social diversity, and Alaska has increased in both respects since statehood. The state population has more than doubled since 1959, and Alaska is no longer America's least populous state. For a region of fewer than 700,000 residents, Alaska has a rich array of economic, ethnic, environmental, social, fraternal, and political groups. Civil society also includes private media such as newspapers, radio, and television stations, and now the Internet. One might also add the state's extensive university system, which—although not strictly part of civil society because of its reliance on state budgetary allocations and governance by a board of regents appointed by the governor—is a source of independent research on the economic, social, political, public education, and environmental impacts of the industry.

When the oil producers constructed TAPS in 1973–1977, a small number of groups and individuals monitored the process. Although this coincided with the rise of the national environmental movement, most environmental NGOs were national and not local. In the early twenty-first century, Alaska hosts more than fifty environmental organizations, and they easily form alliances among themselves and with national environmental organizations. Labor unions closely follow oil development activities, as do most of the state's Native-owned corporations and nonprofit organizations. Even individuals have specialized in monitoring oil industry activities, such as Fairbanks watchdog Richard Fineberg.[9] Many groups within Alaska civil society strongly support the oil industry, such as chambers of commerce in large cities, oil field workers organized into associations such as the Alliance and VECO, and of course industry employees. But the network of groups is not an oil industry chorus, and groups criticizing the influence of oil multinationals on occasion are as vocal as those who identify closely with the industry.

The system characteristics—transparency, populism, administrative capacity, and civil society—are *variable* over time and may not change in tandem. During Governor Murkowski's negotiations with gas producers in 2005–2006, for example, transparency was low, populist forces were rising in influence, and the Alaska civil society was robust. Altogether, we argue that these characteristics of Alaska's maturing political system, along with the statutory and constitutional powers of the state within the federal union, have brought Alaska closer to rough parity with multinational oil and gas corporations doing business in the state. We see a mature but dependent state dealing more effectively with a dominant but constrained industry.

Throughout, we have mentioned the growing capacity of the state to manage its own destiny. Also, we have discussed elements of uncertainty and vulnerability that give the oil and gas multinationals potential future advantages in a global economy. Resource-dependent economies are vulnerable because of technological developments beyond their control, which can negatively affect the value of their resources (for example, the effect of synthetic rubber on Indochina and Brazil). As well, lack of diversification leads to the "oil curse" and the "Dutch disease." For these reasons, the new relationship between the state and industry is fragile and always subject to change.

## ▓ Notes

1. Stephen Haycox, *Alaska: An American Colony* (Seattle: University of Washington Press, 2002), p. 156.

2. Jeannette Paddock Nichols, *Alaska: A Short History of Its Administration* (Cleveland, OH: Arthur H. Clark, 1924).

3. See William H. Wilson, "Alaska's Past, Alaska's Future," *Alaska Review* 4, no. 1 (1970); Claus-M. Naske and Herman Slotnick, *Alaska: A History of the Forty-ninth State*, 2nd ed. (Norman: University of Oklahoma Press, 1987); and Terrence Cole, "The History of a History," *Pacific Northwest Quarterly* 77 (October 1986). Also see George Rogers, *The Future of Alaska: The Economic Consequences of Statehood* (Baltimore: The Johns Hopkins Press, 1962), ch. 3 and 5.

4. The $1.6 billion in additional revenue for FY 08 matches the difference between actual revenues and those projected by the state Department of Revenue for the 2006 PPT at the same high prices, when the legislature passed the bill in August 2006. It was this forecasting error that attracted the governor's attention, and, of course, her support for changing the tax was critical to its enactment. See Alaska Special Session Reports, Vol. 2, no. 5 (November 9, 2007) and Vol. 2, no. 7 (November 19, 2007), Juneau; and the Bradners' Alaska Economic Report, November 28, 2007.

5. Nevertheless, it should be noted that from the 1994 elections through 2006, both houses of the Alaska Legislature were under the control of a nearly veto-proof Republican majority. This majority introduced a $250 million, five-year budget reduction plan following its election. Several members of the majority targeted positions for elimination in state resource agencies because they believed state regulatory policy was too strict.

6. Steve Quinn, "Memo Cites Concerns over Murkowski's Pipeline Plan," *Fairbanks Daily News-Miner*, January 26, 2007, p. 6.

7. See http://money.cnn.com/magazines/fortune/fortune_archive/2007/07/23/1001385836/index.htm.

8. See Gerald A. McBeath and Thomas A. Morehouse, *Alaska Politics and Government* (Lincoln: University of Nebraska Press, 1994), p. 70.

9. Fineberg is a former University of Alaska faculty member, advisor to Governor Cowper, and freelance journalist who publishes a newsletter on oil and gas issues. See www.finebergresearch.com.

# Acronyms

| | |
|---|---|
| ACES | Alaskan's Clear and Equitable Share |
| ACIR | Advisory Commission on Intergovernmental Relations |
| ACMP | Alaska Coastal Management Plan |
| ADFG | Alaska Department of Fish and Game |
| AFN | Alaska Federation of Natives |
| AGIA | Alaska Gasline Inducement Act |
| AHF | Alberta Heritage Savings Trust Fund |
| AHFC | The Alaska Housing Finance Corporation |
| AIDEA | Alaska Industrial Development and Export Authority |
| Alpetco | Alaska Petrochemical Company |
| AMBBA | Alaska Municipal Bond Bank Authority |
| ANCSA | Alaska Native Claims Settlement Act |
| ANGTS | Alaska Natural Gas Transportation System |
| ANILCA | Alaska National Interest Lands Conservation Act |
| ANS | Alaska North Slope |
| ANWR | Arctic National Wildlife Refuge |
| AOGA | Alaska Oil and Gas Association |
| AOGCC | Alaska Oil and Gas Conservation Commission |
| APFC | Alaska Permanent Fund Corporation |
| APIC | Alaska Public Interest Coalition |
| APOC | Alaska Public Offices Commission |
| ARCO | Atlantic Richfield Company |
| AS | Alaska Statute |
| ASLC | Alaska Student Loan Corporation |
| ASRC | Arctic Slope Regional Corporation |
| BIA | Bureau of Indian Affairs |
| BLM | Bureau of Land Management |
| BP | British Petroleum |
| CBR | Constitutional Budget Reserve |

| | |
|---|---|
| CBRF | Constitutional Budget Reserve Fund |
| CEO | chief executive officer |
| CIRI | Cook Inlet Regional Incorporated |
| COE | Corps of Engineers |
| CPI | consumer price index |
| CWA | Clean Water Act |
| DCRA | Department of Community and Regional Affairs |
| DEC | Department of Environmental Conservation |
| DGC | Division of Governmental Coordination |
| DMWM | Division of Mining and Water Management |
| DNR | Department of Natural Resources |
| DOG | Division of Oil and Gas |
| DOL | Division of Land |
| EA | environmental assessment |
| EIA | Energy Information Administration |
| EIS | environmental impact statement |
| ELF | Economic Limit Factor |
| EPA | Environmental Protection Agency |
| FECA | Federal Elections Campaign Act |
| FOIA | Freedom of Information Act |
| FWS | US Fish and Wildlife Service |
| FY | fiscal year |
| HSS | Health and Social Services |
| IHA | Incidental Harassment Authorization |
| ISER | Institute of Social and Economic Research |
| JPO | Joint Pipeline Office |
| K–12 | kindergarten through twelfth-grade |
| LDCs | less-developed countries |
| LMEICO | Lease Monitoring and Engineering Integrity Coordinating Office |
| LNG | liquefied natural gas |
| LPGs | liquefied petroleum gases |
| MES | minimum efficient scales |
| MMS | Minerals Management Service |
| MNCs | multinational corporations |
| NEPA | National Environmental Policy Act |
| NGLs | natural gas liquids |
| NGOs | nongovernmental organizations |
| NGPA | Natural Gas Policy Act |
| NMFS | National Marine Fisheries Service |
| NOAA | National Oceanic and Atmospheric Agency |
| NPDES | National Pollution Discharge Elimination System |
| NPF | Norwegian Petroleum Fund |
| NPR-A | National Petroleum Reserve–Alaska |

| | |
|---|---|
| OCS | Outer Continental Shelf |
| OPEC | Organization of Petroleum Exporting Countries |
| OPMP | Office of Project Management and Permitting |
| PACs | political action committees |
| PF | Permanent Fund |
| PFD | Permanent Fund Dividend |
| PIRG | Public Interest Research Group |
| POMV | percent of market value |
| PPT | profit-based production tax |
| PSD | Prevention of Significant Deterioration |
| ROGDAB | Royalty Oil and Gas Development Advisory Board |
| ROWs | rights-of-way |
| RSAs | reimbursable-services agreements |
| SGDA | Stranded Gas Development Act |
| TAPS | Trans-Alaska Pipeline System |
| TEK | traditional ecological knowledge |
| USGS | US Geological Survey |
| VSMs | vertical support members |
| WOGA | Western Oil and Gas Association |

# Bibliography

*Alaska Budget Report* (Juneau), selected issues.

*Alaska Business Monthly* (Anchorage), selected issues.

Alaska Department of Revenue. *Revenue Sources Book: Forecast and Historical Data* (Juneau: Oil and Gas Audit Division, 1998, 1999, 2005, 2006, 2007).

Alaska Division of Lands, *Annual Reports* (Anchorage: Department of Natural Resources, 1966, 1967, 1968).

Alaska Division of Oil and Gas. *Alaska Oil and Gas Report* (Anchorage: Department of Natural Resources, 2004).

*Alaska Economic Report* (Juneau), selected issues.

Alaska Housing Finance Corporation. *2006 Annual Report* (Anchorage: 2007).

Alaska Industrial Development and Export Authority. *2006 Annual Report* (Anchorage: 2007).

Alaska, The Long Range Financial Planning Commission. "The State Long Range Financial Planning Commission Report," October 1995.

Alaska Permanent Fund Corporation. *2006 Annual Report* (Juneau: 2006).

———. *Alaskans Speak Out on Public Policy Choices. Trustees' Papers,* Vol. 6 (Juneau: 1999).

———. *An Alaskan's Guide to the Permanent Fund,* 11th ed. (Juneau: 2005).

———. *Changes to the Investment World During the Permanent Fund's First Two Decades. Trustees' Papers,* Vol. 4 (Juneau: 1997).

———. *The Early History of the Alaska Permanent Fund. Trustees' Papers,* Vol. 5 (Juneau: 1997).

———. "Making the Case for Complete and Protected Inflation-Proofing." *Trustees' Papers,* Vol. 7 (Juneau: 2001).

———. *Wealth Management—A Comparison of the Alaska Permanent Fund and Other Oil-Generated Savings Accounts Around the World. Trustees' Papers,* Vol. 3 (Juneau: 1988).

Alaska Petrochemical Company. *Preliminary Proposal to Purchase Alaska State Royalty Crude and to Construct a Petrochemical Refinery Complex in Alaska* (Houston: 1977).

Alaska Review of Social and Economic Conditions. *Sustainable Spending Levels from Alaska State Revenues* (Anchorage: University of Alaska, Institute of Social and Economic Research, 1983).

*Anchorage Daily News*, selected issues.

Ansolabehere, Stephen, John M. P. de Figueiredo, and James M. Snyder, "Are Campaign Contributions Investment in the Political Marketplace or Individual Consumption? Or 'Why Is There So Little Money in Politics?'" MIT Sloan Working Paper No. 4272-02 (October 2002).

Becker, David G., and Richard L. Sklar. "Introduction." In David G. Becker and Richard L. Sklar, eds. *Postimperialism and World Politics* (Westport, CT: Praeger Publishing Group, 1999), 1–10.

Berman, Matthew. "Caveat Emptor: Negotiated Fiscal Regimes," *Journal of Petroleum Finance and Development* 2, no. 1 (1997): 25–43.

———. "Economic Development Through State Ownership of Oil and Gas: Evaluating Alaska's Royalty-in-Kind Program," *International Journal of Global Energy Issues* 26, no. 1–2 (2006): 83–103.

Berman, Matthew, Eric Myers, William Nebesky, Karen White, and Teresa Hull. *Alaska Petroleum Revenues: The Influence of Federal Policy* (Anchorage: Institute of Social and Economic Research, 1984).

Berry, Mary Clay. *The Alaska Pipeline: The Politics of Oil and Native Land Claims* (Bloomington: University of Indiana Press, 1975).

BP Exploration (Alaska) Inc. *Environmental Performance on Alaska's North Slope* (Anchorage: February 1998).

British Petroleum. *BP in Alaska: 40 Years of Risks and Rewards* (Anchorage: 2001).

Browning, Martin, and M. Dolores Collado. "The Response of Expenditures to Anticipated Income Change: Panel Data Estimates," *The American Economic Review* 91, no. 3 (June 2001): 681–692.

Cameron, Raymond D., Kenneth R. Whitten, Walter T. Smith, and Daniel D. Roby. "Caribou Distribution and Group Composition Associated with Construction of the Trans-Alaska Pipeline," *The Canadian Field Naturalist* (1993): 155–163.

Cardoso, Fernando Henrique. "Associated-Dependent Development: Theoretical and Practical Implications." In Alfred Stepan, ed. *Authoritarian Brazil: Origins, Policies and Future* (New Haven, CT, and London: Yale University Press, 1973).

Cardoso, Fernando Henrique, and Enzo Faletto. *Dependency and Development in Latin America* (Berkeley: University of California Press, 1979).

Cashman, Kay. "ARCO's 40 Years in Alaska," *Alaska Journal of Commerce*, September 18, 1995.

Cheney, Dick, Colin Powell, Paul O'Neill, Gale Norton, Donald L. Evans, and Norman Minetta. *National Energy Policy: Report of the National Energy Policy Development Group* (Washington, DC: US Government Printing Office, 2001).

Coates, Kenneth. "The Discovery of the North: Towards a Conceptual Framework for the Study of Northern/Remote Regions," *The Northern Review* 12/13 (1994).

Coates, Peter A. *The Trans-Alaska Pipeline Controversy: Technology, Conservation, and the Frontier* (Fairbanks: University of Alaska Press, 1993).

Cole, Terrence M. "The History of a History," *Pacific Northwest Quarterly* 77 (October 1986).

———. *Blinded by Riches: The Permanent Funding Problem and the Prudhoe Bay Effect* (Anchorage: Institute of Social and Economic Research, University of Alaska, January 2004).

Cooley, Richard. *Politics and Conservation: The Decline of Alaska Salmon* (New York: Harper & Row, 1963).

Dam, Kenneth W. *Oil Resources: Who Gets What How?* (Chicago: University of Chicago Press, 1976).

The Dow-Shell Group. *Petrochemical Development for Alaska: A Proposal* (Midland, MI: Dow Chemical, 1980).

————. *Alaska Petrochemical Industry Feasibility Study: A Report to the State of Alaska* (Midland, MI: Dow Chemical, 1981).

Eisner, Mark A., Jeff Worsham, and Evan Ringquist. *Contemporary Regulatory Policy* (Boulder, CO: Lynne Rienner Publishers, 2000).

Evans, Peter. *Dependent Development: The Alliance of Multinational, State and Local Capital in Brazil* (Princeton: Princeton University Press, 1979).

*Fairbanks Daily News-Miner*, selected issues.

Federal Task Force on Alaska Native Affairs. *Report to the Secretary of the Interior* (Washington, DC: December 1962).

Fischer, Victor. *Alaska's Constitutional Convention* (Fairbanks: University of Alaska Press, 1975).

Flanders, Nicholas E., Rex V. Brown, Yelena Andre'eva, and Oleg Larichev. "Justifying Public Decisions in Arctic Oil and Gas Development: American and Russian Approaches," *Arctic* 51, no. 3 (September 1998): 275–278.

Francis, John G., and Clive S. Thomas. "Influences on Western Political Culture." In Clive S. Thomas, ed. *Politics and Public Policy in the Contemporary American West* (Albuquerque: University of New Mexico Press, 1999), 23–54.

Frank, Andre Gunder. *Capitalism and Underdevelopment in Latin America: Historical Studies of Chile and Brazil* (New York: Monthly Review Press, 1969).

Freedman, Paul, Michael Franz, and Kenneth Goldstein. "Campaign Advertising and Democratic Citizenship," *American Journal of Political Science* 48, no. 4 (October 2004).

Fried, Neal, and Brigitta Windisch-Cole. "The Oil Industry," *Alaska Economic Trends* 23, no. 9 (September 2003): 3–12.

Goldsmith, Oliver Scott. "Safe Landing: A Fiscal Strategy for the 1990s," *ISER Fiscal Policy Papers,* no. 7 (Anchorage: Institute of Social and Economic Research, University of Alaska, July 1992).

————. "From Oil to Assets: Managing Alaska's New Wealth," *ISER Fiscal Policy Papers*, no. 10 (Anchorage: Institute of Social and Economic Research, University of Alaska, June 1998): 1–8.

Goldsmith, Scott, and Eric Larson. "What Does $7.6 Billion in Federal Money Mean to Alaska?" *UA Research Summary,* no. 2 (Anchorage: Institute of Social and Economic Research, University of Alaska, November 2003).

Goldsmith, Oliver Scott, and Jeff Wanamaker. *The Economic Impact of the Permanent Fund Dividend* (Anchorage: Institute of Social and Economic Research, 1989).

Goldsmith, Scott, Linda Leask, and Mary Killorin. "Alaska's Budget: Where the Money Came From and Went 1990–2002," *ISER Fiscal Policy Papers*, no. 13 (Anchorage: Institute of Social and Economic Research, University of Alaska, May 2003).

Gramling, Robert. *Oil on the Edge: Offshore Development, Conflict, Gridlock* (Albany: State University of New York Press, 1996).

Grayson, George W. *The Politics of Mexican Oil* (Pittsburgh, PA: University of Pittsburgh Press, 1980).

Greene, Jeffrey D., and John R. Brueggeman. "Montana." In Carl Mott, ed. *Proceedings: Roundtable on State Budgeting in the 13 Western States, January 2006* (Salt Lake City: Utah Center for Public Policy and Administration, 2006).

Groh, Clifford J., and Gregg Erickson. "The Permanent Fund Dividend Program: Alaska's 'Nobel Experiment.'" In *The Early History of the Alaska Permanent Fund. The Trustee Papers*, Vol. 5 (Juneau: Alaska Permanent Fund Corporation, 1997).

Gross, Donald A., Robert K. Goidel, and Todd G. Shield. "State Campaign Finance

Regulations and Electoral Competition," *American Politics Research* 30 (March 2002): 143–165.

Hammer, Heather-Jo, and John W. Gartrell. "American Penetration and Canadian Development: A Study of Mature Dependency." In Mitchell A. Seligson and John T. Passé-Smith, ed. *Development and Underdevelopment: The Political Economy of Global Inequality* (Boulder, CO, and London: Lynne Rienner Publishers, 1998), 337–352.

Hannesson, Rognvaldur. *Investing for Sustainability: The Management of Mineral Wealth* (Norwell, MA: Kluwer Academic Publishers, 2001).

Harrison, Gordon S. "The Economics and Politics of the Alaska Permanent Fund Dividend Program." In Clive S. Thomas, ed. *Alaska Public Policy Issues* (Juneau: Denali Press, 1999).

———. *Alaska's Constitution: A Citizen's Guide,* 4th ed. (Juneau: Alaska Legislative Affairs Agency, 2002).

Haycox, Stephen. *Alaska: An American Colony* (Seattle: University of Washington Press, 2002).

Haynes, Geoffrey. *Review of Alaska Royalty Oil* (Juneau: Alaska Department of Natural Resources, 1983).

Hickel, Walter J. *Crisis in the Commons: The Alaska Solution* (Oakland: ICS Press, 2002).

Hsieh, Chang-Tai. "Do Consumers React to Anticipated Income Changes? Evidence from the Alaska Permanent Fund," *The American Economic Review* 93, no. 1 (March 2003).

Hymer, Stephen. "The Multinational Corporation and the Law of Uneven Development." In Jagdish N. Bhagwati, ed. *Economics and World Order: From the 1970s to the 1990s* (New York and London: The Free Press, 1972).

Institute of Business, Economic, and Government Research (IBEGR), "Alaska's Economy in 1967," *Monthly Review of Alaska Business and Economic Conditions* 5 (1976).

———. "The Petroleum Industry in Alaska," *Monthly Review of Alaska Business and Economic Conditions* 1 (University of Alaska, Fairbanks) (August 1964).

Institute of Social and Economic Research. "The Alaska Citizen's Guide to the Budget" (Anchorage: 2002).

———. *Understanding Alaska: People, Economy, and Resources* (Anchorage: University of Alaska, 2006).

Jacobson, Gary C. *The First Congressional Elections after BCRA* (Washington, DC: The Campaign Finance Institute, 2005).

Johnson, Stephen. "The Alaska Legislature." In Gerald A. McBeath and Thomas A. Morehouse, eds. *Alaska State Government and Politics* (Fairbanks: University of Alaska Press, 1987).

Joint Pipeline Office. *Summary of Public Scoping Comments: Trans-Alaska Pipeline System Right-of-Way Renewal Environmental Impact Statement* (Anchorage: November 2001).

Kalman, Gary, and Adam Lioz. *Raising the Limits: A Bad Bet for Campaign Finance Reform* (Washington, DC: US PIRG Education Fund, 2006).

Kason, Joan. "The Creation of the Alaska Permanent Fund: A Short History." In *The Early History of the Alaska Permanent Fund: The Trustee Papers*, Vol. 5 (Juneau: Alaska Permanent Fund Corporation, 1997).

Katzenstein, Peter, ed. *Between Power and Plenty* (Madison: University of Wisconsin Press, 1978).

Kemp, Alexander. *Petroleum Rent Collection Around the World* (Halifax: The Institute for Research on Public Policy, 1987).

———. "Development Risks and Petroleum Fiscal Systems: A Comparative Study of the U.K., Norway, Denmark, and the Netherlands," *The Energy Journal* 13, no. 3 (1992): 17–39.

Klapp, Merrie. "The State—Landlord or Entrepreneur?" *International Organization* 36, no. 3 (1982).

Knapp, Gunnar, Scott Goldsmith, Jack Kruse, and Gregg Erickson. *The Alaska Permanent Fund Dividend Program: Economic Effects and Public Attitudes* (Anchorage: Institute of Social and Economic Research, 1984).

Kresge, David, Daniel Seiver, Oliver S. Goldsmith, and Michael Scott. *Regions and Resources: Strategies for Development* (Cambridge: MIT Press, 1984).

Landau, Martin. "Redundance, Rationality, and the Problem of Duplication and Overlap," *Public Administration Review* 29 (July/August 1969): 346–358.

Lewis, Charles, and the Center for Public Integrity. *The Buying of the President 2000* (New York: Avon Books, 2000).

Lovecraft, Amy, and Jerry McBeath. "Alaska." In Carl Mott, ed. *Proceedings: Roundtable on State Budgeting in the 13 Western States* (Salt Lake City: University of Utah, 2005).

Lovejoy, W. F., and P. T. Homan. *Economic Aspects of Oil Conservation Regulation* (Baltimore: The Johns Hopkins Press for Resources for the Future, 1967).

Makinson, Larry. *Open Secrets: The Price of Politics in Alaska* (Anchorage: Rosebud Publishing, 1987).

McBeath, Gerald A. "Transformation of the Alaska Blanket Primary System," *Comparative State Politics* 15, no. 4 (1994): 25–42.

———. *The Alaska State Constitution: A Reference Guide* (Westport, CT: Greenwood Press, 1997).

McBeath, Gerald A., and Thomas A. Morehouse. *The Dynamics of Alaska Native Self-Government* (Lanham, MD: University Press of America, 1980).

———. *Alaska Politics and Government* (Lincoln: University of Nebraska Press, 1994).

———. "Reforming Alaska's Political and Governmental System." In Clive S. Thomas, ed. *Alaska Public Policy Issues: Background and Perspectives* (Juneau: Denali Press, 1999).

McBeath, Gerald A., Thomas A. Morehouse, John Barkdull, and Linda Leask. *Natural Resource Issues and Policies on Alaska's North Slope* (Anchorage: Department of Natural Resources, July 1981).

McBeath, Jerry. Annual reports on Alaska's fiscal policymaking. In *Proceedings of the Roundtable on State and Local Budgeting* (retitled *Annual Western States Budget Review* in 2007) (Salt Lake City: Center for Public Policy and Administration, University of Utah, 1992–2007).

———. "Campaign Finance Reform and Alaska's 1998 Elections: A Preliminary Report." Paper presented to the Western Regional Science Association Conference in February 2000, Kauai, Hawaii.

———. "Changing Capabilities of Northern Communities: Environmental Protection," *Northern Review* 23 (2002).

———. "Oil Transportation Infrastructure: The Trans-Alaska Pipeline System and the Challenge of Environmental Change." In M. Ruth, ed. *Smart Growth and Climate Change: Regional Development, Infrastructure and Adaptation* (Northampton, MA: Edward Elgar, 2006): 129–152.

McBeath, Jerry, and Carl E. Shepro. "The Effects of Environmental Change on an Arctic Native Community: Evaluation Using Local Cultural Perceptions," *The American Indian Quarterly* 31, no. 1 (Winter 2007): 44–65.

McDonald, Stephen L. *Petroleum Conservation in the United States* (Baltimore: The Johns Hopkins Press for Resources for the Future, 1971).

———. *The Leasing of Federal Lands for Fossil Fuels Production* (Baltimore: The Johns Hopkins Press for Resources for the Future, 1979).

Mercer Inc., *Norwegian Government Pension Fund–Global: Annual Performance Evaluation Report 2006* (London: Mercer, 2007).

Meurs, Pedro van. "Proposal for a Profit Based Production Tax for Alaska" (manuscript, Juneau, February 14, 2006).

Mieszkowski, Peter, and Eric Toder. "Taxation of Energy Resources." In Charles E. McLure Jr. and Peter Mieszkowski, eds. *Fiscal Federalism and the Taxation of Natural Resources* (Lexington, MA: D. C. Heath and Co., 1983), 65–92.

Mitchell, Donald. *Sold American: The Story of Alaska Natives and Their Land* (Hanover, NH: University Press of New England, 1997).

———. *Take My Land Take My Life* (Fairbanks: University of Alaska Press, 2001).

Morehouse, Thomas, and Lee Huskey. "Development in Remote Regions: What Do We Know?" *Arctic* 45, no. 2 (June 1992).

Mumey, Glen, and Joseph Ostermann. "Alberta Heritage Fund: Measuring Value and Achievement," *Canadian Public Policy* 16, no. 1 (1990).

Naske, Claus-M., and Herman E. Slotnick. *Alaska: A History of the Forty-Ninth State*, 2nd ed. (Norman: University of Oklahoma Press, 1987).

National Petroleum Council, Committee on Arctic Oil and Gas Resources. *Report of the Exploration Task Group* (Washington, DC: 1981).

National Research Council. *Cumulative Environmental Effects of Oil and Gas Activities on Alaska's North Slope* (Washington, DC: The National Academies Press, 2003).

Neely, Burr. "Oil and Gas Industry Campaign Contributions and Election Outcomes: An Analysis of the 1998 and 2000 Legislative Elections in Alaska," Paper delivered to the Western Regional Science Association Conference in Monterey, California, February 2002.

*New York Times*, selected issues.

Nichols, Jeannette Paddock. *Alaska: A Short History of Its Administration* (Cleveland, OH: Arthur H. Clark, 1924).

Nielson, Jon M. *Beaufort Sea Study—Historic and Subsistence Site Inventory: A Preliminary Cultural Resource Assessment* (Barrow: North Slope Borough, 1977).

Noreng, Oystein. *Crude Power: Politics and the Oil Market* (London and New York: I. B. Tauris Publishers, 2002).

Ostrom, Vincent. *The Intellectual Crisis in American Public Administration* (Tuscaloosa: University of Alabama Press, 1974).

Philip, George D. E. *The Political Economy of International Oil* (Edinburgh: Edinburgh University Press, 2004).

Picraux, Danice R., and Gilbert K. St. Clair. "New Mexico Budget—FY 2006." In Carl Mott, ed. *Proceedings: Roundtable on State Budgeting in the 13 Western States, January 2006* (Salt Lake City: Utah Center for Public Policy and Administration, 2006).

Pretes, Michael. "Underdevelopment in Two Norths: The Brazilian Amazon and the Canadian Arctic," *Arctic* 41, no. 2 (1988).

Primo, David M., and Jeffrey Milyo. "Campaign Finance Laws and Political Efficacy: Evidence from the States," *Election Law Journal* 5, no. 1 (2006).

Rafuse, Robert W., Jr. *Representative Expenditures: Addressing the Neglected Dimension of Fiscal Capacity,* Information Report M-174 (Washington, DC: Advisory Commission on Intergovernmental Relations, 1990).

Rakestraw, Lawrence. *A History of the U.S. Forest Service in Alaska* (Juneau: US Department of Agriculture, Forest Service, Alaska Region, 2002).

Roderick, Jack. *Crude Dreams: A Personal History of Oil and Politics in Alaska* (Fairbanks: Epicenter Press, 1997).

Rodney, Walter. *How Europe Underdeveloped Africa* (Washington, DC: Howard University Press, 1981).

Rogers, George. *The Future of Alaska: The Economic Consequences of Statehood* (Baltimore: The Johns Hopkins Press for Resources for the Future, 1962).

Rosenbaum, Walter A. *Environmental Politics and Policy*, 5th ed. (Washington, DC: CQ Press, 2002).

Rosenberg, Jonathan. "Persistent Patterns: Oil and Gas Industry Contributions to Alaska Legislative Races, 1986 and 1996." Paper delivered at the Western Regional Science Association Conference in Hawaii, February 1997.

Ross, Ken. *Environmental Conflict in Alaska* (Boulder: University Press of Colorado, 2000).

Rural Research Agency. "Alaska's Permanent Fund: Legislative History, Intent, and Operations." In *The Early History of the Alaska Permanent Fund: The Trustee Papers*, Vol. 5 (Juneau: Alaska Permanent Fund Corporation, 1997).

Scherer, F. M., Alan Beckenstein, Erich Kaufer, and R. D. Murphy. *The Economics of Multi-Plant Operation: An International Comparisons Study* (Cambridge: Harvard University Press, 1975).

Schultz, Paul. "Laboratories of Democracy: Campaign Finance Reform in the States," *Public Integrity* 6, no. 2 (Spring 2004).

Seligson, Mitchell A., and John T. Passé-Smith, eds. *Development and Underdevelopment: The Political Economy of Global Inequality* (Boulder, CO, and London: Lynne Rienner Publishers, 1998).

Sklar, Richard L. "Postimperialism: A Class Analysis of Multinational Corporate Expansion," *Comparative Politics* 9 (1976).

———. "Postimperialism: Concepts and Implications." In David G. Becker and Richard L. Sklar, eds. *Postimperialism and World Politics* (Westport, CT, and London: Praeger Publishing Group, 1999), 11–36.

Smith, Peter. "The Politics of Plenty: Investing Natural Resource Revenues in Alberta and Alaska," *Canadian Public Policy* 17 (1991): 139–154.

Strohmeyer, John. *Extreme Conditions: Big Oil and the Transformation of Alaska* (New York: Simon and Schuster, 1993).

Szabo, D. J., and K. O. Meyers. "Prudhoe Bay: Development History and Future Potential." Paper presented to the Society of Petroleum Engineers Western Regional Meeting, Anchorage, May 1993.

Thomas, Clive S. "The West and Its Brand of Politics." In Clive S. Thomas, ed. *Politics and Public Policy in the Contemporary American West* (Albuquerque: University of New Mexico Press, 1991), 1–22.

Tuck, Bradford, Lee Huskey, Dona Lehr, and Eric Larson. *Alaska Economic Growth and Change: Opportunities for Import Substitution* (Anchorage: Institute of Social and Economic Research, 1988).

Tussing, Arlon, and Lois Kramer. *Hydrocarbon Processing: A Primer for Alaska* (Anchorage: Institute of Social and Economic Research, 1981).

Tyson, Ray. "Causeway Compromise," *Alaska Business Monthly* (March 1991).

US Department of the Interior, Bureau of Land Management. *Draft Environmental Impact Statement: Renewal of the Trans-Alaska Pipeline System Right-of-Way* (Washington, DC: 2002).

Walker, D. A., P. J. Webber, E. F. Binndian, K. R. Everett, N. D. Lederer, E. A.

Northstrang, and M. D. Walker. "Cumulative Effects of Oil Fields on Northern Alaskan Landscapes," *Science* 238 (1996): 757–759.

Warrack, Allan, and Russell Keddie. "Alberta Heritage Fund vs. Alaska Permanent Fund: A Comparative Analysis." Alaska Permanent Fund Corporation, unpublished papers, no date.

Well, P. G., J. N. Butler, and J. S. Hughes, eds. *Exxon Valdez Oil Spill: Fate and Effects in Alaskan Waters* (Philadelphia: ASTM, 1995).

Wilson, William H. "Alaska's Past, Alaska's Future," *Alaska Review* 4, no. 1 (1970).

Yergin, Daniel. *The Prize: The Epic Quest for Oil, Money and Power* (New York: Simon and Schuster, 1992).

# Index

Administrative distance, 15

Agnew, Spiro, 38

Aid to Families with Dependent Children, 133

Alaska: administrative capacity of government, 245; administrative distance and, 15; basic industry reliance on oil in, 149; civil society in, 245–246; comparison with other oil-producing regions, 233–235; construction costs in, 147; control of use of resources by, 8; cuts in spending in, 83; decline in federal government employment in, 149; Democratic Party in, 1–2, 45, 57; dependence on oil, 2, 4–5, 235–243; dependency theory and, 7–11, 235–243; discovery of oil in, 24–29; diversification strategies of, 115; as economic colony, 233, 234; economic development through oil in, 145–166; employment sectors in, 148*fig*; establishment of proprietary role over oil/gas bearing lands in, 14; "exceptionalism" of, 5–7; executive/legislative budget rivalry, 129, 130, 143*n33*; federal funding and, 135–137; fiscal gap in, 83; fiscal regime in, 84–104; fisheries in, 12, 18, 23, 29, 124, 166*n2*; history of oil resources in, 23–53; influence on oil policies in, 11; lack of bureaucratic expertise in, 29; lack of diversification in, 4–5; lack of early interest in oil in, 23; management of oil wealth by, 171–192; market constraints on, 6; military advice against statehood for, 53*n1*; military installations in, 23; mining in, 12; "neglect thesis" of history in, 233; oil as chief source of income in, 29; oil price shocks and, 115, 125; percentage of United States oil produced by, 113; petroleum revenues, 83–105; population, 23, 149, 150; preservation of gains from use of natural resources, 171–192; prodevelopment electorate in, 57; relationship to federal government, 9; relations to global energy markets, 6; Republican Party in, 1, 2, 15, 45, 52, 57; reputation as recipient of federal "pork," 136; resident/nonresident employment in, 147, 167*n12*; resource-based economy in, 1; response to crisis of low oil prices, 119–127; restrictions on autonomy of territorial government, 23; revenue shortfalls, 98; risk sharing with oil companies and, 15, 87–89; share of oil revenues, 83; statehood for, 16, 23, 27, 113; "Take Back Our State" ballot iniative, 58, 63; transportation costs, 147–148; underdeveloped infrastructure in, 234; undeveloped oil reserves in, 234; vulnerability of economy in, 12

Alaska Action Committee, 37

Alaska Aerospace Development Corporation, 176

# About the Book

Does Alaska's reliance on oil and gas mean that it inevitably will be controlled by corporate energy interests? Or can the state use its vast resource holdings to manage a more symmetrical partnership? *The Political Economy of Oil in Alaska* investigates the complex relationship Alaska has with its most precious commodity.

Offering a new perspective on the challenges of oil-dependent development, the authors explore the dynamic balance between the power of a subnational government—as the owner of resources, possessor of fiscal authority, and regulator of safety and environmental conditions—and the ability of Big Oil to develop energy resources, affect the state economy, and influence state policies. The result is a comprehensive study of an often contentious alliance.

**Jerry McBeath** is professor of political science at the University of Alaska Fairbanks, where he has taught since 1976. He was educated at the University of Chicago and at the University of California–Berkeley (PhD, political science, 1970). His areas of research interest and publication include comparative politics (with a focus on East Asia, particularly China and Taiwan), Alaska state and local government, the Alaska Constitution, Alaska Native politics, education reform in the United States, government and politics of circumpolar northern nations, and North American, Asian, and European environmental politics. He is responsible for Chapters 2, 7, 8, and 9.

**Matthew Berman** is professor of economics at the Institute of Social and Economic Research, University of Alaska Anchorage. He attended Harvard College and completed his graduate studies in economics at Yale University (PhD, 1977). He first came to Alaska in 1978 as a Rockefeller Foundation postdoctoral fellow in environmental affairs, and joined the UAA faculty in 1981. His primary areas of interest include economic organization and social-ecological systems. Recently, he has published on spatial economics of marine ecosystems, sustainability of arctic mixed economies, resource management institutions and uncertainty, and health and safety policy for rural areas. He is responsible for Chapters 4 and 6.

**Jonathan Rosenberg** is professor of political science at the University of Alaska Fairbanks, where he has been on the faculty since 1993. He holds degrees in political science from Pennsylvania State University and the University of California–Los Angeles (PhD, 1992). Specializing in comparative politics and international political economy, he has published on the political economy of post-revolutionary Cuba and Mexico, sustainable development and stakeholder participation in the Eastern Caribbean, the role of official assistance in environmentally sustainable development, and the effects of globalization on the environment in the Americas. He is responsible for Chapters 1 and 5.

**Mary F. Ehrlander** is assistant professor of history and co-director of northern studies at the University of Alaska Fairbanks, where she has taught since 2001. She earned degrees (in political science and northern studies) at UAF, and a PhD in government at the University of Virginia in 1999. Her research interests include history and politics in the circumpolar North; northern alcohol cultures, policies, and problems; and education policy in the United States. She is responsible for Chapter 3.